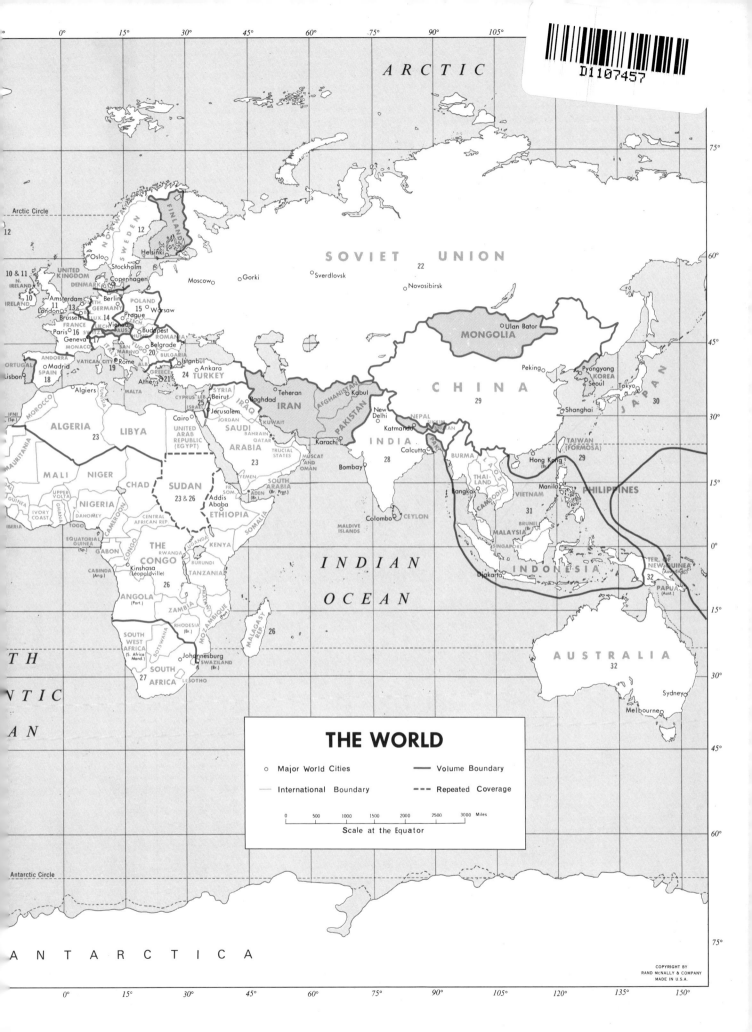

THE WORLD

○ Major World Cities
—— Volume Boundary
— International Boundary
- - - Repeated Coverage

Scale at the Equator

LIFE WORLD LIBRARY

HANDBOOK OF THE NATIONS

AND INTERNATIONAL ORGANIZATIONS

TIME LIFE BOOKS ®

LIFE WORLD LIBRARY

HANDBOOK OF THE NATIONS

AND INTERNATIONAL ORGANIZATIONS

by The Editors of LIFE

TIME INCORPORATED   NEW YORK

COVER: Flags of United Nations member
countries, in alphabetical order, ripple in the
breeze outside U.N. Headquarters in New York.
From right to left in the foreground they are:
Czechoslovakia *(red and white visible),* Dahomey,
Denmark and Dominican Republic *(not
distinguishable),* Ecuador *(shield insigne on yellow,
blue and red),* El Salvador *(blue and white),*
Ethiopia *(green, yellow and red),* Finland *(blue
and white),* France *(not distinguishable),* Gabon
(green, yellow and blue), Gambia *(not visible),*
Ghana *(red, white and green),* and Greece *(blue
and white stripes).*

TIME-LIFE BOOKS

EDITOR
Maitland A. Edey
TEXT DIRECTOR   ART DIRECTOR
Jerry Korn   Sheldon Cotler
CHIEF OF RESEARCH
Beatrice T. Dobie
Assistant Text Directors:
Harold C. Field, Ogden Tanner
Assistant Art Director:
Arnold C. Holeywell
Assistant Chiefs of Research:
Monica O. Horne, Martha Turner

•

PUBLISHER
Rhett Austell
General Manager: Joseph C. Hazen Jr.
Circulation Director: Joan D. Manley
Marketing Director: Carter Smith
Business Manager: John D. McSweeney
Publishing Board: Nicholas Benton, Louis Bronzo,
James Wendell Forbes

LIFE MAGAZINE

EDITOR: Edward K. Thompson
MANAGING EDITOR: George P. Hunt
PUBLISHER: Jerome S. Hardy

LIFE WORLD LIBRARY

SERIES EDITOR: Oliver E. Allen
Editorial Staff for *Handbook of the Nations:*
Assistant Editors: David S. Thomson, Jay Brennan
Designer: Ben Schultz
Chief Researcher: Grace Brynolson
Researchers: Sondra Albert, Paula von Haimberger Arno, Lea Guyer,
Evelyn Hauptman, Helen Muller, Louise Samuels, Ruth Silva,
Clover Vail, Sandra Van Doren, Diane Wynne, Ellen Youngblood

EDITORIAL PRODUCTION
Color Director: Robert L. Young
Copy Staff: Marian Gordon Goldman, Patricia Miller,
Dolores A. Littles
Picture Bureau: Margaret K. Goldsmith, Barbara Sullivan
Art Assistants: Douglas B. Graham, John M. Woods

The text for this book was written by Sam Halper, Peter Meyerson,
Frederick K. Poole, John Stanton and John von Hartz. Valuable help
was also provided by the following individuals and departments of
Time Inc.: LIFE staff photographers Margaret Bourke-White, Larry
Burrows, Dmitri Kessel, Francis Miller; United Nations Bureau Chief
Frederick Gruin; the Chief of the LIFE Picture Library, Doris O'Neil;
the Chief of the Time Inc. Bureau of Editorial Reference, Peter Draz;
the Chief of the TIME-LIFE News Service, Richard M. Clurman.

Credits and Acknowledgments: Page 156

Handbook of the Nations and International Organizations
© 1966 Time Inc. All rights reserved.
Published simultaneously in Canada.
Library of Congress catalogue card number 66-14914.
School and library distribution by Silver Burdett Company.

Contents

	Page
Introduction	6
Gazetteer of the Nations	8
International Organizations	33
Nations Not Covered in Other Volumes	
Portugal	73
Austria	81
Finland	93
Liechtenstein	100
Andorra	101
San Marino	102
Monaco	103
Vatican City	104
Iran	107
Afghanistan	119
Pakistan	124
Nepal, Bhutan and Sikkim	134
Ceylon	137
Outer Mongolia	142
Korea	147
Oceania	152
Index to This Volume	157
Guide to Major Topics in the LIFE WORLD LIBRARY	161

Introduction

This volume marks the culmination of a project that has taken almost six years to complete: the publication of a series of 34 books, totaling 5,600 pages, that comprise the Life World Library.

The aim of this series has been to present a comprehensive interpretation, in text and photographs, of the principal nations and peoples of the contemporary world. We have thought of our typical reader as a person who welcomes an evocative summing up of all the facets of a nation's life so that he will have a deeper understanding of events and personalities in the news. He may not be planning a visit abroad—but reading one of these volumes should help him, if he is fortunate enough to travel, to enjoy a better grasp of the contemporary scene wherever he goes.

In order to achieve a measure of detachment toward often controversial matters, the editors from the outset adopted a policy of having the text chapters in each volume written by a person intimately acquainted with his subject but not native to the country or area he is writing about. Understandably, a majority of the authors have been Americans, but almost a third have been British; most have made refresher trips—sometimes covering thousands of miles—before sitting down to write. Each author has been supplemented by a staff of writers, researchers and designers in New York and by photographers and correspondents working out of Time-Life Bureaus around the world. The result is a collaborative work that has been translated into 13 languages and is now distributed in more than 90 countries.

We have urged our authors to write in their own individual styles, and in this and other ways we have tried to bring variety to the series. But we hardly needed to stress the differences among nations, for they are endlessly diverse. Yet in preparing these volumes we have been struck over and over again by two truisms of world history so obvious that they are often little appreciated. One of these is that the luck of geography plays a large role in the story of

---

THE LIFE WORLD LIBRARY

EUROPE

THE BALKANS (Albania, Bulgaria, Romania, Yugoslavia)

BRITAIN (England, Scotland, Wales, Northern Ireland)

EASTERN EUROPE (Czechoslovakia, Hungary, Poland)

FRANCE

GERMANY (West Germany, East Germany)

GREECE

IRELAND

ITALY

THE LOW COUNTRIES (Belgium, Luxembourg, Netherlands)

RUSSIA

SCANDINAVIA (Denmark, Norway, Sweden)

SPAIN

SWITZERLAND

AFRICA

SOUTH AFRICA

TROPICAL AFRICA (all countries between the Sahara and South Africa)

THE MIDDLE EAST

THE ARAB WORLD (Algeria, Iraq, Jordan, Kuwait, Lebanon, Libya, Morocco, Muscat and Oman, Saudi Arabia, Sudan, Syria, Tunisia, United Arab Republic, Yemen)

ISRAEL

TURKEY

any people; whether a land happens to have good natural resources or is fortunate enough to be easily defended from invasion or domination can markedly affect its fate for centuries. The second is that, although nations differ in character and custom, most of the problems they face are universal and repeat themselves endlessly through history.

In choosing the subject for each volume in the series, two criteria have been used: (1) the importance of the country or region on the contemporary political scene or in world history and (2) its special relevance to American readers. Thus each of the major countries of the world—France, Russia, Britain, Japan and the like—has received a volume to itself, as have certain smaller but especially meaningful countries, such as Ireland and Switzerland. Other countries have generally been grouped into regional volumes like *Eastern Europe* or *Central America*. Inevitably, some countries either did not seem to warrant a single volume or did not fit into any major regional political or geographic grouping. To compensate for this, countries not previously treated in earlier books are covered in this volume, starting with Portugal on page 73.

The scope of this volume—which is staff written —goes further than that, however. The book also contains a Gazetteer (pages 8-31), a Guide to Major Topics covered in all the volumes of the World Library (pages 161-176), and a comprehensive digest of all the major international organizations such as the United Nations and the European Community (pages 33-71).

The complete LIFE World Library consists of the 34 volumes listed below: 32 books on countries; the *Handbook of the Nations*, which you are now reading; and an *Atlas of the World* to serve as a companion volume to all the rest.

OLIVER E. ALLEN
Editor, LIFE World Library

ASIA

CHINA *(both mainland China and the Taiwan-based Republic of China)*
INDIA
JAPAN
SOUTHEAST ASIA *(Brunei, Burma, Cambodia, Indonesia, Laos, Malaysia, North Vietnam, Philippines, South Vietnam, Thailand)*

CENTRAL AMERICA AND THE WEST INDIES

CENTRAL AMERICA *(Costa Rica, El Salvador, Guatemala, Honduras, Nicaragua, Panama)*
MEXICO
THE WEST INDIES *(Cuba, Dominican Republic, Haiti, Jamaica, Puerto Rico, Trinidad and Tobago, and the U.S., British and French possessions)*

SOUTH AMERICA

THE ANDEAN REPUBLICS *(Bolivia, Chile, Ecuador, Peru)*
BRAZIL
COLOMBIA AND VENEZUELA AND THE GUIANAS
THE RIVER PLATE REPUBLICS *(Argentina, Paraguay, Uruguay)*

NORTH AMERICA

CANADA
THE UNITED STATES

OTHERS

AUSTRALIA AND NEW ZEALAND
HANDBOOK OF THE NATIONS AND INTERNATIONAL ORGANIZATIONS
ATLAS OF THE WORLD

Gazetteer of the Nations

ON this and the following 23 pages is a gazetteer of the nations of the world grouped geographically. Colonies and overseas territories are listed at the end of the geographical group in which they lie. The area and population statistics for each country were derived from United Nations sources in September of 1965. For the sake of uniformity in this volume the proportions and colors of flags do not always conform exactly to official national stipulations. At the end of the entry on each country there is a reference either to another volume in the LIFE World Library in which the country has been discussed or to another section of this volume, *Handbook of the Nations,* in which there is further material on the country (e.g.: *"See:* Page 101, HBK" for additional material on Andorra). A full list of the abbreviations used in these references will be found at the bottom of pages 161-175 in this book.

EUROPE

The second-smallest continent (after Australia), Europe occupies only 8 per cent of the earth's land mass. Yet Europe contains more than 20 per cent of the world's population and is a virtually inexhaustible reservoir of cultural and economic productivity. Europe begins in the east at the Ural Mountains in Russia and stretches past the British Isles to include Iceland in the Atlantic; it runs from the barren northlands of Russia and Scandinavia to the warm Mediterranean Sea in the south. Its plains and grasslands, when not desecrated by war, yield a prodigious agricultural output, and its intricate network of navigable rivers and canals supplies good transportation routes as well as water for power and irrigation. The seas that lap the continent have always borne a copious harvest of seafood, offering everything from shellfish to blue whales. But perhaps Europe's greatest gift from nature is its impressive reserves of minerals and raw materials—reserves so plentiful that they have yet to be depleted even after centuries of exploitation. The continent is still the world's leading producer of coal, iron and lignite. Two thirds of the world's mercury comes from Europe and scores of other industrial raw materials are produced there.

Given these riches and the energetic and creative spirit of its people, Europe became a power that dispatched culture, conquerors and settlers to the rest of the world; its influence and its thinking made an impact felt to this day. Industry continues to flourish despite the ravages of scores of local wars and two world wars. Europe has always been able to raise itself from its own ashes. World War II left the continent near total ruin, with millions dead or maimed, proud cities wasted and a formidable industrial complex in chaos. But from these depths Europe has entered one of the most prosperous times of its history. Since 1938 European hydroelectric output has increased more than 200 per cent. Automobile production over the same period leaped by more than 300 per cent while the output of steel and iron soared proportionately. Europe exported $11.5 billion worth of goods in 1938; by the mid-1960s exports had surpassed the $85 billion mark.

ALBANIA Tucked between marshy plains along the Adriatic and the peaks and valleys of southern spurs of the Dinaric Alps, minuscule Albania is one of Europe's most primitive countries. It is also one of the proudest: although ruled by a Communist regime, it was the second nation in Europe (after Yugoslavia) to break with the monolithic Soviet bloc.

Principal Cities: Durrës, Elbasan, Korçë, Shkodër, Tirana (cap.), Vlorë. *Population:* 1,814,000. *Area:* 11,100 sq. mi. *Government:* Communist dictatorship. *Economy:* Mainly agricultural. *Religion:* About 70 per cent Moslem. *Language:* Albanian. Two dialects: Gheg in the north, Tosk in the south. *See:* BAL.

ANDORRA High in the Pyrenees between France and Spain, Andorra is a land of mountain valleys whose inhabitants specialize in the raising of sheep and the smuggling of goods. Self-governing, it owes titular allegiance to both Spain and France.

Principal City: Andorra la Vella (cap.). *Population:* 11,000. *Area:* 175 sq. mi. *Government:* Coprincipality. *Economy:* Agriculture and smuggling; some tourism. *Religion:* Roman Catholic. *Language:* Catalan. *See:* Page 101, HBK.

AUSTRIA The second Austrian republic was born out of the German defeat of 1945. A first republic, born out of the defeat of 1918, had been taken over by Hitler's Germany in 1938. Once the imperial queen of two great Empires, the Holy Roman and the Austro-Hungarian, present-day Austria is a tiny country of magnificent scenery, clinging to the sides of three ranges of Alps that cross the country from west to east. The capital, Vienna, home for almost one in every four Austrians, still proudly wears the elegant necklace of palaces, theaters, concert halls, opera houses, museums and gardens of the Habsburg era and seems to ring with the music written there by many great men: Franz Joseph Haydn, Wolfgang Amadeus Mozart, Ludwig van Beethoven, Franz Schubert, Johannes Brahms, Anton Bruckner, Johann Strauss, Gustav Mahler, Richard Strauss and Arnold Schönberg. Prosperous and well content, today's Austrians work oil fields; mine iron, magnesium, copper and zinc; process steel; farm; and tend their forests. But their No. 1 business is to cater to the tourists who flock in by the thousands winter and summer to visit one of the loveliest countries on earth.

Principal Cities: Graz, Linz, Salzburg, Vienna (cap.). *Population:* 7,215,000. *Area:* 32,374 sq. mi. *Government:* Federal republic. *Economy:* Agriculture, forestry, manufacturing, tourism. *Religion:* 90 per cent Roman Catholic, 6 per cent Protestant. *Language:* German. *See:* Page 81, HBK.

BELGIUM A manufacturing nation since the Middle Ages, when its textile mills were Europe's most important, Belgium is today one of the most heavily industrialized countries on the Continent. It is still a major producer of textiles; its coal deposits are among the world's richest; it is also a major manufacturer of steel and of petrochemicals. Belgium's location on the North Sea, its inland port Antwerp, and its network of canals, rivers and railroads help to make it one of the Continent's major importers and exporters. Although Belgium is also an important agricultural producer, it is forced to import food for its basically urban population. Despite the fact that Belgium is a leader in the European unity movement (with the Netherlands and Luxembourg, it formed the economic-cooperation group known as Benelux, forerunner of the Common Market), it has certain divisive problems at home. There are strong tensions between the Flemish-speaking Roman Catholics of the north and the largely anticlerical French-speaking people of the south.

Principal Cities: Antwerp, Brussels (cap.), Ghent, Liège. *Population:* 9,378,000. *Area:* 11,779 sq. mi. *Government:* Constitutional monarchy. *Economy:* Highly industrialized; produces most of its own food. *Religion:* Roman Catholic. *Languages:* Flemish and French; some German. *See:* LCO.

BULGARIA Poor and primitive, with half of its people engaged in agriculture, Bulgaria is the Soviet Union's most loyal ally and the only remaining Russian satellite that makes the U.S.S.R. appear economically advanced. Large amounts of the country's best products (tobacco, meat and dairy products, and fruit) are exported to the Soviet Union, while Bulgaria must content itself with second best. Some industry has been established since World War II, yet Bulgaria still imports petroleum products, textiles, machinery and motor vehicles. More than 50 per cent of such imports come from the Soviet Union. Bulgaria's friendship with Russia is based partly on sentiment: the original Bulgars were Turkic tribesmen who adopted the customs and speech of the Slavs of nearby Russia; it was Russian pressure

that enabled Bulgaria, after 500 years of Ottoman rule, to throw off the Turkish yoke to become independent in 1908.

Principal Cities: Plovdiv, Sofia (cap.), Varna. *Population:* 8,144,000. *Area:* 42,729 sq. mi. *Government:* Communist dictatorship. *Economy:* Agricultural. *Religion:* Mainly Eastern Orthodox. *Language:* Bulgarian. *See:* BAL.

CZECHOSLOVAKIA A nation in existence only since 1918, when it was created out of fragments of the Austro-Hungarian Empire, Czechoslovakia is in effect two countries: Bohemia-Moravia to the west, where the urbanized Czechs live, and Slovakia to the east, agricultural homeland of the Slovaks. Before and after World War II, Czechoslovakia not only was able to feed itself with home-grown foods but also was the most industrialized nation in Eastern Europe. On February 25, 1948, under Russian pressure, the country succumbed to a Communist coup d'état; within a fortnight Foreign Minister Jan Masaryk, a democratic leader and son of Thomas Masaryk, founder and first President of Czechoslovakia, was found dead under still-unexplained circumstances. Eduard Beneš, second President of the republic and a leading figure in the establishment of independence, died later that year. Under inept Communist planning, the country's economy foundered; while it remains a producer of armaments, locomotives and shoes, it is today only a step ahead of its neighbors and is a food importer.

Principal Cities: Brno, Pilsen, Prague (cap.). *Population:* 14,058,000. *Area:* 49,370 sq. mi. *Government:* Communist dictatorship. *Economy:* Important industrial producer; some agriculture. *Religion:* About 70 per cent Roman Catholic. *Languages:* Czech and Slovak. *See:* EEU.

DENMARK Within Denmark's borders lies some of the most fertile soil of the European plain. Profits derived from the export sale of cattle, pigs, dairy goods, fruit, grains and potatoes, processed and marketed through a highly developed system of farmers' cooperatives, are the bulwark of the economy. With the income from such exports, mineral-poor Denmark has been able to purchase raw materials for its industries (shipbuilding, chemicals and machinery), to supply to its citizens a stable government and a great variety of social services, and to create in its capital, Copenhagen, one of the most sophisticated cities of Europe. A less prosperous part of Denmark is the ice-covered Atlantic island of Greenland, considered a Danish county.

Principal Cities: Arhus, Copenhagen (cap.), Odense. *Population:* 4,720,000. *Area:* 16,619 sq. mi. *Government:* Constitutional monarchy. *Economy:* Agriculture important; also an exporter of machinery, furniture and textiles. *Religion:* Lutheran. *Language:* Danish. *See:* SCN.

FINLAND Standing between the international poles of East and West, and lying partially above the Arctic Circle and partially in the North Temperate Zone, Finland represents a human triumph in a severe political and physical environment. It was conquered in 1155 by Sweden, and it was for centuries the cockpit for Swedish-Russian wars. In 1809 the Russians gained control of the country, and Finland became a self-governing entity inside the autocratic Russian empire. It broke away from Russia in 1917 but unfortunately it continued to be involved in power struggles. It fought and lost a 1939-1940 war to keep the Russians from using Finnish territory to build defenses against Germany. In 1941, to recover its lost territory, it joined Nazi Germany in a second war on Russia and lost again. Finland paid the Soviet Union a huge indemnity, but it also managed to keep its independence.

Principal Cities: Helsinki (cap.), Tampere, Turku. *Population:* 4,613,000. *Area:* 130,119 sq. mi. *Government:* Republic. *Economy:* One of the leading producers of timber, pulp and paper. Agriculture highly mechanized. *Religion:* Predominantly Lutheran. *Languages:* Finnish, Swedish. *See:* SCN.

FRANCE A much-admired nation, France was long the world's cultural leader. Until very recently every educated man had two languages, his own and French. Even countries at war with France, countries invaded by or invading France, countries driven mad by France, all love France. In America this affection is mingled with gratitude; French armies and fleets came to the aid of the colonies during the American Revolution. In the early 1960s the affection was mixed with a wry wrath as France, whose burgeoning postwar prosperity was born in massive Marshall Plan aid from the U.S., sought to dismantle the European collective-security system set up by the U.S. when Europe feared a Russian invasion, and slowed the European unity movement the U.S. had done so much to encourage. But politicians come and go and the affection remains—based, as is all the world's, on reasons ranging from the sensual to the sublime. One admires them, for they know how to live, these French. Their wines and cheeses and fruits and vegetables and cookery surpass all others on earth. Memories of the charms of their women can set old men in China, Australia, Chile and the Congo, who studied in Paris, dreaming young men's dreams. And everywhere in this land is the proud evidence that these people never neglected man's civilizing mission. At Lascaux in southern France 20,000 years ago man painted on the walls of caves. At Vix in eastern France 500 years before Christ man placed in the tomb of a Celtic princess works of art made in Greece. In Brittany in western France are the stone monuments at which Celtic priests once performed dark rites. Everywhere are the Romanesque churches of early Christianity, and at Chartres rises one of the finest examples of the great Gothic cathedrals that grew out of the religious devotion (and local ambition to outdo the next town) of the Middle Ages. Modern man's philosophy was largely hammered out in the Paris Latin Quarter, his political ideas evolve from the French Revolution, and the artistic eye with which modern man looks at his brothers was trained by the painters of France.

Principal Cities: Lyons, Marseilles, Nice, Paris (cap.), Toulouse. *Population:* 48,417,000. *Area:* 211,207 sq. mi. *Government:* Republic. *Economy:* Leading agricultural producer of Western Europe; also important industrially. *Religion:* Mainly Roman Catholic. *Language:* French. *See:* FRA.

GERMANY The Federal Republic of Germany (West Germany) fairly bristles with activity. Along its 2,000 miles of superhighways roar 10 million Volkswagens, Porsches, Opels and Mercedeses. Across the country rise modern factories turning out an endless tide of products: 2.9 million cars, buses and trucks each year, 5.9 million radio and television sets, 37 million metric tons of steel. Two decades after the devastation of World War II, West Germany is the most prosperous nation in Europe. It is also a partner in the Western alliance. Formed out of the American, British and French zones of occupation

in 1949, the Federal Republic signed a "peace contract" with the U.S., Britain and France in 1952. It attained full sovereignty (and recognition by Soviet Russia) in 1955, the same year that it became a member of the North Atlantic Treaty Organization and pledged itself (upon French insistence) never to manufacture nuclear arms. In the postwar years West Germany established a functioning democratic system, but questions inevitably arise about the depth of the West German belief in democratic values. Fifty-five per cent of today's West Germans grew up after the Nazi era; a British journalist notes that every day in West Germany someone anxiously asks: "But they *are* completely different from their parents—aren't they?"

Far less prosperous and far more of an enigma is the German Democratic Republic (East Germany). Formed out of the Soviet zone of occupation in 1949, it is recognized as an independent state only by members of the Communist bloc; in policy it is an abject follower of the Soviet Union. Drab and gray, it is nonetheless an important producer of petrochemicals and machinery, ranking sixth among European states in industrial output (West Germany is third). Few of its products, however, reach its own citizens; East Germany's role is that of a Soviet-bloc supplier. Within its borders lies the former German capital, Berlin, a Western outpost still garrisoned by Allied troops.

East Germany. Principal Cities: Dresden, East Berlin (cap.), Karl-Marx-Stadt, Leipzig. *Population:* 17,000,000. *Area:* 41,815 sq. mi. *Government:* Communist dictatorship. *Economy:* Industry becoming increasingly important. *Religion:* Predominantly Protestant. *Language:* German. *See:* GER.

West Germany. Principal Cities: Bonn (cap.), Hamburg, Munich, West Berlin. *Population:* 58,290,000. *Area:* 96,114 sq. mi. *Government:* Federal republic. Democracy. *Economy:* Largely industrial. *Religion:* Protestant in the north, Roman Catholic in the south. *Language:* German. *See:* GER.

GREECE A stony, mountainous peninsula jutting out into the Mediterranean Sea, Greece has been one of the least favored lands on earth. Only its narrow valleys are fertile, the omnipresent hills suitable only for herding sheep. The victims of a grudging nature, the Greeks have also suffered at the hands of man. They have been invaded, conquered and controlled by neighboring powers for most of the past two millennia: by the Romans, by the Byzantine Empire, by the Ottoman Empire, and most recently by Italian and German armies in World War II. But poverty and misfortune are not the whole, or true, story of Greece or the Greeks, for this was the place and the people that in the 10 centuries before Christ created perhaps the noblest and most intellectually creative civilization ever seen. The Greeks invented democracy and almost the entire substructure of ideas and concepts that underlie Western civilization.

They also colonized many areas around the Mediterranean. But then, as if punishing themselves for what their own ethical system taught was the worst of sins, intellectual pride, the Greeks went a long way toward destroying their civilization in the Peloponnesian Wars. Through all their catastrophes, however, the Greeks have endured. The winning of the modern nation's independence in 1821 by no means brought tranquillity, but since the trials of World War II and a subsequent four years of civil war, the Greeks have built an increasingly prosperous society. Shipbuilding and other maritime activities flourish, modern agriculture is making the ancient land more productive, industries such as textiles, chemicals and mining are growing swiftly, and tourism is on the rise. This growing economy was further stimulated when Greece became an Associate Member of the European Economic Community in November 1962.

 Principal Cities: Athens (cap.), Piraeus, Salonika. *Population:* 8,510,000. *Area:* 50,944 sq. mi. *Government:* Constitutional monarchy. *Economy:* Mainly agricultural; some industry. *Religion:* Greek Orthodox. *Language:* Greek. *See:* GRE.

HUNGARY A country of flat plains, Hungary has long been an important agricultural producer. In partial consequence, it has also been a target for invaders. Its name derives from a Magyar tribe known as the On Ogurs, fierce horsemen from Central Asia who established an independent kingdom on the Danube plain in the 10th Century. Turks held control of much of the area from 1526 to 1699; eventually it fell under the complete control of the Austrian House of Habsburg. Not until the end of World War I did Hungary again attain a separate existence; after World War II it was scooped into the Soviet orbit. Despite a heroic rebellion in 1956, Hungary still lies in the Russian shadow. While the Communists have managed to build sufficient industry to account for more than half of the national output, the country's economy has been troubled in recent years; both agricultural and industrial productivity remain low.

 Principal Cities: Budapest (cap.), Debrecen, Miskolc. *Population:* 10,146,000. *Area:* 35,919 sq. mi. *Government:* Communist dictatorship. *Economy:* Primarily agricultural, but becoming increasingly industrialized. *Religion:* Mainly Roman Catholic. *Language:* Magyar. *See:* EEU.

ICELAND First settled by Norsemen in the Ninth Century and later populated by immigrants from Sweden and the British Isles, the island republic of Iceland is Europe's westernmost democracy. Much of the island is covered with glaciers, hot geyser spray or lava; Icelanders live mostly on coastal shores. Fishing is the major industry; cod, herring and such fishing by-products as cod-liver oil account for more than 80 per cent of Iceland's exports. A part of Norway from 1264 to 1380 and then under Danish control or domination until World War II, Iceland retains close ties with Scandinavia. It was one of the founding members of the Nordic Council (see page 57) and it holds a typically Scandinavian interest in education. Its numerous free schools help to give it one of the world's highest literacy rates.

 Principal City: Reykjavik (cap.). *Area:* 39,768 sq. mi. *Population:* 189,000. *Government:* Republic. *Economy:* Fishing; some agriculture. *Religion:* Lutheran. *Language:* Icelandic, a tongue similar to Old Norse. *See:* SCN.

IRELAND A land the British essayist G. K. Chesterton once characterized as one where all the wars are merry and all the songs are sad, Ireland spent seven and a half centuries under frequently repressive British rule, a fact reflected in the present-day division of the island into two separate political entities: the independent republic of Ireland (Eire) and the six counties that constitute Northern Ireland, a part of the United Kingdom (see page 14). Foreign domination did not help Ireland. In the 1840s blight struck the potato crops that were the basic diet of its people. A million and a half Irishmen died; another million emigrated. Today, Ireland has only half as many people as it had in 1845. The crop disaster also caused a revolution in Irish farming; nowadays, utilizing its legendary, grand grass, Ireland specializes in dairying and the raising of cattle, horses and sheep.

Since attaining independence in 1921, the Irish have also succeeded in establishing considerable light industry; exports of such goods as paper, machinery and textiles are on the rise. But perhaps the finest Irish export has been in a less tangible field: literature. Ireland has produced not only William Butler Yeats, a poet who stands among the giants, and the novelist James Joyce, who has been described as the greatest master of the English language since John Milton, but a host of other writers whose output and achievement would do proud a far larger country than Ireland.

 Principal Cities: Cork, Dublin (cap.), Limerick. *Population:* 2,855,000. *Area:* 27,135 sq. mi. *Government:* Republic. *Economy:* Agriculture, light industry. *Religion:* Roman Catholic. *Languages:* Gaelic official; English. *See:* IRE.

A GUIDE TO NATIONAL NAMES

To designate the countries listed in this gazetteer and discussed elsewhere in this volume, the editors have followed the official usage of the United States Department of State. Virtually all of the nations of the world have both a short-form and a long-form name. Afghanistan's long-form name, for example, is Kingdom of Afghanistan; Zambia's long-form name is Republic of Zambia. Short forms like Afghanistan or United States or Zambia are commonly used except on official documents or on formal occasions. In cases where, by reason of historical circumstances, a country has two rival governments, both have been listed and discussed together. East Germany and West Germany, for example, are discussed under the entry "Germany"; Communist China and Nationalist China are discussed under "China."

ITALY Flanked by the Tyrrhenian and Adriatic Seas, the mountainous peninsula of Italy sweeps 730 miles into the Mediterranean from the southern coast of Europe. Once the homeland of the most powerful nation on earth, Italy dissolved into a collection of bickering petty kingdoms and papal states after the disappearance of Roman authority in the Fifth Century A.D., not to re-emerge as one country until the 19th Century, when dedicated nationalists waged the wars that eventually led to unification under King Victor Emmanuel II of Sardinia. Unity did not bring stability. In 1922, after years of economic unrest, Benito Mussolini became Premier of Italy and, as its dictator, set Italy upon the fateful road of Fascism, empire and alliance with Nazi Germany. After defeat in World War II the country was an economic and political shambles. Abolishing the monarchy and establishing a republic, Italy began to rebuild with American aid. By the 1950s it was in the midst of an amazing economic expansion, known not only for its traditional exports of fruits, wines and cheeses but for sleek autos, well-designed machinery,

Gazetteer

efficient electronic products and high-fashion clothes. Most of these products came from the bustling cities of Milan, Turin and Genoa in the northern Po valley, where hydroelectric power from the Alps and the valley's complex of rivers was used to overcome Italy's critical shortage of coal and other industrial fuels. The Po valley is also Italy's agricultural heartland. Central Italy contains the historic cities of Rome, Florence and Pisa, which help to attract more than 23 million visitors each year. The south, with its barren soil and overpopulation, is the most economically retarded section of Italy. Recent measures by the Government have inspired massive public-works projects. But the poverty in the south is so severe that Italy still possesses one of the lowest per capita income levels in Western Europe.

 Principal Cities: Genoa, Milan, Naples, Rome (cap.), Turin. *Population:* 51,090,000. *Area:* 116,303 sq. mi. *Government:* Republic. *Economy:* Industry, agriculture, tourism. Exports textiles, motor vehicles, agricultural produce. *Religion:* Roman Catholic. *Language:* Italian. *See:* ITA.

LIECHTENSTEIN A tiny pastoral country perched between Austria and Switzerland, Liechtenstein is ruled by a 15-member Landtag and a hereditary prince of the House of Liechtenstein. It has no army, and only 18 policemen, and lives largely by providing a tax shelter for foreign firms.

 Principal City: Vaduz (cap.). *Area:* 61 sq. mi. *Population:* 18,000. *Government:* Constitutional monarchy. *Economy:* Light industry, cattle raising. *Religion:* Roman Catholic. *Language:* German. *See:* Page 100, HBK.

LUXEMBOURG A large and major power in the Middle Ages, Luxembourg was divided or seized by its neighbors time and again over the centuries; not until 1867 did the European nations grant it independence. Today it is small but prosperous; its land is intensively farmed and large deposits of iron ore help to make it Western Europe's sixth-largest steel producer.

 Principal City: Luxembourg (cap.). *Population:* 328,000. *Area:* 999 sq. mi. *Government:* Constitutional monarchy. *Economy:* Mainly industrial. *Religion:* Roman Catholic. *Languages:* French, German, Luxembourgian. *See:* LCO.

MALTA For 35 centuries one world sea power or another ruled Malta, coveting its strategic location in the Mediterranean. Independent since 1964, the barren country is developing industry and tourism for the money to meet its deficit in food and goods.

 Principal City: Valletta (cap.). *Population:* 324,000. *Area:* 122 sq. mi. *Government:* Member British Commonwealth. *Economy:* Efforts being made to develop exports. *Religion:* Roman Catholic. *Languages:* Maltese, English.

MONACO In Europe's smallest principality, Monaco, the major industry is tourism; an annual two million visitors are drawn by the country's mild climate, gambling casino, and its rulers, Prince Rainier III and his consort, the former Grace Kelly of Philadelphia and Hollywood.

 Principal Cities: Monaco-Ville (cap.), Monte Carlo. *Population:* 22,000. *Area:* .8 sq. mi. *Government:* Constitutional monarchy. *Economy:* Tourism, gambling. *Religion:* Roman Catholic. *Language:* French. *See:* Page 103, HBK.

A GROWING NUMBER OF COUNTRIES

The dissolution of European colonial empires since World War II has brought about a vast increase in the number of independent states. Before the war 71 countries were independent; today there are more than 125. In Europe itself, which contains 33 states, the number has remained relatively constant for decades; Austria-Hungary, Montenegro and Serbia disappeared after World War I, but were replaced by four new countries: Austria, Hungary, Czechoslovakia and Yugoslavia. During World War II the number was reduced by three when Estonia, Latvia and Lithuania were forcibly incorporated into the Soviet Union. Some of the world's smallest states—Andorra, Liechtenstein, Monaco, San Marino and Vatican City—are to be found in Europe; together they cover an area less than a quarter the size of Rhode Island.

NETHERLANDS An astonishing range of industrial and agricultural products makes the Netherlands (familiarly known as Holland) one of the world's busiest trading centers. With a modern, efficient industrial complex built out of the rubble of World War II, Holland produces, among other things, steel, ships, textiles, chemicals, and such diverse goods as chinaware and electrical appliances. Holland's agricultural output is equally prodigious, with exports of dairy products, vegetables and grains, as well as the famous tulip and other flower bulbs. As a result, Holland's main port, Rotterdam, moves more goods than any other world seaport. It handles more than 100 million tons each year, regularly surpassing the port of New York. Holland has always reclaimed land from the North Sea with sturdy systems of dikes, ditches and pumping stations. The land is needed for the country's 12 million people, who give it a density of more than 1,000 per square mile, one of the highest in Europe. More than a quarter of Holland's land is below sea level. Once a major seafaring nation, Holland now has scattered territories in South America (Surinam) and the Antilles.

 Principal Cities: Amsterdam (cap.), Rotterdam, The Hague (seat of Government). *Population:* 12,127,000. *Area:* 12,978 sq. mi. *Government:* Constitutional monarchy. *Economy:* Agriculture, trade and industry. *Religion:* About 40 per cent Roman Catholic, 40 per cent Protestant. *Language:* Dutch. *See:* LCO.

NORWAY With deep waterways called fjords slicing far into its mountainous countryside, Norway has a coastline of more than 2,000 miles on the western part of the Scandinavian peninsula, and it has long been a nation wedded to the sea and ships. It has the fourth-largest merchant fleet in the world; fishing is a major industry. Less than 4 per cent of the land is cultivated, but there is considerable dairying, and vast forests give rise to lumbering and pulp and paper making. Water and mountains provide the country with another blessing: cheap power. The harnessed mountain streams and rivers make Norway the most hydroelectrified nation in the world in proportion to population.

Principal Cities: Bergen, Oslo (cap.), Trondheim. *Population:* 3,695,000. *Area:* 125,181 sq. mi. *Government:* Constitutional monarchy. *Economy:* Shipping, lumbering, fishing, tourism. *Religion:* Lutheran. *Languages:* Riksmål, a dialect of Danish; Landsmål, derived from Old Norse. *See:* SCN.

POLAND A nation that has battled through the centuries to remain intact, Poland is a land marked by tragedy. In the middle of the 18th Century the country covered 280,000 square miles of Eastern Europe. But in 1772 Russia, Prussia and Austria partitioned a third of Poland. In 1793 Russia and Prussia claimed half the remaining land and finally, in 1795, the three countries swallowed Poland whole, wiping it from the map of Europe. The country was briefly reconstituted by Napoleon; in 1864 Russia incorporated it within its own territory, renaming it Vistula Land. It was not until after World War I, in 1918, that Poland again emerged as a nation. Germany invaded in 1939, precipitating World War II and making Poland a battleground of Europe. Then, only a short time after the fighting had ceased, the Communists gained control of the state and Poland was trapped behind the Iron Curtain. Today, Poland is struggling to increase its markets for machinery, textiles and glass in the West. More than half the country is still agricultural.

Principal Cities: Cracow, Lódź, Warsaw (cap.). *Population:* 31,420,000. *Area:* 120,359 sq. mi. *Government:* Communist dictatorship. *Economy:* Agricultural, but increasingly industrialized since World War II. *Religion:* Predominantly Roman Catholic. *Languages:* Polish, German, Russian. *See:* EEU.

PORTUGAL One of the poorest of European states, Portugal is also one of the most beautiful. Its exports consist of such products as olive oil, cork and port wine, but its hills are adorned with lovely castles and cathedrals, mementos of the great empire that Portugal built in the 15th and 16th Centuries. Oddly, it has once again become the world's leading colonial power, the only country still controlling large areas in Africa. Portugal has been a dictatorship since 1932, when Dr. António de Oliveira Salazar took control of the country.

Principal City: Lisbon (cap.). *Area:* 35,510 sq. mi. *Population:* 9,167,000. *Government:* Officially a republic. *Economy:* Mainly agricultural. *Religion:* Roman Catholic. *Language:* Portuguese. *See:* Page 73, HBK.

ROMANIA Traditionally an oil, timber and food producer, Romania is a country of mountains and long plains. Like its neighbors, it fell under Communist control after World War II. Despite Russian pressure that it remain a supplier of oil, wood and wheat to the Soviet bloc, Romania has been rapidly industrializing; its growth rate in recent years has averaged 15 per cent, the highest in Europe. Long regarded as one of the more subservient Soviet satellites, Romania has in fact been a leader in the drive for economic independence.

Principal Cities: Bucharest (cap.), Cluj, Timisoara. *Population:* 18,927,000. *Area:* 91,699 sq. mi. *Government:* Communist dictatorship. *Economy:* Industrializing. *Religion:* Eastern Orthodox. *Language:* Romanian. *See:* BAL.

SAN MARINO The oldest republic in the world, San Marino is perched on a mountaintop in northeastern Italy. Usually politically stable, San Marino shocked the West when Communists took control of the Government in 1945 and held it until 1957. Tourism and stamps bring in the bulk of San Marino's revenue.

Principal City: San Marino (cap.). *Population:* 17,000. *Area:* 24 sq. mi. *Government:* Republic. *Economy:* Predominantly agricultural; considerable tourism. *Religion:* Roman Catholic. *Language:* Italian. *See:* Page 102, HBK.

SPAIN This is a country with a long, eventful and often tragic history. A site of Greek colonies, and later a part of the Roman Empire, it was largely conquered and controlled by the Moors from the Eighth to the 15th Centuries. Then the monarchs of Aragon and Castile, Ferdinand and Isabella, married, united their kingdoms and expelled the Moors. In the fateful year 1492, Isabella and Ferdinand dispatched Christopher Columbus westward, a move that eventually gave Spain control over the major portion of South and Central America. The gold that flowed in from these vast realms made Spain rich—but brought it into violent and sustained conflict with other expanding countries. In 1588 a British fleet destroyed the Spanish Armada off English shores; in many eyes the defeat reflected imperial Spain's inherent weaknesses. After it, Spain began the long decline into the poverty that has characterized the country in recent centuries. Wracked in the 1930s by one of the modern era's cruelest civil wars, Spain has tried, and is trying, to make bearable the lot of the farmers who work its fields and of the workers who mine its coal and run its slowly expanding industries.

Principal City: Madrid (cap.). *Area:* 194,833 sq. mi. *Population:* 31,604,000. *Government:* Officially a monarchy; in fact a dictatorship. *Economy:* Primarily agricultural; industry developing slowly. *Religion:* Roman Catholic. *Languages:* Spanish, Catalan, others. *See:* SPA.

SWEDEN Hidden behind its snowy mountains on the eastern side of the Scandinavian peninsula, Sweden is a land of energetic, bustling people who have in times past played large-scale roles in European history. During the Thirty Years' War they led the Protestant side, and in the reign (1697-1718) of Charles XII they all but conquered the whole north of Europe, Russia included. After the Napoleonic Wars ended in 1815, Sweden turned its energies in other directions, building what is today a thriving economy based on lumber, hydroelectric power and a high-grade steel industry. Sweden is also a producer of merchant ships and fine glassware, and its fishing fleets are world-renowned. Executive power in Sweden, a neutral nation for more than 150 years, is vested in the king, who in practice acts only with the consent of the Swedish parliament.

Principal City: Stockholm (cap.). *Population:* 7,661,000. *Area:* 173,665 sq. mi. *Government:* Constitutional monarchy. *Economy:* Becoming increasingly industrialized. *Religion:* Lutheran. *Language:* Swedish. *See:* SCN.

SWITZERLAND High in the Alps, Switzerland is a nation poor in natural resources that waxes prosperous on unlimited water power, the superb skills of its people and the beauty of mountains that attract more than five million tourists a year. The Swiss turn out all manner of things: watches, precision machinery, textiles, chocolates and chemicals. The country is also one of the world's banking centers. A seven-man executive committee, chosen by the legislature, runs traditionally neutral Switzerland, with one of its members serving as president each year. But important matters are decided by popular referendum.

Principal Cities: Basel, Bern (cap.), Geneva, Zurich. *Population:* 5,874,000. *Area:* 15,941 sq. mi. *Government:* Federal republic. *Economy:* Industrial, agricultural. *Religions:* Protestant, Roman Catholic. *Languages:* German, French, Italian, Romansch. *See:* SWI.

UNION OF SOVIET SOCIALIST REPUBLICS
Geographically the largest single nation in the world, the land traditionally known as Russia sprawls across one seventh of the earth's surface. Covering so vast an area, Russia is inevitably a country of climatic extremes: northeastern Siberia is one of the coldest regions inhabited by man; the Central Asian deserts are bleak and windswept; the Black Sea region resembles the Mediterranean coast. The country is also endowed with a variety of natural resources, being rich in manganese, coal, iron ore, potash and gold. After the U.S., this once-backward nation now produces more steel, oil, electric power, aluminum and cement than any other country. In 1949 the U.S.S.R. became the second nation to produce an atom bomb, and in 1957 it became the first to place a satellite into orbit. Such achievements are a partial result of the fact that since the 1930s the Soviet state has placed strong emphasis on the development of heavy industry, frequently to the detriment of agriculture and the production of consumer goods. In recent years the country's rate of economic expansion has slowed, and in the mid-1960s Russia began experiments with the decentralization of economic controls to restimulate growth. Agriculture, too, remains a problem, for while the country is among the world's largest producers of grains and other basic foodstuffs, output from the tightly controlled (and widely unpopular) state and collective farm system has been relatively static, there is little additional land available for cultivation, and the Soviet population is increasing at the rate of 3.5 million persons each year. Perhaps in part because of a desire to devote attention to such domestic problems, the Soviet Union has, since the death of Joseph Stalin in 1953, adopted a more moderate attitude toward the West.

Principal Cities: Leningrad, Moscow (cap.). *Population:* 227,687,000. *Area:* 8,649,489 sq. mi. *Government:* Communist dictatorship. *Economy:* Mainly industrial. Coal, iron ore, steel, lumber, fur, oil, caviar, manganese, chromium exported. *Religion:* Mainly Russian Orthodox. *Languages:* Russian; 145 other languages. *See:* RUS.

UNITED KINGDOM
Hard hit by the strains of World War II, in which the bonds of its empire were weakened, in which its financial resources were virtually exhausted and in which its traditional leadership in world trade passed to the United States, this island country—known officially as the United Kingdom of Great Britain and Northern Ireland and less formally as Britain—is trying hard to adjust to the new world order. Still one of the most highly industrialized nations in the world, Britain is a leading producer of coal, iron and steel and of heavy machinery, automobiles, aircraft and textiles. Nevertheless, this industrial structure has begun to show cracks and, worse, an increasing inability to compete successfully abroad. Even so, seen against the austere background of the late 1940s, individual Britons seem prosperous. One out of eight owns an automobile and nearly that many manage vacations abroad each year. Moreover, despite the fact that it has since the war granted independence to more than 20 states encompassing 700 million people, Britain is still a major political force in the world. As a leading member of the Western alliance, it maintains an overseas defense force of 158,000 men stretching from Germany to Aden, as well as a substantial force in Malaysia, and gives more than $500 million a year in aid to underdeveloped nations, many of them former members of the empire and now associated with Britain in the British Commonwealth of Nations (see page 62). Almost all of them paid Britain the compliment of modeling their governments on that of Westminster—or, at the least, they emulate the trappings of British democracy. In 1965 Britain celebrated the 700th anniversary of the birth of Parliament in 1265, an event, Winston Churchill once observed, that "lighted a fire never to be quenched in English history"—and, he might have added, the world's.

Principal Cities: Birmingham, Glasgow, London (cap.). *Population:* 54,213,000. *Area:* 94,220 sq. mi. *Government:* Constitutional monarchy. *Economy:* Highly industrialized; iron and steel manufacturing, trade, tourism important. *Religions:* Anglican; Presbyterian (Scotland). *Languages:* English, Gaelic, Welsh. *See:* BRI.

VATICAN CITY
An independent sovereign state since 1929, Vatican City is a triangle of churches, palaces, courts, gardens and the renowned Basilica of St. Peter. It is the residence of the Roman Catholic pope and a shrine to three great artists who built and decorated much of it: Bernini, Michelangelo and Raphael. The area also contains a number of the world's most important museums and the oldest (15th Century) public library in Europe.

Population: 900. *Area:* 108.7 acres (excluding certain churches in Rome and the pope's villa at Castel Gandolfo, which are technically parts of the Vatican City state). *Government:* The pope is absolute sovereign and proprietor, but in practice he delegates the greater proportion of his temporal powers to a lay governor and a council. *Economy:* Aside from contributions from the faithful throughout the world, the Vatican obtains revenue from investments, particularly in Italian industry and real estate. *Languages:* Latin is official for Church matters; Italian for the Vatican City state. *See:* Page 104, HBK.

YUGOSLAVIA
The largest of the Balkan states, Yugoslavia has in the years since World War II been more fortunate than its neighbors. Pulpwood and lumber taken from its extensive forests are important products, and although agriculture still occupies half the population, the exploitation of rich mineral resources has enabled Yugoslavia to take significant strides toward industrialization. Moreover, the striking beauty of the country attracts tourists at the rate of 3,300,000 a year. A composite of independently minded peoples, Yugoslavia came into existence after World War I; Marxism arrived at the end of World War II with Josip Broz Tito, who used his position as chief of the wartime Partisan movement to establish a Communist Government after the Nazis' withdrawal. In 1948 Yugoslavia became the first Communist state to break with Russia.

Principal City: Belgrade (cap.). *Population:* 19,279,000. *Area:* 98,766 sq. mi. *Government:* Communist dictatorship. *Economy:* Agriculture important: increasingly industralized. *Religions:* Eastern Orthodox, Roman Catholic. *Languages:* Serbo-Croatian, Slovenian, Macedonian. *See:* BAL.

AFRICA

Africa, the second-largest continent, spans 5,000 miles from the Mediterranean to the Cape of Good Hope and spreads 4,700 miles at its broadest. Its 294 million people speak some 800 languages and dialects, giving Africa an almost crippling linguistic diversity. Its nations are no less disparate. Africa contains some two score individual countries, ranging in culture and politics from such Arabic North African states as Morocco, Algeria, Libya and Egypt through the often poverty-stricken nations of Tropical Africa to the troubled Republic of South Africa. Most African nations emerged only recently from the colonial empires built by European states in the 19th Century. Many of these, though nominally republics, are in reality military regimes. The northwestern coast of Africa on the Mediterranean is a mild land of citrus groves, olive trees and vineyards. This placid environment is dramatically altered to the south by the three-million-square-mile wastes of the Sahara. Below this formidable barrier is a belt of grasslands and tropical rain forests astride the equator. In East Africa snow-capped mountains rise. The Kalahari Desert intrudes to the south, only to give way to rich grasslands and croplands that extend to the tip of the continent.

ALGERIA For 200 miles inland from the Mediterranean shore, Algeria is similar in climate to southern France and is heavily populated. But south of this fringe, beyond the Sahara Atlas Mountains, yawns the Sahara itself—the vast desert that occupies two thirds of Algeria. Predominantly agricultural, Algeria produces grains, citrus fruits and wine. It has not been a quiet land. In 1830 France conquered Algiers, and in 1848 it declared Algeria a part of France itself. The indigenous Algerian Moslems and the French settlers clashed continuously, their struggle erupting in brutal and bloody war in 1954. Finally, in 1962, France abandoned the fight and Algeria became independent.

Principal Cities: Algiers (cap.), Bône, Constantine, Oran. *Population:* 11,600,000. *Area:* 919,-590 sq. mi. *Government:* Republic. *Economy:* Agriculture, petroleum, iron ore, phosphates. *Religions:* Moslem; Catholic minority. *Languages:* Arabic, French. *See:* ARW.

BOTSWANA Roughly the size of France, the former British colony of Bechuanaland achieved independence in 1966. A poor country, just north of South Africa, Botswana is landlocked and two thirds desert (the Kalahari). Its only arable land lies along its eastern border, where 80 per cent of its population lives.

Principal City: Gaberones (cap.). *Population:* 559,000. *Area:* 22,000 sq. mi. *Government:* Republic; member British Commonwealth. *Economy:* Livestock raising, subsistence farming, migrant labor to South Africa. *Religion:* Animist. *Languages:* English, Tswana. *See:* SAF.

BURUNDI A former Belgian colony, Burundi became independent in 1962 after splitting from its sister state Rwanda. Burundi is an agricultural nation that exports coffee and cotton but whose budget nonetheless continually shows a deficit.

Principal City: Bujumbura (cap.). *Population:* 2,650,000. *Area:* 10,747 sq. mi. *Government:* Constitutional monarchy. *Economy:* Subsistence agriculture. *Religions:* Traditional animist beliefs; about half the population has been converted to Roman Catholicism. *Languages:* Kirundi, French. *See:* TAF.

CAMEROON A federation of former French and British West African territories, Cameroon is populated by people of a number of different tribes, and encompasses a wide variety of lands (savanna to rain forest) and climates (temperate to tropical). It exports bananas, cocoa and coffee; some aluminum is made.

Principal Cities: Buea, Douala, Yaoundé (cap.). *Population:* 5,103,000. *Area:* 183,568 sq. mi. *Government:* Federal republic. *Economy:* Agricultural. *Religions:* Traditional animist beliefs; Christian and Moslem minorities. *Languages:* English and French official. *See:* TAF.

CENTRAL AFRICAN REPUBLIC Located in the heart of Africa, the Central African Republic lies on a rolling plateau, with a giant rain forest covering the southern half. About 90 per cent of the country's people live in rural areas and more than 95 per cent of them are illiterate. The country is landlocked; exports must be taken 900 miles to a seaport. Formerly known as Ubangi-Shari, the nation gained its independence from France in 1960.

Principal Cities: Bangui (cap.), Mbala. *Population:* 1,352,000. *Area:* 238,224 sq. mi. *Government:* Republic. *Economy:* Basically agricultural; exports cotton, coffee, peanuts, diamonds. *Religions:* Animist beliefs; Christian and Moslem minorities. *Languages:* French official; local dialects. *See:* TAF.

CHAD Landlocked in north-central Africa, Chad consists of a sterile northern desert and a tropical southern region. About 96 per cent of the people of this lightly populated land, which is more than twice the size of France, are farmers or herdsmen. Cotton accounts for about 80 per cent of exports.

Principal Cities: Fort-Archambault, Fort-Lamy (cap.), Moundou. *Population:* 3,300,000. *Area:* 495,752 sq. mi. *Government:* Republic. *Economy:* Agricultural. *Religions:* Moslem, traditional animist beliefs. *Languages:* French official; various Arabic and African dialects. *See:* TAF.

CONGO (BRAZZAVILLE) A former French colony, the Congo (whose capital is Brazzaville, on the north bank of the Congo River) is hot and humid with little good farmland. Almost 80 per cent of the people are subsistence farmers; wood and its by-products constitute over half the exports. An economic asset is Pointe Noire, the Congo's seaport, which handles goods from surrounding nations. The Congo's left-leaning government has warmly welcomed assistance from Communist China and Cuba, and has provided Communism with its firmest foothold in Africa.

Principal Cities: Brazzaville (cap.), Pointe Noire. *Population:* 826,000. *Area:* 132,046 sq. mi. *Government:* Republic. *Economy:* Based on agriculture. *Religions:* Traditional animist beliefs; large Christian minority; some Moslems. *Languages:* French official; various native languages. *See:* TAF.

15

CONGO (KINSHASA) To distinguish this huge country, once known as the Belgian Congo and now called the Democratic Republic of the Congo, from its small neighbor to the northwest (see page 15), the convention evolved of appending to each the name of its capital. The muddle was made worse when, in 1966, after six years of chaos following the withdrawal of Belgium, the country purged itself of European place names. The capital, Leopoldville, became Kinshasa. By whatever name, the country, though unstable politically, is rich in natural resources, exporting 70 per cent of the world's industrial diamonds, 60 per cent of its cobalt, and 10 per cent of its copper and tin.

Principal City: Kinshasa (cap.). *Population:* 15,300,000. *Area:* 905,562 sq. mi. *Government:* Republic. *Economy:* Mainly agricultural. Important mineral deposits. *Religions:* Traditional animist beliefs; large Christian minority; some Moslems and Jews. *Languages:* Many native languages. *See:* TAF.

DAHOMEY Tucked under the West African geographic bulge, Dahomey is a long, narrow tropical land that is chiefly agricultural. Products obtained from palm trees, particularly oil, make up 65 per cent of Dahomey's exports. As a French colony, Dahomey developed an able corps of civil servants who often have been sought by other French-speaking African nations.

Principal Cities: Cotonou, Porto-Novo (cap.). *Population:* 2,300,000. *Area:* 44,696 sq. mi. *Government:* Republic. *Economy:* Mainly agricultural; exports palm products, coffee. *Religions:* Animist beliefs; Christian, Moslem minorities. *Languages:* French official; tribal languages. *See:* TAF.

ETHIOPIA A country of high plateaus with abundant rain, low humidity and an average annual temperature of 55 degrees, Ethiopia, in northeastern Africa, has some of the most fertile croplands on the continent. Coffee has been part of Ethiopian farming for so many centuries that some experts believe the word "coffee" derives from Kaffa, an agricultural region in the southwest. Grains, oilseeds and hides are also exported. Ethiopia's longtime ruler, Haile Selassie I, gained power in 1930. He was overthrown during the 1935-1936 Italian invasion, but was restored to the throne when Ethiopia was liberated from the Italians in 1941. Ethiopia's days as a landlocked nation ended in 1952 when Eritrea, a United Nations Trust Territory on the Red Sea, became a part of the country. The Eritrean port of Assab can handle up to 660,000 tons of goods yearly.

Principal City: Addis Ababa (cap.). *Population:* 22,200,000. *Area:* 457,266 sq. mi. *Government:* Constitutional monarchy. *Economy:* Mostly agricultural; some industry and manufacturing. *Religion:* Ethiopian Orthodox. *Languages:* Amharic and English official; many native languages. *See:* TAF.

GABON Discoveries of iron ore, uranium, oil and gold, plus large manganese deposits, have given Gabon a viable economy. A former French territory on the equator in West Africa, Gabon has long sold lumber from its rain forests. It has a light population density, and almost 90 per cent of its children attend school.

Principal Cities: Libreville (cap.), Port-Gentil. *Population:* 462,000. *Area:* 103,089 sq. mi. *Government:* Republic. *Economy:* Forestry, mining and agriculture. *Religions:* Christian majority; large minority following animist beliefs. *Languages:* French official; many native languages. *See:* TAF.

GAMBIA No more than 30 miles wide and about 300 miles long, the ex-British territory of Gambia extends along the banks of the winding Gambia River in West Africa. About 90 per cent of its small export earnings comes from peanuts.

Principal City: Bathurst (cap.). *Population:* 330,000. *Area:* 4,003 sq. mi. *Government:* Independent member British Commonwealth. *Economy:* Agricultural; exports peanuts, rice and beeswax. *Religion:* Predominantly Moslem. *Languages:* English; various native languages. *See:* TAF.

GHANA In 1957 the British Colony of the Gold Coast became one of the first African nations to gain independence and was looked to as a leader of pan-Africanism. Potentially Ghana is rich. Some 300,000 independent farmers produce more than one third of the world's cocoa. Hardwoods are exported, as are diamonds, gold, manganese and bauxite. However, a decade of increasingly tight dictatorial rule, during which the country's finances were grossly mismanaged, left it on the verge of bankruptcy and precipitated a military coup. Since then, recovery has been slow.

Principal Cities: Accra (cap.), Cape Coast. *Population:* 7,340,000. *Area:* 91,843 sq. mi. *Government:* Republic; member British Commonwealth. *Economy:* World's largest producer of cocoa; also exports minerals, timber. *Religion:* Animist beliefs. *Languages:* English; local languages. *See:* TAF.

GUINEA A primarily agricultural nation situated on the west coast of Africa, Guinea also has rich bauxite deposits. In 1958 Guinea became the only former French African colony to break all ties with France. This hampered its economy, and subsequently new trade and cultural agreements were signed with France.

Principal Cities: Conakry (cap.), Kankan. *Population:* 3,420,000. *Area:* 94,925 sq. mi. *Government:* Republic. *Economy:* Largely agricultural; exports bananas, palm nuts, coffee, bauxite, iron ore, diamonds. *Religions:* Predominantly Moslem; animist beliefs. *Languages:* French; native languages. *See:* TAF.

IVORY COAST The third-largest coffee exporter in the world, the Ivory Coast is a self-sufficient nation. About 90 per cent of its people farm, fish or cut timber. The Ivory Coast gained its independence from France in 1960 and is one of the most economically prosperous of the former French West African colonies. Industry is limited, but manganese and diamonds are mined.

Principal Cities: Abidjan (cap.), Bouaké. *Population:* 3,750,000. *Area:* 124,503 sq. mi. *Government:* Republic. *Economy:* Mostly agricultural. *Religions:* Traditional animist beliefs predominate; Moslem and Christian minorities. *Languages:* French official; many African languages. *See:* TAF.

KENYA Independent since 1964, this former British colony bestrides the equator on the east coast of Africa. An agricultural nation with coffee its main export, Kenya is one of the few African countries with a major dairy industry. Its industrial complex, moreover, is expanding, as is the tourist revenue from its seven game parks. Kenya was torn asunder in the years 1952 to 1956 when insurgent tribesmen known as the Mau Mau terrorized the white colonials, demanding the return of tribal lands, self-government for native tribes and independence from Britain. After much slaughter on both sides, the revolt subsided by 1956. That year the franchise was extended to all Kenyans, and in 1960 a new constitution gave Africans a majority in the Legislative Assembly.

Principal City: Nairobi (cap.). *Population:* 9,365,000. *Area:* 224,960 sq. mi. *Government:* Republic; member British Commonwealth. *Economy:* Mainly agricultural. *Religions:* Animist beliefs predominate; large Christian minority. *Languages:* English; Swahili; tribal languages. *See:* TAF.

LESOTHO Awkwardly situated entirely within the Republic of South Africa, the former British Crown Colony of Basutoland achieved sovereignty in 1966. With not enough arable land to support its population of nearly one million Basuto tribesmen, this mountainous country is relying on the development of its hydroelectric potential.

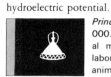

Principal City: Maseru (cap.). *Population:* 975,000. *Area:* 11,716. *Government:* Constitutional monarchy. *Economy:* Agriculture, migrant labor to South Africa. *Religions:* Protestant, animist minority. *Languages:* English, Sesotho.

LIBERIA A nation on the western shore of Africa, Liberia was founded by freed slaves sent there by American philanthropical societies in the 1820s. Clashes between the former slaves and the indigenous tribesmen were frequent. Today, the descendants of the slaves make up only 1 per cent of the population. Basically agricultural, Liberia has recently discovered iron-ore deposits.

Principal City: Monrovia (cap.). *Population:* 1,066,000. *Area:* 43,000 sq. mi. *Government:* Republic. *Economy:* Mostly subsistence agriculture; exports iron ore, rubber, diamonds, coffee. *Religions:* Officially Christian; some Moslems. *Languages:* English official; tribal languages and dialects. *See:* TAF.

LIBYA The fourth-largest country in Africa, Libya nonetheless lacks sufficient arable land; 95 per cent of its territory is desert. About 80 per cent of its people therefore cluster along the coast of the Mediterranean Sea or near oases where some meager farming is possible. Made an Italian colony in 1911, Libya was liberated in 1943 after the North African desert campaigns. After Libya attained independence in 1951, its economic future seemed bleak. Then, in 1959, a major oil discovery was made. Estimated oil revenues between 1962 and 1965 amounted to more than $400 million.

Principal Cities: Benghazi, Tripoli (joint caps.). *Population:* 1,559,000. *Area:* 679,358 sq. mi. *Government:* Constitutional monarchy. *Economy:* Agriculture and oil important. *Religion:* Moslem. *Language:* Arabic. *See:* ARW.

MALAGASY REPUBLIC Comprising the island of Madagascar, Malagasy was settled by East Indians long before the French took over in 1896. In 1947, only 13 years before giving the island independence, France put down a revolt costing some 80,000 Malagasy lives. Malagasy has a self-sufficient agricultural economy. It also possesses some fascinating fauna: 800 varieties of butterflies and nearly 300 kinds of birds, half of them found nowhere else.

Principal Cities: Tananarive (cap.), Tuléar. *Area:* 230,035 sq. mi. *Population:* 6,180,000. *Government:* Republic. *Economy:* Agriculture. *Religions:* Animist beliefs; large Christian minority. *Languages:* Malagasy, French. *See:* TAF.

MALAWI Like other new African nations, Malawi, formerly British Nyasaland, is dependent on subsistence agriculture. It relies on Portuguese Mozambique for a port and on racist Rhodesia for imports and so, unlike other newly independent states, it leans toward compromise with these bastions of "white colonialism," and this causes great internal friction.

Principal City: Zomba (cap.). *Area:* 46,066 sq. mi. *Population:* 3,753,000. *Government:* Republic; member British Commonwealth. *Economy:* Basically subsistence agriculture. *Religions:* Animist beliefs; Moslem, Hindu, Christian minorities. *Language:* English official. *See:* TAF.

MALI Suffering from high illiteracy among its people and from a shortage of arable land, Mali has tried to handle its problems by federating with more advanced neighbor states. However, a linkup with Senegal collapsed in 1960, while a projected union with Ghana and Guinea never materialized.

Principal City: Bamako (cap.). *Area:* 464,872 sq. mi. *Population:* 4,576,000. *Government:* Republic. *Economy:* Subsistence agriculture, fishing. *Religions:* Moslem; traditional animist beliefs; small Christian minority. *Languages:* French; tribal languages. *See:* TAF.

MAURITANIA When Mauritania won its freedom from France in 1960, prospects were grim. This arid nation, whose 900,000 people have a per capita income of less than $80 a year, was nevertheless coveted by Morocco. Since then matters have improved. Large iron-ore reserves are being developed, Mauritania has dispensed with its four-million-dollar subsidy from France, and Morocco has ceased its annexation efforts.

Principal City: Nouakchott (cap.). *Population:* 900,000. *Area:* 419,229 sq. mi. *Government:* Republic. *Economy:* Nomadic livestock raising. *Religion:* Officially Moslem. *Languages:* French; Arabic; native languages. *See:* TAF.

MOROCCO This North African kingdom proudly traces its history back 1,200 years. But only 20 per cent of its people are literate, their per capita income is only $160 a year, and their life expectancy is only 40 years. Taken over by France and Spain early in the 20th Century, Morocco did not regain its freedom until 1956. Half the work force is unemployed or underemployed, and from 1963 to 1965 the Moroccan House of Representatives was able to pass only four laws. In mid-1965 King Hassan set about imposing a strong government.

Principal Cities: Casablanca, Rabat (cap.), Tangier. *Population:* 12,959,000. *Area:* 171,305 sq. mi. *Government:* Monarchy. *Economy:* Agriculture, mining. *Religion:* Officially Moslem. *Languages:* Arabic, French, Spanish. *See:* ARW.

NIGER Two and a half times France's size, this landlocked back country is part jungle, part savanna and part desert. About 2 per cent of the land has enough water for cultivation; its central plateau is roamed by nomads.

Principal Cities: Niamey (cap.), Tahoua, Zinder. *Population:* 3,193,000. *Area:* 489,189 sq. mi. *Government:* Republic. *Economy:* Agriculture and stock raising important. *Religions:* Predominantly Moslem; animist minority. *Languages:* French; many native languages. *See:* TAF.

NIGERIA Africa's most populous nation, rich in natural resources and talented people, did remarkably well during its first years of independence from Britain. Foreign capital poured in at the rate of some $90 million yearly. However, early hopes for Nigeria have been shattered by bloody tribal fighting.

Principal Cities: Ibadan, Kano, Lagos (cap.), Nsukka. *Area:* 356,668 sq. mi. *Population:* 56,400,000. *Government:* Republic; member British Commonwealth. *Economy:* Agricultural. *Religions:* Moslem; animist and Christian minorities. *Languages:* English; many native languages. *See:* TAF.

RWANDA This former Belgian trust territory has the lowest per capita income in Tropical Africa. Moreover, its major tribe, the Bahutu, periodically wars on a minority group, the Watusi.

Principal Cities: Gisenyi, Kigali (cap.), Nyanza. *Population:* 3,018,000. *Area:* 10,169 sq. mi. *Government:* Republic. *Economy:* Mainly subsistence agriculture. *Religions:* Traditional animist beliefs, Roman Catholicism. *Languages:* French official; various native languages. *See:* TAF.

SENEGAL Despite the fact that Dakar, its modern capital, is the foremost port in West Africa, a result of the fact that it was once the showcase of French West Africa, Senegal is basically poor; peanuts constitute 75 per cent of the nation's exports.

Principal City: Dakar (cap.). *Area:* 76,124 sq. mi. *Population:* 3,400,000. *Government:* Republic. *Economy:* Agricultural; exports peanuts and peanut products and phosphates. *Religions:* Moslem, animist beliefs, Roman Catholicism. *Languages:* French; many native languages. *See:* TAF.

SIERRA LEONE This country became a British colony in 1808, and independent in 1961. It supplies 25 per cent of the world's diamonds, but most of its people are illiterate and poor.

Principal Cities: Bo, Freetown (cap.), Kenema, Makeni. *Area:* 27,925 sq. mi. *Population:* 2,190,000. *Government:* Republic; member British Commonwealth. *Economy:* Agriculture and mining important. *Religion:* Animist beliefs. *Languages:* English official; various native languages. *See:* TAF.

SOMALIA This nation combines poverty and pugnacity. No Somali youth considers himself well-dressed without an iron bracelet—won only by killing two men in combat—and the country has aggressive plans for a "Greater Somalia."

Principal City: Mogadishio (cap.). *Population:* 2,300,000. *Area:* 246,201 sq. mi. *Government:* Republic. *Economy:* Livestock raising, subsistence agriculture. *Religion:* Officially Moslem. *Languages:* Somali official; Arabic, English, Italian, native tongues. *See:* TAF.

SOUTH AFRICA Covering the lower tip of Africa, South Africa is a land that abounds in valuable minerals (it mines more than half of the world's gold and millions of dollars' worth of diamonds annually) and fertile croplands and grasslands. Economically South Africa is secure, but its policy of "apartheid," or separation of its white population from the nonwhites, makes the country the object of a worldwide controversy. The nation is firmly controlled and governed by the descendants of European settlers, who account for one fifth of the population.

Other South Africans may work for the whites but may not mingle socially with them or live outside special nonwhite areas.

Principal Cities: Cape Town (cap.), Durban, Johannesburg. *Population:* 17,892,000. *Area:* 472,358 sq. mi. *Government:* Republic. *Economy:* Mining, engineering, chemical, petroleum industries; agriculture also important. *Religion:* Predominantly Christian. *Languages:* Afrikaans, English official; many native languages. *See:* SAF.

SUDAN The largest country in Africa, Sudan has a Middle Eastern flavor in the north, where its Arabic-speaking Moslem people dwell. In the south live Negroid tribes. Clashes between the two groups have been a constant torment to the Sudan. Independence, but not stability, came in 1956 after 56 years under the control of an Anglo-Egyptian consortium. A military coup overthrew the parliamentary Government in 1958. In 1964 the military leaders were in turn replaced by a civilian Government.

Principal Cities: Khartoum (cap.), Omdurman, Port Sudan. *Population:* 13,540,000. *Area:* 967,498 sq. mi. *Government:* Republic. *Economy:* Agricultural; cotton exporter. *Religions:* Moslem; animist, Christian minorities. *Languages:* Arabic official; African languages in south. *See:* TAF.

TANZANIA Created by a political union between Tanganyika and the offshore islands of Zanzibar and Pemba, Tanzania came into existence in 1964. Sisal, sugar, cotton and coffee are grown on the mainland; cloves are the major export of the islands.

Principal Cities: Dar es Salaam (cap.), Tanga, Zanzibar. *Area:* 362,820 sq. mi. *Population:* 10,179,000. *Government:* Republic. *Economy:* Subsistence agriculture; exports sisal, cotton, coffee, cloves. *Religions:* Animist beliefs, Christian, Hindu, Moslem. *Languages:* Swahili, English official. *See:* TAF.

TOGO Its boundaries drawn arbitrarily by France, Germany and Britain in the 1880s, Togo is a narrow strip in West Africa, never more than 124 miles wide. Some cocoa and coffee are exported, and exploitation of phosphate deposits brings some revenue.

Principal City: Lomé (cap.). *Area:* 21,853 sq. mi. *Population:* 1,603,000. *Government:* Republic. *Economy:* Agricultural; exports coffee, cocoa, phosphates. *Religions:* Traditional animist beliefs; Christian and Moslem minorities. *Languages:* French official; numerous native languages. *See:* TAF.

TUNISIA The smallest of the North African states, Tunisia is also very poor. Agricultural products provide two fifths of the national income. The country has rich deposits of phosphates and mines iron ore and lead, but it also has severe overpopulation and an additional 200,000 persons are born yearly. Long under French control, Tunisia became independent in 1956, but tensions between it and France remained. In 1961 Tunisia tried to seize the French base at Bizerte; more than 1,000 Tunisians were killed. When the Tunisian Government in 1964 appropriated all foreign-owned lands, France withdrew most economic aid.

Principal Cities: Bizerte, Tunis (cap.). *Population:* 4,565,000. *Area:* 48,332 sq. mi. *Government:* Republic. *Economy:* Agriculture, mining. Exports phosphates, wheat, olive oil, iron ore, wine. *Religions:* Moslem; Christian, Jewish minorities. *Languages:* Arabic official; French widely used. *See:* ARW.

UGANDA Blessed with fertile soil and an agreeable climate, Uganda is a self-sufficient agricultural nation in east-central Africa. Cotton and coffee represent more than three fourths of Uganda's export earnings, and copper is also profitably exported. A British protectorate, Uganda is a federation of four once-separate kingdoms. Uganda's beauty is legendary: its scenic wonders include the Mountains of the Moon and Lake Victoria.

Principal Cities: Jinja, Kampala (cap.). *Population:* 7,551,000. *Area:* 92,525 sq. mi. *Government:* Republic; member British Commonwealth. *Economy:* Mainly agricultural. *Religions:* Animist beliefs; Christian and Moslem minorities. *Languages:* English official; many tribal languages. *See:* TAF.

UNITED ARAB REPUBLIC Occupying the northeast corner of Africa, the United Arab Republic (Egypt) is a land 95 per cent covered by deserts or marshes. As a result about 95 per cent of the country's people live in the fertile Nile River valley. In late summer the Nile habitually floods, not only irrigating the land but depositing rich silt, which makes farming possible in this arid country. Most Egyptians are farmers, cotton being the main cash crop. But the nation is slowly industrializing, and today there are some 3,000 factories in the country. Iron ore is plentiful and more steel factories are being built. Another source of money is tourism: about 400,000 persons visit each year. More than $150 million is added annually to the treasury from tolls paid by the 19,000-odd ships that pass through the Suez Canal, nationalized in 1956 by President Gamal Abdel Nasser, who assumed power after the ouster of the late King Farouk in 1952. Such revenues are being used to bring more of the Egyptian land under irrigation—and for good reason. In an already crowded country, the population is increasing by about half a million persons each year.

Principal Cities: Alexandria, Cairo (cap.), Giza, Port Said, Suez. *Population:* 28,900,000. *Area:* 386,100 sq. mi. *Government:* Republic. *Economy:* Mainly agricultural. *Religion:* Predominantly Moslem. *Language:* Arabic. *See:* ARW.

UPPER VOLTA The main export of this wild, neglected bush country, densely populated for Africa, is its manpower. Large numbers of workers go to Ghana as farm laborers. Another 200,000 men draw pensions from Paris for former service in the French Army. These remittances, plus an annual subsidy from France, ruler until 1960, constitute the main sources of income.

Principal Cities: Bobo-Dioulasso, Koudougou, Ouagadougou (cap.). *Population:* 4,716,000. *Area:* 105,869 sq. mi. *Government:* Republic. *Economy:* Agricultural; some gold mining. *Religions:* Traditional animist beliefs; Moslem minority. *Languages:* French; numerous native languages. *See:* TAF.

ZAMBIA Copper gives Zambia the third-highest per capita income in Africa. However, Zambia must depend on European engineers to keep its mines in production. Landlocked Zambia also depends on neighboring, racist Rhodesia for its smelting coal and on the Rhodesian railway to export the copper.

Principal Cities: Kitwe, Lusaka (cap.), Mufulira, Ndola. *Population:* 3,710,000. *Area:* 288,129 sq. mi. *Government:* Republic; member British Commonwealth. *Economy:* Copper mining, farming. *Religions:* Animist beliefs; some Christians. *Languages:* English official; many native languages. *See:* TAF.

BRITISH AFRICA The rush to freedom that has diminished Britain's once-extensive African empire ran out in the mid-1960s. Of its colonies, protectorates and dependencies—in all, a total of 23 separate political entities—only three remain, and in 1965 one of these, Rhodesia, declared its independence of Britain. With the exception of South Africa, each state upon achieving sovereignty has elected to remain within the Commonwealth (see page 62).

Rhodesia In this sun-drenched, rolling land, just north of South Africa, 220,000 white settlers have carved out a tidy, affluent existence based on tobacco, cattle and small industry. For whites, wages are sufficient to permit a relatively high living standard. In 1961 Britain refused to grant independence to Rhodesia, a self-governing colony since 1923, unless the white ruling minority recognized the rights of Rhodesia's four million Africans. In 1965 Rhodesia's government defied Britain and unilaterally declared itself independent. Britain countered by taking its case to the United Nations, which voted economic sanctions against the rebellious country.

Seychelles On these 92 islands 1,000 miles east of Africa some 46,000 people of mixed European and African ancestry are supported by exports of copra, cinnamon, vanilla and guano.

Swaziland Lush and mineral-rich, Swaziland boasts one of the world's largest asbestos mines plus large deposits of iron ore.

FRENCH AFRICA In 1945 France was by far the largest African power, with 44 million people in four million square miles of territory. The postwar reaction against colonialism reduced French Africa to the two small colonies listed below.

Comoro Islands The Comoros consist of four main islands northwest of Madagascar. On them live 207,000 people who grow coffee and cacao.

French Somaliland Here live 82,000 people clustered around the capital of Djibouti. Terminus of the Ethiopian railway, Djibouti is a relatively busy port.

PORTUGUESE AFRICA Traditionally reluctant to change, Portugal retains the largest colonial empire remaining in Africa. It runs all—the Cape Verde Islands included—with a firm hand. In the 1960s Portugal began countering agitation for freedom by promulgating educational and other social reforms.

Angola This producer of diamonds, oil and coffee, together with its sister colony of Mozambique, provides more than half of Portugal's national income.

Mozambique From Mozambique tea, coffee, cashew nuts and cotton flow to Lisbon. Through its Indian Ocean ports pass Zambia's copper, Rhodesia's tobacco and South Africa's gold.

Portuguese Guinea This impecunious sliver of 12,700 square miles and 525,000 people lives off farming.

SPANISH AFRICA This small empire consists of the two areas cited below, plus the equatorial provinces of Fernando Po and Río Muni. Comprising 10,830 square miles and 246,000 people, they produce coffee and cacao for export.

Ifni An enclave on the Moroccan coast, this Spanish territory ekes a meager living from fishing and livestock raising.

Spanish Sahara Some 24,000 people inhabit the 103,000 square miles of this colony. It has some interior settlements, a few coastal towns and a hinterland of raw emptiness.

MIDDLE EAST

The Middle East, also called the Near East or the Levant, has always been one of the world's most important crossroads; here Europe, Asia and Africa are joined. This land was the cradle of powerful ancient civilizations (like those of Babylonia and Assyria). Here were spawned the three great monotheistic religions—Christianity, Judaism and Islam. Today more than 90 per cent of the population follows the path of Islam and two thirds of the people cling to life by subsistence farming. In the struggle to achieve more modern economies, some Middle Eastern nations, particularly on the Arabian peninsula, have received help through the discovery of oil; the Middle East sprawls over two thirds of the world's known oil reserves. Advanced irrigation systems also offer hope by opening new land to farming. But the Middle Eastern population increases about 5 per cent every year, creating a demand for more produce than the newly developed lands can yield.

CYPRUS The mountainous island of Cyprus in the eastern Mediterranean has been seized by one power after another over the centuries. In 1878 the Turks gave control of it to Britain, and it was formally annexed by Britain during World War I. In 1960 the island became independent. Its subsequent history has been one of conflict between its Greek-speaking peoples, who want union with Greece, and the Turkish-speaking minority.

Principal City: Nicosia (cap.). *Area:* 3,572 sq. mi. *Population:* 587,000. *Government:* Independent republic; member British Commonwealth. *Economy:* Mines and exports some copper and iron pyrites; agriculture. *Religions:* Greek Orthodox, Moslem. *Languages:* Greek, Turkish. *See:* TUR.

IRAQ With only a narrow outlet on the Persian Gulf, Iraq is virtually landlocked in the Middle East. Most of its oil, its most valuable export, is piped to ports on the Mediterranean. Oil aside, Iraq is an agricultural country. In the fertile valley of the Tigris and Euphrates Rivers, Iraq grows dates, grains, rice and vegetables. The country has not been politically stable since King Feisal II was killed during an Army coup in 1958.

Principal Cities: Baghdad (cap.), Basra, Mosul. *Population:* 7,004,000. *Area:* 173,259 sq. mi. *Government:* Republic. *Economy:* Oil production, agriculture. *Religions:* Moslem; small Christian minority. *Language:* Arabic. *See:* ARW.

ISRAEL A country one quarter the size of Maine, Israel is an island of Judaism in an Arab, Moslem sea. The result of years of agitation by Zionist leaders who wished to establish a national homeland for Jews in the "land of Canaan" promised to the Biblical Abraham, it proclaimed itself a nation in 1948 after Britain, which had held the area under a mandate from the League of Nations, withdrew its troops. Neighboring Arab states immediately invaded but were repulsed by Israeli forces. Since no

peace treaty has ever been agreed upon, Israel and the Arab states are to this day technically, and at times actually, in a state of war. Israel has had other troubles as well: the difficulties of integrating into the society the one million Jewish refugees, many of them survivors of Nazi concentration camps, who have come to Israel since 1948; the problem of building a forceful economy, in the face of Arab trading boycotts, in a predominantly desert land. To a considerable extent the country has succeeded—citrus fruits are a principal export; large areas of the Negev desert are being brought under cultivation by mammoth irrigation projects. Israel also produces a wide range of industrial goods. Tourism is a major force in the economy; more than 200,000 visitors come each year.

Principal Cities: Haifa, Jerusalem (cap.), Tel Aviv. *Population:* 2,476,000. *Area:* 7,992 sq. mi. *Government:* Republic. *Economy:* Basically agricultural; some light industry. *Religions:* Judaism; small Moslem, Christian minorities. *Languages:* Modern Hebrew, Arabic. *See:* ISR.

JORDAN Inland from the Mediterranean, arid Jordan is all but landlocked, with only a 15-mile-wide opening on the Gulf of Aqaba. Less than 20 per cent of the country is arable, yet more than 80 per cent of the people are farmers or nomadic herdsmen. The old, historical part of the holy city of Jerusalem lies in Jordan, giving impetus to a thriving tourist trade. Some 200,000 visitors come to Jordan each year. Jordan was formerly Transjordan, part of the British mandate for Palestine. Its current boundaries stem from the armistice that Israel and the Arab states signed in 1949. Jordan's population includes more than half a million Arab refugees from Israel.

Principal Cities: Amman (cap.), Jerusalem. *Population:* 1,898,000. *Area:* 37,301 sq. mi. *Government:* Monarchy. *Economy:* Agricultural; exports fruit and vegetables. *Religion:* Moslem. *Language:* Arabic. *See:* ARW.

KUWAIT A hot, barren scrap of land on the northwestern shore of the Persian Gulf, Kuwait possesses 25 per cent of the world's oil reserves. Before 1952, when the oil boom began, Kuwait was desperately poor. Today the country's reserves are estimated to be worth more than $100 billion.

Principal City: Kuwait (cap.). *Area:* 6,000 sq. mi. *Population:* 371,000. *Government:* Sheikdom. *Economy:* Oil production; industry developing. *Religions:* Moslem; small Christian minority. *Languages:* Arabic, English. *See:* ARW.

LEBANON Situated at the extreme eastern end of the Mediterranean, Lebanon is a prosperous Middle Eastern country. Trade is brisk, for Beirut, Lebanon's capital, includes a free zone which charges no customs duties. About 500,000 tourists annually visit Lebanon's beaches, mountains and ancient ruins. The Lebanon Mountains occupy some 50 per cent of the country, and while less than half of the land is arable, about 40 per cent of the Lebanese are farmers who grow grains, olives, citrus fruits and cotton. The mountain slopes were once resplendent with the famous cedars of Lebanon but now only 400 remain.

Principal City: Beirut (cap.). *Area:* 4,015 sq. mi. *Population:* 2,200,000. *Government:* Republic. *Economy:* Essentially agricultural. *Religions:* Christian, Moslem. *Languages:* Arabic, French, English. *See:* ARW.

MUSCAT AND OMAN A sultanate in the eastern corner of the Arabian peninsula, Muscat and Oman is a traditional ally of Britain. From fertile oases come such crops as cereals, pomegranates, limes, dates and tobacco. Oil was discovered in 1964.

Principal Cities: Muscat (cap.), Nizwa. *Population:* 565,000. *Area:* 82,000 sq. mi. *Government:* Sultanate. *Economy:* Basically agricultural. *Religion:* Moslem. *Languages:* Arabic; Indian languages. *See:* ARW.

SAUDI ARABIA A sprawling land of sun-baked terrain and rocky mountains, Saudi Arabia occupies about four fifths of the Arabian peninsula. The country receives only four to 12 inches of rain yearly, has no big rivers, and suffers from the shifting sand dunes and sandstorms that regularly claim tillable land. Nevertheless, irrigation projects, often drawing water from underground, make Saudi Arabia an agricultural country, the fourth-largest producer of dates in the world. Grains and other fruits are also grown. Oil, nonetheless, gives the economy substance. With 10 per cent of the world's reserves, Saudi Arabia collects oil revenues of more than $400 million a year, 80 per cent of its income. Pilgrims who visit the Islamic holy cities of Mecca, where Mohammed was born, and Medina, where he is buried, also contribute to the Saudi Arabian income. More than 250,000 pilgrims from outside Saudi Arabia visit the cities yearly. Since the late 1950s new Government programs have begun to modernize Saudi Arabia with new schools, buildings, docks, jetports and highways, and larger irrigation systems.

Principal Cities: Mecca (religious cap.), Riyadh (royal cap.). *Area:* 869,999 sq. mi. *Population:* 6,600,000. *Government:* Absolute monarchy. *Economy:* Agricultural; oil producer. *Religion:* Moslem. *Language:* Arabic. *See:* ARW.

SYRIA Placed near the crossroads of Europe, Africa and Asia, Syria has until recently been both a battleground and an occupied territory. It shook off French domination after World War II and in 1958 joined Egypt to form the United Arab Republic. In 1961 it seceded from the U.A.R. after an Army coup, the first of several that plagued the country in ensuing years. Syria is mountainous, but fertile croplands, particularly near the Mediterranean coast and along the Euphrates valley, yield wheat, cotton, figs, olives, fruits and tobacco. In all, some 75 per cent of Syria's people are farmers whose crops provide about one third of the national income. Oil and minerals have been discovered but have not been fully developed. Syria does receive rentals on oil pipes that cross its land en route from Saudi Arabia and Iraq to Mediterranean ports.

Principal City: Damascus (cap.). *Population:* 5,399,000. *Area:* 71,227 sq. mi. *Government:* Socialist state (legislative and executive powers vested in a National Revolutionary Council). *Economy:* Mostly agricultural. *Religions:* Moslem; Christian minority. *Language:* Arabic. *See:* ARW.

TURKEY Lapped by the waters of the Mediterranean, Aegean and Black Seas, Turkey is a peninsular land bridge linking Europe and Asia. Today a staunch ally of the West, Turkey was conquered by warrior tribes that migrated into the region from Central Asia from the 11th to the 13th Centuries, and it rose to greatness in the 15th Century as the Islamic conqueror of Constantinople (Istanbul), the capital of the Byzantine Eastern Christian Empire. From the 14th through the 17th Centuries the Turks' Ottoman Empire expanded to include a territory ranging through North Africa and the Middle East and extending deep into the Balkans. Peace treaties following World War I finally dissolved the ailing empire, which had fatally sided with Germany. Beginning in 1923 Turkey made a series of dramatic and cataclysmic moves to re-establish itself as a viable nation. Proclaiming itself a republic under the leadership of Mustafa Kemal Atatürk, a strong-minded soldier turned statesman, the country set out to remodel its institutions and its way of life on those of the West, its longtime foe. To an extent the effort succeeded—literacy rates rose 29 per cent in the period from 1927 to 1960, and the elements of a Western democratic system were established—but the first flush of optimistic vision has faded in Turkey. Unemployment is high, and agriculture still occupies three quarters of the population, providing 40 per cent of the national income. Moreover, Turkish democracy has been troubled by coups, and not all of its people, particularly rural citizens, are convinced of the value of Western ways.

Principal Cities: Ankara (cap.), Istanbul. *Population:* 31,118,000. *Area:* 301,380 sq. mi. *Government:* Republic. *Economy:* Agricultural; industry slowly developing. *Religion:* Moslem. *Language:* Turkish. *See:* TUR.

YEMEN Made up in large part of sun-baked mountains and deserts, Yemen also has irrigated highlands that are among the most fertile on the Arabian peninsula. Cereals and fruits are cultivated on this land and Mocha coffee is an important export. Politics in Yemen have been unstable since 1962 when insurgents proclaimed the country a republic. Clashes broke out between them and tribesmen loyal to the Imam, Yemen's ruler.

Principal City: San'a (cap.). *Area:* 75,289 sq. mi. *Population:* 5,000,000. *Government:* Provisional republic. *Economy:* Agricultural; coffee exporter. *Religion:* Moslem. *Language:* Arabic. *See:* ARW.

PROTECTORATES AND COLONIES

The term "British protectorate" used to describe some of the smaller states of the Arabian coast is an official British designation for a territory whose external and internal affairs are administered by the British under an agreement with the local ruler. A British protectorate differs from a colony in that its citizens are referred to as "British protected persons," rather than as British subjects. The term "colony" means that the administration of the territory has been legally ceded to the British Crown, which is represented locally by a governor, administrator or commissioner. There is no difference between a colony and a "Crown Colony"; some colonies, like the Crown Colony of Bermuda or the Crown Colony of Hong Kong, simply prefer that designation.

STATES OF THE ARABIAN COAST Scattered along the Persian Gulf and the Arabian Sea, the states of the Arabian coast consist of a number of tiny sultanates, sheikdoms and emirates. Existence is difficult in these hot, dry, desolate lands; only three states, Bahrain, Qatar and Abu Dhabi, have large oil reserves. One, Aden, survives as a free port. Others receive British aid.

Bahrain An archipelago in the Persian Gulf, Bahrain has income from oil, grows dates and vegetables, and builds dhows.

Federation of South Arabia Composed of Aden and 16 of 20 states along the Arabian Sea, the Federation is mainly desert. All of the states but Aden are British protectorates.

Qatar Once a poor sheikdom on the Persian Gulf, the country now receives in excess of $50 million yearly in oil revenues.

Trucial States Seven sheikdoms on the Persian Gulf, the Trucial States are impoverished; only one, Abu Dhabi, has oil.

ASIA

A third of the world's land mass and 60 per cent of its people are contained in Asia. Yet 37 per cent of the continent is controlled by the Soviet Union, a power based in Europe (see page 14). Until well into the 20th Century the fate of the rest of Asia was largely decided by Europeans and Americans, who dominated much of the continent politically, and most of it economically. Since Japan began its Asian expansion in the late 1930s, however, national consciousness has grown. Today the futures of most Asians—whether living in the giant nations of China or India, the smaller states of Pakistan, Afghanistan, Mongolia, Japan, Ceylon or Burma, or the tiny mountain countries of Nepal, Sikkim and Bhutan— are largely in the hands of fellow Asians. One reason Asia remained a world backwater for so long is its inhospitable topography. Great plateaus and ranges extend diagonally 4,500 miles across the continent. Most of the people live in the lowlands near the big rivers and their tributaries. To the west are the Tigris and Euphrates, in whose valley once flourished the earliest civilizations known to man.

Western domination of Asian lands took many forms. The Portuguese and Dutch, and later the English and French, came to the Far East in search of riches and stayed to colonize. The U.S. also established strong economic influence in the region, and remains an important force. Today, with virtually every state on the continent bent on determining its own course, the countries of Asia have engendered a patchwork of political approaches, ranging from the tentative democracy of India to the firm state control of China.

AFGHANISTAN Landlocked in Central Asia, Afghanistan is a dry, mountainous land, 25 per cent covered by deserts. But there are also fertile plains, some of them irrigated, where cotton and fruits are raised. About 90 per cent of the people are small farmers or herdsmen, some of whose products—karakul-lamb hides, known as Persian lamb, and Afghan wool rugs—are world-renowned. Being strategically placed (it is surrounded by Russia, China, Iran and West Pakistan), Afghanistan is courted by East and West. Aid programs are helping to provide roads, airports and irrigation and to enlarge the educational system to combat the almost 90 per cent illiteracy of the population.

Principal City: Kabul (cap.). *Area:* 253,861 sq. mi. *Population:* 14,900,000. *Government:* Constitutional monarchy. *Economy:* Essentially agricultural. *Religion:* Moslem. *Languages:* Pushtu, Persian. *See:* Page 119, HBK.

BHUTAN Squeezed high in the Himalayas between India and Tibet, Bhutan is a nation of pastures and farmland and lofty mountain spires. Its forests are replete with exotic wildlife and its people are noted for their metalwork. Bhutan's king has absolute power at home, but external affairs of the country are controlled by India, as are those of neighboring Sikkim.

Principal City: Thimbu (cap.). *Area:* 18,147 sq. mi. *Population:* 715,000. *Government:* Monarchy. *Economy:* Agricultural, pastoral. *Religion:* Buddhism. *Languages:* Tibetan dialects, Nepali. *See:* Page 134, HBK.

BURMA The Burmese, long known as being among the most friendly and easygoing of the peoples of Southeast Asia, are also among the most productive. The paddies of the vast Irrawaddy River delta, the most densely populated part of the country, constitute one of the world's most important rice-growing areas. Much of the country's industry involves the processing of agricultural products and timber, but mining, metal processing (especially of tin) and the refining of local oil are becoming an increasingly more significant, if still small, part of the economy. Surrounding the Irrawaddy Valley are wild mountains, spurs of the eastern Himalayas; in the north there still live primitive Mongoloid tribes, including the Naga head-hunters. Minority tribesmen, particularly the Shans and the Karens, have constituted a threat to the country's stability since Burma became independent from Britain in 1948. Another threat has been the possible encroachment of Communist China. In 1962 an Army group with a strong socialist bent seized control of the country. The group has maintained correct relations with, and has received aid from, both China and the West.

Principal Cities: Mandalay, Rangoon (cap.). *Population:* 24,229,000. *Area:* 261,788 sq. mi. *Government:* Military dictatorship. *Economy:* Largely agricultural. *Religions:* Buddhism; Christian, Hindu, Moslem minorities. *Languages:* Burmese; tribal languages. *See:* SEA.

CAMBODIA Once the seat of an empire in Southeast Asia which stretched from Burma to the South China Sea, Cambodia is today a small nation that plays a vigorous if sometimes contradictory role in world affairs. Under the leadership of Prince Norodom Sihanouk, Cambodia, which won independence from France in 1953, has variously opposed or favored the policies of France, China and the United States. The nation possesses rich rice fields and rubber plantations, a capital (Phnom Penh) that is becoming increasingly more cosmopolitan, and the spectacular 12th and 13th Century temple ruins of the Khmers' Angkor Wat.

Principal City: Phnom Penh (cap.). *Population:* 5,900,000. *Area:* 69,899 sq. mi. *Government:* Independent monarchy. *Economy:* Essentially agricultural. *Religion:* Buddhism. *Languages:* Khmer (Cambodian), French. *See:* SEA.

CEYLON A 270-mile-long, pear-shaped island off the southeast tip of India, Ceylon is noted for its varied natural beauty. Coconuts are grown along the coast; paddies predominate in the southwestern lowlands; in the mountainous interior are rubber and tea plantations. Once the independent kingdom of the Sinhalese, Ceylon was successively encroached upon by the Portuguese, Dutch and British. The British took control in the late 18th Century and ruled until independence was granted in 1948.

Principal City: Colombo (cap.). *Area:* 25,332 sq. mi. *Population:* 10,965,000. *Government:* Parliamentary democracy; member British Commonwealth. *Economy:* Basically agricultural. *Religions:* Buddhism; Hindu, Christian minorities. *Languages:* Sinhalese, Tamil, English. *See:* Page 137, HBK.

CHINA Officially there are two Chinas: the Republic of China (Nationalist China), which controls the island of Taiwan, and the People's Republic of China (Communist China), which controls the long-neglected mainland. When the Communists took over in 1949, after the Nationalists' flight, they set out to modernize a vast and diverse region in which mountains rise more than 24,000 feet and lowlands lie more than 500 feet below sea level. In the western two thirds of the nation, where minority groups such as Tibetans and Mongols live, mountains and dry plateaus sharply reduce the cultivable land; 90 per cent of the people live in the eastern third, drained by the great Amur, Yellow, Yangtze and West Rivers. The climate ranges from subtropical in the south to bitter cold in the north. An estimated 400 million people speak Mandarin, the national language, but the rest of China's more than 700 million people use so many languages and dialects that no accurate count has ever been made. Still unable to produce enough food to feed its people, China is trying to industrialize and to double its agricultural production. At the same time, its leaders, having broken with the Russian Communists, are attempting to take over the ideological leadership of the entire underdeveloped world.

Nationalist China holds only the Pescadores islets and the little islands of Quemoy and Matsu, as well as the Taiwan island group, but it is recognized by many governments as the official Chinese regime. Between 1950 and 1965 the Nationalists received $1.5 billion in American economic aid. The aid program ended in 1965 after Nationalist and American officials agreed that Taiwan's economy had become self-sufficient. The Nationalists continue to receive military aid.

Communist China. Principal Cities: Canton, Peking (cap.), Shanghai. *Area:* 3,691,502 sq. mi. *Population:* 735,000,000. *Government:* Communist dictatorship. *Economy:* Essentially agricultural; attempting industrialization. *Religions:* Buddhism, Taoism. *Language:* Mandarin Chinese. *See:* CHI.

Nationalist China. Principal City: Taipei (cap.). *Population:* 12,070,000. *Area:* 13,884 sq. mi. *Government:* Independent republic. *Economy:* Mainly agricultural. *Religion:* Buddhism. *Language:* Mandarin Chinese. *See:* CHI.

INDIA With nearly 480 million people crammed into a subcontinent a third the size of the United States, India contains 567,000 villages, most of them impoverished; its people speak 845 languages and dialects; and the members of two large and ancient cultures, the Hindi-speaking Indo-Aryan in the north and the Telugu- and Tamil-speaking Dravidian in the south, are almost continually at odds. India is, in short, a nation beset by manifold problems. In the struggle to achieve a viable, economically strong democracy it does, however, possess certain assets. When the British departed in 1947 after almost two centuries of rule, they left a functioning governmental structure and a corps of well-educated leaders—many of them men who, like Mohandas Gandhi, had been among the foremost opponents of British rule. But despite intense efforts at industrialization by such leaders as Jawaharlal Nehru and Lal Bahadur Shastri, the nation remains primarily agricultural. In addition to the difficulties of expanding the country's agricultural and industrial output to meet the needs of a rising population—an attempt hampered by traditional Hindu attitudes of passive acceptance and caste stratification—the Government has also had to contend with aggression from the Chinese and conflicts with Pakistan. But it has managed to improve the educational system and make slow but steady gains in raising living standards.

Principal Cities: Bombay, Calcutta, Madras, New Delhi (cap.). *Population:* 471,627,000. *Area:* 1,176,150 sq. mi. *Government:* Republic; member British Commonwealth. *Economy:* Agricultural; industry developing. *Religions:* Hindu; Moslem, Christian, Sikh, Parsi minorities. *Languages:* Hindi; English; more than 800 other languages, dialects. *See:* IND.

INDONESIA The more than 3,000 islands that make up Indonesia constitute the largest nation in Southeast Asia, and there is evidence that it would like to be still larger. Indonesia has already expanded into New Guinea, taking West Irian from the Dutch, and has sent guerrillas into northern Borneo, which is part of Malaysia. Like Java, the most developed island, Sumatra has a railroad, but transportation on the other islands is mainly by riverboat and jungle track. The majority of Indonesians are Moslems who work at subsistence farming. Since winning independence from the Netherlands in 1949, Indonesia has experienced extreme political stresses. Among the major forces have been the strong Communist Party; the nationalist-minded Army; and the country's longtime President, Sukarno, a man of kaleidoscopic political views.

Principal Cities: Bandung, Djakarta (cap.), Surabaja. *Area:* 575,893 sq. mi. *Population:* 100,045,000. *Government:* Independent republic. *Economy:* Oil production, agriculture, mining. *Religions:* Moslem; Hindu, Christian, Buddhist minorities. *Languages:* Bahasa Indonesian, English. *See:* SEA.

IRAN All but floating on a vast pool of oil that has fueled British warships in two world wars and in peace helped turn the wheels of Europe's industries, Iran, whose northern neighbor is Russia, ranks importantly in the world's strategic calculations. Its bustling capital, Teheran, contains nearly two million people, such tourist attractions as palaces and fine shops, and such signs of prosperity as monumental traffic jams. A ring of drowsy lesser cities shows fewer signs of prosperity. At least 60 per cent of the country's people are farmers and another 15 per cent are nomadic shepherds, all living far outside the scope of Teheran's oil-based bustle. In ancient ways they raise wheat, barley and rice for themselves and some of the world's finest fruits and nuts for export.

Principal Cities: Esfahan, Mashhad, Tabriz, Teheran (cap.). *Population:* 22,860,000. *Area:* 636,293 sq. mi. *Government:* Constitutional monarchy. *Economy:* Oil production and refining; bulk of people employed in agriculture. *Religion:* Moslem. *Language:* Persian. *See:* Page 107, HBK.

JAPAN Less than 20 years after its unconditional surrender to the Allies, Japan became the wonder of Asia. With a population density of 678 persons per square mile, it is one of the most overcrowded nations in overcrowded Asia, and yet it is by far the most prosperous country in the East and by far the region's leading industrial center. The four major islands and hundreds of tiny ones that make up the Japanese archipelago constituted one of the most isolated nations in the world when Japan was first opened up to the West by Commodore Matthew C. Perry of the U.S. Navy in 1853. But 52 years later, when its military forces defeated those of Russia, Japan emerged as a major world power, and for a time it appeared that it would be a dominant one. In World War II the Japanese spread out across Asia and the Pacific to the edges of India and Alaska before being driven back. The occupying Americans introduced a policy of democratization. By 1952 Japan had regained its independence; by 1957, when it was admitted to the United Nations, its war-devastated economy had been rebuilt. Today it is one of the world's leading shipbuilders and a top producer of steel, transistor radios, television sets, motor vehicles and textiles. Tokyo, with a population of 10.6 million, is the world's largest metropolis and has more neon signs and movie theaters than any other city. The main shopping section, the Ginza, is almost as crowded every evening as New York's Times Square on New Year's Eve. Choice property in the Ginza sells at $18 million an acre. Because of Japan's many mountains, only a sixth of the land is under cultivation. But the Japanese, unlike most Asians, have practiced conservation for centuries, and hence the land is green and has a higher yield per unit than that of any other country. With its economy burgeoning on every front, Japan is now in search of an identity. Traditional elements from its feudal days exist side by side with elements from the modern West. Many a businessman spends his day in a way that would not be unfamiliar to a New York executive, and at the end changes into traditional dress and spends the evening in a home furnished much as it would have been centuries ago.

Principal Cities: Osaka, Tokyo (cap.). *Population:* 96,906,000. *Area:* 142,726 sq. mi. *Government:* Parliamentary democracy (Emperor is symbol of state but has no governing power). *Economy:* Industry, agriculture. *Religions:* Shinto; Buddhism; Christian minority. *Language:* Japanese. *See:* JAP.

KOREA A nation plagued by wars and foreign occupations, Korea has paid for its strategic location on a peninsula of the Asian mainland. World War II ended a half century of Japanese domination but split the nation in two along the 38th Parallel of latitude. Northern Korea was seized by Russian-trained Communists and became the Democratic People's Republic (North Korea), while southern Korea formed the Republic of Korea (South Korea). In 1950 the North invaded the South, precipitating a struggle that eventually involved Chinese Communist forces on the side of the North Koreans and U.N. forces led by the U.S. on the side of the South Koreans. The fighting did not

end until 1953, when the border between the North and the South was again stabilized along the 38th Parallel. All of Korea is essentially agricultural, but the North is more industrialized.

North Korea. Principal City: Pyongyang (cap.). *Population:* 10,700,000. *Area:* 46,540 sq. mi. *Government:* Communist state. *Economy:* Agriculture; some industry. *Religion:* Buddhism. *Language:* Korean. *See:* Page 147, HBK.

South Korea. Principal City: Seoul (cap.). *Population:* 27,633,000. *Area:* 38,004 sq. mi. *Government:* Republic. *Economy:* Agricultural. *Religions:* Buddhism, Christianity. *Language:* Korean. *See:* Page 147, HBK.

LAOS The nation of Laos, which has figured so prominently in the East-West struggle, is a former part of French Indochina composed of river valleys isolated from each other by mountains and jungles. Laos has few roads. Most of its people are Thai Buddhists. The major cash item in the Laotian economy has been the American aid given to assist the nation during the lengthy struggle between neutralists, rightists and Communists. In recent years stability of a sort has come through an alliance between the neutralist Government and the rightists. The Communists—nominally, along with the rightists, a part of the Government—have boycotted all Government activities.

Principal City: Vientiane (admin. cap.). *Population:* 1,925,000. *Area:* 91,428 sq. mi. *Government:* Monarchy. *Economy:* Agricultural. *Religion:* Buddhism. *Languages:* Lao; French; tribal languages. *See:* SEA.

MALAYSIA The Federation of Malaysia, a rubber- and tin-rich British Commonwealth nation enjoying one of the highest standards of living in Southeast Asia, was born in 1963 as the result of two years of deliberations among several states: Malaya, a sovereign member of the Commonwealth; Britain's two Crown Colonies on the island of Borneo, Sarawak and Sabah; and the Commonwealth island state of Singapore. The main stumbling block to federation had been the Malayans' fear that Singapore's 1.8 million persons of Chinese ancestry might lean toward Communism, and the fact that inclusion of Singapore meant that Malayans would be outnumbered. Until 1965 Malaysia functioned as a single nation, in spite of the Malayans' fears. But political rivalry between the Malayans and the Chinese from Singapore led to the separation of Singapore from the Federation that year.

Principal City: Kuala Lumpur (fed. cap.). *Population:* 9,137,000. *Area:* 50,700 sq. mi. *Government:* Parliamentary democracy; member British Commonwealth. *Economy:* Agricultural; exports tin and rubber. *Religions:* Moslem, Buddhism. *Languages:* Malay, English. *See:* SEA.

MALDIVE ISLANDS A British airfield on one of the 2,000 coral islands that make up the Maldive group is virtually the only sign of the outside world in this new Indian Ocean nation. The people are almost all Moslem fishermen who market their goods in Ceylon to the north. Since little can be grown on their atolls, the Maldivians also depend on Ceylon for food other than fish.

Principal City: Male (cap.). *Population:* 93,000. *Area:* 115 sq. mi. *Government:* Independent sultanate. *Economy:* Fishing; exports limited amounts of coir yarn and copra. *Religion:* Moslem. *Language:* Maldivian.

NEPAL The immense Himalayan peaks that form Nepal's northern border with Chinese-controlled Tibet and the rugged mountain spurs and deep valleys that flow southward to its border with India dominate the land. Roads are rare, and most goods still travel on the backs of yaks, mules or men. Nepal is, however, emerging from its ancient isolation, admitting foreigners and aid funds, and taking hesitant steps to emerge from the poverty of an agricultural economy into the modern era.

Principal City: Katmandu (cap.). *Population:* 9,700,000. *Area:* 54,362 sq. mi. *Government:* Monarchy. *Economy:* Agricultural. *Religions:* Buddhism, Hinduism. *Language:* Nepali. *See:* Page 134, HBK.

OUTER MONGOLIA Lying between the U.S.S.R. and China, the Mongolian People's Republic is, after Russia, the second-oldest Communist nation. According to many Western observers, it is also one of the most independent. When the new state was founded in 1921 with the aid of Lenin's Red Army, Outer Mongolia was one of the most backward regions in the world, stagnating in poverty after centuries of Chinese rule. Outer Mongolia's herdsmen were offered virtually no education or medical care. In addition, nearly half of its men were unproductive Buddhist lamas, and there were no modern cities or towns. Today most of Outer Mongolia's people are still herdsmen, but there is universal education, a doctor for every thousand persons, and growing industry. In international Communist disputes, the Mongolians side with the Russians against the Chinese, but no Russian troops are stationed on Mongolian soil.

Principal City: Ulan Bator (cap.). *Population:* 1,019,000. *Area:* 592,663 sq. mi. *Government:* Republic. Communist dictatorship. *Economy:* Pastoral, agricultural. *Religion:* Buddhism. *Language:* Mongolian. *See:* Page 142, HBK.

NONALIGNMENT: AN ASIAN CONCEPT

The roots of neutralism or nonalignment in the Cold War were planted in Asia. In 1948, just after India was freed from British rule, Prime Minister Jawaharlal Nehru announced that he and his countrymen would not "align ourselves" with either East or West. In ensuing years the concept of nonalignment spread to such diverse nations as Yugoslavia, Egypt and most of the emergent African countries. The nonaligned nations on occasion still exercise an important influence on world events.

PAKISTAN Created in 1947 by the division of the Indian subcontinent into basically Hindu India and basically Moslem Pakistan, this nation consists of two sections separated by 1,000 miles of Indian territory. During the first year of independence, under the firm leadership of Mohammed Ali Jinnah, a British-educated barrister, the Pakistanis settled an estimated six million refugees from India and made progress toward building a stable nation. In 1948 Jinnah died and for the next 10 years Pakistan was beset by governmental ineffectiveness and corruption and by bitter quarrels between its two sections, whose only real bond is the Moslem religion. In 1958 General Mohammed Ayub Khan staged a military coup and took control of the Government. Since then Pakistan has enjoyed a measure of stability and economic progress.

Principal Cities: Karachi, Rawalpindi (cap.). *Population:* 100,762,000. *Area:* 365,528 sq. mi. *Government:* Republic; member of the British Commonwealth. *Economy:* Agricultural; industry developing. *Religions:* Moslem, Hindu. *Languages:* Urdu, Bengali, others. *See:* Page 124, HBK.

PHILIPPINES Granted independence by the United States in 1946, the Philippines is a functioning, Western-style democracy. By the mid-1950s the Philippines had suppressed its Communist Huk rebellion and come a long way toward recovery from the devastation of World War II. But despite such important cash crops as sugar, timber and copra, the country remains undeveloped, corruption is rampant, and there are wide gaps between rich and poor. The big islands of Luzon and Mindanao and the 7,000 lesser ones that make up the Philippines were ruled by Spain for more than three centuries. As a result of the Spanish legacy, most of the people are still Roman Catholics and much of the architecture is Spanish-influenced. The islands were ceded by Spain to the U.S. in 1898, two years after the people had tried unsuccessfully to set up an independent republic.

Principal Cities: Cebu, Davao, Manila (cap.). *Population:* 31,270,000. *Area:* 115,707 sq. mi. *Government:* Republic. *Economy:* Agricultural. *Religion:* Predominantly Roman Catholic. *Languages:* Tagalog, English. *See:* SEA.

SINGAPORE The smallest nation in Southeast Asia, Singapore is an island 27 miles long and 14 miles wide. When Singapore became independent from Malaysia in 1965, it retained trade and defense ties with the Federation. Malaysia needs the highly industrialized island to process Malaysian tin and rubber—and also because Singapore contains one of the world's major ports and is the banking center of Southeast Asia. Singapore needs Malaysia for raw materials and markets.

Principal City: Singapore (cap.). *Population:* 1,820,000. *Area:* 224 sq. mi. *Government:* Democracy; member British Commonwealth. *Economy:* Financial center of world rubber and tin markets. *Religions:* Moslem, Christian, Buddhist, Hindu. *Languages:* Malay, Chinese, Tamil, English. *See:* SEA.

THAILAND Serving as the West's major bastion in Southeast Asia, Thailand is the only nation in the area that has never been colonized by a European power. Threatened by Communism in its northern provinces, it has received vast amounts of American military aid in recent years. In Bangkok, its fairyland capital, is the headquarters for SEATO (see page 48).

Principal City: Bangkok (cap.). *Area:* 198,455 sq. mi. *Population:* 29,700,000. *Government:* Monarchy. *Economy:* Agricultural; light industry developing. *Religion:* Buddhism. *Language:* Thai. *See:* SEA.

VIETNAM In 1954 an agreement was signed in Geneva ending France's eight-year war against the Communist Viet Minh forces of Vietnam. Under the Geneva accord Vietnam won independence and was divided into two zones—North Vietnam and

South Vietnam. Under the leadership of the Viet Minh revolutionary Ho Chi Minh, North Vietnam became a Communist state, one which clearly intended to enlarge its frontiers and those of Communism. President Ngo Dinh Diem of South Vietnam came under increasing harassment from the Communist guerrillas of the Viet Cong, successor to the Viet Minh. In 1963 the Diem Government was overturned by a military coup. After that, the war intensified. In 1965 the U.S. began bombing strategic points in North Vietnam and added 176,500 servicemen to the 23,500 military advisers it had already stationed in the South. The two tiny, rice-producing Vietnamese states thus became the focal point in Southeast Asia and the world in the military and ideological struggle between East and West.

North Vietnam. Principal City: Hanoi (cap.). *Population:* 17,800,000. *Area:* 61,293 sq. mi. *Government:* Republic. Communist dictatorship. *Economy:* Agricultural. *Religion:* Buddhism. *Language:* Vietnamese. *See:* SEA.

South Vietnam. Principal City: Saigon (cap.). *Population:* 15,715,000. *Area:* 65,948 sq. mi. *Government:* Republic. No political parties. *Economy:* Basically subsistence agriculture. *Religions:* Taoism, Buddhism, Roman Catholicism. *Languages:* Vietnamese, French, English. *See:* SEA.

Brunei The British protectorate of Brunei on North Borneo has only about 98,000 people but amasses an annual income of about $36 million from oil and investments abroad.

Hong Kong The colony of Hong Kong, a major trade center and Western listening post, encompasses Hong Kong Island, small sections of the Chinese mainland and some smaller islands.

Sikkim Smallest of the Himalayan kingdoms, Sikkim grows a variety of crops. Its foreign affairs are controlled by India, which also supplies aid and domestic advisers.

CENTRAL AMERICA AND THE WEST INDIES

As the brassy sun signals noon each day, Central America seems a place untouched by the 20th Century. A fly-buzz quiet settles over the cobblestone streets of Tegucigalpa, Honduras. In El Salvador a member of one of the Fourteen Families that run the country glides by limousine to his club for an afternoon of bridge high above the smells of acres of shacks. There is a distressing sameness to the regional profile: population explosions, lack of housing and jobs, too many soldiers, too few schools, single-crop economies, landless peasants, and family oligarchies that skim off the thin gravy. The heritage of Spain—feudal, dogmatic, fatalistic—seems still to overlie much of the region. But now leaders are beginning to launch programs to give the plain people a stake in their countries. After sitting still for nearly 500 years, the region is poised for change.

BARBADOS Most easterly of the Caribbean islands and also the most densely populated, Barbados has been linked with Britain since settlement in 1627. The island has had an elected legislature since 1639, and has been fully self-governing since 1961.

Principal City: Bridgetown (cap.). *Population:* 250,000. *Area:* 166 sq. mi. *Government:* Constitutional monarchy; member British Commonwealth. *Economy:* Tourism, exports sugar. *Religion:* Anglican. *Language:* English.

COSTA RICA Coffee-based Costa Rica was settled by a healthy Spanish middle class of artisans, farmers and shopkeepers who learned to do their own work after warfare wiped out the indigenous Indians. Now it is Central America's most prosperous, literate, democratic and law-abiding country. It has no army, merely a Civil Guard; a quarter of the budget goes to education. There are 1,200 policemen and more than 1,800 schools, and the president travels without a bodyguard.

Principal City: San José (cap.). *Population:* 1,391,000. *Area:* 19,575 sq. mi. *Government:* Republic. *Economy:* Agricultural. *Religions:* Roman Catholic; Protestant minority. *Languages:* Spanish, English. *See:* CTA.

CUBA From 1868 to 1898 the Cubans fought their Spanish overlords until they won independence at a cost of some 250,000 Cuban and Spanish lives in the first decade of the struggle alone. However, in the next 35 years the U.S. felt impelled to intervene a number of times in Cuba's internal affairs. In 1933 Cuba ousted Gerardo ("the Butcher") Machado, and the U.S. then relinquished its right to intervene. Nevertheless, Cubans continued to feel that the U.S. was interfering in Cuba. This anti-U.S. feeling explains some of the acclaim given to Fidel Castro when he proclaimed a new, nationalistic Cuba after coming to power in 1959. Within two years Castro had tied Cuba to Communist Russia, and Cubans resumed the struggle for independence.

Principal City: Havana (cap.). *Area:* 44,218 sq. mi. *Population:* 7,631,000. *Government:* Republic. Communist dictatorship. *Economy:* Largely agricultural. *Religions:* Roman Catholic, Protestant. *Language:* Spanish. *See:* WIN.

DOMINICAN REPUBLIC Forced to expel Spanish, French and Haitian overlords to gain independence in 1844, the Dominican Republic has since that time continued to abuse its hard-won freedom. In 1916 U.S. Marines intervened to restore order. The Marines left in 1924; Rafael Leonidas Trujillo became dictator in 1930. He built good roads and a showy capital, and looted the country of almost one billion dollars. Trujillo was assassinated in 1961. The ensuing struggle between Army and people fostered chaos and further U.S. intervention (in 1965).

Principal City: Santo Domingo (cap.). *Population:* 3,452,000. *Area:* 18,816 sq. mi. *Government:* Republic. *Economy:* Agricultural. *Religions:* Roman Catholic; Protestant, Jewish minorities. *Language:* Spanish. *See:* WIN.

EL SALVADOR The smallest and most crowded nation in Central America, El Salvador is a land of dangerous ferments. It leads the area in yield per acre of coffee and cotton and has been enjoying an industrial boomlet. This has meant great prosperity for the Fourteen Families, a small clique that owns virtually everything in El Salvador. But it has increased resentment among the poverty-stricken peasants and common laborers. Alarmed, the military and a few advanced members of the Fourteen Families have, with U.S. help, launched a program of social reform.

Principal City: San Salvador (cap.). *Population:* 2,824,000. *Area:* 8,260 sq. mi. *Government:* Republic. *Economy:* Agricultural; some industry. *Religion:* Roman Catholic. *Language:* Spanish. *See:* CTA.

GUATEMALA

New cars and buildings dominate the bustling downtown streets of Guatemala's capital, Guatemala City. Food-processing factories and cosmetics and tire plants have been built near it, supplementing coffee and bananas, the country's old economic standbys. The Maya Indians, who compose more than half the population, remain outside the money economy.

Principal City: Guatemala City (cap.). *Population:* 4,304,000. *Area:* 42,042 sq. mi. *Government:* Republic. *Economy:* Agricultural. *Religions:* Roman Catholic; Protestant minority. *Languages:* Spanish; Indian dialects. *See:* CTA.

HAITI

The world's richest colony when echoes of the French Revolution at home sent half a million slaves rising against France's despotic colonial rule in 1791, Haiti became independent in 1804, but the revolt wrecked the country. Today, Maryland-sized Haiti has the lowest literacy rate, per capita income rate and life expectancy rate in the hemisphere.

Principal Cities: Cap-Haïtien, Port-au-Prince (cap.). *Population:* 4,551,000. *Area:* 10,714 sq. mi. *Government:* Dictatorship. *Economy:* Agricultural. *Religions:* Roman Catholic, *vodou.* *Languages:* French, Creole. *See:* WIN.

HONDURAS

The least-developed republic in Central America, Honduras has only some 200 miles of paved roads. It is often called a typical "banana republic," but its own people wryly call it "the land of the 70s: 70 per cent illiterate, 70 per cent rural, 70 per cent illegitimate"—and, they might add, 70 per cent unstable. In almost a century and a half of independence, Honduras has had 136 revolutions and only two constitutionally elected presidents who completed their full, legal terms.

Principal City: Tegucigalpa (cap.). *Population:* 2,092,000. *Area:* 43,277 sq. mi. *Government:* Republic. *Economy:* Agricultural. *Religions:* Roman Catholic; Protestant minority. *Languages:* Spanish; Indian dialects. *See:* CTA.

JAMAICA

Birth rate and industrialization gallop neck and neck in this new Caribbean nation, which gained independence from Britain in 1962. New enterprises—largely the production of bauxite and women's clothing—which have been attracted by Jamaica's favorable tax laws and the availability of literate, low-cost labor have helped the Government to increase industrial output markedly, but 20 per cent of Jamaica's workers remain unemployed. What keeps Jamaica more stable than its neighbors is the legacy of 300 years of British rule, which left it with a democratic constitution and a real two-party system.

Principal City: Kingston (cap.). *Population:* 1,728,000. *Area:* 4,232 sq. mi. *Government:* Constitutional monarchy; member of British Commonwealth. *Economy:* Agricultural; bauxite mining. *Religions:* Protestant; Roman Catholic, other minorities. *Language:* English. *See:* WIN.

MEXICO

The first Latin American country to carry out a generally successful social revolution, modern Mexico is one of the most prosperous nations in the region. The first phase of the revolution began in 1910, took seven years, mobilized thousands of peasant soldiers, including women, destroyed the oligarchy that had dominated the country, broke the power of the Roman Catholic Church and opened the way to a democratic, middle-class society. The establishment of a new way of life was jeopardized over the next quarter of a century by militarists, *caudillos* and rebellious churchgoers. With the inauguration of President Lázaro Cárdenas in 1934, the revolution hit its stride. Cárdenas expropriated the properties of American and British oil companies and launched a broad agrarian-reform program. During World War II, thrown back on its own resources, Mexico took steps toward large-scale industrialization. Today its gross national product is increasing at the rate of 6.3 per cent a year. The process of industrialization has pulled one third of the once-somnolent population into a new and vital middle class. There are still thousands of landless peasants and an illiteracy rate of about 30 per cent. Still, Mexico is one of the very few hemisphere nations whose Government is attempting to create a 20th Century society.

Principal City: Mexico City (cap.). *Population:* 40,913,000. *Area:* 761,600 sq. mi. *Government:* Federal republic. *Economy:* Primarily agricultural; industry expanding. *Religions:* Roman Catholic; Protestant, Jewish minorities. *Languages:* Spanish; numerous Indian languages. *See:* MEX.

NICARAGUA

Revolutions kept Nicaragua turbulent for almost a century following the country's achievement of independence in 1838. Then in 1936 Anastasio ("Tacho") Somoza took control. Somoza amassed a $60 million personal fortune, but he also helped to develop Nicaragua. Somoza was assassinated in 1956, and Nicaragua is still struggling toward democracy.

Principal Cities: Granada, León, Managua (cap.). *Population:* 1,597,000. *Area:* 57,143 sq. mi. *Government:* Republic. *Economy:* Agricultural. *Religions:* Roman Catholic; Protestant minority. *Language:* Spanish. *See:* CTA.

PANAMA

This country produces bananas—and little Panamanians at the explosive birth rate of 4 per cent annually. Badly housed and poor, Panamanians emerge periodically from slums to riot against the Americans whose well-built homes stand in the nearby Canal Zone. During these disturbances the Twenty Families, who own the TV stations, sugar mills and coffee plantations, and who generally select the presidents, worry nervously that the anger will boomerang against them.

Principal City: Panama City (cap.). *Population:* 1,210,000. *Area:* 29,208 sq. mi. *Government:* Republic. *Economy:* Agricultural; Canal Zone revenues. *Religions:* Roman Catholic, Protestant. *Language:* Spanish. *See:* CTA.

TRINIDAD AND TOBAGO

Although 40 per cent of its people are Negroes and 35 per cent are East Indians—a combination that makes for explosive tensions in neighboring British Guiana—Trinidad remains calm. Its relative tranquillity is probably the result of the fact that there is an opportunity for economic advancement on this comparatively wealthy island, whose oil production helps to give it the fifth-highest per capita income in the hemisphere. The island of Tobago, 30 air minutes away, gives itself over to tourism and the raising of cacao and sugar.

Principal Cities: Arima, Port-of-Spain (cap.), San Fernando. *Population:* 949,000. *Area:* 1,980 sq. mi. *Government:* Monarchy; member British Commonwealth. *Economy:* Oil producing, food processing. *Religions:* Protestant, Roman Catholic, Hindu, Moslem. *Language:* English. *See:* WIN.

U.S. TERRITORIES Long a forceful presence in Central America and the West Indies, the United States nonetheless has avoided formal colonization. Today it holds only the U.S. Virgin Islands and technical sovereignty over small strips of land paralleling the Panama Canal.

Canal Zone This narrow outpost of the U.S. flanks the Canal and bisects Panama. In 1965 the U.S. agreed to renegotiate the treaty that gives it control over the Zone.

Puerto Rico Unique among states, Puerto Rico is neither a nation nor a possession, but a commonwealth joined with the U.S., officially a "Free and Associated State." With the help of the U.S. (which liberated it from Spain in 1898) and the imagination of its first elected Governor, Luis Muñoz Marín, this Caribbean island, once a poorhouse, has increased production of all goods and services an average of 9 per cent annually since 1950, making it one of the world's fastest-growing countries.

Virgin Islands The Virgins came under U.S. rule in 1917. They remained backward until the 1950s when cheap plane fares made them easily accessible to American tourists and their credit cards.

BRITISH TERRITORIES Many isles and islets in the West Indies remain British colonies, although a number have been given self-rule. Some export a few agricultural products; many more have become sunny havens for vacationers.

Bahamas Some 700 islands—20 inhabited—make up the Bahamas, which lie about 50 miles off the coast of Florida. The main island, New Providence, is the focus of the tourist trade.

Bermuda One of Britain's oldest colonies, Bermuda is now virtually self-governing. The chief town is Hamilton; the chief products include pharmaceuticals, fruits—and golf and sun.

British Honduras A small, isolated remnant of the Empire, British Honduras sits rather forlornly on the northeast corner of Central America, producing timber, especially mahogany, and some sugar and other agricultural products.

British Virgin Islands Britain shares the cluster of islands called the Virgins with the U.S. The islands are near Puerto Rico and exist largely by farming, although there are some tourists.

British West Indies Many clusters of islands, such as the Windwards and the Leewards, make up the British West Indies. The largest islands, such as Jamaica, have become independent.

FRENCH ANTILLES In the 18th Century France owned many of the Caribbean islands, but it lost most of them to the British in 1782. Today, aside from a section of St. Martin, it owns only two: Guadaloupe and Martinique.

Guadaloupe Settled by the French in 1635, Guadaloupe is composed of two main islands, Guadaloupe and Grande Terre. Primarily agricultural, the islands export sugar and bananas.

Martinique Like Guadaloupe, 426-square-mile Martinique is mainly agricultural; it exports bananas, sugar and rum.

NETHERLANDS ANTILLES Two groups of islands make up the Netherlands Antilles. One group, the Leewards, includes Aruba, Bonaire and Curaçao. The other, the Dutch Windwards, includes some islets and the southern part of the island called St. Martin by the French and Sint Maarten by the Dutch.

Aruba The chief business of semiarid Aruba, as of Curaçao, is refining and shipping oil imported from Venezuela.

Bonaire With 110 square miles, Bonaire is somewhat larger than 70-square-mile Aruba but, lacking refineries, is not nearly so prosperous. Its 7,000 people raise some livestock.

Curaçao In Dutch hands since 1816, Curaçao has a booming oil business and a growing tourist trade.

Sint Maarten This small island in the Windwards is shared with the French. Its main activities are growing and shipping livestock and making sun-seeking tourists welcome.

SOUTH AMERICA

This continent is far richer in resources than its output would indicate. Its barely known Amazon, whose drainage basin covers an area about the size of the United States, excluding Alaska, is the center of a great fan-shaped system of rivers and streams providing 2,300 miles of navigable waterways. Brazil possesses large, undeveloped iron-ore reserves; Venezuela is the world's third-largest oil producer. But only 4 per cent of the land has been put to the plow; the continent has only 22 persons per square mile. Yet most peasants are either landless, or jammed onto small farms on the poorest soil, or crammed into the slums of Rio, Lima or Caracas. The potential is there; what is lacking is the social, intellectual and political framework on which to build.

ARGENTINA This is the melting pot of South America. Discovered by Spanish conquistadors in 1536 and first colonized by Spain, Argentina has since, like the U.S., attracted immigrants from all over Europe. There are many people of British and German descent, and there are more Italian names in the telephone book of Buenos Aires, the capital, than Spanish. The second-largest country in South America (after Brazil), Argentina is most noted for its vast plains, called the Pampa, which contain some of the best cattle country in the world. Farther south, on the often cold and windy grasslands of Patagonia, sheep ranches and recently developed oil wells predominate. Free of Spanish rule since 1810, Argentina has been anything but serene politically, often being ruled by demagogues. Since the expulsion of its most prominent strongman, Juan Perón, in 1955, Argentina has had democratic rule punctuated by violence and military coups.

Principal City: Buenos Aires (cap.). *Population:* 22,045,000. *Area:* 1,072,067 sq. mi. *Government:* Federal republic. *Economy:* Wheat, cattle. *Religions:* Roman Catholic; Protestant, Jewish minorities. *Language:* Spanish. *See:* PLA.

BOLIVIA Landlocked in the Andes, Bolivia is rich in minerals, including tin (of which it is the world's third-largest producer), but it is desperately poor. Three quarters of Bolivia consists of fertile, tropical lowlands producing rubber and Brazil nuts. But 75 per cent of the population, mostly Indians, clings to a marginal life on the barren, high plateau where the Incas once nursed the soil to fertility. In 1952 a revolution nationalized the tin mines and brought comprehensive social reforms, but the country is not yet politically stable.

Principal Cities: La Paz (cap.), Sucre (const. cap.). *Population:* 3,653,000. *Area:* 424,162 sq. mi. *Government:* Republic. *Economy:* Agriculture, mining. *Religion:* Roman Catholic. *Languages:* Spanish; Indian languages. *See:* AND.

BRAZIL Occupying almost half of South America's total area, Brazil is the fifth-largest country in the world—only the Soviet Union, Canada, China and the U.S. are bigger. This sprawling nation is a mixture of vast forests and huge cities, and its people are an integrated blend of the descendants of settlers from Europe, Indians, Japanese and Negro slaves. Farmers constitute more than half of the working force even though less than 5 per cent of the land is cultivated. The agricultural output is nonetheless highly diversified: Brazil supplies nearly half of the world's coffee, is one of the world's largest producers of cocoa beans, and includes sugar, cotton, oranges and tobacco among its range of exports. Brazil is also rich in minerals, containing, for example, an estimated 14 per cent of the world's total reserves of iron ore. Its iron and steel industry is the largest in Latin America. Power fuels seem to be lacking in quantity, but Brazil's wide network of rivers is a potential source of hydroelectric power. Brazilian growth has been hampered in recent years by chaotic politics and rising inflation.

Principal Cities: Brasília (cap.), Recife, Rio de Janeiro, São Paulo. *Population:* 78,809,000. *Area:* 3,286,470 sq. mi. *Government:* Republic. *Economy:* Major agricultural and livestock producer; steel, machinery industries. *Religions:* Roman Catholic, Protestant. *Language:* Portuguese. *See:* BRA.

CHILE In many ways Chile is the most civilized country in South America. The military respects the fair and honest elections; only once since 1891 has the nation veered from constitutionalism. Chile also has a free press and intelligent economic planning. But there are some uncomfortable facts behind the comfortable façade: wealth (derived largely from the mining of copper and other minerals) is concentrated in a few hands, the infant mortality rate is one of the world's highest, living costs are exorbitant, peonage is common, and inflation is rampant. One result is that Chile has a strong and voluble Communist Party. However, a left-wing Christian party bested the Communists in late 1964 and began leading Chile in a search for democratic solutions to its problems.

Principal Cities: Santiago (cap.), Valparaíso. *Population:* 8,492,000. *Area:* 286,396 sq. mi. *Government:* Republic. *Economy:* Mining of copper, other minerals. *Religion:* Roman Catholic. *Language:* Spanish. *See:* AND.

COLOMBIA This is a relatively prosperous country producing fine coffee. The capital city is gray under the fog rising toward the mountains, and businessmen clutch umbrellas and wear English wool suits. They spend their evenings in intellectual talk;

Bogotá has 11 universities, a number of museums and five daily newspapers. Colombia was politically stable until the assassination of the Liberal idol Jorge Gaitán in 1948 provoked a 12-day riot. The great riot led to continuing violence that rolled up a death toll of 200,000 in 15 years. To abate the violence, the rival Liberal and Conservative Parties finally agreed to share political power equally, alternating the presidency every four years. However, Colombian democracy does not really function; the strangely chosen Government is feeble.

Principal City: Bogotá (cap.). *Area:* 439,512 sq. mi. *Population:* 15,434,000. *Government:* Republic. *Economy:* Agricultural; a major exporter of high-grade coffee. *Religions:* Roman Catholic; small Protestant, Jewish minorities. *Language:* Spanish. *See:* COL.

ECUADOR "A rich country inhabited by a poor people" is what ex-President Galo Plaza (1948-1952) calls Ecuador. The economy of South America's second-smallest country (after Uruguay) depends on exports of bananas, coffee and cacao—commodities whose prices fluctuate nervously. Equally unstable is government; in almost a century and a half of independence Ecuador had 16 constitutions. The Indians who dwell in poverty in the chill highlands, and who constitute half of Ecuador's population, are a prime source of instability.

Principal Cities: Guayaquil, Quito (cap.). *Population:* 4,877,000. *Area:* 104,506 sq. mi. *Government:* Republic (Constitution suspended, 1963). *Economy:* Primarily agricultural. *Religions:* Roman Catholic; Protestant minority. *Languages:* Spanish; Indian languages. *See:* AND.

GUYANA Ninety per cent of the population of this former British colony on the northeast shoulder of South America lives along its narrow coastline. Like much of Holland, this land lies partly below sea level and must be protected by dikes.

Principal City: Georgetown (cap.). *Population:* 650,000. *Area:* 83,000 sq. mi. *Government:* Constitutional monarchy; member British Commonwealth. *Economy:* rice, sugar, bauxite and manganese. *Religions:* Christian, Moslem, Hindu. *Language:* English.

PARAGUAY Wars and dictatorships have left Paraguay a sleepy backwater. In a bloody five-year war that began in 1865 against Brazil, Argentina and Uruguay, the country's population was chopped from 525,000 to 221,000. The Chaco War with Bolivia in the 1930s cost another 20,000 lives. In more recent years thousands have emigrated. With an economy based largely on cattle, this landlocked country remains desperately poor.

Principal City: Asunción (cap.). *Population:* 1,949,000. *Area:* 157,047 sq. mi. *Government:* Republic. *Economy:* Agricultural, pastoral. *Religions:* Roman Catholic, Protestant. *Languages:* Spanish, Guarani. *See:* PLA.

PERU Nature has dealt harshly with Peru, which is divided into three major parts: the narrow, accessible coastal desert, where most of the cities and industries are situated; the unyielding Andes, where subsistence farming is carried on by poor Indians; and the virtually inaccessible eastern lowland jungle. Peru is otherwise divided: a small minority of the population garners the bulk of the national income; the bottom half averages an annual per capita income of $50, and a third of the people speak

Principal City: Lima (cap.). *Area:* 496,221 sq. mi. *Population:* 11,650,000. *Government:* Republic. *Economy:* Agriculture, fishing, mining. *Religions:* Roman Catholic, Protestant. *Languages:* Spanish, Quechua. *See:* AND.

URUGUAY A peaceful, democratic, cattle- and sheep-raising state long known as the "Switzerland of America," Uruguay is now a worried little nation awash in red ink. The socialism launched by President José Batlle y Ordóñez in the 1910s simply ran away with itself. Government bureaucracy is vast; workers labor six hours a day, enjoy 44 legal holidays a year and retire with full-pay pensions at 55. As a result of such well-meant social benefits, Uruguay's productivity is declining.

Principal Cities: Montevideo (cap.), Paysandú, Salto. *Population:* 2,715,000. *Area:* 72,172 sq. mi. *Government:* Republic. *Economy:* Pastoral, agricultural. *Religions:* Roman Catholic; Protestant minority. *Language:* Spanish. *See:* PLA.

VENEZUELA Oil, of which Venezuela is the world's leading exporter, earns the country roughly 20 per cent of its national income and helps to give Venezuela the highest per capita income in South America. But Venezuela faces increasing competition from other oil producers. Moreover, the national revenues are badly distributed. A third of the Venezuelans are illiterate and half of them live on a bare subsistence level. Aware of that fact, recent governments have, with strong U.S. support, worked to accelerate land reform, improve educational facilities and develop the mineral resources of eastern Venezuela.

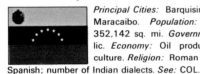

Principal Cities: Barquisimeto, Caracas (cap.), Maracaibo. *Population:* 8,427,000. *Area:* 352,142 sq. mi. *Government:* Federal republic. *Economy:* Oil production, mining, agriculture. *Religion:* Roman Catholic. *Languages:* Spanish; number of Indian dialects. *See:* COL.

THE GUIANAS To Sir Walter Raleigh this was the long-sought "El Dorado." Later explorers did find gold. But most of the people of the Guianese regions listed below subsist on farming.

French Guiana This former penal colony has been in a continuous decline for years. Its exports, particularly of sugar, used to pay for imports; now French Guiana is virtually bankrupt.

Surinam Bauxite deposits, assistance from the home Government, and hard-working immigrants have made this part of the Netherlands into the most prosperous spot in the Guianas.

NORTH AMERICA

The vast continent of North America, abundant in raw materials and fertile agricultural lands, supports two highly industrialized nations, the United States and Canada, whose 3,987-mile mutual border is the longest continuous undefended frontier in the world. Although much of North America has been developed there still remain sparsely populated areas, particularly in Alaska and northern Canada. To the geographer, North America includes all the land that stretches from northern Canada south to the Isthmus of Panama, as well as the West Indies, and the island of Greenland, politically a part of Denmark (see page 9). In this gazetteer Mexico and the Central American nations are discussed under "Central America and the West Indies" (see page 26).

CANADA First colonized by the French under Champlain in the early 17th Century, Canada fell to the English in 1763 and became a British colony. Some measure of self-rule was achieved by 1849, and since 1931 Canada has been self-governing. The land is staggeringly large—it is the second-largest nation (after the Soviet Union) on earth—but with only 19 million people it is thinly populated. The 1.5-million-square-mile Northwest and Yukon Territories contain less than 1 per cent of the population and their great mineral resources remain largely untapped. But Canada is by no means poor: it has wide stretches of excellent farmland and produces quantities of oil, natural gas, zinc, copper, iron ore and timber. Much of this growing industry is controlled by Canadians of British (especially Scottish) descent, and this helps create what is perhaps Canada's prime political problem: French Canadians feel cheated and periodically demand independence for the French-speaking province of Quebec.

Principal Cities: Montreal, Ottawa (cap.), Toronto. *Area:* 3,851,802 sq. mi. *Population:* 19,604,000. *Government:* Monarchy; member British Commonwealth. *Economy:* Large industrial, agricultural output. *Religions:* Roman Catholic, Protestant. *Languages:* English, French. *See:* CAN.

UNITED STATES In 1940 the gross national product of the United States amounted to about $100 billion. By the 1960s it had reached $600 billion, more than 40 per cent of the output of the rest of the Free World alone. The U.S. produces more than 25 per cent of the world's steel, more than 35 per cent of its electric energy, almost 50 per cent of its automobiles, nearly half of its radios, television sets and refrigerators, and three quarters of its airplanes. It spends more than $50 billion a year for military preparedness to maintain its role as defender of democracy throughout the world. It gives some $3.5 billion a year in aid to less-developed nations. This miracle of productivity and affluence was accomplished in a land made up almost entirely of immigrants from established, older nations and their descendants. At first the home of aboriginal Indian tribes, America was settled by small groups of British, French, Dutch and Swedes; successive waves brought in Scotch-Irish, Germans, Irish, Scandinavians, peoples from Eastern Europe and the Middle East, and others from Spain and Portugal. French and Spanish colonizers in the South and West were absorbed, and to the West eventually came Asian immigrants. At least 10 per cent of the population is made up of descendants of slaves from Africa. While vast problems in the areas of civil, economic and educational rights remain, these groups have to an astonishing degree become part of the diverse yet homogeneous American society. The first to come were mainly farmers who worked a land that varies from fruitful coastal areas to rugged mountains to plains and deserts. Gradually their descendants and the new immigrant waves populated the vast country. From 1790 to 1965 the geographic center of population moved from 23 miles east of Baltimore to a point in central Illinois. An equally significant trend has been the shift in population from the land to urban areas; by 1960 seventy per cent of all Americans had become city dwellers.

 Principal Cities: Chicago, Detroit, Los Angeles, New York, Philadelphia, San Francisco, Washington, D.C. (cap.). *Population:* 194,583,000. *Area:* 3,615,204 sq. mi. *Government:* Federal republic. *Economy:* World's leading economic power, with broad industrial and agricultural base. *Religions:* Protestant; large Roman Catholic minority; small Jewish, Eastern Orthodox minorities. *Language:* English. *See:* USA.

OCEANIA

Oceania stretches 8,000 miles east across the South and Central Pacific from Australia. Its thousands of islands can be broadly classified into three groups: Polynesia, which forms a triangle encompassing Hawaii, New Zealand and Easter Island; Micronesia, a region northwest of Polynesia; and Melanesia, which runs from New Guinea to the Fijis.

AUSTRALIA Discovered by a Dutch captain in 1606, Australia was long an unknown land used by Britain as a penal colony. The entire continent, larger than the continental United States without Alaska, was not even traversed until 1861. Organized as a commonwealth in 1901, the present-day nation, a prosperous and bustling Western presence in the East, has fewer than 12 million people since much of the interior remains virtually uninhabitable. The aborigines who were living in Australia before the British arrived have dwindled in numbers.

 Principal Cities: Canberra (cap.), Sydney. *Population:* 11,360,000. *Area:* 2,971,020 sq. mi. *Government:* Monarchy; member British Commonwealth. *Economy:* Agricultural-pastoral; growing industry. *Religions:* Protestant, Roman Catholic. *Language:* English. *See:* ANZ.

NEW ZEALAND Noted for its South Seas beauty and the British flavor of its life, New Zealand is a pastoral nation. Chiefs of the Maoris, a branch of the Polynesians, ceded sovereignty over it to the British in 1840. The island is now a Commonwealth member with Maoris represented in its Parliament.

 Principal Cities: Auckland, Wellington (cap.). *Population:* 2,640,000. *Area:* 103,736 sq. mi. *Government:* Monarchy; member British Commonwealth. *Economy:* Agricultural. *Religion:* Protestant. *Language:* English. *See:* ANZ.

WESTERN SAMOA A German colony before World War I, Western Samoa has more recently been governed by New Zealand, first under a League of Nations Mandate and later as a U.N. Trusteeship Territory. In 1962 it became independent. The nation consists of nine islands, two of them inhabited.

 Principal City: Apia (cap.). *Area:* 1,097 sq. mi. *Population:* 119,000. *Government:* Monarchy. *Economy:* Agricultural; exports copra, cocoa, bananas. *Religion:* Protestant. *Languages:* English, Samoan. *See:* Page 152, HBK.

ANTARCTICA: UNKNOWN CONTINENT

Antarctica, the most inhospitable and least explored of the continents, spreads out from the South Pole to meet the Atlantic, Pacific and Indian Oceans. It contains 90 per cent of the ice in the world; winds hit velocities of 200 miles an hour and temperatures plunge to 125 degrees below zero. The continent may have been first sighted by an American whaler in 1820, a claim disputed by the British. A British expedition in 1899 was the first to winter on the continent, and a Norwegian was the first to plant a national flag on the Pole. Various nations have made claims to slices of Antarctica, but have cooperated in its exploration since 1957-1958, the International Geophysical Year.

AUSTRALIAN DEPENDENCIES The northeastern part of the island of New Guinea is a U.N. Trusteeship administered by Australia, as are the islands of New Britain, New Ireland, Bougainville and the Admiralty group. Papua, in southeastern New Guinea, is Australian territory.

BRITISH DEPENDENCIES Tonga is a self-governing kingdom of about 150 islands under British protection in western Polynesia. Some of the Solomons, located in Melanesia, are a British protectorate. The Fiji Islands are a Crown Colony. The New Hebrides are governed by an Anglo-French Condominium.

CHILEAN DEPENDENCY Chile's only inhabited possession in Oceania is 63.9-square-mile Easter Island.

FRENCH DEPENDENCIES France's major Overseas Territory in the Pacific is French Polynesia, taking in the Society (including Tahiti and Bora Bora), Tuamotu, Gambier, Austral and Marquesas Islands. France also rules the New Caledonia group in Melanesia. Like French Polynesia, the Wallis and Futuna Islands function as an Overseas Territory of France.

NEW ZEALAND DEPENDENCIES The Cook Islands, lying between Tahiti, Samoa and Tonga, are administered by New Zealand as an external territory. Other New Zealand islands include the Tokelaus, north of Samoa, and lonely Niue, which subsists on copra and bananas.

U.S. DEPENDENCIES The Trust Territory of the Pacific Islands, administered by the U.S. under the U.N. Security Council, takes in more than 2,000 islands, 64 of them inhabited, in Micronesia, including the Marshalls, Carolines and Marianas. Natives of Guam, at the southern end of the Marianas, are U.S. citizens. American Samoa is a U.S. Territory. Other areas under U.S. administration include the Ryukyu group, which takes in Okinawa; the Bonins; the Volcano Islands, where Iwo Jima is located; the Midway Islands; isolated Marcus, Wake and Johnston Islands; and some of the Phoenix and Line Islands.

The tall, thin slab of the U.N. Secretariat towers over nearby New York buildings as well as the domed General Assembly to its right.

International Organizations

IT is a truism that men wish to live in peace; it is equally true that they do not necessarily wish to live under rules established by their neighbors. The concept of mutual cooperation for protection against the encroachments of belligerent and covetous enemies is therefore by no means new. As early as the Fifth Century B.C. the Greek cities on the Gulf of Corinth formed themselves into the cooperative Achaean League, first for defense against marauding pirates and later against the legions of Philip II of Macedon, one of the earliest of history's great conquerors. The rise of the Roman Empire (which eventually took over Philip's conquests and most of those of his son, Alexander the Great) established a concept of a unified world in which all men could live in peace that lingered long past the final fall of the empire in the Fifth Century A.D.; perhaps the entire history of Europe since Rome's disintegration—and, by extension, that of much of the rest of the earth—can be seen

CONTENTS OF THIS SECTION

UNITED NATIONS AND
ALLIED ORGANIZATIONS

History of the U.N.   34-35
Secretariat   35-36
General Assembly   36-37
Security Council   38
Economic and Social Council
  (ECOSOC)   38
Trusteeship Council   39
International Court of Justice   39
Other United Nations
  Organizations   40
Specialized Semi-Independent
  Organizations
  Related to the U.N.   40-42

THE WORLD'S REGIONAL
ORGANIZATIONS: MILITARY

North Atlantic Treaty
  Organization (NATO)   43-45
Western European Union (WEU)   46
Eastern European Mutual Assistance
  Treaty (Warsaw Pact)   46-47
Central Treaty
  Organization (CENTO)   47-48
South-East Asia Treaty
  Organization (SEATO)   48-49
ANZUS Treaty   49

REGIONAL ORGANIZATIONS:
ECONOMIC AND SOCIAL

The European Community   50-51
European Coal and Steel
  Community (ECSC)   51-52
European Economic Community (EEC) 52-54
European Atomic Energy
  Community (Euratom)   54-55
Benelux   55
Organization for Economic
  Cooperation and Development
  (OECD)   55-56
Bank for International Settlements
  (BIS)   56
Council of Europe   56-57
Nordic Council   57
European Free Trade Association
  (EFTA)   57-58
Council for Mutual Economic
  Assistance (Comecon)   58-59
Organization of American States
  (OAS)   59-60
Organization of Central American
  States (ODECA)   60-61
Central American Common Market
  (CACM)   61-62
Latin American Free Trade
  Association (LAFTA)   62

The Commonwealth   62-63
The Colombo Plan for Co-operative
  Economic Development in South
  and South East Asia   64
African Regional Groups   65
The Arab League   66
Association of Southeast Asia   66-67
South Pacific Commission (SPC)   67

ORGANIZATIONS FOR NONPOLITICAL
COOPERATION

International Red Cross   68
European Conference of Ministers
  of Transport (ECMT)   68-69
Danube Commission   69
Central Commission for
  the Navigation of the Rhine   69
International Chamber of Commerce
  (ICC)   69
Bureau of International
  Expositions (BIE)   70
European Broadcasting Union (EBU)
  and International Radio and
  Television Organization (OIRT)   70
International Criminal Police
  Organization (Interpol)   70
World Council of Churches (WCC)   70-71
International Olympic Committee   71

as an attempt to re-establish, sometimes by conquest and sometimes by cooperation, the unity of the world. Not until the end of World War I, however, did a body come into existence that attempted to establish a real, planet-wide society of nations. The League of Nations, which was established largely because of the dedicated urgings of President Woodrow Wilson of the Unites States, failed to prevent another world conflict partly because the U.S. ultimately refused to become a League member and, more broadly, because the League lacked the power to coerce member nations into peaceful compromise. After World War II the nations of the world tried again to establish an instrument for the keeping of the world's peace. In the spring of 1945, again in part because of U.S. urging, 51 countries founded the United Nations in San Francisco. This section discusses the activities of the United Nations and those of other organizations dedicated to international cooperation.

The United Nations and Allied Organizations

THE HISTORY OF THE UNITED NATIONS

The League of Nations, born of World War I, had failed. World War II was shattering Europe and Asia. Scientists were at work devising a bomb that could incinerate the world. At this point the democratic nations resumed the search—begun in ancient Greece with the Achaean League—for an effective international organization to keep the peace. The effort commenced on June 12, 1941, when 14 Allied nations (nine of them represented by governments-in-exile) issued the London Declaration calling for "a world . . . relieved of the menace of aggression." A few weeks later Winston Churchill of Britain and Franklin D. Roosevelt of the United States proposed, in the Atlantic Charter, the establishment of "a permanent system of general security." On January 1, 1942, a declaration issued in Washington first used the phrase "United Nations," coined by F.D.R. to describe the wartime alliance. In Moscow on October 30, 1943, the foreign ministers of the United States, Britain, Russia and China formally called for "establishing at the earliest practicable date a general international organization . . . for the maintenance of international peace and security."

A year and a half later, on April 25, 1945, the day U.S. and Russian soldiers linked up at the Elbe, the representatives of 50 nations met in San Francisco's Opera House to consider a draft of a United Nations Charter submitted by the major powers. After nine weeks of discussion they produced the 111-article U.N. Charter, which pledged them jointly "to save succeeding generations from the scourge of war" and to "promote social progress." The Charter was ratified by the necessary number of governments by October 24, 1945. The Charter was hailed by its enthusiasts as the dawning of the millennium and disparaged as spongy liberalism by its detractors.

In retrospect, the Charter was less forward-looking than it might have been. It was written by professional statesmen with large-minded objectives but stingy notions about granting the new organization the means to achieve those objectives. If one paragraph of the Charter declared that members "shall settle their international disputes by peaceful means," another stressed the sovereign equality of member states. The Security Council, run by the five great powers, would be the U.N.'s executive arm. It would decide for the organization when the peace was being threatened and what steps should be taken. A key article specified, however, that Council actions could be vetoed by any of the five permanent members of the Council: the U.S., Britain, Russia, France and China. A General Assembly in which all the members had an equal voice and vote could debate all germane issues and act as the U.N.'s conscience and complaint box—but little more. A Secretary-General was to be the administrative chief of a permanent bureaucracy.

Basic to U.N. success, obviously, was the idea that the Big Five, after alliance in war, would work together for peace. There was no provision for coercing these giants. If anyone were coerced it would be the vetoless small fry. The U.N. has always been caught in a contradiction between its promise of absolute sovereignty for important members and its mandate to keep the peace.

The constitutional arrangement did not have a chance. The Cold War split the Big Five from the start. At the first General Assembly meeting, which opened on January 10, 1946, Russia clashed with the West over electing the Assembly's president. On January 19, 1946, two days after it opened for business, the Security Council received its first complaint, Iran charging that the Soviet Union was interfering in its internal affairs. Two days later the Soviets countercharged that the British were interfering in the internal affairs of Greece, and a few weeks after that the Soviets cast their first veto. The Council's first major success in bringing an international force into action against an aggressor was the result of an accident. In 1950, just before the eruption of the Korean War, Moscow's delegate walked out of the

THE U.N. FLAG, approved in 1947, shows the U.N. emblem in white on a light blue field. The emblem consists of a north polar projection of the world, symbolizing world unity, cradled by olive branches, since ancient times the symbol of peace.

Council to protest its failure to admit Red China. His absence enabled the Council to order police action taken against North Korea.

Realizing that the Russians would not again make the same mistake, the U.S. hastened to push through the General Assembly (where the U.S. controlled a sizable majority) the "Uniting for Peace" resolution. This resolution empowered the Assembly to recommend the use of "armed force when necessary" if trouble came and the Security Council were vetobound. The embittered Russians vented their rage over this action on the U.N.'s first Secretary-General,

U.N. delegates sit and chat before a General Assembly meeting.

Trygve Lie, until in 1952 he felt forced to resign.

Nevertheless, for at least five years the U.N. was able to function through the Assembly, with the West's guaranteed majorities in that body being used to circumvent the East's Security Council vetoes. The General Assembly of 1955 was the turning point. In that session West and East by agreement stopped blocking each other's new membership applications, and in a "package deal" 16 new states took seats in the Assembly. This radically altered the old power balance: no longer could the Assembly be counted on to make the U.N. effective. In these circumstances it was fortunate that the Swedish economist-diplomat Dag Hammarskjöld had been appointed the second Secretary-General in 1953. Brilliant, forceful and ingenious, Hammarskjöld was instrumental in compelling France, Britain and Israel to halt their 1956 invasion of Egypt, and in arranging in 1958 for U.N. observation groups to be in

Lebanon and Jordan to prevent interference from Egypt. He sent a U.N. representative to troubled Laos in 1959 against Russia's wishes and organized the peace-keeping operation in the Congo. In 1961, as the angered Russians were proposing that he be replaced, Hammarskjöld was killed in a plane crash while on duty in the Congo.

The U.N. had been able to do its job by a series of Security Council-to-Assembly-to-Secretary-General forward passes of power. When one arm faltered or was stymied, another took over and kept the world organization moving. Working largely in this pragmatic fashion, the U.N. has racked up some formidable victories. It has been an occasional peacemaker in smaller disputes, a decompression chamber for larger quarrels and a forum for the airing of differences among nations. It has aborted at least five wars. There have been U.N. failures, too, most spectacularly its inability to stop the Russian subjugation of Hungary in 1956 and its inability to get India to permit a U.N.-supervised plebiscite in Kashmir.

The end of the Hammarskjöld era brought with it the end of the era of brilliant improvisation. The third Secretary-General, U Thant, faced a different situation. The key problem of the U.N.—how to reconcile national sovereignty with the keeping of the peace—had finally to be faced. On the organization's 20th anniversary *The New York Times* made a bitter assessment: "The big powers have used the organization selfishly—when at all." The liberal U.S. Jesuit weekly *America* said: "The U.N. can never be effective without the power to curtail the freedom of its members. . . . The hour has arrived . . . when we have to choose between unlimited national sovereignty and effective international organization."

THE UNITED NATIONS SECRETARIAT

The chief of the U.N.'s Secretariat, the Secretary-General, is both the top administrative officer and the head janitor of the United Nations. He and his 8,934-man force—"such staff as the organization may require" in the Charter's phrase—arrange the U.N.'s conferences, collect the necessary background information for its meetings, see to it that speeches are translated into five languages, and keep the public informed of U.N. activities through television and radio and through publications in some 60 languages. In a single year some 350,000 index cards are needed simply to keep track of U.N. documents, and these are made out and filed by Secretariat personnel. The Secretariat also makes sure that the 6,600 windows and the 26 miles of carpeting in the U.N.'s New York headquarters buildings are kept clean, that the flags fly out front and that the garage in the basement is properly run. About two thirds of the total staff of the Secretariat is spread around the globe looking after U.N. business—peace-keeping, U.N. technical-assistance programs, communications —in 80 countries.

The U.N. Charter also gives the Secretary-General a single, and it has turned out, most important, political task: to "bring to the attention of the Security Council any matter which in his opinion may threaten . . . international peace." That sentence—because of the deadlock in the Security Council and the near-anarchy in the Assembly—has elevated the Secretary-General to a position of being in some respects the chief executive of the world. Successive Secretaries-General have won the right not merely to speak their minds but to make major political proposals to the U.N., to suggest missions of inquiry when the Security Council balks, to criticize member governments publicly, to negotiate with heads of state and even to establish U.N. armies as large as 20,000 men. Dag Hammarskjöld once told the malfunctioning U.N. that he "was prepared to fill any vacuum" that the organization left in providing for the safeguarding of peace; and he proceeded to do so, on one occasion defying a Security Council veto. Often left without a clear mandate, Hammarskjöld nevertheless developed what had been designed as a purely administrative job into a crucial post. Trygve Lie, his predecessor, said: "This is the most impossible job in the world."

THE U.N. GENERAL ASSEMBLY

The General Assembly is the closest the world has ever come to having a Parliament of Man. All 121 U.N. members, representing 2.3 of the world's 3.2 billion people, have one vote apiece in the Assembly and are entitled to a double row of seats and a green-topped desk in the sloping chamber. Sessions convene on the third Tuesday of every September and usually last 10 to 12 weeks. What the meetings accomplish is less predictable. The Assembly is the amorphous, free-floating conscience of the U.N. Its franchise—to discuss anything within the scope of the U.N. Charter and make recommendations on whatever the Assembly wishes—is so broad as to be meaningless. Or it can be meaningful if one of the great powers really wants the Assembly to act.

But to get meaningful action from the Assembly takes some doing, for the Assembly is only half a legislative body; it can make recommendations, but it cannot enforce them. As if to compensate for this lack of power, the Charter gives the Assembly at least the appearance of being the center of the U.N. organization. The Assembly has control over the U.N.'s budget, and it elects most of the members of the three Councils—Security, Trusteeship, and Economic and Social (see below)—all of which must also report back to it. It also appoints the Secretary-General, new U.N. members and World Court judges (see page 39), and approves Charter amendments— after the Security Council has proposed them.

This arrangement, which gives the power to the Security Council and the voice to the General Assembly, was a compromise between 1945's prevailing idealism and the member governments' *Realpolitik*. In 1950 the Assembly's inherent possibilities were

The U.N. General Assembly meets in its large New York auditorium to hear an address by Ethiopia's Emperor Haile Selassie.

The hub of the United Nations is the General Assembly. Every branch of the U.N. reports to the General Assembly either directly or indirectly. One of these branches, the Security Council, has under its jurisdiction the Military Staff Committee (1), the Disarmament Commission (2), and U.N. peace-keeping forces and military observers (3). Another U.N. organ linked to the Assembly is the Economic and Social Council, which in turn has connections with the regional economic commissions (4), functional commissions (5), the Trade and Development Board (6), the U.N. Conference for Trade and Development (7), UNICEF (8), the U.N. High Commissioner for Refugees (9), the Administrative Committee on Coordination (14), the U.N. Development Program (15) and the International Atomic Energy Agency (16). ECOSOC coordinates the following specialized agencies: the International Labor Organization (17), Food and Agricultural Organization (18), U.N. Educational, Scientific and Cultural Organization (19), World Health Organization (20), International Development Association (21), World Bank (22), International Finance Corporation (23), International Monetary Fund (24), International Civil Aviation Organization (25), Universal Postal Union (26), International Telecommunication Union (27), World Meteorological Organization (28), Inter-Governmental Maritime Consultative Organization (29), and General Agreement on Tariffs and Trade (30). Attached directly to the Assembly are the Main Committees of the General Assembly (10), the Procedural Committees (11), Standing Committees (12) and other subsidiary bodies (13), as well as the U.N. force in the Middle East (31), the agency for Palestine refugees (32) and the Administrative Tribunal (33).

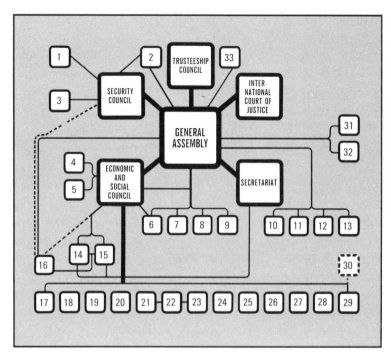

turned to advantage by the U.S. In despair over the Security Council's inability to act in the face of repeated Soviet vetoes, Washington pushed through the "Uniting for Peace" resolution empowering the Assembly to conduct peace-keeping operations when the Security Council deadlocked. This gave the Assembly, and the West, a new measure of power, but it was undercut in 1955 when the U.N. took in new members, initiating an expansion that transformed the Assembly from a West-dominated group into one with an Afro-Asian plurality of more than 50. The U.S.'s ability to use the Assembly thereupon declined—but the Russians' enthusiasm for the Assembly rose, for they saw in it a means of propaganda and of action against the West.

And so it went. In 1958, for example, in a remarkable switch, Nikita Khrushchev proposed to transfer from Council to Assembly discussion of the British-U.S. "armed intervention" in Lebanon and Jordan. In 1964, in another Cold War turn, the U.S. saw a chance to use the Assembly once more against the U.S.S.R. over the matter of Russia's refusal to pay its share of the maintenance of the U.N.'s forces in Egypt and the Congo. Moscow was two years in arrears and was in danger of forfeiting its Assembly vote. On second thought, however, the U.S. decided against enforcing the penalty, which might well have imperiled the U.N.'s very existence. The 1964

Assembly convened but never took a vote on a substantive matter, thus avoiding the issue of whether or not the Soviets still had a vote.

Unfortunately, the do-nothing 1964 session further depressed Assembly prestige. One major reason why the U.S. stood by and let this happen was voiced in a 1965 *Saturday Evening Post* editorial: "The pro-Western majority that we once counted on has vanished because of the flood of new Afro-Asian members who now dominate the Assembly." The article went on to point out that "four of those African nations have a combined population smaller than that of Georgia."

The result has been a number of proposals for "weighted voting" to replace the "one country one vote" formula by which some 200 million Americans are equated with, say, 1.6 million Togolese. If carried out, weighted voting might not benefit the West as much as would appear. For example, the founders of 1945 included all the little Central American republics, whose combined population barely outstrips that of newcomer Tanzania. In addition, if the Assembly went to weighted voting, the U.S. would get 120 votes to Togo's one, but Red China, if admitted to the U.N., would get 470—more than twice the total for all Western Europe. The solution may lie less in playing the numbers game than in making a true effort at international cooperation.

THE UNITED NATIONS SECURITY COUNCIL

MEMBERS: (Permanent) China, France, U.S.S.R., United Kingdom, United States. Ten member countries elected by General Assembly.

The Security Council, directed by the U.N. Charter to take "primary responsibility" for maintaining world peace, is the key element in the United Nations. Structurally, it consists of five permanent members (the U.S., Russia, China, Britain and France) plus 10 others elected for two-year terms by the General Assembly. It is the only U.N. organ whose decisions are subject to one member's veto.

This veto power, which enables one country to paralyze the Security Council, has been much deplored. It was, however, a most necessary part of the Charter, for without it both the U.S. and the U.S.S.R. would have stayed out of the U.N.; neither of the two nations was prepared to yield its sovereignty by joining an organization over whose actions it did not have a final say. In any case, it was assumed that the great powers would be able to agree on what constituted a threat to the peace. It did not, of course,

The Security Council convenes in its New York headquarters.

work out that way. Hostility rather than cooperation between East and West marked the postwar world, and the Russians again and again used their veto. The Council was able to carry out its peace-keeping mandate in Korea in 1950 and in the Congo in 1960, but otherwise its job has largely been taken over by the Secretary-General and the General Assembly.

As the U.N.'s cop on the beat, the Council is organized to "function continuously," and it has summoned meetings in as little as six hours. In the early years Council meetings were frequent, but as the Council became less effective it met less and less. Recently, however, the French have joined the Russians in working for a return to the Council, and there are signs that the U.S. is thinking in the same direction.

THE ECONOMIC AND SOCIAL COUNCIL

The Economic and Social Council, or ECOSOC, is the U.N.'s social worker, and a very busy one at that. Charged with fostering worldwide advances in economic, social, cultural and humanitarian fields, it began, says a British expert, "by pursuing every social and economic objective in sight, with an extravagant faith in . . . the value of proliferating committees and commissions." By 1965 it had spawned eight principal commissions, 14 specialized agencies, and a score of miscellaneous bodies, lesser commissions and committees. It had also set up semiofficial relations with more than 300 non-U.N. organizations such as the Movement for Calendar Reform and the Council on World Tensions, Inc.

ECOSOC's 27-delegate Council, elected for three years by the U.N.'s General Assembly, meets twice yearly, once every spring for about a month at the U.N.'s Manhattan headquarters and again every summer in Geneva. Ad hoc and standing committees review the U.N.'s technical-assistance program; deal with ECOSOC's specialized agencies, ranging from the Universal Postal Union to the World Health Organization (see page 42); and study and report on women's rights, the narcotics trade and dozens of other matters. Additionally, ECOSOC is responsible for four Economic Surveys, one each for Europe, Asia and the Far East, Africa, and Latin America. Especially well regarded are the Economic Survey for Europe, headed from 1947 to 1957 by the eminent sociologist Dr. Gunnar Myrdal, and ECLA, its opposite number for Latin America, run from 1950 until 1963 by Dr. Raúl Prebisch. (Prebisch now directs UNCTAD, a newborn ECOSOC affiliate concerned with the development of backward nations.)

With its erratic, sprawling organizational chart and its social-worker stance, ECOSOC tends to look like a billowing, do-gooding spinster trying to cope with an oversized brood of rambunctious children. Naturally, the quality of its service ranges from very good to empty talkativeness. However, some experts rate ECOSOC very highly, considering it potentially the most important organ in the world body. Peace and security matters make up most of the news about the U.N., but they are only a small part of the U.N. at work. Seventeen of every 20 U.N. employees and 80 cents of every U.N. dollar are engaged in economic, social and technical enterprises.

THE U.N. TRUSTEESHIP COUNCIL

MEMBERS: There are three categories—(1) states that administer Trust Territories, (2) permanent members of the Security Council, and (3) as many additional members as needed to make equal the number of trusteeship and nontrusteeship states.

The U.N.'s Trusteeship Council was set up in 1946 to supervise the administration of dependent territories placed under the international trusteeship system and to promote their "progressive development towards self-government." It has succeeded so well that it may not be needed much longer. The Council started with 11 Trust Territories—former League of Nations Mandates and colonies of the nations defeated in World War II. They ranged in size from Tanganyika, which was bigger than Texas, to Nauru, a dot in the ocean. By 1965 the Council had only three remaining Trust Territories—Nauru, New Guinea and the Pacific Islands. The Council sends detailed questionnaires to the states administering these areas—Australia, New Zealand, Britain and the U.S.—to find out about economic, social and educational conditions and about the steps that have been taken toward self-government. It also considers petitions from aggrieved natives. Periodically, the Council sends out "visiting missions." So well has the Council done in the past that it now has less and less to do. Even its chamber in New York has been made over so that it can be used by other organizations.

THE INTERNATIONAL COURT OF JUSTICE

FOUNDED: June 1945 in San Francisco. **HEADQUARTERS:** The Hague, Netherlands. **MEMBERS:** 117 U.N. members plus Liechtenstein, San Marino and Switzerland.

The International Court of Justice, the U.N.'s principal judicial body, is a vestige of the old League of Nations. Although World War II spelled the final end of the League, the League's Permanent Court of International Justice continued to exist throughout the conflict in the Peace Palace built in 1913 at The Hague, Holland. The 1945 U.N. organizing conference in effect admitted its inability to improve substantially on the League's Court when it specified that the new Court take over the old's statutes, precedents and meeting place, dropping only the first word of the Court's old name, "Permanent."

The Court has 15 justices, each of whom is elected by the General Assembly and the Security Council to serve for a nine-year term. The Court has two

functions. First, it hands down "advisory opinions" requested by the Assembly, the Councils or other major U.N. bodies. Second, it decides "contentious" cases submitted to it by member governments. Member governments automatically include all U.N. members as well as some non-U.N. members, such as Switzerland, which agreed to comply with certain conditions. About one third of the members (but, notably, none of the Communist states) have pledged themselves to accept the Court's decisions, allowing

The International Court of Justice hears a case in its chamber.

themselves, however, a few caveats. Some put a time limit on the Court's compulsory jurisdiction; the U.S. insists on excluding matters of "domestic jurisdiction"—and also insists that it alone be the judge of when this applies. Despite the West's caveats, the East's cold shoulder and its own lack of a police force, the Court has handed down—and made stick —a number of decisions. Among them are judgments that Norwegian fishermen could have exclusive rights to certain waters, that the Colombian Embassy in Lima was not required to surrender to Peruvian authorities a Peruvian Leftist who had taken asylum there, and that islets in the English Channel belonged to Britain, not France.

However, the Court has had its failures, too. In 1962 it handed down an advisory opinion that all U.N. members must help pay for the U.N. armies in the Middle East and the Congo. Russia and France, against whom the decision was directed, continued to refuse to pay. Like the rest of the U.N., the Court is a compromise between a growing movement to world peace and order and a residual passion for national sovereignty.

OTHER UNITED NATIONS ORGANIZATIONS

The U.N. has aided in the creation of four bodies that foster progress in the fields of economic and social development, of world trade, of atomic energy and in the care of the world's destitute children.

The United Nations Development Program

The U.N. Development Program was formed in 1965 as a consolidation of the United Nations Special Fund and the Expanded Program of Technical Assistance. Its purpose is to bring together the resources of 119 countries to further worldwide economic and social development. Its activities include making surveys of natural resources to determine the economic potential of various regions, setting up research and training centers, and providing advisory services in a number of technical fields.

General Agreement on Tariffs and Trade (GATT)

Immediately following World War II, the U.N. initiated discussions on world trade with an eye toward lowering such restrictive barriers as high tariffs. When these talks met with unexpected difficulties, some of the interested nations agreed on tariff concessions among themselves. The concessions were incorporated in a contract called the General Agreement on Tariffs and Trade which went into effect in 1948. Today there are 80 participating governments in GATT, representing 80 per cent of the world's trade. Based in Geneva, Switzerland, GATT has a modest budget, but its work is impressive. Its Director-General has called it "the most comprehensive instrument for trade liberalization that ever existed." Among GATT's recent negotiations have been the so-called Kennedy round of talks, aimed at across-the-board tariff reductions and at promoting through trade the economic health of the underdeveloped countries.

International Atomic Energy Agency (IAEA)

The International Atomic Energy Agency was organized in 1957 under the auspices of the U.N. to promote peaceful uses of atomic energy and to distribute atomic fuel. It was not very successful in distributing fuel since many nations had already made other arrangements to get it. As a result, IAEA changed course and today places much of its emphasis on inducing nations voluntarily to submit their

nuclear plants to IAEA control. Other activities include giving assistance to developing nations in the uses of nuclear energy in medicine, agriculture and industry, and the distribution of nuclear information.

The United Nations Children's Fund (UNICEF)

One of the best-known programs of the United Nations is the Children's Fund, originally conceived under the title of United Nations International Children's Emergency Fund and still popularly known as UNICEF. Created in 1946 to provide much-needed food and clothing to children in war-torn countries, UNICEF continues to this day to help the young with health, nutrition and education programs. Its annual budget of some $35 million is contributed by governments, private organizations and individuals. The best-known sources of UNICEF revenue in the U.S. are the Halloween Trick or Treat collection and the sale of Christmas and greeting cards.

Pakistani children attend a school that is aided by UNICEF.

SPECIALIZED SEMI-INDEPENDENT ORGANIZATIONS RELATED TO THE U.N.

Many intergovernmental agencies that work for cooperation among nations are loosely affiliated with the United Nations but operate autonomously, with their own governing bodies and budgets.

International Bank for Reconstruction and Development (World Bank)

The International Bank for Reconstruction and Development, better known as the World Bank, was conceived at the Bretton Woods Conference in 1944 to promote the economic development of the member nations. Since that time it has made long-term loans worth more than nine billion dollars and sent financial experts to aid in planning the development of 40 countries. A Board of Governors, with representatives from each of the member nations, delegates most of its authority to 20 Executive Directors and a President based in Washington, D.C. By its Articles of Agreement the World Bank makes loans to

An atomic plant, built with World Bank aid, helps power Rome.

member governments and to private enterprises with government guarantees when money cannot be obtained from other sources. Its first loans were for reconstruction in Europe. Since 1948 most World Bank loans have gone to countries in Asia, Africa, Europe and Latin America.

International Development Association (IDA)

The International Development Association, an affiliate of the World Bank (see above), was set up in 1960 to promote progress in underdeveloped nations. Although it is administered by the World Bank's officers and staff, IDA has its own funds. Unlike the World Bank, its loans are all interest-free. The more highly developed nations among the 103 members contribute to the organization's funds in gold or in convertible currencies, the less developed nations primarily in their own national currencies. Loans so far have totaled more than one billion dollars—primarily for development in transportation, agriculture and industry.

International Finance Corporation (IFC)

By making its own investments in private enterprise and by stimulating international investment in underdeveloped countries, the International Finance Corporation supplements the operations of the World

Bank and the International Development Association (see above). Formed in 1956 as a World Bank affiliate, the 78-member IFC has its own funds and staff but draws on services provided by the World Bank. The IFC's investment and underwriting commitments had totaled $137 million by 1965 and had earned a net income of $22 million.

International Monetary Fund (IMF)

The International Monetary Fund was set up in 1946 to promote a freer system of world trade and payments, and to encourage currency-exchange stability. By 1965 more than 20 nations had eliminated exchange restrictions with the encouragement of the IMF, and many more had taken advantage of its technical-assistance program. The Fund is controlled by a Board of Governors made up of one Governor and one Alternate from each of the 103 member nations. Many of its operations are run by a Managing Director and a Board of Executive Directors.

International Civil Aviation Organization (ICAO)

The International Civil Aviation Organization came into being in 1947, replacing the older International Commission for Air Navigation and the Pan American Convention on Commercial Aviation. Its 110 members cooperate to promote international air safety standards and to encourage superior aircraft design. An assembly of ICAO members chooses a Council and the Council, in turn, elects a Secretary-General. Both work to carry out the organization's programs. Based in Montreal, the ICAO has field offices located around the world.

Food and Agriculture Organization (FAO)

The goal of the 110-member (plus four associate members) Food and Agriculture Organization is to eliminate hunger from the world. To accomplish this ambitious objective, FAO attempts to increase efficiency in the production and distribution of food and thus to raise levels of nutrition and standards of living. Specific programs cover such areas as the development of water resources, use of fertilizers, soil-erosion control and international exchange of agricultural information. Based in Rome, FAO is governed by a Conference composed of its members. The programs recommended by the Conference are translated into action by a Council and a Director-General who has an international staff.

International Organizations

Inter-Governmental Maritime Consultative Organization (IMCO)

The 60 member states of the Inter-Governmental Maritime Consultative Organization, a U.N. agency, work to bring about cooperation and exchange of information on all technical matters that affect shipping and to coordinate maritime safety efforts. Since IMCO began operating in 1959, its activities have included programs to simplify shipping documents and procedures and to revise the international Code of Signals. IMCO is directed by an Assembly, made up of representatives from the member states, which draws up programs that are carried out by a Secretary-General under the supervision of a Council.

International Labor Organization (ILO)

Established in 1919 by the Treaty of Versailles as an autonomous part of the League of Nations, the International Labor Organization in 1946 became the first specialized agency to be associated with the U.N. Its goal is the attainment of peace through social justice. Every year two Government delegates, an employers' delegate and a workers' delegate, from each of the 115 member nations meet in Geneva to set world labor standards and discuss a wide range of social and labor questions. ILO's programs are carried out by the Geneva-based secretariat, which has branches in major world capitals.

International Telecommunication Union (ITU)

The International Telecommunication Union, which celebrated its centenary in 1965, produces international regulations governing the operation of telegraphy, telephony and radio networks throughout the world. The ITU also publishes information and in general seeks to maintain and extend international cooperation for the improvement of telecommunications of all kinds. Recently it acquired responsibility for outer-space radio communications.

United Nations Educational, Scientific and Cultural Organization (UNESCO)

The United Nations Educational, Scientific and Cultural Organization came into being in 1946 to stimulate progress and cooperation in the fields from which it takes its name. Its policies are formed in a General Conference held every two years with representatives from the 120 member nations plus three associate members. Operating from headquarters in Paris, UNESCO's Secretariat carries out programs

Delegates to a meeting talk in UNESCO's Paris headquarters.

of worldwide scope, with emphasis on underdeveloped countries. Projects include international exchange of teachers and publications, cultural programs to bring Asia and the West closer together, scientific research on water, application of science and technology to the industrialization of developing countries, and modernization of educational facilities.

Universal Postal Union (UPU)

The Universal Postal Union, one of the oldest international organizations, dates from 1874, when 22 nations held a conference in Bern, Switzerland, to work out greater uniformity in postal services. Affiliated with the U.N., the UPU has its headquarters in Bern, where representatives from its 127 member nations strive for uniformity in such matters as weight limits and charges.

World Health Organization (WHO)

The World Health Organization came into being in April 1948 with the ambitious goal of "the attainment by all peoples of the highest possible level of health." Since that time it has freed hundreds of millions of people from disease and has proved one of the most effective arms of the United Nations. Its activities range from coordinating international health efforts to standardizing drugs.

World Meteorological Organization (WMO)

The World Meteorological Organization provides the current framework through which nations carry on and expand their century-old practice of exchanging weather information. An arm of the U.N., WMO works to improve weather reporting, the application of meteorology to aviation, shipping and farming, and research and training. It is controlled by the World Meteorological Congress.

The World's Regional Organizations: Military

NORTH ATLANTIC TREATY ORGANIZATION (NATO)

FOUNDED: April 1949 in Washington, D.C. **HEADQUARTERS:** Brussels. **MEMBERS:** Belgium, Canada, Denmark, France, German Federal Republic, Greece, Iceland, Italy, Luxembourg, Netherlands, Norway, Portugal, Turkey, United Kingdom, United States.

The single most important alliance in the Western world, NATO is a defensive grouping of 15 nations stretching from Iceland to Turkey, encompassing 8,579,659 square miles and 5.5 million men under arms. As a military organization it has worked so well that it may soon be out of a job.

The North Atlantic Treaty Organization was formally launched in 1949 by representatives of the 12 original NATO nations apprehensively gathered in Washington to seek ways to protect Western Europe against Soviet invasion. The Russians, not satisfied with wartime annexations of Estonia, Latvia and Lithuania, together with parts of Finland, Romania, Poland, Germany and Czechoslovakia, had greeted the 1945 peace by intensifying their expansionist drive. While Allied forces in Europe demobilized, the Soviets kept their armies on near-war footing. As

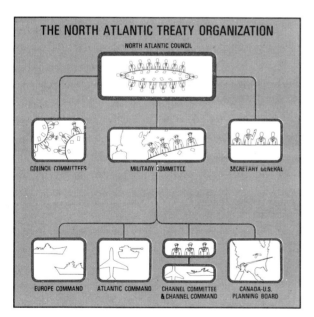

The highest ruling body in the North Atlantic Treaty Organization is the North Atlantic Council *(top)*, composed of civilian representatives of the member nations. Directly beneath this Council are the Council Committees, the Secretary General and the top military authority in NATO, the Military Committee, which oversees the activities of NATO's three military Commands and its Planning Group.

early as 1945 they stirred civil war in Greece and brought pressure on Turkey and Iran. In 1947 the Communists seized power in Hungary, Bulgaria, Romania and Poland; in 1948 Czechoslovakia fell. The Communist International, dissolved during the war, was revived in 1947 and renamed the Cominform, with the frank mission of attacking and destroying the Western political complex.

Not surprisingly, the wartime dream of a world order resting on the United Nations vanished like smoke in a cold Siberian wind. What was more, the Soviet Union could, and did, hamstring the U.N.'s Security Council (see page 38) with its use of the veto power. Instead of providing a forum where the great powers could hammer out differences, the U.N. had become an instrument of their rivalry.

The U.S. had traditionally avoided alliances with European nations. But now, faced by the continuing Russian menace, the U.S. Senate on June 11, 1948, authorized the Government for the first time during a period of peace to associate itself with such collective defense arrangements as would contribute to the nation's security. President Truman's Administration deliberated and then, in April 1949, ten European nations and Canada gathered in Washington to league together with the U.S. and form NATO. The Berlin Blockade, then in its 10th month, dramatized the extent to which Western Europe lay in the shadow of Soviet might, and all 12 powers eagerly signed the treaty. (Three nations—Greece, Turkey and the German Federal Republic—subsequently joined NATO's original 12, bringing the pact's membership to 15.)

The 14-clause North Atlantic Treaty said that an attack on one member was to be considered an attack on all. It provided against aggression by calling first for mutual assistance to build the means of resistance, next for consultation in the event of threats and finally for common action in case of attack. The treaty remained just that, a treaty, until 1950. What then put NATO on its feet, turning it into an armed and effective alliance, was an event not in Europe but in Asia—the Communist invasion of South Korea. "The attack upon Korea," said President Truman, "makes it plain beyond all doubt that Communism has passed beyond the use

Jet fighters from seven different NATO air forces point their needle noses at each other on an airfield in Europe during maneuvers.

of subversion to conquer independent nations and will now use armed invasion and war." The U.S. began to rearm, not just to fight in Korea but also to beef up its forces in Europe. Most of the other NATO nations also increased their defense expenditures, promising to ship battle-ready divisions to man the East-West border. From a simple guarantee that would bring the U.S. to the defense of Western Europe for the next 20 years, NATO evolved toward a much more permanent and complex arrangement for integrating and pooling U.S. and European military resources.

NATO's structure evolved correspondingly and today encompasses a labyrinth of commands, subcommands and subsidiary bodies. At the top of the organizational chart—and NATO's top political authority—is the North Atlantic Council. The Council meets at the "ministerial level" two or three times a year when high-ranking officials from each of the

NATO'S FLAG has a blue background, symbolizing the Atlantic Ocean; a circle, the symbol of unity; and a four-pointed star representing a compass, a guide on the voyage to peace.

member countries get together and chart long-range policy. The Council's day-to-day work is done by the Permanent Representatives, who meet at least once a week. A secretariat, which itself has five major functional subdivisions, executes Council policy.

On the military side NATO's top organ is the Military Committee, which is made up of Chiefs of Staff of the member nations, and provides strategic guidance for NATO's forces. These forces, which *are* NATO in the final reckoning, are divided into three main commands and one regional planning group. The most important is Allied Command Europe, which is headed by the Supreme Allied Commander Europe. This commander and his staff are usually known by the initials SACEUR, and they are quartered in SHAPE (Supreme Headquarters Allied Powers Europe) in southern Belgium. SACEUR controls all land, sea and air operations in its area. Operations in the Atlantic are the responsibility of NATO's principal naval commander, Supreme Allied Commander Atlantic, known as SACLANT. NATO's third command, and by far the least important, is Allied Command Channel, which looks after matters involving the English Channel and the southern North Sea. Significantly, two of the most important parts of NATO's structure—the Military Committee and SACLANT—are headquartered in the United States. It is also significant that the chiefs of the European and Atlantic commands have always been U.S. officers.

NATO's first phase, its growth from 1949 to 1955, was in some ways the easiest. Stalinist Russia's hostility cemented the alliance, making all the Allies grateful for the U.S.'s headlong rush from isolationism to participation in European affairs. It has been the second phase, from 1955 to the present, that has proved to be NATO's time of troubles.

What happened, at least in part, is that NATO worked too well. Since the signing of the North Atlantic Treaty, not another inch of European territory has fallen under Soviet domination. Additionally, Western Europe, thanks again to U.S. help, has made an astounding comeback, recovering its economic health. Simultaneously, events on the enemy side— Stalin's death, the Soviet thaw, the Sino-Soviet split —have helped create a real sense of lessened tension. The effect of the decrease in the Eastern threat and the increase in Western strength—in themselves sufficient developments to make a tight alliance with America seem less necessary—has been enhanced by a bitter division within the NATO alliance itself.

The main cause of division, at least indirectly, was Russia's success in producing an atom bomb and then a hydrogen bomb. The U.S., of course, continued to maintain that if necessary it would defend its NATO allies with its nuclear weapons (over which it alone exerted final control). But since this could well mean that the U.S. would be destroyed by Russian nuclear weapons, some European members of NATO became skeptical, doubting that the U.S. would risk such a fearful penalty just to defend, say, Berlin. They felt that they could only be safe if NATO shared nuclear control with the U.S., and their view drew widespread support. "In the past," wrote ex-U.S. diplomat Ronald Steel, "nations could solemnly pledge themselves to one another's aid in the event of attack. . . the risks, while grave, were within the realm of toleration. Today this no longer seems true. . . . No nation can be expected to accept its own incineration to help out a friend."

By 1959 even the late Christian Herter, a former U.S. Secretary of State, was forced to admit to a Congressional hearing that he could not "conceive of the President of the United States involving us in an all-out nuclear war unless the facts showed clearly that we are in danger of devastation ourselves." France's Charles de Gaulle was the first European

GIs join Italian soldiers on NATO maneuvers in Turkey.

leader to raise the nuclear issue publicly, but Britain was not far behind. The debate found the U.S. unwilling to share control, while at the same time deploring France's decision to build and maintain its own nuclear bombs and delivery system. Once France had built its own bomb, de Gaulle felt confident enough to take the next step and withdraw French forces from all NATO's integrated military commands. Moreover, he ordered all foreign forces to leave French soil by April of 1966. This meant abandonment of the big, white, A-shaped building which had been built especially for NATO in 1959 near Paris' Bois de Boulogne, in favor of an office building in downtown Brussels. It also meant that SHAPE, NATO's military headquarters, was banished from a comfortable Paris suburb to a remote village in southern Belgium.

Some authorities say that the true cause of friction within NATO is simply that it has been such a success that the alliance no longer seems truly necessary. If there were still a pressing need for NATO, if it were still vitally important to close ranks against Russian advances in Europe, de Gaulle might have lessened his insistence on France's right to act independently and other NATO members might somehow have found a way to resolve their differences. However, during the mid-1960s the problem of how to defend Western Europe against Iron Curtain countries became a question of less moment than how to carry on trade with them. It was clear that if NATO could accommodate itself to this new order it might survive; if not it would cease to function. In either case, nobody could deny its triumphs in the past.

WESTERN EUROPEAN UNION (WEU)

FOUNDED: May 1955 in London. **HEADQUARTERS:** London. **MEMBERS:** Belgium, France, German Federal Republic, Italy, Luxembourg, Netherlands, United Kingdom.

The Western European Union, which has played an important role in many of the major postwar European efforts to achieve military and economic cooperation, has its origin in the Brussels Treaty of 1948. At that time Britain, France, the Netherlands, Belgium and Luxembourg signed an agreement providing, in effect, that hostilities against any treaty member would involve war with all five. The treaty also called for economic, social and cultural collaboration among the members. When it was signed it created the tightest international association in European history. And it was one of the first big steps toward formation of the North Atlantic Treaty Organization for collective defense (see pages 43-45) and the Council of Europe for economic cooperation (see pages 56-57).

France's rejection in 1954 of the idea of a European Defense Community led to the remaking of the Western European Union in its current form. Concerned primarily with finding a way to associate the defense efforts of West Germany with NATO, the foreign ministers of the Brussels Treaty nations, plus those of West Germany, Italy, the U.S. and Canada, met in London. They drew up a document which ended the Allied occupation of West Germany and strengthened the former Brussels Treaty, and invited Germany and Italy to sign it. The decisions of 1954, ratified by the nations concerned the following year, brought the WEU into being as a seven-nation body, including West Germany and Italy.

The body's major organ is the Council of the WEU—made up of the foreign ministers or ambassadors of the six Continental member nations resident in London plus an undersecretary of the British Foreign Office. The Council, under the chairmanship of a Secretary-General, formulates over-all policy and is charged with ensuring cooperation with NATO. An Assembly, composed of the WEU nations' delegates to the Council of Europe, meets twice a year, usually in Paris, and may make recommendations to the WEU's Council. The WEU's social and cultural activities were transferred to the Council of Europe in 1960, but the WEU still maintains an Agency for the Control of Armaments and a Standing Arms Committee.

In 1963, when Great Britain was denied membership in the European Economic Community (see pages 52-54), whose six members all belong to the WEU, a WEU Liaison Commission was set up to study closer economic cooperation between London and the EEC. It was also agreed that the Council of the WEU should hold regular quarterly meetings during which member governments could exchange views on Europe's political and economic problems.

EASTERN EUROPEAN MUTUAL ASSISTANCE TREATY (WARSAW PACT)

FOUNDED: May 1955 in Warsaw. **HEADQUARTERS:** Moscow. **MEMBERS:** Albania, Bulgaria, Czechoslovakia, German Democratic Republic, Hungary, Poland, Romania, U.S.S.R.

The Eastern European Mutual Assistance Treaty, signed in Warsaw by the Communist nations of Eastern Europe on May 14, 1955, was originally meant as a reply to the integration of West German forces into the North Atlantic Treaty Organization, and actually did little more than legalize the presence of Soviet troops in the satellite countries. But the organization, better known as the Warsaw Pact, has come increasingly to resemble NATO as a body

Envoys from Russia and its allies draw up the Warsaw Pact.

coordinating the military forces of separate nations.

The 20-year pact was signed by representatives from the Soviet Union, Albania, Bulgaria, Czechoslovakia, East Germany, Hungary, Poland and Romania. It stipulated that the armed forces of the member states would have a joint command and that all would be obligated to come to the defense of any member under attack. The pact supplemented the several existing bilateral treaties and became the binding force among the Communist nations.

The structure of the pact is similar to that of NATO. At the top is the organization's Political Consultative Committee, which roughly corresponds to NATO's Council. Like NATO's forces, those of the Warsaw Pact are made up of units drawn from the armies of the signatory nations. Again like NATO, the Warsaw Pact really involves not just the forces assigned to it but, should war occur, the total military establishments of the member nations.

At the start it was clear that the pact was set up far more for the benefit of Russia than for the other members. One of its effects was to consolidate a buffer zone protecting the Soviet frontiers. East Germany, Poland and Czechoslovakia formed a line of defense between Russia and Western Europe; Romania and Bulgaria bolstered Russia's control of the Black Sea and its potential for control of the Dardanelles; Albania provided a site for Soviet submarine bases.

Changes within the Communist world, however, have altered Russia's relationship with its Communist allies and hence the nature of the pact. The 1956 uprising in Hungary showed that the first loyalty of satellite troops could be to their own nations instead of to the Russian-dominated alliance. Albania, although still technically a pact member, has sided with China in all recent disputes between the two Communist giants and has not participated in pact activities since the end of 1961. Romania's late President Gheorghe Gheorghiu-Dej did not attend pact meetings for a period of 18 months. The other members, to different degrees, have established positions independent from the U.S.S.R., and the Russians seldom get agreement on anything except routine matters.

Despite the growing insistence of the nations of Eastern Europe on running their own business, the Warsaw Pact is by no means a dead letter. The military forces of the member nations, especially those of East Germany, Czechoslovakia, Poland and the U.S.S.R., have been increasingly integrated, and they have held several joint maneuvers. In addition, Russia has helped modernize its allies' armies. In short, the Warsaw Pact remains a formidable military expression of the ideological and economic ties that still exist among most of the European Communist nations.

CENTRAL TREATY ORGANIZATION (CENTO)

FOUNDED: February 1955 in Baghdad, Iraq. **HEADQUARTERS:** Ankara, Turkey. **MEMBERS:** Iran, Pakistan, Turkey, United Kingdom.

The Central Treaty Organization was intended to be a major link in a worldwide, Western-oriented system of mutual defense against encroachments from the Communist world. Concerned with the Middle East, it has ties in the West with NATO (see pages 43-45) and in Asia with the nations of the South-East Asia Treaty Organization (see below). Although CENTO has fallen short of achieving military solidarity in the Middle East, it nonetheless has had considerable success in promoting the technological advance of the region.

CENTO began as the Baghdad Pact in February 1955, when a mutual-defense treaty was signed by Turkey and Iraq. Later in that same year Britain, Pakistan and Iran joined the Pact. In 1958 the Pact's

Officers of CENTO forces discuss military exercises in Iran.

headquarters was transferred from Baghdad to Ankara, Turkey, and the next year, 1959, one of the Pact's original members, Iraq, withdrew. As a result, the alliance's name was changed to the Central Treaty Organization. The United States, although not a full member, belongs to CENTO's Military, Economic and Counter-Subversion Committees, sends observers to meetings of its Council, and has signed bilateral military and economic agreements with Iran, Pakistan and Turkey.

CENTO's successes have been more economic than military, although it has helped to contain Russian influence. Under CENTO development programs, roads, railroads and telecommunications have been established linking Turkey with Iran and with Pakistan. Another program was responsible for modernization of the Turkish ports of Iskenderun and Trabzon. Assistance in agriculture and public health has also been provided. CENTO training and research centers are maintained in Teheran and Kraj, Iran, and in Malir, Pakistan.

SOUTH-EAST ASIA TREATY ORGANIZATION (SEATO)

FOUNDED: September 1954 in Manila, Philippines. **HEADQUARTERS:** Bangkok, Thailand. **MEMBERS:** Australia, France, New Zealand, Pakistan, Philippines, Thailand, United Kingdom, United States.

On September 6, 1954, eight alarmed nations met in Manila and in three swift days wrote and signed the SEATO treaty. Their objective: to contain the Communist surge into Southeast Asia. Four months before, the French fortress of Dienbienphu had fallen to Red assault and France had lost Indochina. At the moment Communist guerrillas were beleaguering the British in Malaya and causing trouble in Burma and the Philippines. For weeks U.S. Secretary of State John Foster Dulles had been shuttling between European capitals seeking a pact "to save all of Southeast Asia if it can be saved; if not, to save essential parts of it." The SEATO pact was the result. Going into force early in 1955, the treaty pledged action by the signatories against armed attack on any one of them. Additionally, SEATO set forth a special mid-20th Century sort of commitment, providing that in cases of political subversion from outside which threaten to take over a member country, all signers will "consult immediately in order to agree on the measures which should be taken for the common defense."

Codicils tacked onto the SEATO treaty attest to divergences among the partners. An ancillary Pacific Charter, designed to reassure newly independent countries like the Philippines, proclaims the "principle of equal rights and self-determination of peoples." Another divergence among the partners appeared when the U.S. working draft of the treaty called for the pact to be directed specifically against "Communist aggression." At the insistence of the other signatories the U.S. excised the word "Communist." In a separate declaration the U.S. made plain, however, that it meant to fight Red aggression only and not get involved in non-Communist

brawls like the India-Pakistan battle over Kashmir.

The treaty roused no great enthusiasm at birth. One major problem is that Western members outnumber Asian members five to three—a fact quickly pointed out by Red propagandists—and of these three, the Philippines are an island nation and Pakistan is somewhat off course. (Cambodia, Laos and South Vietnam have also been granted SEATO protection as "protocol" states.) Many vital areas are not covered. The three Asian lands with the largest non-Communist armies (South Korea, Taiwan, India) are outside SEATO and so is the nation with the greatest industrial potential (Japan). Indonesia, India, Ceylon and Burma disdain the organization.

SEATO's organizational framework is modest. Overall direction rests with a Council of Foreign Ministers which convenes in annual meetings that rotate from capital to capital. When this Council is not in session, the Council Representatives, generally the members' Ambassadors to Thailand, meet monthly at the rambling headquarters building in Bangkok, administering the political program and SEATO's modest budget of a little more than one million dollars annually. A Secretary-General with a small staff completes the permanent apparatus. There

During SEATO meetings a U.S. admiral sees a Thai official.

is an intelligence assessment committee as well as a number of expert committees and study groups in other areas to advise the organization in carrying out its various programs. For example, there is a research center in Bangkok which helps to keep track of Communist activities. A cultural exchange program and institutions in the fields of engineering, administration, vocational training, medical research and community development have been established. SEATO also sponsors conferences on economic and social matters.

SEATO, however, stands or falls on its military effectiveness. Unlike NATO, it has no military high command or forces in being. The joint eight-member international planning staff is a shadow group, mostly turning out contingency plans on how aggression should be met. Military liaison offices in Bangkok shuttle messages between the military authorities in the eight SEATO countries, and twice a year the military chiefs meet. The most tangible signs of military cooperation are the annual maneuvers, staged in Thailand and the Philippines and in the South China Sea. But the fact is that if an emergency arose, SEATO's military response would depend entirely on how each Government answered the call for assistance. With France advising neutralism in Asia and with British power diminished, the hard-rock military strength of SEATO is the striking power of the U.S. Seventh Fleet.

SEATO, in fact, has less muscle than the United States's bilateral defense arrangements with Thailand, the Philippines and South Vietnam, and there have been moments when the organization's future has seemed doubtful. In 1959, during the Bangkok Foreign Ministers Meeting, many observers thought the organization was finished when the U.S. pressed for a strong communiqué condemning Communist intervention in Laos and the French overrode everyone with their veto. Yet SEATO survived and modified its previous rule requiring unanimity before it could move. Later, in President John F. Kennedy's Administration, a strong feeling arose in some quarters that SEATO had become a divisive rather than a uniting force against Communism, segregating India, Burma, Indonesia and Ceylon. SEATO survived that, too. Even with its limitations, it has offered the United States the widest politico-military base available so far for action against Communism in Asia.

ANZUS TREATY

SIGNED: September 1951. **SIGNATORIES:** Australia, New Zealand, United States.

The ANZUS Treaty, which has become a bulwark of free-world security in the Pacific, came into being almost casually. After World War II, when China had become a Communist state, Washington began to look upon Japan as its chief Asian ally; this required negotiating a much friendlier peace treaty with Tokyo than is usual with an ex-enemy. To get approval for a treaty that would greatly strengthen Japan, the U.S. had to give guarantees to both Australia and New Zealand, which feared a resurgence of Japanese militarism. Thus on September 1, 1951, a week before the peace pact with Japan was concluded, Australia, New Zealand and the U.S. signed the ANZUS Treaty, stating "publicly and formally their sense of unity so that no potential aggressor could be under the illusion that any of them stand alone in the Pacific Area." In the event of attack, each signatory is pledged to move against the common danger "in accordance with its constitutional processes." The treaty's mechanism is simplicity itself: there are periodic meetings (usually annual) of the Foreign Ministers or their deputies, and there is a group of military advisers that by custom consists of the U.S. Pacific Area Commander and high-ranking representatives of Australia and New Zealand.

ANZUS initially meant more to Australia and New Zealand than to the U.S. But Chinese Communist aggression in Korea and elsewhere soon lent new meaning to the pact. Today the problem is not that it encompasses too little but that events may become too complicated for the pact to handle. The territory within its purview bestrides the confrontation area between the U.S. and Red China, and each new crisis becomes a test of the pact's effectiveness. But the treaty is broad enough for it also to be invoked to meet problems not necessarily related to the Communist threat, such as Australia's dispute with Indonesia over New Guinea. Thus Washington has wondered whether its antipodal partners would—or could—help if the U.S. became involved in hostilities with China over Taiwan. Australia, for its part, has wondered whether the U.S. would have responded had fighting erupted between Australian and Indonesian forces. What the crises of the future may involve for the ANZUS partners and how effective the pact will prove remain serious questions.

Regional Organizations: Economic and Social

THE EUROPEAN COMMUNITY

MEMBERS: Belgium, France, German Federal Republic, Italy, Luxembourg, Netherlands. The European Coal and Steel Community was founded in April 1951 in Paris and is headquartered in Luxembourg. The European Economic Community and the European Atomic Energy Community both were founded in March 1957 in Rome and both are headquartered in Brussels.

For 2,000 years, from Caesar to Churchill, a united Europe has been the aim of dreamers, schemers, conquerors and assorted political experts. What finally created a form of European union was the devastation and demoralization caused by the most terrible of Europe's wars. In 1945 an eminent British historian voiced the common belief that the physical and

The 1959 European Parliament convenes in Strasbourg, France.

moral damage done by World War II was so great that the end of European history was at hand. Precisely because the old Europe seemed dead, the long-talked-of new Europe appeared necessary. Meeting secretly in Geneva in the spring of 1944, resistance leaders from France, Italy and the Netherlands issued a call for a federated Europe. Meanwhile in London, where they were operating governments-in-exile, leaders of Holland and Belgium talked seriously of bringing their two countries together, adding Holland to BLEU, the Belgium-Luxembourg Economic Union founded in 1922. In September 1944 BLEU became Benelux when the Netherlands joined. With the end of the war, proposals for such unions became

the rage. Among those suggested were FRANCITA (a Franco-Italian customs union), FRITALUX (a union of FRANCITA and Benelux) and UNISCAN (United Kingdom-Scandinavia).

The first concrete step toward founding an actual Europe-wide community, however, was taken by the U.S. Congress. The European Recovery Act of April 3, 1948, setting up the Marshall Plan, stressed the importance of developing "a large market with no internal trade barriers," such as that in the United States. To push Europe toward community, Congress conditioned U.S. aid on the European nations' getting together to share and administer the funds according to a joint program based on mutual cooperation. Out of this came the 16- (later 18-) nation OEEC (Organization for European Economic Cooperation). Aside from apportioning Marshall Plan aid and setting up the EPU (European Payments Union) to facilitate trade and currency exchange, OEEC encouraged joint consultation.

In 1946 Winston Churchill had come out strongly for European unity, saying in a famous speech in Zurich, "We must build a kind of United States of Europe." Late in 1947 unity movements had become so numerous that an International Committee of the Movements for European Unity was formed, which proceeded to get all the groups together in May 1948 for a "Congress of Europe" at The Hague. This meeting led to the establishment of the Council of Europe (see pages 56-57), which was inaugurated in Strasbourg the following year. Grandiose in design but undernourished in real power, the Council was invited to build a new Europe by nations that, jealous of their sovereignty, refused it any means for independent action. Up to then this disparity had been the fatal flaw of Pan-Europeanism.

One observer, however, had the answer. The self-taught French economist Jean Monnet, a onetime League of Nations official and France's postwar planning chief, turned his back on the old dreams. Instead he proposed to start with a practical, simple, acceptable formula: first involve nations in a very limited area of cooperation; then, on the basis of the mutual confidence they would develop, proceed to coordinate their activities in more advanced sectors. An assistant explained Monnet's theory of how to move Europe toward community: "You think of a mountain path. From the bottom, there is one view; from a point part way up, another; from the top, quite another. A man standing at the bottom cannot possibly have the view of a man standing at the top. . . . To change his view, you must get him to start moving up, however slowly." In 1950 Europe began to climb.

The point that has been reached to date is a generalized concept, the "European Community." The two words sum up three real Communities already in operation—the Coal and Steel Community, the Economic Community and the Atomic Energy Community (see below). For the first few years the trio shared only a common parliament, court and ministerial council; in 1965 an executive was set up to operate all three Communities. By a resolution of the common European Parliament, "the three Communities stem from one political idea and concept, and form three separate elements in a single entity." Hopefully the time may soon arrive when the existing Communities will themselves merge and expand, and the European Community will then become a real, tangible force rather than a verbal convenience and a vision.

European Coal and Steel Community (ECSC)

At 4 o'clock in the afternoon of May 9, 1950, French Foreign Minister Robert Schuman read newsmen a proposal from his Government that U.S. political observer Walter Lippmann later described as "the most audacious and constructive since the end of the war." On its face Schuman's proposal simply called on France and Germany to pool and modernize their coal and steel industries under one directing authority. This proposed European Coal and Steel Community, however, actually incorporated several revolutionary breakthroughs. First, it answered one of the dilemmas of the moment: how to enlist West Germany's resources in the defense of Western Europe against Communism while maintaining curbs on Germany's proved aggressiveness. The very act of combining France's and Germany's steel resources would make war between the two not only unthinkable but militarily unworkable. Second, the plan, which had been drafted for Schuman by France's prophet of European unity, Jean Monnet (see above), promised to be the first practical step toward a possible federation of Europe. Third, it could speed the

reconstruction of the ruined economies of Germany and France by combining the two vital ingredients of heavy industry—French iron ore and German coal.

The ECSC Treaty—which was printed in Louis XIV type with German ink on Dutch vellum bound in Belgian parchment adorned with an Italian-silk marker—was signed by six of Europe's democratic nations on April 18, 1951, and the first European organization with federal characteristics was launched. Previous international groups had always been composed of members' representatives, and their decisions were usually the result of fragile compromises between national rivalries. The ECSC for the first time set up a supranational organization to which member governments transferred part of their sovereign powers and whose executive carried out its tasks independently.

Delegates initial a pact creating the Coal and Steel Community.

The executive branch of the ECSC is a High Authority of nine men who are chosen by the six member governments but thereafter freed of all national control. The treaty gave the High Authority great powers: for example, it can tax the coal and steel production of one area and use the proceeds to solve common problems; or it can limit production and set minimum and maximum prices.

The High Authority is accountable to a 142-member European Parliament (chosen by and from the memberships of the parliaments of the six member nations), which by a two-thirds vote of censure can oust the High Authority, and to a seven-man Court of Justice with binding power to decide whether the

Authority's acts are within the bounds of the treaty. For certain financial and economic decisions the Authority needs at least majority consent of the Council of Ministers, which is made up of six men, one from each of the member nations. This Council is the only part of ECSC's apparatus which, by its one-nation-one-vote make-up, harks back to the days of jealous nationalism rather than of *inter*nationalism.

Jean Monnet's daring innovation quickly showed signs of working. During ECSC's first five years steel production within the Community rose 43 per cent. As for coal, which is fighting a losing competitive war with fuel oil, the ECSC tidied up the industry, increasing output from 1.4 tons per man shift underground in 1957 to 2.4 tons in 1964, reducing the labor force by more than 30 per cent and closing 154 marginal mines. As early as 1953, Monnet, who became the first president of the ECSC High Authority, was able to say that the ECSC "is the first expression of the Europe that is being born."

European Economic Community
(EEC, also known as the Common Market)

The biggest postwar surprise in Europe has been the European Economic Community, usually called the Common Market. Uniting six war-devastated nations —the same six that compose the European Coal and Steel Community (see above)—the Market has become the fastest-growing economic area in the West. EEC is the world's biggest trader, the biggest importer, the second-biggest exporter (after the U.S.) and the leading market for raw materials. In its first years the Market's gross product expanded twice as fast as that of the U.S. and its industry grew four times as fast.

While no single nation in the Market has a population of more than 60 million, together the EEC's six countries boast 180 million people, nearly as many as live in the United States. Their active work force of 74 million is actually greater than that of the U.S. The Common Market's emergence as a powerful unit on the world scene is in some ways comparable to that of the U.S. in the 19th Century and to Soviet Russia's emergence in the 20th. It is the world's newest economic giant.

The Common Market is a natural outgrowth of the European Coal and Steel Community. It simply applies to all goods the ECSC's successful principles. Signed March 25, 1957, atop the Capitoline Hill in

Rome, its 387-page treaty called for a customs union among the six member nations. Tariffs on goods shipped between the six were to disappear by stages and all were to align the tariffs they charged on imports from outside the Market. On January 1, 1958, the Market began operating, with the first 10 per cent cut in members' tariffs scheduled for January 1, 1959. This and a second internal tariff cut worked so well—trade between the six rose 50 per cent in two years—that EEC members thereafter happily accelerated the timetable. All internal tariffs on industrial and agricultural goods were to be abolished by July 1, 1967 (the original target date had been 1970), and proposals have been made to put a common external tariff into effect at the same time.

The objective of EEC, however, is to be more than a customs union; the Market anticipates that in its final stage, investments, labor, currency and services will be able to move across the national boundaries as freely as goods. Already the EEC countries have

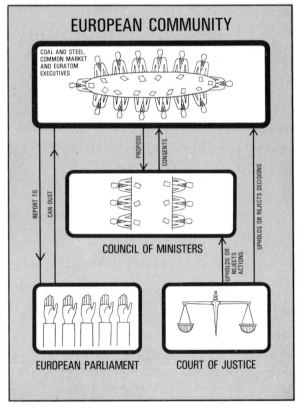

The structure of the European Community, shown above, is headed by the Coal and Steel, Common Market and Euratom Executives. Attached to them is the Council of Ministers. A 142-man European Parliament, elected from the legislatures of member countries, can oust the Executives by a two-thirds vote. The seven-judge Court of Justice rules on the acts of both Executives and Council Ministers.

Delegates talk informally around paper-strewn tables after the adjournment of a meeting of the Commission of the Common Market.

taken joint steps against inflation and monopolies.

It has not all been smooth sailing. Europe's farmers are rigidly protectionist-minded, and a farm crisis occurred in the Market's fourth year. Originally, farm products had been put in a special "Schedule G," which provided for slower tariff-cutting arrangements. French farmers, notably more efficient than Germany's, wanted some of the same accelerated tariff-cutting on farm products that Germany's industrialists, who are notably more efficient than France's, were enjoying in the field of manufacturing. France's President Charles de Gaulle threatened that France would refuse to participate in the further development of the Market if no agreements on grain prices were reached. This threat forced the Market to hold marathon negotiations, and after some 200 hours of talks a single, common farm policy emerged. This agreement was immediately hailed as a signal that the Market had now passed the point of no return, for, according to a clause ingeniously written into the Rome treaty, its signing completed the Market's Stage Two. The next stage provides that a member nation has the power to veto proposals that would slow EEC progress, but cannot veto forward moves.

On Europe's traditionally tariff-sheltered businessmen, longtime followers of a low-volume, high-profit philosophy, the Common Market has had an exhilarating effect. Imitating in many ways U.S. production methods and marketing techniques, they have chopped profit margins and lengthened production lines. A new predilection for the word "Europe" has led to a rash of strange neologisms, such

as Euromalt (malt makers) and Euromaisers (corn producers). A West German adman remarked: "I don't know what to do about this Europe craze. Once all you had to do to sell a product was to say 'Made in Germany.' Now, to make our German brands competitive, we have to imply that people are smoking them all over Europe. It's the same from soup to schnapps—you have to show people using it in Paris, in Brussels, in Rome."

The structural framework of this booming Market is delicately and ingeniously balanced. At the top is the Common Market Commission, which meets every Wednesday morning on the dot of 10: nine men and their advisers gather around a mahogany table in a room on the ninth floor of a concrete-and-glass building in Brussels. The two members apiece from France, West Germany and Italy, and the one each from the Benelux countries, plot the grand strategy and supervise the daily tactics of the Market. The rest of the apparatus operates in much the same way as that of the ECSC. The Market also has a court, a parliament and a ministerial council that provide checks and balances to the power of the Market's nine-man Commission. The arrangement has continued to move toward increasing community. By a vote taken in 1965, all three components of the Community—ECSC, EEC and EURATOM (see below)—will presently share a common executive, making the entire apparatus uniform.

In some respects, however, the EEC has begun to show a contrary tendency toward inflexibility. In 1961 Britain (which four years before had declined to enter the Market) capitulated and pressed hard for entry. After 17 months de Gaulle (who tends to regard the Market as a cozy Continental club) uttered a regal "Non!" saying: "England is, in effect, insular, maritime, linked by its trade, its markets and its food supply to the most diverse and distant countries. . . . How can England be brought in with such a system?"

Crowds at a Brussels auto show admire sleek European cars.

The EEC survived this crisis, but expert observers began to take a closer look at the institution and found more reason for concern. Said one: "The Rome Treaty was made with the promise of broadening out to embrace more countries. If the Common Market had worked tolerably well its officials would have welcomed the idea of more members asking to join, of more progressive steps being taken. But because it worked so unbelievably well, they became exclusive and nearly arrogant. With the boldest international venture of our time, a new isolationism sprang into being." The 7,500 "Eurocrats" staffing the Community, whom the London *Economist* once hailed for their "dynamism," have themselves altered, according to one Common Market founding father who says: "They came to Brussels as pioneers. Now the adventure has worked so well that they don't want to risk tampering with it."

This is not the first time that successful revolutionaries have become defenders of a new status quo. Walter Hallstein, the head of the Market Commission, has announced that "we are not in business; we are in politics. We are building the United States

of Europe." Despite Hallstein, the standpatters were becoming increasingly formidable in the EEC in the mid-1960s. While Europeanists continued to talk of moving to new and closer forms of unity, de Gaulle derided "those Simple Simons who believe in supranationalism" and advocated "the Europe of fatherlands," that is, a loose confederation of sovereign states linked by contact between leaders and Cabinets rather than by supranational institutions.

De Gaulle's notions have been widely criticized as impractical, obstructionist and calculated to seriously slow European progress. Hallstein continued to insist that "Europe must find its unity as a community or not at all." But de Gaulle continued to proclaim that "we do not want a supranational Europe. For us that would be to want to disappear." Thus, in the short and brilliant history of the Common Market, an impasse loomed.

European Atomic Energy Community (Euratom)

The third European Community institution is Euratom, an organization set up to develop peaceful uses of atomic energy for the six nations that belong to the Common Market and the ECSC (see above). Launched on the same day as the Common Market by another treaty signed in Rome, Euratom was designed to fill a need that seemed imperative. Europe was doubling its electricity requirements every 10 years and by 1980 would need twice as much power from all sources than in 1960. Unless it started generating nuclear energy economically, the European Community, which spends two billion dollars annually to import coal from the U.S. and oil from the Middle East and Eastern Europe, would be expending six billion dollars by 1980. To avoid these crippling costs, Euratom was to furnish one fourth of the Community's electricity needs by 1980.

Euratom, which has set up its own centers for research in Belgium, Germany, Italy and Holland, is directed by a five-man Euratom Commission that functions in much the same way as the governing Commission of the European Economic Community. Euratom's executive is also responsible, like those of the ECSC and the EEC, to the European Community's ministerial council, court and parliament.

Euratom has so far proved the least important of the three groups that make up Europe's Community. In the first place, it has had to revise its original estimate of how the Community's energy requirements

Delegates sign the 1957 pacts creating the EEC and Euratom.

should be met. Conventional fuels have become more plentiful and less expensive, while creating atomic energy has proved more costly than was expected. Euratom also had trouble with President de Gaulle. In line with his consuming ambition to make Europe independent of the U.S., de Gaulle withheld support from Euratom in favor of French national efforts to develop atomic skills and weapons. Despite de Gaulle, Euratom continues its low-key efforts to further the peaceful uses of the atom, and many experts feel that this undervalued agency will eventually become a most important part of the Community.

BENELUX

FOUNDED: September 1944 in London. **HEADQUARTERS:** Brussels. **MEMBERS:** Belgium, Luxembourg, Netherlands.

Benelux, Europe's pioneer economic union, all but unites the economies of Belgium, the Netherlands and Luxembourg (hence its name BE-NE-LUX). Initially suggested back in 1851, this first step toward a common market (see pages 52-54) actually got its start in 1921 as a two-nation arrangement between Belgium and Luxembourg; it formally became a trio when the Netherlands joined in 1944. By 1957, a full year before the Common Market started, 97 per cent of all Benelux's internal trade was moving freely within its 25,755-square-mile area. Since the formation of the larger Common Market in 1958,

Benelux has presented the somewhat confusing spectacle of a common market within a common market. It is not yet, however, superfluous since, among other virtues, it operates so smoothly. In addition, Benelux's practices are still ahead of the Market's in some respects, particularly in the free exchange of labor. In other areas the Market has outstripped Benelux's pace, specifically in the freer exchange of farm produce. Benelux's 16 committees are limited to giving advice, but its Council and Executive can make decisions that are binding on their Governments. The Market owes much to Benelux's daring supranationalism and to its bold tariff-cutting. Not only has the Market come close to Benelux's goals of tearing down most customs barriers but its success presages the moment when Benelux will become—like all successful pioneers—redundant.

ORGANIZATION FOR ECONOMIC COOPERATION AND DEVELOPMENT (OECD)

FOUNDED: September 1961 in Paris. **HEADQUARTERS:** Paris. **MEMBERS:** 18 European nations plus the United States, Canada and Japan. Finland and Yugoslavia have special status.

The Organization for Economic Cooperation and Development is a successor to the famous post-World War II European Recovery Program popularly known as the Marshall Plan, after the then U.S. Secretary of State George C. Marshall, who first outlined it in a Harvard commencement speech in 1947. The Marshall Plan provided funds (some $13 billion) from the United States for the reconstruction of the Western European industrial and agricultural complex, which had been devastated by six years of war. The Plan made direct money loans and grants, helped settle debts and claims between member nations with extensions of credit, and provided aid for countries with balance-of-payment deficits. The main stipulation imposed by the United States was that the Western European nations compose their differences and cooperate in the economic sphere.

The Plan was an unqualified success. From the ruins of war rose an economically strong Western Europe that took further strides toward economic union with the formation in 1952 of the European Coal and Steel Community (see pages 51-52) and in 1957 of the European Economic Community (see pages 52-54). Europe was also, however, divided. For the Common Market included only six European nations (Belgium,

France, Italy, Luxembourg, the Netherlands and West Germany), leaving the others out in the cold. As a result, Britain led six other Western European nations not included in the Common Market (Austria, Denmark, Norway, Portugal, Sweden and Switzerland) into their own European Free Trade Association (see pages 57-58) in the hope of creating a viable economic group of their own that would someday enter the Common Market as a bloc. This group

Paris' Château de la Muette houses OECD's headquarters.

eventually came to be known as the "Outer Seven."

Significant contributions to the economic integration of Western Europe were made by the old Organization for European Economic Cooperation, the body that had administered the Marshall Plan funds. This grouping was reorganized in 1961 as the Organization for Economic Cooperation and Development, or OECD. The OECD includes the "Six," the "Seven," Greece, Iceland, Ireland, Spain and Turkey as well as the U.S., Canada and Japan. The goals of the organization are to maintain the economic stability of member nations, to expand world trade and, although the OECD does not itself disburse funds, to try to help underdeveloped nations by encouraging aid to them from its members. Through the OECD the restored Europe participates on an equal basis with the countries of North America and Japan in initiating economic policies of international scope.

BANK FOR INTERNATIONAL SETTLEMENTS (BIS)

FOUNDED: May 1930 in Basel, Switzerland. **HEADQUARTERS:** Basel. **MEMBERS:** Central banks of 26 European countries and banking groups in the U.S.

Founded in 1930, the Bank for International Settlements originally had a dual purpose: to handle Germany's payment of World War I reparations and to provide for cooperation between central banks of European nations. Subscriptions for its capital were provided by the central banks of Belgium, Great Britain, France, Italy and Germany and by banking groups from Japan and the United States. By 1956 most of the U.S. shares and all of the Japanese shares were in European hands. In addition to promoting cooperation among European banks, BIS, which is headquartered in Basel, Switzerland, provides facilities for various international financial operations and acts as trustee or agent for international settlements. It also serves as a meeting place for the governors of Europe's central banks and is a center for research and information on monetary and economic matters. Its administration is made up of men who are governors or presidents of the central banks in several of the member nations. The organization is capitalized at 500 million gold Swiss francs, or some $116.3 million.

COUNCIL OF EUROPE

FOUNDED: May 1949 in London. **HEADQUARTERS:** Strasbourg, France. **MEMBERS:** Austria, Belgium, Cyprus, Denmark, France, German Federal Republic, Greece, Iceland, Irish Republic, Italy, Luxembourg, Malta, Netherlands, Norway, Sweden, Switzerland, Turkey, United Kingdom.

One of the first tangible expressions of the postwar enthusiasm for European unity was the Council of Europe, which was founded in 1949 following a meeting of nearly 1,000 leading Europeans. The Council has fallen somewhat short of the original high hopes, however, partly because Britain's theoretical enthusiasm for a united Europe is actually inhibited by its close relations with the Commonwealth and the U.S. The Council's statute, signed in London, calls vaguely for European nations to join together "for the purpose of safeguarding . . . the ideals . . . which are their common heritage." The Council itself has been greatly overshadowed by the success of the European Communities. Composed of a Committee of Ministers (one member per nation) and a 147-member Consultative Assembly, the Council has done useful work in human rights, social security and legal coordination and provides an important sounding board for European opinion. However, when matters requiring sacrifices of sovereignty arise, the Council becomes a paper organization, hamstrung by its own Committee of Ministers, in which one member representing one Government can, and usually does, exert an absolute veto.

THE NORDIC COUNCIL

FOUNDED: February 1953 in Copenhagen, Denmark. **MEMBERS:** Denmark, Finland, Iceland, Norway, Sweden.

Launched in 1953 "to develop further cooperation between the Nordic countries," the Nordic Council has set no worlds on fire. Annual meetings of the 69-member Council, which is composed of delegates chosen from the members' parliaments, can make suggestions only. Nevertheless, the Council exerts considerable influence on the politicians of the five countries in the field of Nordic concerns. Thanks to the Council, Scandinavia's 21 million citizens can move throughout the area without passports. They may also take jobs freely in any of the five countries,

Danish Prime Minister Jens Krag addresses the Nordic Council.

and when visiting or living in a member state they automatically receive the same social security benefits enjoyed by its citizens. The Council has set up uniform rates for transport and communications and has established an atomic research center. Its scope is limited—military questions and foreign relations with non-Scandinavian states are automatically taboo, principally for fear of alarming Russia, which is occasionally suspicious of the Council. Lacking supranational powers, the Council nonetheless shows that even a modestly endowed organization can be useful.

EUROPEAN FREE TRADE ASSOCIATION (EFTA) (Also known as the Outer Seven)

FOUNDED: January 1960 in Stockholm, Sweden. **HEADQUARTERS:** Geneva, Switzerland. **MEMBERS:** Austria, Denmark, Norway, Portugal, Sweden, Switzerland, United Kingdom. **ASSOCIATE MEMBER:** Finland.

The European Free Trade Association started out as a marriage on the rebound. Seven nations that could not—or would not—join the Common Market (see pages 52-54) got together in 1960 in a belated, defensive and admittedly temporary free-trade bloc that was to last only until they could make some arrangement with the Market. During the first phase of its uneasy existence, the European Free Trade Association began to eliminate internal tariffs on industrial goods among members. But even here the main purpose was to keep in step with the Common Market so as to make future association easier. There were, however, real differences between the Outer Seven (as EFTA is often known) and the Inner Six (a nickname for the Common Market). Unlike the

Six, the Seven had no plans to reduce tariffs on agricultural products or to establish a common external tariff or, most important of all, to set up supranational institutions that would help prepare the way for ultimate political union.

EFTA's limited franchise reflected the thinking of Britain, its largest member, which has half the total population and international trade represented by the Seven, and Finland, an associate member. Tied strongly to its far-flung Commonwealth and to the U.S., Britain had no appetite for building the kind of tightly European, supranational community envisioned by the Market.

Within its limitations, EFTA worked. Members cut internal industrial tariffs 70 per cent in six years and increased trade with one another by 80 per cent. In the summer of 1961, Britain, its economy lagging, its pound sterling under attack, and seeing greater dangers ahead, pressed vigorously to join the Common Market. The rebuff administered to Britain in January 1963 by French President Charles de Gaulle chilled EFTA, yet paradoxically gave it vigor. At a ministerial meeting in May of that year, EFTA shifted subtly from being a holding operation to an organization with plans of its own.

The EFTA Ministers decided to speed the Outer Seven timetable and eliminate all remaining quota restrictions on industrial trade within EFTA along with all tariffs by the end of 1966. They also set up an Economic Development Committee with a franchise to make the most free-ranging studies and suggestions and to act as a clearinghouse through which the specialized knowledge of one EFTA country can be put at the disposal of any other requiring it. Even in a marriage of convenience, custom weaves its own bonds, and the Outer Seven nations found themselves looking more to one another and less to the Inner Six.

COUNCIL FOR MUTUAL ECONOMIC ASSISTANCE (COMECON)

FOUNDED: January 1949 in Moscow. **HEADQUARTERS:** Moscow. **MEMBERS:** Albania, Bulgaria, Czechoslovakia, German Democratic Republic, Hungary, Mongolian People's Republic, Poland, Romania, U.S.S.R.

The Moscow-based Council for Mutual Economic Assistance, known in the West as Comecon, has been called the Communists' Common Market. Founded in 1949, it was originally little more than a formal

A Czech plant makes shoes and tires for other Comecon nations.

structure through which the Soviet Union could use the resources of its satellites to bolster its own war-shattered economy. Later, as Russia's economy improved, Comecon aid began to flow the other way, toward the satellites. More recently, Comecon has undergone further changes that reflect the growing independence of East European Communist nations.

When Comecon was formed in January 1949, its membership consisted of the U.S.S.R., Bulgaria, Czechoslovakia, Hungary, Poland and Romania. Albania joined later in 1949, but ceased attending Comecon meetings in 1961 because of the Russian-Chinese split. East Germany joined in 1950 and Mongolia in 1962. Yugoslavia is also represented, but not as a full member. Cuba, China, North Korea and North Vietnam send observers to Comecon meetings.

At the start Comecon enabled Russia to give a quasi-legal color to what was, in reality, exploitation. The Russians took coal, for example, from Poland, paying the Poles about $1.50 a ton when the current world price for coal ranged from $14 to $20 a ton. The first big change in the nature of the organization occurred in 1956 when the Hungarian and Polish uprisings forced Russia to take another look at its dealings with its satellite states and to pour $1.5 billion in emergency aid into their economies. Plans for Comecon were completely revamped, and member nations were assigned tasks for which they were presumably best qualified. Czechoslovakia, whose gigantic Skoda arms factories had been important to the World War II Axis military machine, was to specialize in heavy industry. Poland began concentrating on coal mining and the construction of transport equipment. Hungary was assigned to concentrate on aluminum processing; East Germany on chemicals, building materials and precision machinery; Bulgaria on its orchards, vineyards and Black Sea workers' resorts; and Romania on petroleum production.

But within a few years the satellite countries started to balk at their assigned roles and to insist, as the Romanians put it, on the "right of every nation to develop and plan its economy in accordance with its own national interests." The Eastern European countries turned toward the West looking for trade. Romania's late party chief Gheorghe Gheorghiu-Dej defied Russia by buying iron ore from India and turning to an Anglo-French consortium to build a big steel-rolling mill. Romania also has a West German-installed plastics plant and a French-built phosphoric acid and fertilizer plant. In the early 1960s the country's trade with the West rose from 15 per cent to 40 per cent of its total foreign trade. Czechoslovakia and East Germany were reluctant to go along with Russian plans for an Eastern European industrial development fund for fear that they would be forced to supply most of the capital. Hungary and Bulgaria, unhappy with Comecon plans to emphasize their mining and agricultural output, began to develop other industries on their own.

One major reason for the satellites' economic rebellion has little to do with either Communist ideology or fear of Russian domination: it is simply that Comecon has failed to bring the prosperity that former Premier Nikita Khrushchev promised when he said that by 1965 the Communist states would have more than half the world's industrial production. Instead of going up, the growth rates in the member countries went down from 13.3 per cent in 1955 to 10.4 per cent in 1960 and 8.6 per cent in 1963. The disappointment registered even in Moscow. The Soviet magazine *International Life* has admitted that "hopes of Comecon countries of producing 50

per cent of the world's industrial goods by the end of 1965 have been shattered." The magazine went on to declare that catching up with the West is not the simple matter that some Russian planners had claimed it to be, but rather is a "complicated and contradictory process of divergent tendencies, intricate problems and often sharply contrasting trends."

ORGANIZATION OF AMERICAN STATES (OAS)

FOUNDED: March-May 1948 in Bogotá, Colombia. **HEADQUARTERS:** Washington, D.C. **MEMBERSHIP:** Argentina, Bolivia, Brazil, Chile, Colombia, Costa Rica, Cuba, Dominican Republic, Ecuador, El Salvador, Guatemala, Haiti, Honduras, Mexico, Nicaragua, Panama, Paraguay, Peru, United States, Uruguay, Venezuela.

The world's oldest international body of sovereign nations, the Organization of American States dates back to the First International Conference of American States held in 1889 and 1890. The Conference set up the International Union of American Republics whose purpose was to collect and distribute commercial information through a Commercial Bureau in Washington. This Bureau was reorganized as the Pan American Union in 1910. After World War II the whole inter-American system was further reorganized as the OAS, with the Pan American Union as its permanent secretariat. The OAS's goals have been expanded to include the promotion of peace in the Western Hemisphere by providing joint action to counter any threats of aggression, and the fostering of freedom, economic well-being, and social and cultural development.

The Inter-American Conference is the highest authority of the OAS and is made up of delegations from each member state. The Conference is supposed to meet every five years, but the member governments have occasionally postponed its sessions. The Conference is responsible for deciding upon all of the OAS's long-range policies. The most important organ of the OAS, however, is its Washington-based Council, which serves as the executive branch of the OAS. The Council, which usually meets twice a month, is composed of ambassadors from each member country. It is charged with general supervision of the operations of the OAS. It initiates studies of various problems and makes recommendations to the governments to further cooperation. In addition, it handles any other matters assigned to it either by the foreign ministers or by the Inter-American

Conference. The presiding officer of the OAS is its Secretary General, who is elected by the Council for a 10-year term.

Another important organ of the OAS is known as the Meeting of Consultation of Ministers of Foreign Affairs. This group meets at the request of any member Government, subject to the approval of the Council. Its purpose is to consult for joint action if the security of the hemisphere is threatened or to handle other emergencies. If the Meeting of Consultation

OAS delegates convene at a 1964 meeting in São Paulo, Brazil.

is dealing with an act of aggression, it is assisted by an Advisory Defense Committee made up of top military men from the member states.

The Pan American Union, which continues to perform essentially the same functions it performed before the last reorganization in 1948, serves as an inter-American secretariat. It helps organize all OAS meetings, prepares reports on all OAS activities and maintains cooperative relations with other organizations, such as many of the specialized agencies of the U.N. It has no political functions. Completing the OAS structure are the Specialized Organizations that deal with such matters as health, agriculture and child welfare, and Specialized Conferences that deal with various technical matters. In addition, a new unit called the Inter-American Committee for the Alliance for Progress operates in conjunction with other OAS organizations to coordinate activities of the U.S.-initiated Alliance for Progress, an aid program that provides grants and loans to Latin American nations and to private businesses. The money for these grants comes from both the public and private sectors of the U.S. economy, from financial organs like the International Monetary Fund (see page 41) and from the treasuries of the Latin American nations themselves.

At San José, Costa Rica, the OAS operates the Inter-American Institute of Agricultural Sciences, which offers technical training in modern agriculture. Other OAS economic-development programs cover such fields as education, health and sanitation.

The OAS has been active in peace-keeping roles, such as ending a border war between Costa Rica and Nicaragua and another between Nicaragua and Honduras. It organized sanctions that were effective in undercutting the late Dominican dictator Rafael Trujillo. It sent a peace-keeping force to the Domican Republic after that country's 1965 revolution. Moreover, it often serves as a forum to thrash out differences in times of crisis.

But perhaps the major political role of the OAS in recent years has been as a focus of opposition to Communism in the Western Hemisphere. In 1951 the OAS foreign ministers supported the United Nations' action in Korea. In Caracas, Venezuela, in 1954 the Tenth Inter-American Conference went on record as unalterably opposed to Communism, and this position was re-enforced at the OAS foreign ministers' meeting in Costa Rica in 1960. An important culmination of the policy came in 1962 when the OAS foreign ministers, meeting in Uruguay, suspended Cuba from membership and recommended applying economic sanctions.

ORGANIZATION OF CENTRAL AMERICAN STATES (Spanish abbreviation: ODECA)

FOUNDED: October 1951 in San Salvador, El Salvador. **HEADQUARTERS**: San Salvador. **MEMBERS**: Costa Rica, El Salvador, Guatemala, Honduras, Nicaragua.

ODECA, which was launched in 1951, is at least the 25th attempt to establish some form of unity in Central America. Few unions seem more logical; the five nations share a common history and language and many of the same economic and political problems. They were, in fact, once united in a federation that lasted about 14 years before dissolving in 1838.

ODECA's sponsoring session produced an organizational framework that included a supreme authority composed of the five nations' presidents, which would meet occasionally, and a Conference of Foreign Ministers, which would confer biennially. Other bodies have since evolved, among them an Economic Council, a Cultural and Educational Council and a Secretary-General. The first scheduled foreign ministers' meeting, planned for 1953, was postponed for two years, initially because Guatemala temporarily quit ODECA and then because Costa Rica and Nicaragua were quarreling. Thus the organization did not actually start work until the August 1955 meeting. Another series of later quarrels further inactivated ODECA. In January 1960 Guatemala hopefully proposed a new, improved ODECA. Turned down, Guatemala threatened to quit again. This provoked a 1962 revision of the charter to include a Defense Council and a council to promote economic integration, as well as other changes, which, hopefully, will make ODECA meaningful.

CENTRAL AMERICAN COMMON MARKET (CACM)

FOUNDED: December 1960 in Managua, Nicaragua. **HEADQUARTERS:** Guatemala City, Guatemala. **MEMBERS:** Costa Rica, El Salvador, Guatemala, Honduras, Nicaragua.

Of the many attempts to achieve unity made by the five Central American republics, the most promising by far is the Common Market established in 1960 in Managua, Nicaragua. To apply European-style economic integration to 13 million people, more than 50 per cent of whom are illiterate, with an average annual per capita income of less than $300, with one- or two-crop national economies (bananas, cotton or coffee), and with inadequate communications, transportation and ports, seemed at first like a joke. It recalled cowboy humorist Will Rogers' crack about the Russian Revolution: "They don't have anything, and they're trying to divide it." Surprisingly the new Common Market almost immediately showed signs of health. In less than three years internal trade within CACM far more than doubled—going from $33 million to $82 million—and the proportion of intraregional to total trade rose sharply.

President Kennedy gestures at a 1963 Common Market meeting.

The idea of a Central American Common Market was first proposed in a general way by the U.N.'s Economic Commission for Latin America as early as 1951, but the idea moved slowly until 1960 when, grown impatient, Honduras, Guatemala and El Salvador got together and wrote a tripartite treaty that set 1965 as the target date for the free movement among them of goods, capital and people. Fearful of being left behind, recalcitrant Nicaragua joined up and the all-important General Treaty of Central American Integration was signed, with Costa Rica, the last holdout, joining in 1962. From this point on CACM moved ahead rapidly. By 1965 CACM had erased tariffs on 98.5 per cent of all the products traded among the five countries. A respectable integration structure arose: a common market bank, a single tourist-promotion organization, a common market clearinghouse to facilitate use of national currencies among members, and a problem-solving secretariat based in Guatemala City with a budget of $500,000 yearly.

Two councils oversee CACM: the Central American Economic Council, made up of the members' economic ministers, which meets on any member state's request and which reviews broad policy; and the subordinate Executive Council, composed of one delegate and one alternate per nation, which convenes when necessary to administer the 1960 treaty. The fourfold increase in potential market has suddenly made the long-needed industrialization of Central America seem more attainable. For the first time, locally made shirts, tires, plastics, metal furniture, textiles and paint are available to consumers. But problems remain. Though integration greatly enlarged it, CACM's total trade is still too small. In addition, the five members' economies remain too much alike for the required mutual exchange. Although the members' economic growth rate has averaged 6 per cent a year, these gains have been largely vitiated by a staggering 3.4 per cent annual population growth. Nevertheless, CACM is a going concern. Its member nations are well on their way to achieving a completely free trade zone. In addition, a real attempt to diversify industry is showing considerable success. A Chase Manhattan Bank report says: "So long as the nations of this important region cooperate as closely as they do now, the Central American Common Market is likely to grow in importance as a focus of economic development."

LATIN AMERICAN FREE TRADE ASSOCIATION (LAFTA)

FOUNDED: February 1960 in Montevideo, Uruguay. **MEMBERS:** Argentina, Brazil, Chile, Colombia, Ecuador, Mexico, Paraguay, Peru, Uruguay, Venezuela.

The Latin American Free Trade Association was first proposed in the late 1950s, and the idea generated considerable enthusiasm. Europe, where Latin American countries had sold many of their raw materials, was turning inward, founding its own common market. In addition, trade among Latin American countries was suffering a marked decline and it needed stimulation. So, in 1960, LAFTA's founders—representing three fourths of the population between the Rio Grande and Cape Horn—hammered out a treaty to reduce tariffs 8 per cent annually for 12 years, with free trade in 1973 the objective.

Unfortunately, LAFTA has disappointed expectations. Members have lowered tariffs on 8,500 items, but most of the goods affected are either unimportant or not competitive. All must still pay high tariffs when trading with the nations that make the goods they most need, such as machinery and manufactured items. Trade within LAFTA grew from some $660 million in 1961 to $1.1 billion in 1964, but this represented only about 9 per cent of the members' overall foreign commerce. The less affluent members have tended to fear LAFTA's industrial big three—Argentina, Brazil and Mexico—and have insisted on special tariff concessions. In short, LAFTA has simply not produced a sufficient increase in trade, and even its most sanguine supporters admit that it must start moving or give way to a new plan.

THE COMMONWEALTH

HEADQUARTERS: London. **MEMBERS:** Australia, Barbados, Botswana, Canada, Ceylon, Cyprus, Gambia, Ghana, Guyana, India, Jamaica, Kenya, Lesotho, Malawi, Malaysia, Malta, New Zealand, Nigeria, Pakistan, Sierra Leone, Singapore, Tanzania, Trinidad and Tobago, Uganda, United Kingdom, Zambia.

As imperial Britain and its new Queen, Victoria, were preparing to enjoy the Christmas holiday in 1837, news came from Canada that rebellions were erupting around Montreal and Toronto. The Government was deeply concerned. Was a second American Revolution in the making, 62 years after the first? Instead of dispatching navies and Hessians, Britain's monarch this time sent to the scene Lord Durham, one of the realm's wealthiest men and one of its most radical. After five months in Canada, "Radical Jack" wrote what one historian calls "perhaps the most famous government report in the English language." The Durham Report recommended that Britain give Canada "responsible government"—that is, let the Canadians handle most of their own internal affairs. It was the answer to the problem and it changed the course of empire. Applied first to Canada, spreading then to other colonies, "responsible government" —Britain's way of letting rebellious colonies grow into sister nations—marked the birth of what eventually became the Commonwealth.

By the opening of the 20th Century, British control of domestic affairs in the self-governing white colonies (then called Dominions) had just about vanished. The change was less rapid in foreign relations. In 1914 Britain took itself and the whole Empire into war without asking the Dominions. In 1919, however, the Dominions signed the peace treaties as separate nations and joined the League of Nations as sovereign states. With the Statute of Westminster, passed in 1931, Britain formally relinquished its largely atrophied veto over laws passed by Dominion parliaments.

With World War II, Commonwealth evolution veered sharply in another direction. The Commonwealth that entered the war had been made up of states, such as Canada and Australia, largely populated by white men and governed, in the main, by people of British descent. What developed after the war was a multiracial Commonwealth. In 1947 India and newly created Pakistan became independent countries and joined the Commonwealth, followed by Ceylon, Ghana, Malaya, Nigeria, Cyprus, Sierra

A smiling Queen Elizabeth of Britain is flanked by heads of Commonwealth nations during a Commonwealth Conference in London.

Leone and 14 others—to make a total of 26 members.

The British genius for evolving, for meeting difficulties with pragmatic expedients has created an organization marvelous in its subtlety and adaptability. The apparatus is simple, almost nonexistent. Britain's monarch is the symbolic center. Some members recognize him (or her) ceremonially as their monarch, reigning but not ruling. Others, such as India, regard the monarch as simply Head of the Commonwealth. The Commonwealth's real center is the irregular meetings of its Prime Ministers. At these, occurring about once every 18 months, there is no formal agenda, no published minutes, but rather a chance for the leaders to talk freely and frankly in privacy.

The Commonwealth has no common law applicable to all members; nor does it pledge its members to come to the defense of each other. There are no obligations or set meetings and no joint policies. Members may declare themselves republics or elect kings of their own. Two members have quit—Eire and South Africa. Democratic ideals are sometimes flouted. Australian immigration policies, to give just one example, virtually exclude all nonwhites. Said a British professor: "About the only thing we can't stand is being beaten by one of them at cricket."

What holds this chaotic contraption together? The most important ties probably are British law and parliamentary tradition. From Tasmania to Toronto, courts generally work honestly and lawmaking is orderly. Other ingredients help glue the Commonwealth together, but not so tightly that an exception cannot be found for every rule.

One binding element is common defense. The newly independent Afro-Asian nations, set loose in a cold, forbidding world, believe that the link with Britain helps to make their piping voices heard in world councils and helps to protect them. Member countries swap scientific information and military training and equipment. Another adhesive force has been common trade. The Commonwealth preference system gives tariff concessions to Commonwealth members. Economic ties, however, are becoming less binding. In 1949 half of all Commonwealth exports passed between members. By 1963 the figure had dropped to 30 per cent. Currently Britain trades less with other Commonwealth countries than the U.S. does.

Membership in the sterling area also helps tie the Commonwealth countries together since (except for Canada) they keep the bulk of their foreign exchange and overseas reserves in sterling in London, thus linking themselves to one of the most important trading currencies. From the Commonwealth Relations Office in London's Whitehall pours a constant stream of advice, ideas and expertise. Still another link is schooling. Singapore's Lee Kuan Yew went to Cambridge, Kenya's Tom Mboya to Oxford, Ghana's Kwame Nkrumah to the London School of Economics. The "old school tie" is worn from Manitoba to Malaysia.

It is plain that there is a lot going on in this elusive organization of 750 million people, but a too-close inquiry into its nature can be self-defeating. "The Commonwealth," observed a Whitehall official, "is something that may disappear if you stare at it too hard." Lacking rules and forms, this amalgam of monarchies and republics, democracies and autocracies is a test of how far men of good will are able to work together for their common benefit.

International Organizations

THE COLOMBO PLAN FOR CO-OPERATIVE ECONOMIC DEVELOPMENT IN SOUTH AND SOUTH-EAST ASIA

FOUNDED: 1950 in Colombo, Ceylon. **HEADQUARTERS:** Colombo. **MEMBERS:** (Donors) Australia, Canada, Japan, New Zealand, United Kingdom, United States. (Recipients) Afghanistan, Bhutan, Burma, Cambodia, Ceylon, India, Indonesia, Laos, Malaysia, Maldive Islands, Nepal, Pakistan, Philippines, Singapore, South Korea, South Vietnam, Thailand.

The Colombo Plan is really not a "plan" at all. It is a kind of club that was organized in 1950 at a meeting of the Foreign Ministers of seven British Commonwealth nations. Its purpose was primarily to encourage the economies of the countries of South and Southeast Asia. Lacking the lush financing the United States was then pumping into the Marshall Plan, Colombo's founders set up a loose clearinghouse to discuss economic development and, hopefully, to do something about it. At this stage the Plan seemed little more than a pious wish. Then in 1951 the United States, looking for ways to arrest the spread of Communism in Asia, joined the Plan as a donor nation. From its inception through June 1964 the Plan channeled $17 billion, four fifths of it from the U.S., to needy Asian nations and by mid-1965 had trained some 38,000 technicians. It has become the accepted authority for regional development schemes—which affect a quarter of the world's population. Named after the city of Colombo, the capital of Ceylon, where it was founded and is headquartered, the Plan now has 23 members which are divided, frankly if unofficially, into donors and recipients.

The Plan's organization is simple and low key. Using Colombo as a marketplace, industrialized donor nations make direct deals with "have-not" recipient members, bypassing multilateral talks and the usual bureaucracy. Recipients in turn are not merely passive but are encouraged to help one another. India has received the largest share of donor aid, but at the same time has contributed more than $2.3 million in technical assistance to neighboring Nepal and has trained more technicians for area states than any other recipient member.

Organizationally, says a former director, the Plan is "not tidy, it's an administrative nightmare, but it works." Its governing body, a council of minister-rank delegates, meets only once a year for several days of rambling talks about development. A group of technical advisers carries on with regular conferences in Colombo on the development schemes themselves. The permanent staff is tiny. The Plan's annual report has been described by one observer as "an unreadable and unread compendium." Finally, all the member nations must be unanimous before any program can go into effect. Nevertheless, attempts by the Australians, Americans and others to tighten up the Plan and make it into a more active and efficient organization have perennially failed. The Asians like Colombo's untidy ways. They feel the Plan to be their own and have a proprietary attitude toward keeping it the way it is. So the U.S. does not press hard. Moreover, despite its lack of formal overall scheme, Colombo has yielded some impressive results. Factories, hydroelectric plants and highways have sprouted among the recipients. The original goals set in 1950 (17 per cent more irrigated land, 10 per cent more food production, 67 per cent more electricity) have long since been exceeded. Food output has been rising 3 per cent per year. Unfortunately, the recipient populations since 1950 have increased by 170 million, or 2 per cent annually, so that living standards have risen only slightly. Had it not been for Colombo, however, standards might have plummeted dangerously. At a recent meeting measuring the progress of the Plan against the increase of the population, a delegate observed: "Our problem is babies."

Students aided by the Colombo Plan study in New Zealand.

AFRICAN REGIONAL GROUPS

Since African nations began winning their independence they have formed themselves into a variety of groupings. But the Organization of African Unity was the first continent-wide body designed to provide a framework for pursuing the long-elusive goal of solidarity between the African states. Its creation at Addis Ababa, Ethiopia, in 1963 followed nearly a decade of talk and action by rival groups taking different approaches to the question of Pan-African cooperation. The OAU's membership included all of Africa and Madagascar except for the few white-dominated states and territories of the south.

The charter signed at Addis Ababa proclaimed the purposes of the OAU to be the achievement of political and economic coordination, and cooperation in the areas of culture, health, science and defense. It also called for the elimination of all vestiges of colonialism on the continent. The machinery set up to further these policies included an Assembly of Heads of State and Government of the member nations, a council of ministers, a secretariat and a commission to mediate disputes between members.

The Addis Ababa organization incorporated and thus caused the dissolution of two other important groupings of new African nations—the Casablanca Charter Organization and the Inter-African and Malagasy States Organization, the latter better known as the Monrovia Group (after the capital of Liberia, where it was formed). The Casablanca Group—which included Algeria, the United Arab Republic, Morocco, Ghana, Guinea and Mali—took a radical approach to the cause of uniting Africa into one superstate. It advocated revolution and subversion to end "neocolonialism." The Monrovia Group was made up of Ethiopia, the African nations that had been French colonies (except Guinea and Mali), plus the former British colonies of Nigeria and Sierra Leone and long-independent Liberia. It followed a generally moderate course, favoring the development of the individual countries and looking toward close economic cooperation with the former colonial powers.

Other groupings, with lines extending outside Africa, remained in operation after the OAU was formed. The Brazzaville Group, which took in most of French-speaking Africa south of the Sahara, continued to function under different names. Member states cooperate on such matters as standardization of customs and currency; through their close relationship with France they enjoy association with the European Common Market. Likewise, former British colonies—now the independent states of Tanzania, Kenya, Uganda, Malawi, Zambia, Sierra Leone, Nigeria and Ghana—have a special relationship with Great Britain, including trade advantages as members of the Commonwealth (see pages 62-63). Six African states—Morocco, Tunisia, Algeria, Libya, the United Arab Republic and the Sudan—are members of the Arab League (see page 66), which joins them to the Arab nations of the Middle East.

Partly because of such continuing ties, and partly for other political and nationalistic reasons, the

Ethiopians watch as a U.N. building is opened in Addis Ababa.

OAU got off to a slow start. When its heads of state met in Accra, capital of Ghana, in the autumn of 1965, members were already $2.5 million in arrears in paying for the operation of their inadequately staffed secretariat. Only 19 of the organization's 36 heads of state attended the conference, and five of them went home early. Eight French-speaking nations boycotted the conference altogether to protest Ghana's sheltering of their political exiles. The main accomplishment was the passing of resolutions opposing white domination of southern Africa.

THE ARAB LEAGUE

FOUNDED: March 1945 in Cairo, Egypt. **HEADQUARTERS:** Cairo. **MEMBERS:** Algeria, Iraq, Jordan, Kuwait, Lebanon, Libya, Morocco, Saudi Arabia, Sudan, Syrian Arab Republic, Tunisia, United Arab Republic, Yemen.

The Arab League illustrates the dangers of setting up an international organization without the underpinning required for it to function effectively. The League was created in 1945 "to strengthen the ties between the participant states." At the twice-yearly meetings of the League Council—the governing body in which each member state has one vote—the agenda is usually loaded with such topics as: "To establish relations among the Arab countries on the sound basis of love and genuine cooperation." But under this pleasant surface there is considerable animosity. At a 1962 session the Syrian delegate announced that "We have come here to cut off Nasser's head and end his reptile tactics," to which the Egyptians spat back that their fraternal brothers from Syria were "barking dogs."

Arriving in Cairo, the King of Morocco is met by Nasser (right).

After several fistfights the Egyptians walked out and the Secretary-General wept. In short, the 13 delegations may sometimes talk unity, but the heads of the member states have spent millions plotting one another's assassination.

Although the League has a 10-story headquarters in Cairo and a Secretary-General with a staff of 200, it has no real independent existence or strength. It can do nothing unless it has the unanimous consent of all 13 members—and this seldom happens.

The founding pact of 1945 set up a wispy organization devoted simultaneously to "realizing close collaboration" and guaranteeing each member's "independence and sovereignty," in itself something of a paradox. This uncertain framework is inhabited by a violently disparate group of nations—some very rich and some bitterly poor; some ruled by socialists, others by reactionary monarchs and even by feudal chiefs who have in common little more than a taste for authoritarianism. Ten of the 13 members have territorial claims on one another, and many of the states think of Arab unity as conquering their neighbors. Consequently, although a dozen forward-looking agreements have been signed, including treaties for a common market, an all-Arab airline, an all-Arab tanker company and an Arab law court, all the important proposals have been shelved or, at most, feebly implemented. The sole issue that seems capable of unifying the League is hatred of Israel, but even here the members have been unable to agree on concrete proposals for military strategy or a plan to divert the Jordan water from Israel, which uses it for irrigation.

Yet the League cannot be written off. It keeps going on, the sole gathering place for the Arab leaders, and a possible framework for cohesion in the future. Though riddled with dissension, the League gives continued proof of the frustrated but powerful urge to unity in the Arab world.

ASSOCIATION OF SOUTHEAST ASIA (ASA)

FOUNDED: July 1961 in Bangkok, Thailand. **MEMBERS:** Malaysia, Philippines, Thailand.

Ringing words surrounded the birth of the Association of Southeast Asia in 1961: "Our three countries are jointly inspired by a common desire to think and plan for ourselves, adopt and adapt our own ideas for our own area." To some of the Asian nations the existing regional organizations seemed alien, to others insufficient: the Colombo Plan was London-born and Washington-financed; SEATO was seen as ineffective. There was also growing sentiment for a purely Asian group to cope with the threat of the European Common Market. Thus on July 31, Thailand, Malaya and the Philippines, representing 62.6 million of Southeast Asia's 1961 population of 222 million, met to build "a firm foundation for common action to further economic and social progress."

The Association of Southeast Asia's excitingly phrased plans encompassed a number of social, cultural and economic fields. The Association aimed eventually to set up an Asian counterpart to the European Common Market, to fix common standards for university credits, to seek low telegraph and press rates, to promote tourism, and so on. Governing authority was vested in an annual Foreign Ministers' Conference working through the Standing Committee. The press agents pointed out that the group's initials, ASA, were "a happy augury" because the word "means 'hope and expectation' in the three languages of the member countries—Malay, Tagalog and Thai."

But soon unfortunate facts began to intrude. Burma was indifferent to the idea of joining; Indonesia was downright hostile; the Communists called ASA a disguised tool of SEATO imperialists.

Furthermore, the members turned out to be economically incompatible: trade among them came to only a minute percentage of each country's total and they competed with each other for the same foreign markets. This was not a feasible basis for forming a common market, however fashionable the idea. The worst blow came in 1963 when the Philippines refused to recognize the new Federation of Malaysia on the grounds that the new state was neither politically viable nor the answer to Communist expansion in the area. Malaysia then cut its diplomatic ties with the Philippines. Relations between the two countries were later partially restored, but the rift has not helped ASA. Limping along, it can claim a few concrete accomplishments to date, among them the ASA Express, a through railway coach from Kuala Lumpur to Bangkok. Otherwise, ASA has yet to get moving.

SOUTH PACIFIC COMMISSION (SPC)

FOUNDED: February 1947 in Canberra, Australia. **HEADQUARTERS:** Nouméa, New Caledonia. **MEMBERS AND TERRITORIES:** Australia (Nauru, Norfolk Island, Papua and New Guinea), France (French Polynesia, New Caledonia, New Hebrides, Wallis and Futuna Islands), New Zealand (Cook Islands, Niue, Tokelau Islands), United Kingdom (British Solomon Islands Protectorate, Fiji, Gilbert and Ellice Islands, New Hebrides), United States (American Samoa, Guam, Trust Territory of the Pacific Islands), Western Samoa.

The South Pacific Commission came into being because the 1941-1945 war with Japan shattered the Gauguinlike world of the South Sea Islanders. Jeeps, planes, commissaries and cash—if not battles—intruded on what had been in many cases a Stone Age economy. The traditional folkways of the Melanesians, Polynesians and Micronesians who inhabit these islands were uprooted. In January 1947, in an attempt to relieve this problem, six powers with territorial interests in the area—Britain, the U.S., France, the Netherlands, Australia and New Zealand—met in Canberra and in February formed the South Pacific Commission, "a consultative and advisory body" to "encourage the economic and social welfare and advancement" of three million people.

The organization has remained essentially the same, although the Netherlands withdrew in 1962 after they lost New Guinea, and newly independent Western Samoa became a full member in 1964. At the top, the Commission itself—12 Commissioners from the six powers—meets at least once yearly to advise the governments at home and to concert a mutual program locally. In addition, a Secretary-General, headquartered in New Caledonia, working with a Research Council, executes the day-to-day war on ignorance, poverty and disease with a staff of 60 experts and an annual budget of some $900,000.

These bodies are busy and they operate efficiently. What is most exciting about the Commission, however, is its polyglot Conference, which brings together a number of native delegates every three years. The Conference is purely advisory, but it does provide a place where such delegates as High Chief Tuli Le'iato of American Samoa can meet with Mrs. Teupokoina Morgan from the Cook Islands to discuss subjects ranging from "the role of sorcery" to "how to get the best out of tourism."

A fisheries expert conducts a demonstration on New Caledonia.

Organizations for Nonpolitical Cooperation

INTERNATIONAL RED CROSS

FOUNDED: October 1863 in Geneva, Switzerland. **HEADQUARTERS:** Geneva. **MEMBERS:** 106 countries.

In 1859 a 31-year-old Swiss, Jean-Henry Dunant, witnessed at Solferino, Italy, a bloody battle between Franco-Italian and Austrian armies. The carnage stirred young Dunant to write an eloquent book entitled *A Memory of Solferino* urging the formation of voluntary aid societies to assist victims of war. The book stirred Europe, and in 1863, as a direct result of its publication, and Dunant's persistent campaigning, delegates from 16 countries met in Geneva and suggested the creation of a committee in each country to work with army medical services in wartime. The Geneva meeting also urged that casualties and the personnel appointed to care for them be regarded as noncombatants. It also provided for an international emblem—a red cross on a white field, the reverse of the Swiss flag—to mark supplies. In 1864 twelve countries ratified a convention agreeing to care for battlefield casualties, whether friend or enemy, and the International Red Cross was formally in existence. Since that first convention, four more Geneva conventions have been signed. In 1906 one extended aid to the ill as well as to the

A Red Cross nurse in Morocco helps care for emergency patients.

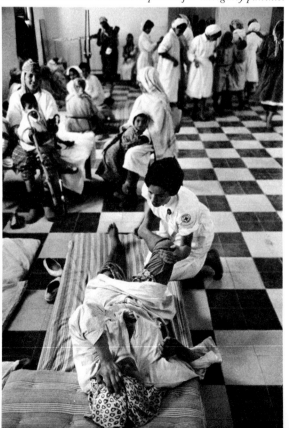

wounded, and in 1907 one was drawn to protect men at sea during wartime. Another, drawn up in 1929, promulgated a code for the treatment of prisoners of war. In 1949 the fourth established rules for the treatment of civilians during wartime.

The work of the Red Cross has expanded with the years. Today it not only cares for the victims of warfare but also offers relief to victims of natural disasters, helps the sick and works toward better public-health standards. The Red Cross now has 106 national societies, all members of the League of Red Cross Societies which, with the International Committee of the Red Cross, forms the heart of the organization. The Committee is composed of 25 Swiss nationals. Its services have not been overlooked. In 1917 and again in 1944 the Committee was awarded the Nobel Peace Prize.

EUROPEAN CONFERENCE OF MINISTERS OF TRANSPORT (ECMT)

FOUNDED: October 1953 in Brussels. **HEADQUARTERS:** Paris. **MEMBERS:** Austria, Belgium, Denmark, France, German Federal Republic, Greece, Ireland, Italy, Luxembourg, Netherlands, Norway, Portugal, Spain, Sweden, Switzerland, Turkey, United Kingdom, Yugoslavia.

When proponents of European political unification realized in the early 1950s that their sweeping proposals were premature (see European Communities, pages 50-51), they fell back on specific economic projects. These limited, pragmatic initiatives not only would accomplish much in their own way but also would result in a greater measure of European cooperation. One of the most successful of these organizations is the European Conference of Ministers of Transport, or ECMT, which was founded in 1953 to reorganize Europe's war-shattered transportation systems. Supervised by a Council of the members' transport ministers and run by a Committee of Deputies, ECMT has encouraged the construction of the seven-mile Mont Blanc tunnel and the four-mile Great St. Bernard tunnel and the canalization of the Moselle River. ECMT engineers have devised uniform road signs for Western Europe and drawn up plans for a system of superhighways and inland waterways. The Conference has also created Eurofima, a joint stock company composed of 16 ECMT members (excluding

Britain and Ireland) that finances the building of standardized freight cars and other railroad equipment. Up to 1963 ECMT's Eurofima had supplied more than 700 locomotives and 10,000 freight cars.

DANUBE COMMISSION

FOUNDED: July-August 1948 in Belgrade, Yugoslavia. **HEADQUARTERS:** Budapest, Hungary. **MEMBERS:** Austria, Bulgaria, Czechoslovakia, Hungary, Rumania, U.S.S.R., Yugoslavia.

The Danube Commission, whose ostensible purpose is to promote free navigation on Europe's longest river, was established at a conference in Belgrade in 1948. This was one of the hottest periods in the Cold War, when Soviet Russia was blatantly wielding its power, and the U.S.S.R. dominated the Belgrade Conference. Securely in control of their Balkan satellites' votes, the Russian representatives rudely ignored the wishes of their former allies and even at one point invited the delegates of Britain, France and the U.S. to pack up and go home. The Western delegates stayed, but they could not prevent the Commission from becoming a device to make the Danube basin into a Russian preserve. In 1953, however, with Stalin dead and with Titoist Yugoslavia making repeated protests, the Russians relaxed and began allowing others to take a minor hand. In 1960 Austria joined the Commission, today West Germany sits in as an observer at the annual meetings, and the Commission is on the way to fulfilling its original mandate to promote navigation on the 1,725-mile river.

CENTRAL COMMISSION FOR THE NAVIGATION OF THE RHINE

FOUNDED: June 1815 in Vienna, Austria. **HEADQUARTERS:** Strasbourg, France. **MEMBERS:** Belgium, France, German Federal Republic, Netherlands, Switzerland, United Kingdom.

The Rhine Commission, first conceived by the Congress of Vienna in 1815, began to function when its members met and adopted rules for navigation at the Convention of Mayence in 1831. It was further strengthened by the Convention of Mannheim in 1868 and enlarged by the Treaty of Versailles. The Commission exists to insure free, equal and safe passage for vessels of all nations along the 580 miles of the Rhine from Basel, Switzerland, to the North Sea. The advent of Nazi Germany disrupted the even tenor of its operations, but at the end of World War II the Commission went back to work,

Barges move majestically down the Rhine, a busy waterway.

clearing the river of bombed bridges and wrecked installations. Concerning itself with such matters as navigational routes and signals and the legal rights of Rhine boatmen, the Commission meets at least twice yearly to do whatever else is necessary to keep traffic flowing along the busiest river (187 million tons of freight in 1964) in Europe.

INTERNATIONAL CHAMBER OF COMMERCE (ICC)

FOUNDED: October 1919 in Atlantic City, New Jersey. **HEADQUARTERS:** Paris. **MEMBERS:** 40 National Committees plus representatives in 35 countries.

A private, nonpolitical body, the International Chamber of Commerce helps in a number of ways to facilitate trade between nations. Its Court of Arbitration provides businessmen with a means of settling disputes arising out of international transactions. It collects information on what is being done in various countries to improve production and distribution. The ICC also sets standard rules for world trade and coordinates the machinery for international transactions. The key organizational units of the ICC are the National Committees of the member nations. These Committees appoint delegates to the International Council, which is the ICC's governing body. Delegates of the National Committees also make up the 40 or so Technical and Regional Commissions that study economic problems and opportunities. And every two years the ICC assembles a Congress that considers all sorts of problems related to international trade.

BUREAU OF INTERNATIONAL EXPOSITIONS (BIE)

FOUNDED: November 1928 in Paris. **HEADQUARTERS:** Paris. **MEMBERS:** 32 countries.

The Bureau of International Expositions was created to oversee the organization of expositions, such as world's fairs, and to control their frequency. To insure that an area is not surfeited with expositions, the Bureau's rules state that major fairs may be held in the same country only once every 15 years and no oftener than once every six years in any one of three zones—European, Pan-American and the rest of the world. The Bureau forbids its member nations to participate in fairs it has not accredited. The recent

Crowds flow past two pavilions at the 1962 Seattle Exhibition.

New York World's Fair (1964-1965) was not recognized by the Bureau for several reasons: the New York fair ran for more than six months, the maximum set by the Bureau; it insisted that exhibiting nations rent space, while Bureau rules require that space be free; and the New York fair came too close on the heels of the Seattle Exhibition of 1962. The Bureau's rules were not binding on New York, however, since the U.S. is not a member of the organization.

EUROPEAN BROADCASTING UNION (EBU) and INTERNATIONAL RADIO AND TELEVISION ORGANIZATION (French abbreviation: OIRT)

EBU was founded in February 1950 in Torquay, England, and has its headquarters in Geneva. **OIRT** was founded in June 1946 in Brussels and is headquartered in Prague.

The European Broadcasting Union deals with radio and television broadcasting on a world scale. With administrative headquarters in Geneva and a technical center in Brussels, EBU develops programs and

arranges the exchange of radio and television news and of educational, agricultural and children's radio and TV programs among the various national networks. One of EBU's better-known subdivisions is Eurovision, an international television exchange in which 23 EBU member organizations participate. In addition to arranging live relays of cultural, news and sports events in Europe, Eurovision exchanges programs with EBU members in North America.

The counterpart of Eurovision in Eastern Europe is Intervision. This is the television branch of the International Radio and Television Organization (the Eastern equivalent of EBU). Intervision links the Soviet Union, Bulgaria, Czechoslovakia, East Germany, Hungary, Poland and Romania.

INTERNATIONAL CRIMINAL POLICE ORGANIZATION (INTERPOL)

FOUNDED: September 1923 in Vienna. **HEADQUARTERS:** Paris. **MEMBERS:** 95 member states.

Its cryptic name suggests continental intrigue, but Interpol (the cable address of the International Criminal Police Organization) is staffed mainly by French deskmen who rarely leave the organization's Paris headquarters. Interpol is primarily a clearinghouse through which the police of many nations exchange information on international criminals and crimes. The idea for Interpol was first advanced in 1914, but World War I intervened and Interpol was not set up until 1923, when delegates from 20 countries convened in Vienna. Interpol ceased to exist during World War II but was revived in 1946.

WORLD COUNCIL OF CHURCHES (WCC)

FOUNDED: August 1948 in Amsterdam, Netherlands. **HEADQUARTERS:** Geneva, Switzerland. **MEMBERS:** 214 member Churches in 90 countries plus eight associated Churches.

The World Council of Churches was formed in 1948 when representatives from 147 different Churches gathered in Amsterdam and wrote the organization's constitution. The most comprehensive interdenominational body in history, it has grown to take in 214 Churches (and eight associates) from no less than 90 countries and territories, including the Orthodox Churches of Russia and other nations and the vast majority of the world's Protestant communions.

The governing body of the WCC is an Assembly made up of delegates from the various member

The bearded Russian Orthodox delegation has a front-row location at the 1961 World Council of Churches Assembly in New Delhi.

Churches which meets every five years. The Assembly appoints the 100 members of the Central Committee, which is divided into several working committees that oversee the various divisions and departments of the WCC. The Executive Committee implements the decisions of the Central Committee. The whole organization is, in essence, an instrument through which Churches can affirm their common bonds and can work to advance Christian causes. Studies conducted under the WCC have examined such matters as the church's role in modern society and the various interpretations of Christian doctrine, the purpose being to clarify the degree to which Churches agree in both doctrine and aims. The WCC also furthers the cause of Christianity by giving emergency financial aid to Churches, by helping refugees (it has resettled 250,000), by providing scholarships for theological students and in many other ways.

INTERNATIONAL OLYMPIC COMMITTEE

FOUNDED: June 1894 in Paris. **HEADQUARTERS:** Lausanne.

The Olympic Games, which have been held every four years since 1896 except during World Wars I and II, are planned and governed by the International Olympic Committee, a group of 72 individuals from 55 of the nations that take part in the competitions. The Committee chooses the locations for the games and is the ultimate authority in enforcing standards of amateurism. It deals with the National Olympic Committees of the 122 nations that are eligible to send competitors to the games and with the International Federations that are in charge of such aspects of the games as supervising tracks and equipment. The Olympics are a revival of competitions held in ancient Greece. In the summer Olympics of 1964, held in Tokyo, 94 nations took part.

Athletes parade around Tokyo's Olympic Stadium during opening-day ceremonies at the 1963 pre-Olympic International Sports Week.

Portugal

ONLY the Portuguese find the independent existence of Portugal an unremarkable state of affairs. To others the most amazing thing about this amazing little country is that it exists at all. It sits in cups of hills, strips of valleys, barren uplands and sandy wastes upon the Atlantic slopes of the Iberian Peninsula, directly under the nose of Spain upon the plain above. Over the centuries the rulers of Spanish Castile have amalgamated by force of arms all the other segments of the Iberian Peninsula—León, Catalonia, Andalusia, the Basque Provinces and the rest —into one country. But not Portugal.

The Portuguese would not have it. Save for one sad span of 60 years they managed to avoid it. They spent their centuries throwing Spaniards (also Romans, Moors, Normans, Britons and French, but mainly Spaniards) out of Portugal, and even today, after a century and a half of peace, a fair definition of a Portuguese is a man who detests Spain.

The second most astonishing thing about Portugal, and stemming from the same hardy Portuguese spirit, is that so small a country managed to seize so large a share of the world and hold it so long. Starting with the *seculo maravilhoso,* the fabulous 15th Century when the navigators Prince Henry, Bartolomeu Dias, Vasco da Gama and the others found sea routes to some of the richest parts of the earth, Portugal built, enjoyed the wealth of, and finally lost great empires in Asia and in Brazil. Ironically, now that the British, French and Dutch empires are in ruins, Portugal is again the world's foremost colonial power.

Besides the Azores and Madeira islands in the Atlantic, which are considered part of the homeland, Portugal possesses the trading settlement of Macao off the south coast of China with some 188,000 people; half the island of Timor in the Sunda archipelago with some 543,000 more people; and five areas in Africa containing 800,000 square miles of territory with 12 million people. This African empire consists of

Angola (whose coffee crop is a big foreign-exchange earner for Portugal), Mozambique, Portuguese Guinea, the Cape Verde Islands, and the tiny islands of São Tomé and Príncipe.

Moreover, Portugal, most of whose overseas territories date back 500 years, has served notice that it does not intend to follow Britain, France and Belgium out of Africa. It denies that its possessions are colonies, and it has refused the United Nations any voice in their affairs. Its legal position is based on a 1951 law that declares all Portuguese colonies to be overseas territories and integral parts of the motherland, and on a 1961 law granting all people living in these regions full Portuguese citizenship.

The nation that controls this far-flung empire is, nevertheless, one of the poorest in Europe, with an average annual per capita income of only $270. Its industrialization program is still in the early stages of development, and its lovely countryside is dotted with farmland that is more scenic than productive. Despite poverty, the people live with an odd air of cheerful elegance, surrounded by monuments of their past magnificence—the palaces, monasteries, universities and cathedrals of the *seculo maravilhoso* and the building renaissance that followed. Special pride is taken in Manoeline architecture, the exuberant

Portuguese woman heads for market with her daughter, donkey and chair.

Portugal

building style whose rich nautical ornamentation testifies to Portugal's long dependence on the sea.

Situated in the extreme southwest corner of Europe, Portugal is a rough rectangle, a shade bigger (34,831 square miles) than the state of Maine and containing about 1.5 million more people (9.1 million) than inhabit New York City. It runs 350 miles from north to south, while the east-west width varies from 70 miles to 140.

Generally speaking, the north and northeast frontiers are the points at which the Spanish tableland breaks and folds into a series of mountain-range fingers pointing southwestward to the sea. Thus there are no natural boundaries to Portugal, only between-the-fingers valleys leading into various parts of the country. Through most of the valleys shallow, fast-water rivers foam and some of these serve as frontier for a bit of the way. Elsewhere the character of the border can range from a high, treeless field to an imaginary line running over rocky flats.

Due south and west the borders are long, scalloped Atlantic Ocean beaches, interrupted occasionally by a river mouth or rocky headland. Over these beaches Portuguese fishermen bring the little anchovies that they split, wrap around slices of stuffed olive, can in olive oil and send forth to the cocktail parties of the world. Canned fish of all sorts is Portugal's third-largest source of foreign exchange.

THE rains that come in over the Atlantic Ocean from the northwest fall more abundantly in the mountainous north than in the south. The difference shows up in the country's color. The south, whose summertime weather holds more than a touch of Africa's searing heat, is tan with sand and ripening wheat. The green begins north of the Tagus River and stretches beyond the highest of Portugal's mountain ranges (6,532 feet), the Serra da Estrêla, to the northern border. In the northwestern part of the country the climate is temperate and the humidity high the year round. The humidity sometimes brings cold fogs but also gives a misty, luminous charm to the countryside.

There are just two large cities in Portugal: Lisbon, the capital (pop. 817,326), where broad plazas, soaring cathedrals and ancient castles punctuate the hills upon which the metropolis rises, and Porto (pop. 305,445), the city of port wine and a cradle of many revolutions. But there are many ancient towns, almost

Three men meet on the sunny ramparts of St. George Castle in Lisbon

all of which display treasures of the past: the Roman ruins of Evora and Coimbra; the Romanesque town hall at Bragança; the castle of Afonso Henriques at Guimarães, the first capital of the first king of Portugal; the 12th Century cathedral of Coimbra; two 14th Century Gothic masterpieces in the monasteries at Alcobaça and Batalha.

Since 1955 some of Portugal's cities have been stirred by modern economic impulses. Roads have been built into all corners of the country. On the mountain streams electric power plants have been built and, linked to them, factories making everything from textiles to superphosphates. But the pace of industrialization is erratic, and the labor pool, while large, has few skilled workers. Since technical training programs are almost nonexistent, more and more Portuguese are emigrating to industrial countries where they can earn in an hour as much as they could make at home in a day.

Thus, Portugal remains a land of fishermen and farmers. Three fourths of its population lives in rural areas. On terraced vineyards in a 30-by-60-mile area of the Douro valley some raise grapes for port, the sweet and heavily fortified (mixed with grape brandy) dessert wine that goes wonderfully well with sharp

The capital city stretches below them to the banks of the Tagus River.

English cheeses or with nuts. The people of the British Isles, in fact, are the chief consumers of Portugal's port wines. English wine merchants established in Porto for 250 years and more dominate the trade. The Portuguese themselves seldom drink port. They prefer table wines like the *vinho verde* that is grown in the northwest and goes best with fish and fish stews. Portugal's second-largest export, after cotton yarn and fabrics, and ahead of canned fish and wines, is raw cork and manufactured cork products. The country sends out a number of other things, among them olive oil, pyrites, resin and turpentine.

The people of Portugal are gentle, sober and friendly. To come among them from the dour villages of western Spain is to encounter sudden warmth and cheerful wit. But both countries share, through a common Moslem influence perhaps, a deep strain of sadness. The prevailing melancholy in Portugal is called *saudade*, which roughly means a nostalgic yearning for a future in which the happiness of the past is revived. Folk songs called *fados* (the word means "fates") deal with the departure of friends, the separation of lovers, the sailings of ships, prolonged goodbyes, sorrows and griefs. But Portuguese cheerfulness is all the warmer for being set amid sadness.

And the Portuguese have other great qualities. They are fiercely faithful to their friends (their Ancient Alliance with Britain is 580 years old). Unlike Protestant Anglo-Saxons, the Portuguese have rarely fallen victims to the disdain for dark skin so prevalent among colonizing nations. Perhaps because of their own racially mixed ancestry, the Portuguese have always maintained intimate contact with the peoples they ruled. Negroes and mulattoes have, for centuries, been able to rise high in the colonial government bureaucracies.

The Portuguese speak to each other in a language better equipped to express emotion than to communicate information. It has the usual five vowels, but by stressing them, nasalizing them, obscuring them, whispering them, unstressing them, diphthonging them (both plain and nasalized), triphthonging them and polythonging them it has acquired more vowel sounds than any language this side of the South Seas. At the same time consonants have disappeared, verbs fight for the head of the sentence, and pronouns in diminutive, superlative and flowery forms wander about in disorderly fashion.

The result is a language most difficult to learn—but one that voices a literature second to none save that of Greece among the small countries of the world. Its poets include one of the country's founding kings, Diniz (1279-1325), whose delicate love poems are still read by the Portuguese; a sometime goldsmith, sometime playwright named Gil Vicente (1470?-1536?), whose plays, pious and merry, are considered the best written in Europe between the time of Euripides and that of Shakespeare; and the 16th Century epic poet, Luis de Camões, whose *Os Lusíadas* has been compared to the *Iliad*.

THE blood of the Portuguese flows from many wells. It first appears in the Lusitanians, themselves probably a mingling of the original Iberians and the Celts, who fought and were defeated (through the treacherous murder of their great leader Viriatus) by the Romans in the second century before Christ. Thereafter for six centuries Rome ruled Lusitania, and when Rome crumbled, first Vandals and then Swabians from the far-off shores of the Danube River set up a kingdom in northern Portugal. The Swabian state lasted 175 years, from 410 to 585, when it was gobbled up by Visigoths who in turn were moved out by Moslems in 711. It took more than 500 years to recover the territory lost to the Arab invaders. But out of the relentless struggle the Portuguese nation was born and its character was defined. Although the first stirrings toward a Christian reconquest began immediately after the Moslem occupation, it was not until the 12th Century that the Christian military orders (such as the Templars) began to form the forces of liberation and initiate large-scale military operations. On a wide front they drove steadily south, sweeping the Islamic armies before them.

BY the end of the 11th Century, despite successes in clearing the Arabs out of northern Portugal, the Portuguese lands were still under the domination of the powerful Spanish kingdom of Castile and León. True independence was another half century away. Ironically, the first steps toward freedom from its neighbor were taken when a Spanish King presented Portugal as a gift to a French Prince: in 1097 Alfonso VI, the ruler of Castile and León, made Portugal a hereditary county and turned it over to his son-in-law, Henry of Burgundy.

But Henry was shrewd and ambitious. He initiated a policy of separation which, after his death, was continued by his wife Teresa. A jealous, arrogant woman, she proclaimed herself Queen of Portugal and precipitated a series of dynastic wars by intriguing against her half sister who ruled nearby León. Teresa even intrigued against her own son, Afonso Henriques, during whose minority she acted as regent. In 1128 Afonso declared war against his mother, and eventually he drove her out of Portugal. It took the young Prince some 15 years to consolidate his position, but in 1143 he managed to gain Spanish recognition as King of the Portuguese, thus becoming the revered founder of the nation.

As King Afonso I, Afonso Henriques redoubled the effort to push the remaining Moslems southward into the sea. Animated by a crusading zeal, he took Santarém and, with the help of a passing party of English, French, Flemish and German crusaders, captured the sleepy seaport of Lisbon. This last was his most important victory, for in the days to come the Moslem south and Gothic north of Portugal would meet and mingle in Lisbon, and there evolve their common Portuguese identity and their common destiny upon the sea. Under Afonso's three successors, who reigned between 1185 and 1279, the Reconquest

of Portugal from the Moslems was completed, the country assumed more or less its present boundaries and, except for periodic skirmishes with Castile, lapsed into relative tranquillity.

These were years of energetic social reorganization, expanded trade and the introduction of more efficient methods of farming the rich but wasted land. Ruling sovereigns, representing the interests of the common people, sought to limit the power of the privileged classes—the nobility and the clergy. Diniz, greatest of the Burgundian kings, forbade the Church to acquire new lands. He also expanded Portugal's relations with the rest of Europe, established a *studium generale* which became the University of Coimbra, enlarged the Navy, and won for himself the title *rei lavrador,* or "farmer king," because of his interest in agriculture and forestry.

After nine kings and 255 years Portugal's long line of legitimate Burgundian rulers ended with the death of Fernando in 1383. The intense internecine conflicts that followed saw the birth of a new dynasty, the House of Avis, which in turn gave birth to the most illustrious era in Portuguese history, the Age of Exploration.

THE idea of overseas expansion had been germinating in the consciousness of the Portuguese ever since the Reconquest, when the victorious princes began to take an interest in Africa, the continent from which the Moslem invaders had come. And at first the Portuguese were content to establish trading posts along the African coast. But as the success of their explorers led to the expansion of trade, the trade routes demanded protection. And with the entry of Spain into the arena of empire builders, national pride required that Portugal dominate and extend its newly acquired territories.

The great age began in 1415 with the conquest of Ceuta, Morocco, directed by Prince Henry the Navigator. At his court on the remote cape of Sagres on the Algarve coast, Henry set up a sailing center that developed navigational instruments and assembled libraries of charts, sailing directions and tidal information. He also built caravels, the finest sailing vessels of their day. These he sent exploring down the west coast of Africa. Yet his own expedition to take Tangier ended in miserable failure. His youngest brother, Fernando, was captured, and the Moslems made it clear they would only surrender him in exchange for

Brightly painted Portuguese fishing boats ride at anchor in the placid little port of Sesimbra near Lis

Ceuta. After nearly six years in captivity Fernando died, still unransomed.

When Henry died in 1460, the pace of exploration slackened until his energetic grandnephew, João II, came to power in 1481. During João's reign Diogo Cão discovered the mouth of the Congo River and Bartolomeu Dias rounded the Cape of Good Hope and reached the east coast of Africa. It was João who, in 1494, negotiated the famous Treaty of Tordesillas with Spain that—with the Pope's blessing—divided between the two countries all the lands already discovered, or that would be discovered. Spain was to have everything lying more than 370 leagues west of the Azores and the Cape Verde Islands and Portugal everything east of there. This gave Portugal title not only to Africa but also to Brazil.

BECAUSE João II's son died before his father, the real inheritor of his expeditions became his cousin Manoel, thereafter known as "Manoel the Lucky." During his reign Vasco da Gama reached India and new Portuguese strong points were established at Cochin, Calicut and Goa in India, at Ormuz on the Persian Gulf, and elsewhere. Other explorers followed, bringing rich new lands under the Portuguese flag. But the small Iberian nation, with a population well under two million, could little afford to provide the manpower and the money needed to maintain its sprawling territories. This, along with internal dissension, the rivalry of other powers and a fall in prices paid for the colonies' tropical products, led inevitably to the empire's slow decline.

By the end of the 16th Century Portugal could no longer withstand the pressure of its aggressive neighbor to the east. In 1580 the Portuguese were forced to form a dual monarchy with Spain in which both nations were ruled by a Spanish king. Even after a successful conspiracy ended the country's "Sixty Years' Captivity," a series of wars with Spain saw the further erosion of Portugal's economic position. By the mid-18th Century, however, the mines of Brazil were fully productive, stimulating an economic and cultural revival. The royal coffers, depleted during the Spanish occupation when Flemish and English traders turned elsewhere for the sugar, tobacco and spices once bought in Lisbon, were swelled by the inflow of Brazilian gold and diamonds. João V launched a period of building and of patronage of the arts unsurpassed in Portuguese history. But in 1755 the catastrophic

Lisbon earthquake, a disaster in which perhaps 13,000 people lost their lives, marked the end of this cultural renaissance.

The earthquake brought to the fore the Marquis of Pombal, a nobleman who displayed great calm and good sense in handling the crisis. Pombal launched many schemes regulating the tobacco, diamond and sugar trade and encouraged fishing and the manufacture of silk. He also set up a monopoly in the wine trade. This enraged the wine dealers, who rioted in Porto. Pombal quelled the riot with an extreme and needless cruelty that made him many enemies. He shocked the pious by expelling the Jesuits, who had opposed his economic plans for Brazil, and enraged the aristocracy by executing one of its foremost members, the Duke of Aveiro, on charges of having plotted the death of the king. When the melancholy Maria I came to the throne, she threw open the prisons that Pombal had filled, restored the Jesuits, pacified the aristocracy and made peace with Spain.

In his old age Pombal was declared guilty of innumerable crimes by Maria and was banished from court; he died a year later. But much of his legacy is still visible in the elegant buildings, wide streets and magnificent plazas of the Lisbon he rebuilt. Beyond that, the Portuguese are indebted to Pombal for another improvement. Returning from a mission to London in 1744, he introduced an odd new instrument—the fork. Within months the entire aristocracy of Portugal stopped eating with its fingers.

FOR Maria the world was nothing but gray sadness. Her husband and eldest son died. The news of the Revolution in France, with the heads of a king and queen rolling in the guillotine's basket, was frightening. By 1792 her mental balance was beyond recapture, and her younger son, the future King João VI, became prince regent just as Portugal entered its years of terrible turmoil. Portuguese soldiers marched against France together with Spain and England, only to have Spain, under the treacherous leadership of Manuel Godoy, sign a separate peace treaty in 1795, leaving Portugal at war. Six years later, in 1801, Spain invaded Portugal's Alentejo region, captured the fortress town of Olivença and forced Portugal to pay a large indemnity.

But still the country's troubles were far from over. In 1806 Napoleon set out to enforce his edict that all continental ports be closed to British shipping. He sent an army under General Andoche Junot across Spain to Portugal. The royal family was packed aboard ships and under British convoy sent off to Brazil for safekeeping. The following year, in 1808, Sir Arthur Wellesley (the future Duke of Wellington) arrived in Portugal with 8,000 troops, defeated the French at Roliça and Vimeiro, and forced Junot out of Portugal. Twice more the French invaded and twice more Wellesley drove them out.

These campaigns caused widespread devastation. This, combined with the absence of the royal family and the weakness of the council of regency, contributed to a deep nation-wide restlessness. The more the royal family in far-off Brazil studied this restlessness the less they wanted to come home. But finally, 10 years after the last battle, João VI, his younger son, Miguel, and his Queen, Carlota Joaquina, started for home. In Lisbon they were presented with a democratic constitution drawn up by a constituent assembly and asked to swear allegiance to it. The King did but the Queen and his son Miguel refused and, after an abortive attempt to abolish the constitution, Miguel was sent into exile.

THIS then was the issue over which Portugal would fight during the first part of the 19th Century: absolutism versus constitutional government. After King João's death his son Pedro, Emperor of Brazil, offered a "charter" to the Portuguese people (the difference between constitution and charter was that the charter was authorized by the monarch and the constitution was based on the sovereignty of the people). However, Pedro refused to leave Brazil and handed over the throne to his infant daughter with Miguel as regent. Miguel proceeded to abolish the constitution and had himself proclaimed king. Seeing this, Pedro abdicated the throne of Brazil, returned to Europe in 1831, raised an army against Miguel and took Porto. A two-year War of the Brothers followed, from which Pedro emerged victorious, only to die of tuberculosis a few months later.

The next years saw the emergence of new parties, the Historicals, or radicals, and the Regenerators, or moderates. These two groups handed the Government back and forth peacefully enough—but lost all connection with popular feeling. A republican movement starting in the 1870s grew stronger. Its climax came in 1908 with the assassination of King Carlos I and his heir Luís. This was followed by the

revolution of 1910 which drove King Manoel II into exile. The republic that took over was a disorderly affair. From 1910 to 1926 it had 43 different governments until a military revolt against the regime broke out and General António Fragoso Carmona was selected to head it. He became President of the Republic and was elected to successive seven-year terms until his death in 1951.

It was Carmona who in 1928 called in "the Doctor," António de Oliveira Salazar, a pale, reticent professor of economics at Coimbra University, to solve the problem of Portugal's muddled finances. Salazar was given complete authority over the expenses of all Government departments, and when his stringent measures turned deficits into surpluses he was made Prime Minister in 1932, a post he was not to surrender for well over three decades. In these years Salazar made for himself a position of unassailable power. This power was founded on three separate police forces, staffed by former Army officers, the most important of them the political police, or PIDE. Undue political curiosity resulted in visits by PIDE and subsequent trips to prisons.

There was scattered and ineffectual opposition from social democratic and Roman Catholic groups. Dom Duarte, Duke and Prince of Bragança, Pretender to the throne, claimed a following of 20,000 Portuguese. There were six revolts between 1946 and 1962. The exploits of the rebels were sometimes spectacular, such as Captain Henrique Galvão's seizure of the liner *Santa Maria* and the wild chase around the seas that followed. General Humberto Delgado was for a time a powerful threat to Salazar, but he was murdered in Spain in 1965. Even Salazar's apologists could claim little more than that the dictator had given Portugal many years of political stability. But Salazar's kind of stability amounted almost to paralysis and did little to foster the economic growth that the nation desperately needs.

FOR FURTHER READING

Bridge, Ann, and Susan Lowndes, *The Selective Traveller in Portugal.* McGraw-Hill, 1961.
Diffie, Bailey W., *Prelude to Empire: Portugal Overseas Before Henry the Navigator.* University of Nebraska, 1960.
Livermore, Harold Victor, *A History of Portugal.* Cambridge University Press, 1947.
Stanislawski, Dan, *The Individuality of Portugal.* University of Texas Press, 1959.

Austria

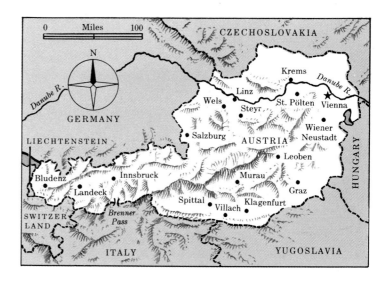

AUSTRIA is what remained after the Austro-Hungarian Empire was dismantled in 1918. About the size of the state of Maine, it is a country of sloping meadows, dark-green forests and glorious, camera-courting mountains. Three massive chains of Alps, each with its supporting spurs, cross Austria from west to east. Dotted everywhere throughout these mountains are lovely little Hansel-and-Gretel country inns and hotels, many of them incorporating parts of medieval castles. Here skiers in stretch pants mix with natives whose mode of dress dates back centuries. Tucked away in the valleys and along the watercourses, straight out of the elegance of the 17th and 18th Centuries, are some of the most remarkably beautiful cities in all of Europe.

All this Austrian charm—the Viennese waltzes, polkas and galopes; the white Lippizaner horses wheeling through their quadrilles in Vienna's Spanish Riding School; the operas, concerts and festivals; the cozy *Gemütlichkeit* of the villages and the genuine 19th Century kiss-the-hand-and-click-the-heels grand manners still found in the cities—all this is Austria's greatest economic resource. The country attracts more than six million tourists—nearly one foreigner for every Austrian—each year. Although many of these visitors are frugal Germans who bring their own box lunches and camp in the fields, there are enough thick billfolds about to produce a yearly cash crop of some $523 million.

Salable charm is by no means Austria's only resource. It has extensive forests and hydroelectric power. The country's spruced-up iron and steel industries export goods worth 5,030,530,000 Austrian schillings ($193.5 million) each year. Many of Austria's steel plants use the Austrian-pioneered Linz-Donawitz oxygen steelmaking process that not only produces high-quality steel more cheaply but also brings in royalties from other countries using the process. There are petrochemical industries clustering around the oil wells of Zistersdorf. Other natural resources include magnesite, copper, lead and salt. Modern plants produce heavy machinery, electrical equipment, paper and cardboard, textiles and clothing. None of these, however, is as important to the Austrian economy as tourism. Charm pays the bills.

Although Austria lags behind most of the other countries of Western Europe, it has seldom been so prosperous, even in the great days of the empire. And it has seldom grumbled more about it. *Das Raunzen,* or grumbling as a fine art, is an Austrian national preoccupation. The true Austrian grumbler is convinced that everything is going to turn out for the worst, but on the other hand it will probably not be as bad as the very worst could very well be. The Austrian has good reason for his pessimistic outlook. Any middle-aged citizen can count his calamities in terms of two world wars lost, an empire gone, fortunes vanished up the inflation spiral, revolutions, violent annexations and city-flattening liberations. This pessimism, almost fatalism, sometimes produces another Austrian trait which the natives call *Schlamperei,* and which can best be translated by the slang word "shlumpiness." It is a tendency to throw up the hands when difficulties arise and go across the street to a coffeehouse.

Despite grumbling and *Schlamperei,* some real progress has been made since the upheavals of World War II. Beyond seasonal adjustments there is no unemployment in Austria. Indeed, the country has to import labor, mostly from Greece and Turkey, although this is partly to make up for the fact that other countries, Germany especially, tap Austria's pool of highly trained people. Austrian factory workers draw an average monthly wage of only $110, but

Villages cluster near the Inn River, which winds through the Austrian Tyrol.

this is augmented by such benefits as controlled rents, socialized medicine, child allowances, an extra month's pay at year's end and adequate retirement pensions. It is also easy for housewives and children to find jobs of their own. According to one estimate, the average Austrian household derives income from one and a half jobs.

Austria's standard of living has been rising steadily. The country, which wobbled out of the rubble of World War II on beaten-up bicycles, had 1,236,000 motor vehicles by 1964, of which 703,000 were passenger cars. On the way to this point Austria passed through an age of the scooter (once Father's necessity, it is now Junior's status symbol) and an age of the Puch, a very miniature Austrian automobile. The present epoch is that of the Volkswagen.

In addition to automobiles, Austrians in 1964 owned 2,238,000 radios and 678,000 television sets, purchased refrigerators in ever-increasing numbers and at the same time, oddly enough, saved money at record rates. Except for an occasional flier in the lottery, savings plans, with home building as the eventual goal, are the favorite Austrian investment.

P RESIDING over this middling opulence is an astonishing Government carefully designed to make sure that no political party will ever wholly achieve its goals. It is a coalition of the conservative People's Party (often called the "Blacks") and the Socialist ("Red") Party that works by *Proporz,* or proportional representation of both parties at all levels of government. The president is usually a Socialist, the chancellor a Conservative and the vice chancellor a Socialist. Every Conservative Cabinet member has a Socialist assistant peering over his shoulder and every Socialist is shadowed by a Conservative. This vastly increases the number of Government posts, as the Austrians themselves jokingly point out, for each job requires a Red and a Black to watch each other and a third man to do the work.

But *Proporz* solved one problem once and is still solving another. During the 10 years of four-power military occupation (Britain, France, the U.S. and Russia) that followed World War II, the coalition enabled Austria to present a united country to the occupying powers, especially to the Russians, who were doing their best to wreck Austrian industry by taking away its machinery as war reparations. And currently it holds off the violent civil strife that

might well result if one of the parties emerged supreme. Sitting side by side in Austrian Cabinets are men who have good reason to hate each other. Some of the Socialists spent time in prison after a short-lived but savage Conservative revolution in 1934. In 1938 some of the Conservatives and some of the Socialists made their peace with Adolf Hitler. Others did not, and found themselves in Nazi concentration camps. The situation obviously calls for delicacy, and the delicacy of agreements worked out in private, rather than noisy and potentially explosive political battling, is what *Proporz* provides.

A full 80 per cent of the people want it this way, or so all the polls seem to indicate. And the almost exactly even split of the voters between Socialists and Conservatives makes compromise possible. Socialist Franz Jonas was elected President in the spring of 1965 by a minuscule majority—50.69 per cent of the votes. The Parliament is likewise almost evenly divided; it is usually in Conservative hands but by so narrow a margin that *Proporz,* if not total peace, has prevailed. This stalemate infuriates the more passionate party leaders, and there is an ever-present danger that one or the other party will drop *Proporz* and go for total victory. Feelings can run high and occasionally riots break out, sometimes over the most unlikely matters: over whether the Austrian Pretender, Otto von Habsburg, may return to the country; over whether a new steamboat on Lake Constance should be named the *Vorarlberg* or the *Karl Renner* (a famous Socialist politician); over how Education Minister Dr. Teodor Piffl-Percevic should deal with professor of economic history Taras Borodajkewycz, an alleged anti-Semite who refuses to be contrite about his Nazi past; over whether the use of labor funds to prop up an ailing Socialist publication should be countenanced; and, finally, over whether the minister dismissed for misusing the funds should be allowed to take secret police files on his enemies home with him. *Proporz* would seem to be a necessity with such a politically volatile people.

I T is often hard to believe that these gale-force political storms can be stirred up in so small a country by such charming people. Young Austrians, statistics say, are eating differently from the way their parents did and are growing thinner and taller. But most Austrians still like to sit comfortably in cafés, reading the newspapers, writing letters, gossiping, drinking coffee *mit Schlag*—topped with thick whipped cream—and eating whipped-cream-filled pastries. In fair weather they tramp the hills west of Vienna looking for the little garlands of pine boughs that are hung out as a sign that this inn, this garden or this vineyard has *Heurigen,* the clear young wine. Then at tables for 12 and more they sit drinking and listening to the musicians until, awash in sentiment and wine, they link arms and sway back and forth in song, using the quiet moments to pour their most intimate secrets into each others' ears.

But the next day everyone is back in his own political niche. Politics in Austria is not so much belief in a set of principles as a way of life. Austrians are born Socialist or Conservative because that is what their fathers were. They go to Socialist or Conservative bookstores to buy the books that shape their young minds. If they become doctors or lawyers they can expect their clients to come from the world of their own political views. If a Socialist becomes interested in such nonpolitical activities as bird watching, stamp collecting, taking photographs or concertgoing, he joins a Socialist nature, stamp, camera or music club. There are similar clubs for the Conservatives.

POLITICS also enter into Austrian big business, not just because all Austrians are such political animals but because many of the biggest businesses are Government-owned. The Austrian economy was so thoroughly wrecked by World War II that only the Government, backed by $962 million in U.S. aid from the Marshall Plan alone, had the means of getting the country's industries going again. As a result some 70 of the nation's largest enterprises—operating in such fields as steel, iron, coal, oil and hydroelectric power—are owned by the Government. The Government also runs the two largest banks, which in turn own 150 more industrial, financial, engineering and trading enterprises.

And here again *Proporz* exerts its pervasive influence on Austrian life. The nationalized industries are run by Section IV of the Federal Chancellery; no matter which party is in power, the opposition has an equal voice in the management of Section IV. The result is that Section IV—and therefore Austrian industry—is run with a cautious, anything-but-daring hand. Section IV argues, of

course, that it is doing a good job, paying taxes equal to those of private industry, and equivalent wages. It admits that the average dividend it pays its single stockholder, the state, is only 1.8 per cent of capital value, but claims that comparison on this score with private industry would be unfair because so much of its gross goes for benefits and plant reinvestment. Efficiency, it claims, is maintained by tight budgets, time studies and automation at least to the general level of European practice. Nevertheless, many Austrians are not happy with the performance. Austrian industry is reasonably healthy, but it is far from booming, and timidity would seem to be one reason. Recently the conversion of a bicycle plant to the manufacture of power mowers was hailed as a daring, decisive step forward. Austrians suspect that they are getting a good deal of *Schlamperei* with the *Proporz.*

IN fact the only good thing to be said about *Proporz* is that it has, so far, worked fairly well —and nothing else has worked at all since the fall of the Austro-Hungarian Empire in 1918. This empire was ruled by what was known as the Dual Monarchy. This was a curious political arrangement, begun in 1867, designed to soothe the Hungarian Magyars' craving for autonomy. The Hungarians were given a measure of self-government and the Habsburg ruler undertook to wear two hats (or crowns), becoming both the King of Hungary and the Emperor of Austria. The arrangement involved three Cabinets, one for Austria, one for Hungary and one for matters involving them both. The Dual Monarchy was vast and seemingly unwieldy, but its parts fitted so wonderfully, if so unwillingly, into one economic and political necessity in Eastern Europe that a great Czech teacher, František Palacký, wrote a century ago that "if the Austrian Monarchy did not exist it would be necessary to create it quickly, in the interest of Europe and of mankind."

The empire reached from Switzerland in the west over the Carpathian Mountains into the present-day Soviet Ukraine in the east, from well inside modern Poland in the northeast to the seaports of Fiume and Trieste on the Adriatic and on down its eastern shore far into what has become Yugoslavia. In 1914 it contained some 51 million people of many restive strains—Germans, Magyars, Czechs, Ruthenians, Romanians, Croats, Serbs, Slovaks, Slovenes, Poles,

Italians, some Moslem Slavs and a handful of Turks.

Hungary was the great breadbasket for all of these people. The other areas concentrated on their specialties: Bohemia, Moravia and Silesia, all now in Czechoslovakia or Poland, provided the rich mines for heavy industry plus hops for the famous breweries of Pilsen. Slovakia produced plump geese and cheeses, Serbia pork, plums and slivovitz (a strong plum brandy). Austria itself offered not only wonderful wines and grapes but also all the charms of a waltzing Vienna, with its lovely women, its glorious music, and its pale-yellow palaces in curved and billowing baroque in which the great men in glittering uniforms who ruled these kingdoms paced back and forth in the summer of 1914, pondering grave matters and coming up with all the wrong answers. The answers led to World War I, and when that was over the Austro-Hungarian Empire, together with 1.2 million of its soldiers, was dead.

IT is difficult to be precise about the origins of either Austria or this doomed empire. Celtic tribes roamed the region's mountains when the Romans came and conquered about 10 B.C. The Romans established their chief camp at Vindobona, later to be called Wenia, or Vienna. Huns and Ostrogoths poured in after the Fifth Century, usually hurrying right on out again toward the warmer climes of Italy. Perhaps Austria's founding father can be said to have been Charlemagne, who conquered parts of present-day Austria in the Eighth Century, organizing them as Mark im Ostland, or "guardian of the eastern approaches" to his own inner citadels, which they remained for more than a century.

But there are others with good claims to be the fathers of Austria. One is Henry the Quarrelsome of Bavaria, who reorganized the Mark im Ostland (which came to be shortened to Ostmark, hence, eventually, Austria) after his grandfather Otto the Great had recaptured the area in 955 from Hungarian Magyar invaders. Another is Leopold, first count of Ostmark and founder in 976 (often cited by Austrians as their nation's birth year) of the Babenberg Dynasty. In 1101 another Babenberg, Leopold III, built a fortress on Kahlenberg Mountain overlooking Vienna. A third nobleman with a claim to be considered Austria's founder is Duke Henry Jasomirgott (the last name being his favorite exclamation, a German agglutination meaning approximately

"Ah, may God help me"), who in the middle 1100s formally established the city of Vienna, built a castle there and dedicated St. Stephen's Church, now Vienna's famous cathedral.

The Babenberg line ran out in 1246 when another Duke nicknamed the Quarrelsome, this one Frederick, was killed battling in Hungary against some marauding Mongols. After a period during which several nobles attempted to seize control, the dukedom went to Ottocar II, the King of Bohemia. By highhanded diplomacy Ottocar pushed his borders southward to the Adriatic; the move so alarmed the rulers of neighboring German principalities that they sought out somebody to curb Ottocar. The man they found, a Swiss landowner of many great estates, had a name that forever after would mean Austria to the rest of the world. Rudolf von Habsburg (Habsburg is a contraction of *Habichtsburg,* or "hawk's castle," this being the name of the family seat in Aargau, Switzerland) was elected German King and was asked to brake Ottocar. This he proceeded to do, forcing the ambitious Bohemian King to disgorge what became after 1282 the basic hereditary Habsburg duchy of German Austria, the cherished, privileged core of all the Habsburgs' future dominions.

In 1363 the Tyrol was added to the Habsburg holdings when Margaretha Maultasch, history's original Ugly Duchess (her name means "pocket mouth"; a portrait alleged to be of her served artist Sir John Tenniel as his model when he drew the Duchess for *Alice in Wonderland),* abdicated in the Habsburgs' favor. A region called the Windisch Mark came their way in 1374 as did parts of the Vorarlberg. The people of Trieste called in the Habsburgs in 1382 to save them from the Venetians, who were constantly attacking them by land and by sea. The Habsburgs also became the real authority in the ecclesiastical sees of Salzburg, Trent and Brixen. Thus the Habsburgs' Austrian domains multiplied almost in spite of themselves.

HABSBURG family law held that all male members jointly inherited all the family's possessions and ruled them in common. This often meant that some members of the family would go into debt to buy the others out peacefully. As often, it meant brutal civil wars, with brothers battling brothers and uncles battling cousins from castle to castle across the unhappy realm. This was for the Austrian people a miserable era: free peasants were forced into slavery, an economic torpor lay upon the land, and in 1348 and 1349, 1369 and again in 1381 the Black Death ravaged the population.

Starting in 1438 the Habsburgs became at least the titular rulers of still more territory—the Holy Roman Empire—when the Empire's Electors established the tradition of electing the head of the Habsburg Dynasty as their emperor. They thus entrusted to them the dream of generations of popes and emperors of uniting Christendom in one political whole. But although parts of present-day France, Germany, Austria, Poland, Czechoslovakia, Italy, Belgium, the Netherlands and Switzerland at one time or another acknowledged themselves part of the Empire, the dream remained just that, and the Habsburgs never made the mistake of favoring this elective Empire over their hereditary possessions.

THESE last they tended judiciously, increasing them not by wars but by marriage, although sometimes a marriage led to a war. Wits gave the family a new motto: *Bella gerant alii; tu, felix Austria nube,* meaning "Let others wage war; thou, happy Austria, marry." Maximilian I was the best, most deft master of the art. He himself in 1477 wed Mary, daughter of Charles the Bold of Burgundy, thereby bringing the Low Countries (which the Burgundians had controlled) under Habsburg rule. Maximilian then arranged the marriage of his son Philip to Joanna of Castile, thus making Philip King of Castile. Castile later became one of the sections of the new Kingdom of Spain, and therefore Philip and Joanna's elder son ascended the Spanish throne in 1516 as Charles I and inherited the overseas realms that Columbus, Cortés and the Pizarro brothers were creating in the Americas and ruled an empire reaching from Peru to the Carpathians. Charles also ruled the Holy Roman Empire from 1519 to 1558 as Charles V. Maximilian, too, arranged the dynastic treaty with Hungary whereby Philip and Joanna's younger son, Ferdinand, became king of that country.

Occasionally the canny Maximilian lost a matrimonial round. In order to remain unmolested in the Netherlands, he was forced to promise the hand of his daughter Margaret, together with a dowry consisting of the territories of Franche-Comté and Artois, to Charles VIII of France. Charles picked up the dowry but did not marry Margaret. Instead he married Anne of Brittany, calmly ignoring the fact that she was already married (by proxy) to Maximilian himself, Mary of Burgundy having died. Maximilian had to go to war to get back Margaret's dowry. But he retrieved matters by marrying her off to Juan of Aragon, thus strengthening the family hold on the Iberian Peninsula.

Known as the "last of the knights" because of his courtly qualities, Maximilian was a man of culture and learning. He in effect subsidized the great Nuremberg engraver Albrecht Dürer, and when there was any cash left over after making dowries for his daughters, he enlarged the Universities of Vienna and Freiburg.

Maximilian's grandson Charles stepped down from the Spanish throne in 1556 and then gave his empire, which included Spain's vast American possessions, Naples, Milan, Sicily and the Low Countries, to his son Philip. Austria, Bohemia and Hungary, albeit Hungary was mainly under Turkish domination at the time, were ruled by his brother Ferdinand. Fortunately, Philip and Ferdinand and their successors supported one another in the years of struggle that followed. In 1683 a Turkish force besieged Vienna, and the garrison nearly starved before a relieving army under King Jan Sobieski of Poland arrived to chase the foe away. There was more fighting in 1697 when an Austrian army under Prince Eugene of Savoy, the best sword for hire in Europe, whipped the Turks out of Hungary, captured Belgrade and finally at Zenta destroyed a Turkish army.

Still more fighting followed: the War of the Spanish Succession (1701-1714), the War of the Polish Succession (1733-1735), the War of Jenkins' Ear (1739-1741), the War of the Austrian Succession (1740-1748). In these many conflicts the Habsburgs lost territory or retrieved old losses or captured new ground—and came out just about even.

ODDLY enough it was just in these years of the loud guns that the loveliness of Vienna was created. Two architects, Johann Fischer von Erlach and Johann Lukas von Hildebrandt, were responsible for most of it. Erlach did the imperial residence; much of the old Hofburg, the Habsburgs' in-town palace; and the Karlskirche, a classic baroque church. Hildebrandt designed the Belvedere Palace as Prince Eugene's summer residence and the lovely Kinsky

Palace. Together they worked on the Schwarzenberg Palace and Prince Eugene's winter residence. Erlach had a hand in the original design for the magnificent royal summer residence of Schönbrunn.

Vienna had its years of greatest cultural achievement in another era of wars and invasions which culminated with the final defeat of Napoleon at Waterloo. In these years, starting in 1781, when Mozart moved from Salzburg to Vienna, and ending in 1828, when Schubert died, four men working in Vienna—Haydn, Mozart, Beethoven and Schubert—created much of the best of what has come to be called classical music. When they were done Vienna would mean just one thing to the world at large—music. Later Bruckner, Brahms, Mahler, Richard Strauss and Arnold Schönberg enriched and deepened the city's musical tradition.

BUT in politics and statesmanship there was little glory. The revolutions of 1848 shook but did not shatter the repressive police state (made endurable by Austrian charm) that the great Austrian diplomat Prince Metternich had fastened on the country in the post-Napoleonic age. Austria's Italian possession of Lombardy was lost in a war with France in 1859, and Austria lost its position as the leading German state in a war with Prussia in 1866. Thereafter Austria faced eastward, toward Russia, and struggled with the problem of containing the nationalistic aspirations of the many different peoples in the empire. It was, of course, an Austrian Archduke, Ferdinand, who was murdered at Sarajevo and thus started the train of events that led to World War I. But it was not the Archduke's assassination that *caused* the terrible conflict. Far more at fault, among other factors, was Austria's fear of Russia and its unreasoning terror of the independence movements breaking out among many of the empire's heterogeneous peoples. At fault, too, was the outmoded Austrian monarchy and its stuffy bureaucrats who could not adjust to modern times and could not imagine what modern war would mean.

The war, in which the badly led Austrian armies suffered costly defeats, tore apart the old Austro-Hungarian Empire. With the blessings of the victorious Allies, the empire was partitioned to form three smaller nations—Czechoslovakia, Hungary and Austria itself. Other segments of the old empire were absorbed by Poland, Yugoslavia, Italy and Romania.

In some cases, as in the Czechoslovakia ruled by Thomas Masaryk, the new nations managed to create miniature Austro-Hungarian Empires of their own by including within their borders mutually hostile ethnic or racial groups. Later an Austrian named Adolf Hitler would make use of these frictions to break up and defeat some of these nations.

Meanwhile, Austria found itself a poor and shrunken thing. The great empire of 51 million people had become a small country of seven million. And it was burdened with a huge capital city of two million people whom it could not hope to feed. Most of the lines of normal economic development had been cut and economists and political scientists saw at once that this miserable land could not live. Austria was divided from its traditional granary, Hungary, and from much of the iron and coal needed to feed its industries; it was also overloaded with administrators left from the era when Vienna ruled more than seven times as many people. Even the Allied statesmen presiding over the carving up of the empire in 1919 shuddered at their work, France's great Georges Clemenceau being the first to call the new Austria just what it was—"leftovers."

This new Austria would be crowded on the north by Germany and Czechoslovakia, on the east by Hungary, on the south by Yugoslavia and Italy, and on the west by Switzerland. Nine provinces, each hotly jealous of its own local authority, were included. A federal Constitution that granted the various provinces a generous autonomy was adopted in 1920 as the first Austrian Republic stumbled into existence. It was shortly in a state of financial collapse, and a League of Nations loan was needed to put it back on its feet again. The League supervised Austria's finances until 1926 and then withdrew hoping that all was well. But it remained clear, especially to Austrians, that this situation could not endure.

ASIDE from its economic difficulties the Austrian Republic had no patriots. The country's three political *lager*, or camps, were not, as in other countries, rivals in the task of making a better Austrian Republic. It was clearly understood by everyone that if any of the three camps gained complete control it would end the Austrian Republic. The Socialist Reds (then called Social Democrats) wanted to make a Marxist workers' republic—a milder version of what was being constructed in Russia. The Conservative

A couple walks through the crisp snow along the Kärntnerstrasse, one of Vienna's liveliest shopping areas

Fresh pastries gleam on the counter of a Vienna "Konditorei.

A smartly dressed woman strides past a chic Vienna shop

Galleryites clap as singers take a bow at the Vienna State Opera.

With newly fallen snow muting the city's sounds, a woman pulls children on a sled along the banks of Vienna's Danube Canal.

Blacks (then called the Christian Socialists) wanted a corporate state—a milder form of what was taking shape in Mussolini's Italy. The "Great German" enthusiasts wished to turn the whole country over to Germany when the time became ripe.

By 1927 the three groups had private armies demonstrating against one another, the Socialist Schutzbund, the Conservative Heimwehr and the Nazi Brown Shirts. In January of that year the Schutzbund and Heimwehr clashed in the town of Schattendorf and an old man and a child were killed. Heimwehr men accused of the murders were acquitted on July 14, and on July 15 the Socialists burned out the Ministry of Justice in Vienna in riots that cost the lives of 85 in the crowds and four policemen. An uneasy peace was re-established, but the private forces continued their drills and soon Austria found itself playing a role far larger than its size in the weakened world's economic troubles.

BY 1931 Austria was again facing economic disaster. Just then, driven by a rising surge of nationalism, the Austrians and the Germans decided that one way out of the economic shackles imposed by the Versailles Treaty was a customs union. France announced that it would oppose this to the utmost, and two months later Vienna's Creditanstalt, a bank that controlled nearly 75 per cent of Austria's industry and was considered one of the best financial houses in Europe, suspended payments on foreign accounts. The resulting shock overwhelmed the Central European banking system, caused severe banking crises in Germany, Hungary and on down the Balkans, and put heavy stress on American, British, French, Dutch and Swiss banks as the Depression settled in heavier than ever.

In this atmosphere Engelbert Dollfuss, a very small man of very large conservative political passions, became Chancellor of Austria with a parliamentary majority of one vote. When Socialist Karl Renner, then serving as president of the Parliament, resigned after a long, hot debate, Dollfuss announced that the Parliament was unworkable anyway and thereafter he governed by emergency decree. In 1933 he made an alliance with Mussolini whereby Austria was to be protected by Italy and serve as a buffer zone between Italy and Germany. In 1934, having decided to crush the Socialists, he provoked their Schutzbund to arms and smashed them with the Conservatives' Heimwehr in four days of battle that took more than 1,000 lives.

Watching, bemused, were the Austrian Nazis. If it were all as easy as that, they thought, then they might as well have a crack at it themselves. Five months later they launched an attack, captured the chancellery, murdered Dollfuss and then were rounded up as the rest of their revolt failed. The murderers were executed—although later, when Hitler had taken Austria, monuments were raised in their memory.

Dollfuss' successor, Kurt von Schuschnigg, a studious and pious but authoritarian man, presided over the final years of Austrian independence, his only reliance the understanding with Italy. But Mussolini was now Hitler's ally, and in 1938 Nazi pressure forced Schuschnigg to visit Hitler at Berchtesgaden in Bavaria. There a shouting, raging Führer ordered Schuschnigg to suppress all evidence of Nazi plots, release all Nazis from Austrian jails and include a leading Austrian Nazi in his Cabinet. Schuschnigg gave in and returned to Austria. There he found members of his Government demanding *Anschluss,* that is, union with Germany. Desperate, Schuschnigg ordered a plebiscite in which the people could vote on whether they, too, wanted *Anschluss,* hoping that the answer would be "no" and that this popular reaction would strengthen his own hand. Hitler evidently also believed the answer would be "no" and sent his army across the border before the plebiscite could take place. Schuschnigg was marched off to join the Socialist leaders in a concentration camp. He emerged at war's end in 1945, to become eventually an American and a professor of political science at Roman Catholic St. Louis University in Missouri.

THE Austria that emerged from German domination at the end of World War II was almost exactly the Austria that had made such a mess of things in its first republican era—the same countryside, the same cities, the same natural resources, virtually the same political parties (although under slightly different names) and even many of the same personalities. But for all that, the atmosphere in this second-chance Austria is notably different from that of the first-chance republic.

For one thing Vienna has become a city of many haunting silences. In the gas ovens of the Nazis it lost much of its former laughter, warmth, love, bustle and fun, its exciting talk, big plans, and great and serious ideas. For this is the city where Sigmund

Freud worked out his theories on psychoanalysis, Gustav Mahler wrote his symphonies, Franz Werfel his novels, Stefan Zweig his biographies, Arthur Schnitzler his plays and novels, and Hugo von Hofmannsthal the plays that Richard Strauss set to music. It is the city Max Reinhardt turned into the leading center of German theater in all Europe. It was, in fact, the world capital of Jewish intellectual life. And now all this is gone. The 300,000 Jews who once did more than their share toward making Vienna a stimulating city are now less than 30,000 and they play nothing like their old role. Without its Jews, Vienna is a diminished city.

THIS the Austrians must live with. But the self-pity that came with the loss of an empire in 1918 no longer exists. The people grumble, but calmly, with an air of being able to count on themselves. The built-in conviction that this small country cannot live has given way to a growing belief that since Austria is alive after all it has been through, then it is at least as viable as Switzerland and Switzerland gets along on comparable terrain quite well.

And this second republic has in both the major parties politicians of ability and integrity, something the first republic generally lacked. They came into existence during the 10 long years of occupation when the common task was to get the country back from the victors, particularly the Russians. The Russians had all sorts of involved schemes to build themselves permanently right into the Austrian economic and political structure. For example, they evolved a proposal for a joint stock company to operate and share the produce of the Austrian oil wells, the Soviet shares to be based on Soviet rights to "German assets" as war reparations. Only by common action of the parties and a growing devotion to Austria as Austria could such plans be turned back.

Little by little Austrians of all political persuasions came to have a bursting pride in the late Dr. Leopold Figl, the Conservative Chancellor and/or Foreign Minister of the period, who tirelessly inveigled and schemed and plotted until he had the Russians completely *eingewickelt*, or bemused, and so won the 1955 State Treaty that ended the occupation. In the course of these negotiations this small but heroic man gave his name to an unofficial unit of liquid measurement, a *Figl* being the amount of alcohol necessary to drink a Russian diplomat quiet.

Austrians are too knowing a people to fool themselves about Russian susceptibility to Figlian charm. They know that the Russians signed the treaty because they believed that they, too, were gaining a lot. They gained a neutral area in mid-Europe and demonstrated to the Germans that when the proper time comes they will be willing to talk and bargain. Besides, in 1955 there was not much more to take out of Austria than they had already taken. The Austrians, dark-cloud watchers always, are also aware that there is a clause in the 1955 treaty forbidding a customs union with Germany. This means, of course, that they cannot join the Common Market—which is a customs union and includes Germany—without being accused by the Russians of violating the treaty's terms. Being barred from the Market threatens the Austrian economy since the prices of the goods they export to the Market (some 50 per cent of their export total) are raised by the duty the Market countries charge on everything coming into the Market from outside. Thus Austrian goods may be priced out of reach of their neighbors. Austria is trying to work out some way that it can become an associate member of the Market. In the meantime it belongs to the "Outer Seven," the British-led European Free Trade Association. This does not solve Austria's problem since only 20 per cent of its exports go to the Outer Seven nations.

Just the same, Austrian pride in the indefatigable Figl has somehow given the people more pride in themselves. It is good to be an Austrian. Austrians were heartily ready to agree with the late U.S. Secretary of State John Foster Dulles when he told them at the treaty-signing ceremonies in Vienna's Belvedere Palace on May 15, 1955: "So today the Austrian people can rejoice not because of what has been given them, but because of what they have won for themselves."

FOR FURTHER READING

Buschbeck, E. H., *Austria*. Oxford University Press, 1949.
Fodor, M. W., *South of Hitler*. Houghton Mifflin, 1939.
Gedye, G.E.R., *Betrayal in Central Europe*. Harpers, 1939.
Kohn, Hans, *The Habsburg Empire, 1804-1918*. D. Van Nostrand, 1961.
Nicolson, Harold, *The Congress of Vienna*. Viking Press, 1946.
Stoye, John, *The Siege of Vienna*. Holt, Rinehart and Winston, 1964.
Taylor, A.J.P., *The Habsburg Monarchy, 1809-1918*. Hamish Hamilton, London, 1948.

Finland

THE Finnish language, a mysterious and vowel-crammed tongue emanating from the Ural Mountains and the Volga River basin and linked obscurely with Hungarian and Estonian, has an almost untranslatable word, *"sisu,"* pronounced *"see-su."* Roughly, it means guts or courage, but it also means stamina, murderous obstinacy and sometimes sheer cussedness. It denotes the Finns' ability to live in icy darkness 51 days a year or to jump from the 212-degree heat of a sauna bath straight into a 40-degree lake. It celebrates the quality that enabled Finland to fight Russia twice in recent decades and then to remain independent—an achievement that Walter Lippmann has called "a political miracle." *Sisu* is the Finns' answer to a savagely harsh physical and political environment.

This northern republic, which is about the size of Italy and has approximately half Greater London's population, is a cold, inhospitable place. Geologically, it occupies probably the hardest land in Europe: granite gneiss and crystalline rock barely covered by shallow, infertile gravels and clays, topped in turn by snow for about 100 days every year. It has few important resources save great stands of pine, birch and spruce—the "green gold" that makes Finland the most forested land in Europe—and some copper. Severe killing frosts make farming perilous. Born to harsh climate, arid soil and isolation, the Finn is reserved, hard-working and independent, and lives with a bone-bred loneliness that he relieves by bouts of hard, dangerous drinking.

The origins of the Finns have always been something of a mystery, but many scholars nowadays believe that they migrated from the region of the upper Volga early in the Christian era. Arriving in what is now southwest Finland, they elbowed the indigenous Lapps into the inhospitable north and settled down.

There, history found them. That is, the Swedes did. Warlike and expansionist, Sweden spread to the east and came marching into Finland in 1155. The Swedes arrived supposedly to crusade for converts to Christianity but they stayed 654 years. It was, as occupations go, remarkably mild and successful. To the Russians across the Gulf of Finland, a Swedish-controlled Finland was an obvious cause for concern, but fortunately the Muscovites had to turn inward during the mid-13th Century to fight off the Mongols racing out of Asia. This gave the Swedes a respite, enabling them to treat Finland generously. Finland, in turn, blossomed with stable institutions.

Swedish nobles were awarded fiefs in Finland and became the country's ruling class. Strangely enough, the Swedes and the Finns got along with a minimum of friction. Further, the Swedish nobles, wanting a role in the affairs of the Government in Stockholm, got for themselves, and for Finland, a large measure of authority and self-rule. After 1362, representatives of Finland had a vote in electing Sweden's kings and a voice in Sweden's parliament. In 1397 Finland got its own currency and court of appeals, and in 1556 it became a grand duchy with, later, its own parliament. By the mid-17th Century, local rule rested in the hands of provincial meetings, a postal system was initiated, new towns were founded and agriculture was encouraged. Education burgeoned; as early as the years 1350 to 1450 Finland sent more students to Paris than any other northern area. In 1640 Finland got its first university, at Turku, later moved to Helsinki.

I T was not all lingonberry-smooth. In the 654 years of its occupation Sweden warred innumerable times with Russia, and in all these wars the Finns of the duchy fought loyally and at great cost. In addition, the Swedish royal habit of awarding Swedish nobles and generals generous tracts of Finnish soil reached enormous proportions in the 17th Century. By 1654 some 60 per cent of Finland was in the possession of Swedo-Finnish nobles, most of them absentee landlords. This, plus excessive taxation and war damage, made the independent Finnish yeomanry into tenant farmers. However, although the Finns occasionally dreamed of independence, they remained, on the whole, loyal to Sweden.

The greatest threat to Swedish rule of Finland was always, of course, Russia, and with the accession of Peter the Great the Russians were turning massively westward at last. In 1703 St. Petersburg (now Leningrad), Peter's magnificent new capital, was begun on the Baltic marshes. After that the absorption of nearby Finland into the Russian sphere was to become a major Russian objective, awaiting only the proper circumstance. The opportunity came in 1807. Napoleon, who was riding high in Europe, asked Sweden to join his Continental blockade against British shipping. Sweden's Gustavus IV, who detested Napoleon, refused. In revenge Napoleon plotted with Russia's Alexander I, promising him a free hand to annex Finland if only he would attack Sweden. In February 1808 Russia invaded. For five months 12,000 Finns held against five times as many Russians, then fell back. Sweden unaccountably failed to send effective aid and in September 1809 surrendered Finland unconditionally. Thus ended six centuries of shared destiny during which Finland achieved its unity, formed its boundaries and received the stamp of Western culture.

The day that Finland had feared had come; it was a conquered possession of Russia. But it was not that bad, at least not at first. Russia's Czar, Alexander I, was a strange and great man who combined

a belief in the divine right of kings with a faith in liberal objectives. Summoning the Diet of the Duchy of Finland, the Autocrat of All the Russias declared that he would rule Finland as a constitutional Grand Duke. He, whose word *was* the law in Russia, would respect the law in Finland; the Constitution would be preserved. Though Alexander ruled an empire of serfs, the Finnish peasants would be free.

The Finns, autonomous to a degree they had never dreamed possible, began to wonder what it meant to be a Finn. Many of them had a Swedish complex. The language and cultural patterns in the Government were Swedish. Among status seekers it was fashionable to be as Swedish as possible, while Finns who clung to Finnish ways and speech were scorned.

T HE growing class of intellectuals counterattacked, in Swedish, of course. The battle cry was given by journalist Adolf Ivar Arwidsson, himself an upper-class Swedo-Finn, who wrote: "Swedes we are not, Russians we can never be; let us therefore be Finns." The Saturday Circle, a group of scholars at Helsinki University who met Saturday evenings, took up the cause. One of them, Elias Lönnrot, a doctor, made it his task to copy down Finnish folk legends. Going from hut to hut, reciting parts of a folk poem, he teased peasants into continuing the recitation. Lönnrot once found a gnarled old farmer, blessed with an astounding memory, who kept him writing two days and part of a third. In 1835 Lönnrot, who thus in effect became Finland's Homer, published the *Kalevala*, the lengthy Finnish epic. The appearance of the *Kalevala* was like discovering a flag around which the Finns could rally; it gave them a sense of nationhood.

A second Saturday Circle member, poet Johan Ludvig Runeberg, directed the attention of the Swedish-speaking upper class to their own peasantry and heroes, writing of their homely virtues and courage in classic style. His *Tales of Ensign Stål*, recounting in poetry the heroism of Finnish troops against the Russian invaders of 1808 and 1809, became the nation's favorite reading (in Swedish, of course), and the dedicatory verse, set to music, is today Finland's national anthem. A third Circle member, philosopher-journalist Johan Vilhelm Snellman, crusaded in Swedish to make Finnish one of the national tongues. His efforts finally bore fruit when, in 1863, the Czar issued an edict which began the process, completed in 1919, of putting Finnish on a par with Swedish as the nation's legal languages.

In the world outside, monarchic fashions were changing. Under pressure everywhere, royalty was shifting from absolutism to constitutionalism. As Russia's monarchs gave under the pressure and then resisted, going from autocracy to liberalism and back, Finland's freedoms also went back and forth: considerable under Alexander I, they were diminished under his tough brother Nicholas, the "Iron Czar," and then enhanced again under gentle Alexander II, who reconvened Finland's Diet after a 54-year hiatus and allowed the duchy a separate currency, distinctive Army units and local self-government. This increased freedom and independence gave the Finns an unparalleled chance for internal development. Industry began elbowing aside landholding; in 1861 the Czar lifted all restrictions on lumbering, thus making the forests that cover 71 per cent of the land of enormous economic importance. Intricate waterway systems were constructed, based on Finland's numerous lakes and rivers, to bring the inland lumber to the sea for export. Plentiful water power prompted the expansion of the textile industry, especially at Tampere, which in time became the "Manchester of Finland" and its second city.

WHEN Alexander II, "the noblest of Finland's Grand Dukes," was killed by Russian revolutionaries in 1881, his embittered son, Alexander III, denounced "the constitutional lie and western ideas." But though reactionary, Alexander III was not stupid and confined himself largely to talk. *His* son, Nicholas II, was both reactionary and stupid, and joined the issue. He dissolved Finland's separate Army units, undermined the Diet and exiled a number of Finnish nationalists, and when more than 500,000 Finns petitioned him to honor the Constitution, he refused to receive their representatives.

Worse yet, Nicholas had posted N. I. Bobrikov to Helsinki as Governor-General. Utterly inflexible and blindly reactionary, Bobrikov began an all-out attack to wipe out Finnish separatism. He made Russian compulsory in the schools, Russified the civil service, and abolished freedom of speech and press. Bobrikov's career came to an abrupt end, however, when a shy, young Finnish bureaucrat named Eugen Schauman shot him down on the capitol steps and then killed himself. One year later,

when Russia's 1905 Revolution threatened to depose the Czar, and when the Finns walked out in a crippling general strike, a terrified Nicholas annulled Bobrikov's decrees and, moving further toward liberalism than anyone before, changed Finland's outmoded Diet to a single chamber elected by the vote of every Finn over the age of 24. Even women got the right to vote, a first in Europe. However, about 1908 the Czar, once more feeling secure, began to take these freedoms back, and a virtual dictatorship was set up. The Finns, for their part, began to make clandestine plans for a rising to free Finland.

THE 1914 war was the break the Finns had waited for. The Czar used the war to complete Russification; Diet meetings were suspended and special taxes imposed. The Finns used the war to prepare for revolution. Helped by nationalist university professors, 2,000 young Finns smuggled themselves into Germany, where they got military training, joined the German Army as the 27th Battalion of Prussian Jägers and waited for a chance to fight the real enemy.

The chance came with the Russian Revolution. On December 6, 1917, Finland's Diet proclaimed the country's independence, and on January 4, 1918, the Soviet Government formally recognized the right of the Finns to do so. The Soviets, however, did not pull back from Finland the 40,000 Russian troops stationed there. These troops allied themselves with the Finnish socialists, who, like the conservative "Whites," were plotting to seize the government. The nationalist Civil Guard began secretly to lay plans to drive the Russians out. A left-wing "Red Guard" of workers and poor peasants, plus the Russian soldiers, made chaotic counterpreparations. The Red Guards seized Helsinki and proclaimed Finland a Socialist Worker's Republic. The Whites set up their own government at Vaasa and the stage was set for civil war.

Led by Carl Gustaf Mannerheim, an aristocratic Swedo-Finn, the Whites attacked the Reds, though outnumbered 2 to 1. The disciplined Jägers returned from Germany in February to instruct and lead the conservative forces. Two companies of Swedish volunteers joined up, and toward the end Mannerheim was forced to ask for a German expeditionary force which helped complete the rout of the brave but uncoordinated Reds. The four-month civil war was

A Finnish housewife fixes supper in a snug but plain kitchen.

over but it left a bitter taste. Some 24,000 from both sides had died, and 73,915 Reds were imprisoned. As many as a quarter of the prisoners died either before firing squads or from starvation. Technically it was an excellent repression, perhaps too successful, for it split Finland almost permanently. Years later a U.S. reporter found not only that there is a large bloc of Communist votes in Finland, but also that many of them are cast by well-to-do families because a father or grandfather was killed by the Whites.

But Finland's troubles were far from over. The new Government of the Whites was so pro-German that it was all but giving the newly freed country to the Kaiser, and had even asked the German ruler to appoint one of his sons king of Finland. The cautious Kaiser instead offered his brother-in-law, Prince Frederich Karl of Hesse. But as it turned out, Germany's World War I armies were on their last legs and Prince Frederich Karl was still studying Finnish when Germany signed the armistice. Mannerheim, who was pro-Allied, replaced the discredited pro-Germans. A republican constitution was soon drawn up and a Progressive was elected president. After more than 750 years Finland had at last won democratic independence.

Though the Finns find it hard to agree among themselves—this nation of uncompromising individualists requires seven political parties to express its discordant views—most of them agreed in 1918 that what had to be done first was to give land to the have-nots. The Government bought up unused land, forced large estates to sell uncultivated holdings and began selling farms of 25 to 50 acres apiece to tenants. By 1935 some 31,000 new farms had been created, two million additional acres had been added to Finland's cultivated area, and the tenancy problem had been materially reduced. This enlightened land policy was a powerful force for stability. So were cooperatives. In 1899 Dr. Hannes Gebhard, a lecturer at Helsinki University, founded the Pellervo Society, named after the Finnish god of fertility. Pellervo flourished and in 1903 there were 189 various cooperative societies. By 1961 Finland had almost 4,000 cooperatives with 1.5 million members, a third of the population.

Finland is a country of slowly won victories, of hardships overcome with bitter work, of small farms hacked out of wilderness by backbreaking effort. There are no fast killings, wheeler-dealing or speculating. Occasionally, however, a certain intemperance in the Finnish nature has showed up in politics. In the 1930s, as the worldwide Depression touched Finland and anxiety about the future increased, Finland produced a substantial Fascist movement. For a while it had the support of the president, the Army and even parliament, and seemed irresistible. It began in 1929 in Lapua, a country village, when farmers beat up and threw out some young red-shirted Communists who had had the temerity to hold a meeting there. Suddenly the idea of a crusade to stamp out Communism, Socialism and all other "ungodly" isms took hold, especially among clergymen, military leaders and industrialists. The black-shirted Lapua Movement was born, with a credo called the Law of Lapua—the right of people to act illegally if necessary against the leftists.

FINNS still call the summer of 1930 "the Lapua Summer." The Law of Lapua produced beatings, murders and even crude deportations to Russia. Finland's venerable first President, Kaarlo Juho Ståhlberg, was considered too democratic by the Lapuans and was kidnaped and almost forced over the border. When the Cabinet did not move fast enough against the Communists, the Lapuans forced it to resign. When the Lapuans made a march on Helsinki, the Government cooperated, giving the "marchers" a 50 per cent reduction on the Government railway. A new parliament compliantly

Hauled by a reindeer, a Laplander brings groceries home to his snow-mantled farm in the bleak far-northern region of Finland.

passed anti-Communist legislation, and the Lapuans demanded more. They threatened to murder the candidate of the Social Democrats in the 1931 presidential election and coerced the electoral college into defeating him by two votes.

However, although the conservative won, the Lapuans lost. The new president whom they had helped elect, while rightist, believed in law and refused to accede to Lapuan demands that he dissolve his Cabinet. In late February 1932 the Lapuans ordered their men to mobilize with four days' rations and prepare for another march on Helsinki, whereupon the president mobilized his generals: "Not even one armed man may come . . . to the capital city. For this you generals will be responsible." Like the McCarthyites in the U.S. later, the Lapuans had overreached themselves. After a tense week they backed off and in March 1932 were themselves illegalized, to be replaced by an insignificant Fascist party, the IKL.

The Russians gazing on from nearby were concerned over the fanatical anti-Communism shown by both the Finnish High Command and the Government. Lapuan proclamations foretelling the glorious day "when the Ural Mountains must serve as the eastern boundary line of Finland" were carefully noted. So was information that Finnish and Polish Army chiefs had held secret *pourparlers* for coordinated action. Russo-Finnish relations improved in the mid-1930s, but then the Hitlerian danger

aggravated Russian unease, and in March 1939 the Soviets asked for a 30-year lease on four islands in the Gulf of Finland to protect Leningrad and the Kronstadt naval base. Mannerheim, Chairman of the Defense Council, urged the Finns to accept. Finland's Government refused. Then, in October 1939, having swallowed Estonia, Latvia and Lithuania, the Soviets came back with increased demands that would have required Finland to yield up some 1,000 square miles of territory, in return for which Russia would cede twice as much territory in Karelia. This time, when negotiations failed, Russia's foreign minister said: "It will now be for the soldiers to negotiate."

On November 30, 1939, Soviet planes bombed Helsinki and war began in the hardest winter in 30 years. To everyone's surprise Finland stopped the invading Russians with enormous losses. The whole world gasped out its admiration for heroic little Finland, and Britain and France sent Finland some 250 planes and 600 cannon, and millions of rounds of ammunition. Despite all the noisy sympathy, the Finns were in a vise and they knew it. Mannerheim coldly counted his supplies—aviation gasoline for one month, heavy shells for 19 days, cartridges for two more months—and urged negotiations. In January 1940 secret meetings began in Stockholm with the Soviet Ambassador, Madame Kollontay, but the negotiations dragged and in February crack troops replaced the chewed-up Soviet units and began smashing through the Karelian Isthmus. On March 12, 1940, on the 104th day of hostilities, having suffered 48,000 casualties, the Finns surrendered.

Finland naturally had to give the Russians more than they had originally demanded, ceding more than 10 per cent of the country's territory. But within a month the Finns were resolutely rebuilding, relocating 450,000 people who elected to quit the ceded area and starting new farms and industrial plants. The resettlement was only one third complete, however, when the ill-fated Finns again became embroiled in a war, this one World War II.

The pause between wars had lasted 15 months. During this time Helsinki twisted and turned, trying for viable defensive arrangements, and ended up boxed in worse than before. Germany was now turning on its Soviet ally, and so mutual enmity toward Russia drew Helsinki to Berlin. On August 17, 1940, Finland's prime minister, acting on his own, agreed to let German troops and matériel pass through Finland, and by the end of September Nazi troops were, in fact, moving through the country. The process acquired momentum. In May 1941 Finnish staff officers conferred in Germany with the Nazi High Command; on June 15 the Germans took command of the defense of northern Finland. When, seven days later, Germany attacked Russia, the Soviets unavoidably began shelling German units on Finnish soil, and the Finns, equally unavoidably, declared war on Russia.

THOUGH fighting on the same side as Germany, the Finns insisted that what they called their "Continuation War" was quite separate from the German conflict. For example, Germany's request that Finland turn over its 1,500 Jews to the Nazis was summarily rejected. Marshal Mannerheim at first refused to join the Germans in attacking Leningrad, concentrating instead on regaining the lost territories, although later Finnish troops did advance into Russia as far as the Murmansk railroad. By early 1943, after the German catastrophe at Stalingrad, a number of Finnish statesmen began to fear that they had thrown in their lot with the losing side, and the Government, seeking a way out, once more started talks with Madame Kollontay.

The situation was desperate. If Finland persisted in trying to reach a separate peace, Berlin would cut off all help and the Russians would break through

and dictate their own terms. On the other hand, the Finns did not want to go down with Germany to ruinous defeat. So, with Mannerheim taking over the presidency, talks were reopened with the Soviets. Russia's terms were severe but they were accepted, and on September 4, 1944, Finland quit its second war with the Soviets. In addition to territory and reparations, the peace conditions required Finland to expel all German troops by September 15.

THUS commenced a new and bitter episode in Finland's fight for freedom. The 200,000 Germans refused to go, and it took 52,000 Finns seven months to battle the excellently equipped Nazis out of Finland and into German-occupied Norway. As they retreated, the Nazis laid waste the whole of Lapland, systematically burning 25,000 buildings and 130 schools, destroying 700 bridges, sowing land mines in woods and fields, poisoning the wells, even cutting down flagpoles. This extra display of organized Teutonic fury cost Finland an additional 764 dead; but on April 27, 1945, the Germans were out and the Finns' five-year nightmare of war ended.

The two wars with Russia killed 85,000 Finns and left another 50,000 wounded or disabled. The country also lost 13 per cent of its area and 11 per cent of its production facilities. Additionally, the Russians handed the Finns the stiffest reparations bill in recorded history, about 11 per cent of the national income for six years. And if two thirds of it had to be paid in ships, cable and heavy metal products for which Finland had little or no manufacturing capability, that was Finland's worry.

Starting almost from scratch, the Finns had to supply such items as 578 vessels, complete with crockery for the galleys and rubber boots for the crews. During that terrible first year, *sisu*, mountainous taxes, and Swedish and American credits brought the Finns through. By 1946 the Russians realized the Finns' good intentions and eased up: they extended the pay-off period from six to eight years. In the final year, 1953, the Russians renounced half of the remaining balance. Oddly enough, the Finns derived some benefits from this long ordeal. The country emerged with a greatly enlarged metalworking industry and with twice the former number of shipyards. The 1944 armistice with the Russians, which limits Finland to a very small Army, Navy and Air Force, has left the country's budget free of the sort of armaments bill that cripples many nations.

After the wars it was obvious that a new course had to be followed. A veteran statesman, J. K. Paasikivi, became president and put Finland on the Paasikivi Line—that is, forget revenge and honor the treaty to the letter. His successor, Urho Kekkonen, elected in 1956, if anything, extended the Paasikivi Line. During one five-year period he called on Chairman Nikita Khrushchev in Moscow every year, probably setting a modern record for next-door visiting by a head of state. Kekkonen hunted with Khrushchev and gave him sauna equipment. On Kekkonen's 60th birthday Khrushchev traveled to Helsinki to celebrate with him, and on Khrushchev's 70th birthday, who should turn up in Moscow but the Finnish President. Some Finns and many Westerners feel Kekkonen went too far. However, the Paasikivi-Kekkonen Line showed some success. In 1956, for example, the Porkkala enclave, 20 miles from Helsinki, "leased" to Russia for 50 years, was returned to Finland.

DESPITE all their hardships, and despite the fact that their living standard is adequate but far from lavish, the condition of the civilizing amenities in Finland today is superb. Finland has an extensive social security system and illiteracy is almost nonexistent. The sale of books per capita is the world's highest. (The average Finn buys four hardcover books a year; the average American one tenth of one hard-cover book.) The Finns also have 40 professional theaters, and local amateur groups give as many as 20,000 performances a year. Composer Jean Sibelius received a pension for most of his life so that he could write music without having to worry about money.

In addition the Finns take great pride in making their country neat and handsome. There is a great elegance in architecture, partly inspired by Helsinki's great railroad station, designed by Eliel Saarinen, which was completed in 1914. (Saarinen's son, Eero, became a leading American architect.) Architectural competition is constant, and Finnish cities esteem their individual architectural excellence. Instead of sprawling in untidy suburbs, Helsinki, a gracious, quiet city of 500,000, has been girdling itself with satellite towns, each placed in a generous-sized site of natural beauty and providing for 8,000 to 15,000 inhabitants. Finnish furniture, fabrics and ceramics are striking and original in form, design and coloring. The plates, saucers, casseroles and urns made by Finland's world-famed Arabia pottery factory are perhaps unequaled for sheer strength combined with beauty.

So the Finns are still a free, creative people—though less free than before. Elections are free, but anti-Russian politicians have been shunted aside and, as though by mutual consent, do not run for high party or Government posts. The press is free, but when a Finnish reporter once described his country's elongated currency as "dollar-type" his editor blue-penciled the phrase, explaining: "We don't want to be needlessly offensive to the Russians." President Kekkonen once said: "We live on fine distinctions."

One has to respect the Finns' judgment, without accepting it entirely. In some 800 years the Finns have won over the glaciers, the forests, the Swedes, the Russians, the Germans, the native Communists, the native Fascists, crushing reparations and even exaggerated *sisu*. It is, in a way, a visible miracle. If on December 6 one stands overlooking Helsinki's Great Square, one sees coming over the snow, in complete silence, long lines of students carrying torches. On and on they come by the thousands, muted, noiseless. There are no bands, no chants, no drums, only the slow onrush of solemn young people bearing several dozen white Finnish flags, one for each year of independence. Unregimented, they march steadily until they mass in the Great Square, still holding their banners, filling the city with a silent, animal alertness; and then, like a crash of muffled thunder into the frosty gloom, they begin to sing Finland's anthem: "Our land, our land, our native land."

FOR FURTHER READING

Jutikkala, Eino, *A History of Finland.* Frederick A. Praeger, 1962.

Mazour, Anatole G., *Finland Between East and West.* Van Nostrand Co., 1956.

Platt, Raye R., ed., *Finland and Its Geography.* Duell, Sloan and Pearce, 1955.

Rintala, Marvin, *Three Generations: The Extreme Right Wing in Finnish Politics.* Indiana University Publications, 1962.

Rosvall, Toivo, *Finland: Land of Heroes.* E. P. Dutton, 1940.

Strode, Hudson, *Finland Forever.* Harcourt, Brace and Co., 1952.

Wuorinen, John H., *A History of Finland.* Columbia University Press, 1965.

Liechtenstein

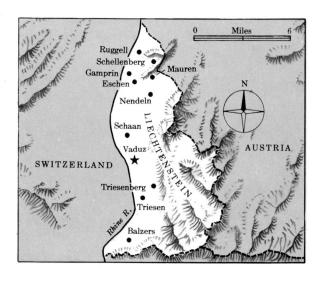

A MAN with a nostalgia for the "good old days" might well find the sovereign state of Liechtenstein a paradise on earth. The tiny 61-square-mile principality, tucked between Austria and Switzerland, spares its 18,000 citizens the traumas induced by billboards and superhighways, radio stations and airports. At the same time the last survivor of the Holy Roman Empire's 343 states spares its people such banes as poverty and slums.

If somewhat lacking in excitement—Liechtenstein has no famous men and plays no role in world affairs—the country's hills and valleys are virtually free of crime, unemployment and political dissension. The majority of its well-clothed and well-fed German-speaking people now earn their living in light industry (most of it postdating World War II) that produces artificial sausage skins, midget calculating machines, needles and false teeth. But 12 per cent are farmers and the tone of the land remains pastoral.

The farmers produce corn, honey and wine, but they are primarily concerned with dairy cattle. In the capital, Vaduz, a city of 3,700 nestled between the Rhine and the towering Castle Vaduz, the traffic is stopped for half an hour each morning and evening as cows are driven through. In the spring and autumn the cows graze in the *Rheintal*, the lowlands; in the summer they are driven to high mountain pastures called *Alpen*. When the cows are brought down in September, the peasants still follow the old Liechtensteinian tradition of honoring the cow in each herd that has given the most milk by decking it out with a broad leather collar, flowers, silver hearts, a big bell with a silver clapper, a three-legged milking stool fixed upside down between the horns, and brightly colored cockades and streamers.

The current state of Liechtenstein dates from 1719, when Emperor Charles VI of the Holy Roman Empire gave the land to a Viennese aristocrat named Liechtenstein, who thereupon became Prince Johann-Adam von Liechtenstein and gave the country his name. The current reigning Prince, Franz Joseph II, 12th of his line, lives in Castle Vaduz, where he keeps his $150 million collection of old masters, one of the most valuable private art collections in the world. One of the 10 richest men in Europe, Franz Joseph has been head of state since 1938, ruling with the assistance of an elected Chief of Government and a unicameral parliament in which two middle-of-the-road parties are represented. A neutral since the Austro-Prussian war of 1866, the country has a police force of only 22 men and no army. Its diplomatic and consular representation, coinage and customs are handled by Switzerland. But an important source of revenue comes from printing its own postage stamps, which are favorites of philatelists.

Austere Castle Vaduz is the home of Liechtenstein's ruler.

Andorra

ANDORRA is a land of "nos": no currency, no income tax, no military conscription, no customs inspection, no newspapers, no railroads, no divorces, no lawyers practicing in court—in fact, no legal code—and no trouble balancing its yearly budget, which somehow manages to exceed $800,000.

What Andorra does have is an august setting high in the eastern Pyrenees on the Spanish-French border; thousands of sheep, cattle, horses and tourists; and ruddy, energetic natives who happily exploit the larceny in their natures by smuggling.

Andorra is an oddity: it is one of the few landlocked free ports in the world. No duty is charged on most goods bought there, and thus the profits from importing duty-free Swiss watches or French cars and then smuggling them across the border to sell in other European countries at much higher prices are substantial. In the old days the Andorran Government used to sell the rights to smuggle, but now it is a freelance undertaking.

Tourists, particularly since the early 1950s, have flocked to Andorra. Some 800,000 visitors a year avail themselves of the low prices of merchandise and the dry, cool summer weather or the skiing in the winter.

About 190 square miles in size, Andorra has a population of some 11,000, only 4,000 of whom are Andorran citizens. All of the citizens are Catholic, and Catalan, as spoken in neighboring Spanish Catalonia, is their native tongue. By way of business, Andorra has two radio stations, seven banks, three ski lifts, more than 70 hotels and inns, and a leaf-tobacco processing plant. Most of the natives, when not engaging in their smuggling forays, are farmers who use every square inch of the country's nearly vertical fields. Some 25,000 head of sheep teeter on Andorra's mountain pastures, as do 3,000 cattle and 1,000 horses.

Andorra is still a medieval state. Since 1278 it has been under the joint sovereignty of "coprinces": the Bishop of Urgel (in Spain) and the ruler of France.

Newlyweds walk along a path in one of Andorra's small towns.

Most governmental business, however, is done by the Andorrans themselves through an elected 24-member General Council. Ancient laws and customs make the head of the house the center of Andorran life. He has the right to appoint his main heir who then inherits three fourths of his estate. The disinherited usually emigrate to France or Spain. Such customs tend to keep the population static and citizenship in Andorra exclusive.

Andorra has gone its own way for hundreds of years, too small and isolated to be worth conquering. But its French and Spanish rulers do exact their price. Each year the Bishop of Urgel receives from Andorra $11.50, plus 12 hams, 12 chickens and 12 Andorran cheeses. The President of France is given a straight $2.50 and no food.

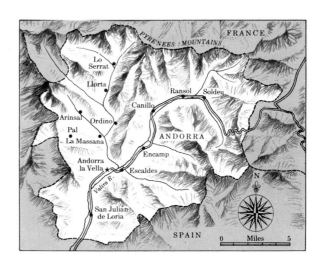

San Marino

ONE reason that San Marino, the world's oldest republic, has remained unmolested through the centuries is that not everyone can find it. An invading army in the 16th Century lost the little mountaintop republic in the fog. The troops searched and searched and when the fog lifted they were too tired to attack. Even on a clear day it is not easy to locate San Marino. Much of its 24 square miles is protected and hidden by Mount Titano, which rises above the plain of Romagna in northeastern Italy. Its main city, also called San Marino, nestles on the 2,438-foot-tall mountain, its three medieval watchtowers resembling extensions of the rugged cliffs.

Legend has it that San Marino was founded by a Christian stonecutter named Marino, who fled the persecutions of the Roman Emperor Diocletian in the Fourth Century A.D. Whatever its origin, the little colony was evolving a republican constitution by about 1000 A.D., and it has remained a republic to this day. The country, known officially as the Most Serene Republic of San Marino, is governed by a Grand Council of 60 members, elected by secret ballot and presided over by two Regents chosen from the Council by its members.

The estimated 17,000 citizens of San Marino depend on tourists and stamps for the money to sustain their independence. About two million tourists visit the country each year, usually just for an afternoon walk along the narrow streets of the capital and to mail fistfuls of postcards bearing the stamps of San Marino. The tiny nation also has a few other businesses: wine making, stonecutting and ceramics. Its fields produce grapes and other fruits and corn.

A crowd gathers in San Marino as a Government is installed.

Other less orthodox ways have been tried for raising the money to balance San Marino's five-million-dollar annual budget. The country was rented to 20th Century-Fox to make the film *The Prince of Foxes*. Although it is 12 miles from the Adriatic Sea, San Marino attempted unsuccessfully in the late 1950s to open a naval register for ships wanting flags of convenience. Mythical titles are also for sale in San Marino, several thousand dollars establishing the buyer as the duke of a local hill.

Usually peaceful in politics, San Marino caused something of a sensation in 1945 when it became the only country west of the Iron Curtain to be controlled by Communists. The Communist majority in San Marino's Council was not militantly Marxist and lost control in 1957 when the Christian Democrats took over.

San Marino may be small and easy for foreigners to take lightly, but the country's Government does not: ridicule of San Marino is a crime punishable by 20 days in jail or a fine.

Monaco

Monaco nestles between the French Maritime Alps and the sea.

MONACO, which once flourished because aristocrats bet fortunes at its gaming tables, now balances its budget through tourism, light industry and postage stamps. Before World War I the fabled casino at Monte Carlo (one of the three sections into which Monaco is divided) accounted for 75 per cent of the country's income, but the casino today brings in barely 4 per cent of Monaco's revenue. It is the yearly two million tourists that provide 40 per cent of Monaco's money. This tourist boom started with the wedding in 1956 of the reigning Prince Rainier III to movie actress Grace Kelly and shows no signs of abating.

Less than a square mile in area—and the smallest principality in Europe—Monaco lies on the beautiful shore where the French Maritime Alps plunge into the Mediterranean Sea. Some 22,000 persons live in Monaco, though only 3,500 of them are citizens. The citizens pay no income tax or death duties. The tax laws for even ordinary residents are liberal and attract firms to open offices in Monaco.

Monaco's light industries include plants that produce beer, plastics and precision instruments. There are also many publishers and printers. The value collectors have attached to Monaco's postage stamps has proved an unexpected boon. The wedding of Prince Rainier and Princess Grace, for example, cost Monaco $450,000—but a stamp commemorating the occasion brought in $512,000.

Always an advantageous, sheltered port, Monaco has been ruled for more than 660 years by a Genoese seafaring family, the Grimaldis. In 1297 François (The Spiteful) Grimaldi captured the harbor's fort by pretending to be a friar seeking a place to sleep. Monaco has been an independent nation ever since François' artful arrival, except for the period from 1793 to 1814 when France controlled the country. Although Monaco is only four miles from the Italian border and the Grimaldis are Genoese, French is the local language, the French franc the currency.

Monaco's well-trimmed gardens, luxury hotels and fine shops have always drawn admirers. But it was the gambling casino, built on the site of a garbage dump in 1863 by one of Prince Rainier's ancestors, Charles III, that began the mass migrations to Monaco. Named by Prince Charles for himself, Monte Carlo became the shimmering symbol of Victorian opulence. Queen Victoria herself, while passing through Monaco during a Riviera sojourn, remained closed in her coach to protest against the gambling. But her jaunty son, who later became King Edward VII, was well known at the casino, and his exploits were not confined to gambling. Only J. P. Morgan was disappointed with Monte Carlo: the 12,000-franc ($636) betting limit was too small to interest him.

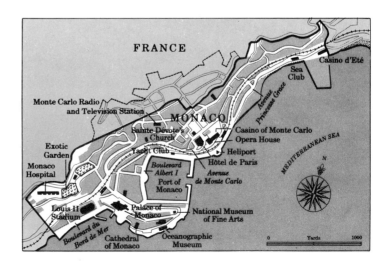

Vatican City

VATICAN CITY, surrounded on all sides by the Italian capital city of Rome, is a tiny, independent state that serves as both the spiritual and administrative center of the vast and ancient Roman Catholic Church. Located on the site of the Emperor Nero's circus, where many early Christians were martyred, it has been a center of Christianity since the first church named for St. Peter—who was the first Bishop of Rome—was erected there in the Fourth Century. Its present magnificent Basilica of St. Peter, built during the Renaissance, is, in effect, the center, or focus, of the worldwide Church.

As old as the papacy is, Vatican City has been an independent state only since 1929, when it was created by the Lateran Treaty. This treaty, so named because it was negotiated in Rome's Lateran Palace, was designed to resolve an awkward situation created in 1870 when King Victor Emmanuel II, the ruler of the newly unified Italian nation, seized Rome, which had for centuries been governed by the pope. Adding insult to injury, Victor Emmanuel moved into the Quirinal Palace, which had been the residence of the popes since the 17th Century. The then

Pope, Pius IX, retreated to the Vatican, announced that he considered himself a prisoner, refused to acknowledge the legality of the King's Government and rejected all offers of indemnity. Pope Pius' successors followed the same unbending course, and in the eyes of millions of Catholics the Italian King stood convicted as an outlaw and a usurper.

The Lateran Treaty resolved this dilemma. In it the Church acknowledged the Kingdom of Italy (and any successor governments) as the legitimate authority in Rome and in all of Italy. In return the Italian Government recognized a 108.7-acre enclosed triangle of churches, palaces, museums and gardens on the west bank of the Tiber River as the free and independent state of Vatican City, thus relieving the popes of all allegiance to Italy or subservience to the ruling House of Savoy.

Also recognized as parts of the state of Vatican City were certain important churches and palaces in or near Rome. Among them were the Lateran Palace itself (now a museum) and the nearby Basilica of St. John Lateran, which is the cathedral church of Rome. Others are the basilicas of Santa Maria Maggiore and St. Paul's Outside the Walls, the palace of San Callisto at the foot of the Janiculum hill, and the papal summer residence at Castel Gandolfo, south of Rome.

Once the treaty was approved, Vatican City assumed the functions of an independent nation. Administratively it was placed in the care of a layman governor and an advisory council. Foreign diplomats, including one from Italy, were received, and the papal State Secretariat sent its nuncios into all parts

Vatican City is dominated by the tall dome of St. Peter's. The Sistine Chapel and the celebrated Vatican museums are to its left.

of the world. The Vatican issued papal passports to its citizen population, minted its own coins and issued its own postage stamps. A Catholic daily, the *Osservatore Romano,* became the voice of Vatican City, and a powerful radio station was built by Guglielmo Marconi himself so that the pope might talk to the world. The Vatican also established a civil and criminal court, although most cases originating in Vatican City wind up in the Italian courts. The long-established ecclesiastical courts of the Church of course continued to operate.

The Vatican also created its own armed forces, part of which is the famous Swiss Guard that dates back to 1505. The Guard is made up of young Catholic men recruited in Switzerland who, dressed in colorful Renaissance uniforms, both attend the pope and stand guard at the main gates of the Vatican.

ASIDE from being the small center of a very large religion, the Vatican is most noteworthy for being one of the world's greatest treasure houses of art and scholarship. Fully half of Vatican City's area is given over to formal gardens of extraordinary beauty. Much of the remainder contains long, three- and four-story structures built with open galleries around courtyards. Into these buildings are packed, with a notable lack of clutter, not only the administrative machinery of the city and Church but also the oldest and still one of the chief public libraries of Europe, the entirely separate Vatican archives, and a whole series of museums, many of them of major importance. Among these museums is the Museo Pio-Clementino of classical antiquities in the Belvedere Courtyard. This collection includes such great examples of Greek sculpture as the *Apollo of Belvedere,* the *Belvedere Torso* and the *Laocoön.* The Vatican also includes the Braccio Nuovo collection and the museums of Egyptian and Etruscan art.

But the museums are only a small part of the artistic wealth of the Vatican; it blazes forth on the walls everywhere. Some of the greatest names of Renaissance art—Raphael, Michelangelo, Botticelli and Ghirlandaio—left examples of their genius here, as did that master of the Baroque period, Giovanni Bernini. Greatest of the works in the Vatican, and perhaps anywhere else, is the vast fresco that Michelangelo painted on the vaulted ceiling of the Sistine Chapel. This heroic work, which took Michelangelo four years to complete, is acknowledged to be one of the world's greatest masterpieces. In addition to it Michelangelo did several other works for the Vatican: the *Last Judgment,* also in the Sistine Chapel; the *Conversion of St. Paul* and the *Martyrdom of St. Peter* in the Pauline Chapel; and a number of sculptures. He served as chief architect for St. Peter's, designed its great dome and saw the work completed to the top of the drum before he died.

Nearly the equal of Michelangelo as a painter and as a contributor to the Vatican was Raphael, who was also a chief architect at St. Peter's until his untimely death of a fever. Raphael converted several rooms over the Borgia Apartments into a monument of Renaissance art, painting tremendous murals depicting the philosophers of Greece and the triumph of religion. On the ceiling are allegorical figures representing Law, Philosophy, Poetry and Theology. And in the Logge next door he covered the walls with frescoes of Biblical scenes, sometimes called "Raphael's Bible."

The third of the great contributors to the Vatican was Bernini, who executed the immense bronze canopy over the High Altar in St. Peter's and the all-embracing colonnades that flank the great piazza in front of the Basilica.

To see all these artistic wonders, to attend Church services, to see the pope and receive his blessing come vast throngs, especially on holy days such as Christmas and Easter. On these occasions Vatican City proves that it has the same crowd and traffic problems as other modern states. It also demonstrates its power, not in size certainly, nor armament, but as the spiritual center of a powerful faith.

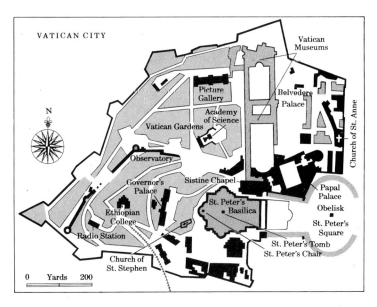

Iran

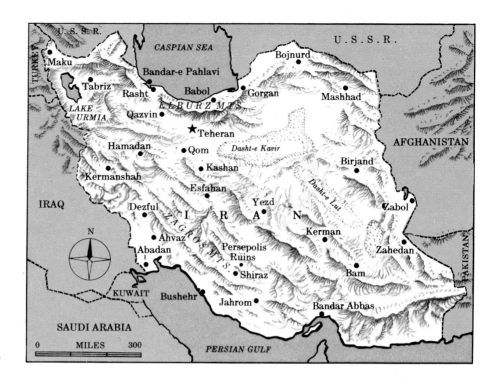

CLIO, the goddess of history, has long granted Iran a major role in her drama. Situated on the strategically important Middle Eastern land bridge linking Asia, Africa and Europe, Iran established the world's first true empire in the Sixth Century B.C., then lost it, and then won it back again. In the course of this, Iran invented the art of empire, that collection of political skills and dirty tricks that any power requires to rule over vast regions of the earth containing many different peoples. In return, down the long roll of the centuries, fierce warriors from all corners of the globe—Alexander of Macedon, Egypt's Ptolemies, cruel Roman and Byzantine emperors, and the merciless Mongols—have come to wreak their violences on Iran, until in many epochs the art of being Iranian was skill in keeping safely out of sight.

Thus while great poets have sung of gentle things in Iran, and philosophers have taught profound things, and inspired people have created civilizing things (not the least of them the luscious peach), most of this was done amidst the clangors of wars, invasions and massacres. There is little catastrophic in the chronicles of man that has not also happened in Iran. Even the Garden of Eden, where the whole catastrophe is said to have begun, is believed to have been located somewhere in Iran's neighborhood.

Oddly enough, Iran is a country that seems to brood in a deep peace. It is a land of scenic grandeur, of long vistas across blazing deserts and of distant, deep-blue mountain ranges. About the size of the United States east of the Mississippi, Iran is mainly contained in a great, irregular V of mountains formed by the Elburz Mountains tumbling across the north and the Zagros Mountains curving through the west and south. To the west of the Zagros range,

down toward the Persian Gulf, lie the incredibly rich oil deposits (the country all but floats on oil) that have fueled the battle fleets of Britain in two world wars, turned the industrial wheels of Europe in peace and brought Iran no end of trouble—and many good things, too.

In the east there are more hills, although they are less mountain ranges than climbing uplands, barren and bleak, where in June the "wind of 120 days" moans alive and with implacable force parches the landscape well into the autumn.

Two low mountain ranges, only faintly resembling the mighty outer bastions, together with some short spurs and shallow valleys, crisscross the inside of the great V, capturing enough clouds and producing enough water to sustain an inner group of oases, farm villages, and such towns as Kerman, Yezd and Qom. But the greater part of the land inside the great mountains is desert over which camel trains move with majestic grace much as they did in the days of Cyrus the Great.

Many of the older cities of Iran—Shiraz, home of poets, gardens and wine; Esfahan, most beautiful of all, and now a center of industry—are on the inner sides of the outer mountain ranges and contain the bones of even older cities. Under Murgab is Pasargadae, the Emperor Cyrus' ceremonial capital in the Sixth Century B.C., whence Cyrus marched on Babylon. And there is Ecbatana, now called Hamadan,

nce the capital of ancient Persia, Persepolis lies in ruins today.

which dates from the 12th Century B.C. and, together with Susa and Babylon, served the Emperor Darius as a working capital.

Two areas of Iran are outside the mountain walls. One is the hot, dry seacoast along the Persian Gulf and Gulf of Oman. In this region dates are grown, packed and exported, but the area of greatest economic importance is the mud flats of Abadan, where the old Anglo-Persian Oil Company, schemed up by Winston Churchill in 1909 when he was converting the British Navy from coal power to oil, built the enormous refinery and the tanker-loading facilities that have brought foreign armies storming into Iran during both of this century's world wars.

THE second area outside the mountains is the Caspian seacoast, the only place in Iran where water is plentiful and the source of some of the finest fruits and nuts in the world—apples, peaches, apricots, grapes, plums, lemons, limes and lovely melons; almonds, pistachios and hazelnuts. And from its end of the Caspian, Iran takes the sturgeon from which comes much of the caviar that the rest of the world assumes is from Russia. The Russians themselves buy a great deal of it.

More then two million of Iran's estimated 22 million people live in the capital, Teheran, which is in the southern foothills of Iran's northern mountain range. This is an imposing city (most of it built since the 1920s) of wide boulevards, impressive palaces and Government buildings, fine shops, movie houses, theaters, a university, newspapers, and a bubbling intellectual and political life. It contains most of the Iranians who in the last 10 years or so have learned how to make refrigerators, stoves, radios, television sets, tires, batteries, steel furniture and detergents, and how to assemble cars, trucks and buses. It also contains many of the aches and pains of modern life: spreading slums, traffic jams and 9,000 tooting taxis, only 3,000 less than there are in New York City.

But if this bustling metropolis looks forward to the Iran of the future, it does not yet represent the Iran of today. Iran remains, for all its historic turbulences, an Oriental country that has tended its affairs unhurriedly for some 2,500 years. Approximately 60 per cent of its inhabitants are farmers who live in small villages, the houses clustered tightly together for protection against the occasional raids of mounted tribesmen. They spend the cruelly cold mountain winters leaning against the warmest wall in town and the blistering summers tending their fields, which are usually small. The land is plowed with iron-shod wooden plows. Water is brought to the fields by underground systems of aqueducts called *qanats*, of a design that was old when Cyrus the Great was young.

When the crop, usually wheat or barley, is harvested, it is divided in fifths: one for the landlord (a wealthy one is known to have owned as much land as would fit in Belgium), another for the water owner, a third for the seed supplier, a fourth for the owner of the draft animals and tools, and a fifth for the peasant himself. A peasant may, of course, have his own animals or his own seed, and thus keep more than one fifth of his harvest. Depending on how many fifths he is entitled to, a peasant's annual income may range from $50 to $100, or in rare cases even more, but then there are not many stores in rural Iran in which to spend even these small sums.

Another 15 per cent of the population is made up of shepherds, many of them what might be called vertical nomads, families that take their flocks up the mountains in the spring and down into the warmer valleys in the winter. These nomads shear their sheep on the trail, dye the wool with colors from roots and bark found along the way, and spin it into colorful rugs for their tents or for sale in city bazaars. Many of them are well mounted and armed and a few still make occasional raids on farm villages. Several elusive groups of raiders have in recent years kept the Iranian Air Force's jet fighters and more than a division of ground troops tied up for months at a time trying to catch them.

CAMEL caravans moving from oasis to oasis far better symbolize the Iranian people than diesel engines panting over the country's fantastic railroads, railroads that may spiral up inside a single mountain and that leap rivers, valleys and gorges on audacious bridges unmatched even in Switzerland. But whether they want to go, the people of Iran are being pushed and shoved toward the diesels, the 20th Century and an industrialized economy. Doing most of the pushing is their shrewd, able and hotly impatient Shahanshah (King of Kings) Mohammed Reza Shah Pahlavi. Actually the modernization drive started with the father of the present Shah,

Reza Pahlavi, an extraordinary man who rose from a cavalry trooper to become ruler of his country in 1925. He created much of present-day Teheran, built a railroad, highways, factories and schools.

The present Shah is convinced that the only solution to the chronic poverty of his country ("It is no honor for me to preside over a nation of paupers," he says) is a "white" revolution directed, in the absence of any other force, from the throne. The Shah wants to see an increase in the production of every sort of commodity until even the most remote Iranian village will feel the need for a higher standard of living. He wants better-educated Iranians (schools are second only to development and defense in the Shah's program), healthier Iranians (hospitals have a high priority), and new industries of all kinds and of all sizes. The Shah is using the country's oil revenues and barter to attract and then to establish the new industries, and he has used land-reform laws to persuade leading landowning families to transfer their capital to more productive industrial investments in the cities.

ALL of this naturally arouses opposition, especially among the landowners and among the Moslem mullahs (religious scholars) whose religious body owns many rural villages. There have been bloody riots in the streets of Teheran, and one of the Shah's most progressive Prime Ministers, Hassan Ali Mansour, was assassinated by people opposed to his plans to modernize the country. The Shah himself once thought it wise to flee briefly to Rome, and he has twice been the target of assassination attempts, once by the Communist Tudeh Party and the second time by a Peking-oriented underground Communist group.

Nonetheless, the Shah's revolution goes on. The Trans-Iranian Railroad from the Persian Gulf to the Russian border, the life line of the southern fronts in Russia during World War II, is sending out branches to link with rail lines in Turkey to the west and Pakistan to the east. Soon, the Shah hopes, a man in Teheran's main railroad station will be able to buy a through ticket to Paris and London or to Karachi and Calcutta. New dams, including the Mohammed Reza Shah Pahlavi Dam, one of the highest on earth, have multiplied power output, and the country has been showered with new airports, canneries, textile plants, telephone and microwave radio networks, oil pipelines, new refineries and new roads.

These bold attempts at modernization as yet touch only a small part of the population. Income distribution remains inequitable; approximately 20 per cent of Iran's inhabitants still receive some 75 per cent of the country's income, leaving the bulk of the people in poverty. And there is another problem that Iranians sum up under the word "corruption," but which refers less to shady dealing than to inefficiency, a lack of practice in thinking out modern problems. When the 80-mile highway from Teheran to the Caspian Sea at Smol was opened up, for example, it was discovered that no one had thought to install a single gas station. As a result many a car zoomed out of town for a weekend at the shore and stalled for lack of gasoline, creating traffic jams in the middle of the Elburz Mountains.

But year by year more people will get more practice dealing with such problems. In one recent three-week period the Iranians signed no less than four major economic agreements. They initialed one with Russia which provides that the Soviets will build a steel mill and machine-tool plant in central Iran (to use Iranian iron ore and coal) and will be paid in natural gas from Iran's oil fields and in agricultural products. A second agreement, this one with Romania, provides that the Romanians will supply Iran with $100 million worth of oil-refinery equipment in return for 30 million tons of oil. A third deal, worth $100 million all told, and signed by the National Iranian Oil Company, the National Petrochemical Company of Iran and the Allied Chemical Corporation of the United States, will establish a petrochemical industry in oil-rich Khuzistan province. The fourth is a $133 million agreement between Iran and a group of American and German companies for the construction of an oil refinery near Teheran. Not since the Roman Emperor Valerian was taken prisoner in the Third Century A.D. and his troops put to work building bridges, dams and aqueducts has Iran managed to inveigle foreign nations into so constructive an interest in its affairs.

IN fact, Iran's relations with the rest of the world have always been a bit askew. The Iranians march into history under the name Persians. This is because two Greek historians, Herodotus and Xenophon, got the name wrong, calling all of present-day Iran (the word means "Land of the Aryans") by the name of one of the country's western districts that was known in those times as Persis. Their extensive and much-read histories naturally perpetuated the error. For epochs upon epochs the Iranians have been trying to set the matter straight. They have gone so far as to refuse to accept diplomatic mail addressed to the Kingdom of Persia. But when, during World War II, Winston Churchill flew into Teheran and rumbled roguishly to the Shah that he refused to be bullied into calling Persia anything else, Iran finally gave up. To Iranians the country fondly remains Iran, but a new law was proclaimed after the war officially recognizing Persia and Iran as interchangeable names.

THE Greeks also painted the Iranians as the world's first, clearly identifiable Bad Guys. They were a luxury-loving lot, the Greeks thought, who wasted their substance in harems. They held themselves superior to foreigners but took what they liked from foreign cultures. In Herodotus' neat double indictment they indulged themselves in pleasures "of all kinds and all borrowed." Worse still, they stood for tyranny, while the Greeks, or at least some of them, stood for democracy and freedom. And it was only natural, under the law of history which says that a great power undeterred by a second great power shall gobble up all its little neighbors, that these Persians should wage war on the Greeks.

Under two of antiquity's greatest Shahanshahs, Darius and Xerxes, Iran twice marshaled armies of terrifying size and hurled them over the seas in ships and across pontoon bridges into the heart of Greece. They scored victories: they massacred the Spartans at Thermopylae and all but destroyed Athens. But at Marathon during the first invasion, and at Salamis and Plataea in the second, they suffered shattering defeats. Superior weaponry probably had as much to do with the Greeks' victories as their courage. Tightly massed and heavily armored Greeks with spears proved superior to the Iranian archers' loose formations and light armor. The seagoing Greeks achieved their victories on water through clever stratagems and more artful seamanship.

All of this was most vividly described by Herodotus in his marvelous *The Persian Wars*. Herodotus was not always completely accurate, as in his use of the name "Persia," although modern archeological finds have several times confirmed as true parts of the

narrative that later historians had long since dismissed as pure fancy. But Herodotus was insatiably curious and, despite his tendency to believe the Greeks more advanced than their neighbors, gives a matchless picture of the Persian world up to 479 B.C., of the world largely ruled by Cyrus, Darius, Xerxes and the other great Iranian shahs. His description of the Greek naval victory at Salamis is a masterpiece of historical narrative, seldom if ever matched by this first great historian's vast army of successors.

Once the Persian Wars—the first ones in history in which a modern man can feel that his concerns were, somehow, involved—were over, Greece once more became a collection of independent and quarrelsome city-states and Iran, despite its defeats, remained the ancient world's leading power. The law of the Persians (and of their cousins, the Medes) was proclaimed over a vast domain stretching from Libya in North Africa around through Egypt into present-day Israel, Syria and Turkey and on eastward into Pakistan and northward into Russia. The shah, accompanied by his seven wise men and the imperial bodyguard of 10,000 "immortals," moved slowly around this extensive realm while relay riders on fast horses brought news from, and carried orders to, every corner of the empire. Officials known as "the eye of the king" went forth to see that the shah's orders were obeyed. Aristophanes and other writers of Greek comedy had a good deal of fun with these officials and what the Greeks considered their outlandish, "barbarian" ways, but that did not make the "Persian" empire any smaller.

IN addition, there were many benevolent aspects to the first great Iranian empire that gave the lie to the harsh views of the Greeks. It was not, of course, democratic and the 20 provinces of the empire were ruled by 20 satraps. But before acting, these officials were required to consult the leaders of native communities in their areas, and the shah himself was required by law to listen to his councilors. Defeated kings were treated with honor and high offices were opened to members of subjugated peoples. The Jews, found in Babylonian captivity by Cyrus the Great, were sent home to Jerusalem with money to rebuild their temple. And the Greek Themistocles, the man who built the Greek fleet that defeated the Iranians at Salamis, when he was subsequently ostracized from

The bright mosaics and minarets of the Mosque of Masjid-i-shah in Esfahan, Iran, are approached by women in black "chadors."

Athens, lived part of his later life as the honored guest of the shahanshah of Iran.

Nor did these ancient rulers neglect their duty to civilization. They built great cities to whose magnificence the ruins of Persepolis, burned by Alexander the Great (perhaps to avenge the destruction of Athens 150 years earlier), stands testimony. Darius built a water basin in Herat to irrigate the steppes, sent ships to explore the Indus River and then continue from its mouth to Suez, built a canal from the Nile to Suez whose course can still be seen, and established ports on the Persian Gulf. And even earlier, many years before the time of Cyrus, the great religious teacher Zarathustra (meaning, perhaps, "Old Camel") called for devotion to Ahura-Mazda, the Wise Lord, at fiery altars burning the gas from Iran's oil deposits. He preached of a life hereafter, the coming of a savior and a final judgment on each immortal soul. Later the liturgy degenerated into debauches, such as a fiesta to Mithras, god of the sun and of light, when the shah traditionally got drunk and danced the royal dance, or the festival honoring Anaitis, the goddess of generation, which came to involve sexual license and the prostitution of young girls.

HOW closely related modern Iranians are to these luminous, if sometimes ill-behaved, peoples of old would baffle a computer. The original people were Aryans—part, that is, of one of the great outpourings of people from Central Asia who form some of the rootstock of nations reaching from India around through the Middle East and into Europe. Adolf Hitler once claimed that the Germans were all Aryans, all pure-blooded and anti-Semitic, but in truth the Aryans were a gregarious lot who mingled much and got around until today the word "Aryan" is diluted to historical nonsense. Iran's original Aryans, for instance, are now mixed with Hittites, Arabs, Egyptians, Greeks, Romans, Mongols and local tribes too numerous to mention. Still, it is a proud thing to look back upon such forebears.

The original Aryans were warriors and horsemen, bringing the horse to Europe and the Middle East about 1700 B.C.; one of the oldest writings in their language is a set of instructions on how to stage a horse race. They fought a number of wars both for and against such ancient cities as Nineveh, Babylon and Elam and established a small enclave of their own at Parsumash under their chieftain Achaemenes. These "sons of Achaemenes," the Achaemenids, were an extremely warlike lot. During one battle the Achaemenid force and the opposing army fell into a shocked peace when a total eclipse, which astronomers calculate occurred on May 28, 585 B.C., obscured the sun. Thoroughly frightened by such a dreadful omen, the two armies forsook battle and went home. The Aryan tribesmen, however, soon recovered their courage and resumed fighting. For a short while they fell under the control of the Medes, but inspired by the leader named Cyrus, who came to be called Cyrus the Great, they revolted and then bound the Medes and other Aryan tribes to them. This group of tribes defeated another coalition consisting of Babylon, Egypt, Lydia and the Greek city of Sparta in the first of the Persian Wars.

IT was during the war, so the books say, that the Persians had the assistance of that unseen hand that wrote upon the walls of Belshazzar's palace among Babylon's hanging gardens the dread words *"Mene, mene, tekel, upharsin."* The prophet Daniel interpreted the words (which in Aramaic mean "It has been counted and counted, weighed and divided") to mean "Your kingdom is lost. You have been weighed in the scales and found wanting." Daniel was right and Babylon fell.

All told, 12 emperors descended from Achaemenes ruled Iran and its empire over a period of more than 220 years. But the Achaemenid rulers grew weak, their satraps became rebellious, and then, suddenly, Alexander the Great of Macedon came riding into Asia astride his battle horse Bucephalus and swept the Iranian armies aside. At the death of Darius III, murdered by his own men because of his failure to halt the Macedonians, Alexander proclaimed himself Great King of Persia. He announced the unification of Persia and Macedonia, forcing his officers to command Iranian troops and his own troops to accept Iranian generals. In a further move for unity he had his officers and some 10,000 of his troops marry Persian wives. Then, after eight years of campaigning through Syria, Egypt, Iran and Turkestan and into India (Bucephalus died of war weariness in his last battle against King Porus of India's war elephants), Alexander, not yet 33, died and the whole empire fell apart. The Macedonians put aside their Persian wives and the Diadochi, Alexander's generals, grabbed for power. The general named Ptolemy got Egypt, Antigonus took Macedonia, and Seleucus became king in Asia Minor and Iran itself, although he swapped off the easternmost provinces of the old empire to India for 500 of those elegant elephants.

Six descendants of Seleucus ruled Iran for nearly a century and helped create a new age in art and spirit that Western writers call the Hellenistic, or Greeklike, Age. The view in Iran, however, is best expressed by the present Shahanshah, who says that "the invaders adopted Persian customs and habits, relied on Persian administrators, married Persian women and in the end were assimilated by the Persian culture." Even after their power was shattered by Rome, members of the Seleucid Dynasty lingered on for another century ruling bits and pieces of the old empire. Then great Pompey of Rome appeared in Syria in 64 B.C. and swept the last Seleucid under history's multicolored rug.

Dynasties succeeded one another in varied arrays of splendor. The nomadic Arsacids of northeast Iran ruled portions of the old empire, now called Parthia, from the Second Century B.C. to the Third Century A.D. They banished the Greek language and returned Iran to its historic role as an Oriental nation. But assassination became a common method of succession. Princes slew their royal fathers (save, sometimes, when fathers got in the first thrust), and the officers of the army were forever intriguing against whoever was on the throne. The king replied with cruelty and treachery which made the situation worse.

THE glories of the Achaemenid empire, destroyed by Alexander, glowed again when a local king named Ardashir I (who was also known as Artaxerxes) revolted against these bloody-minded Arsacid rulers, triumphed over them in three great battles and slew the last of them himself in a hand-to-hand single combat. Thereafter some 30 descendants of Ardashir, whom historians call Sassanian shahanshahs, ruled Iran for nearly four and a half centuries, until 651 A.D. From their palace at Ctesiphon, where the great vaulted hall still stands, they ruled a realm at times nearly as large as the old empire, but there was almost continuous trouble. In the East, Oriental tribesmen required continual chastisement, and in the West the unending war against Iran that Rome inherited, so to speak, from Alexander the Great took on new dimensions of bitterness as

Byzantium took over Rome's role and the war became a religious struggle, the Christian West against the Zoroastrian East.

Despite these tumults Iran was fruitful again. The arts flourished. On the site of Seleucia, just across the Tigris from Ctesiphon, Ardashir built a new city, Veh-Ardashir (Good is Ardashir), and a later Shah, Shapur, transformed ancient Susa into another show-place city, Gunde-Shapur. Pahlavi, a Persian language written in Aramaic script (the present ruling family of Iran adopted the word as its dynastic name), grew popular and a considerable literature developed in it. And in the marvelous gardens for which Iran was (and is) famous, men planted bulbs, and grew such delights as the tulip, a native of Iran, and the rose. A surprisingly advanced medicine grew up. A hospital, medical school and university were founded as early as the Second Century B.C. where Greek teachers combined their knowledge with ancient Indian methods to produce a superior therapy. Medical findings were published for the use of succeeding generations.

THE wars with Rome and Byzantium, continuing over hundreds of years, finally exhausted Iran. When, in 633, squadrons of Arab horsemen came caracoling over the desert sands, Iran had little with which to oppose them, although Yazdegerd III, the last Sassanian dynast, fought them bravely until his assassination in 651. Eventually the various parts of Iran were incorporated into the Islamic Caliphate of Baghdad.

Save in a few pockets Zoroastrianism gave way to the Islamic religion and the Pahlavi language was supplanted by the Arabic. Under wise Moslem leadership, prosperity was widespread, and for a brief moment under Caliph Harun al-Raschid, who ruled in Baghdad at the same time as Charlemagne ruled in the West, a new golden age seemed dawning. Literature bloomed. The Caliph himself comes down to us as a character, along with Sinbad the Sailor, Aladdin, and Ali Baba and the 40 Thieves, in the delightful stories Scheherazade is supposed to have told her husband Schariar during the fabulous "Thousand and One Nights."

But now Iran moved into centuries of extraordinary violence. Revolts against the Arabs arose among indignant taxpayers, outraged noblemen and unemployed frontier warriors. Followers of the Sunni and

Students take exams for Teheran University; 30,000 apply for 6,000 places.

A massive dam, part of Iran's modernization schemes, rises near Teheran.

A market in Teheran, Iran's capital, has gardens and pedestrian walks.

A donkey rider and a bus pass in front of Teheran's new Senate building.

Shah Avenue in Teheran bustles with European autos, scooters and bikes.

the Shiite versions of Islam frequently had at each other's throats. An order of Assassins (led at times by the forebears of two colorful figures of recent days, the Aga and Ali Khan) sprang up in defense of the Shiite cause. The order promised its adherents bliss on earth in palaces full of lovely girls if they killed and came home alive, or similar forms of bliss in heaven if they were killed. The shahs of a new dynasty, the Seljuks, descendants of Turkish mercenary soldiers, found themselves fighting Byzantium, Christian Crusaders and Egyptian invaders. Under the greatest Seljuk ruler, Malik-shah, Iran once again conquered Syria, Egypt and the Middle East. (This happened in the same era as the Norman conquest of England.) But this was no Achaemenid empire peacefully going about its lawful rounds. This was an empire of galloping horsemen and sudden, deadly raids in the night, a land where prudent men kept their scimitars under their pillows when they slept.

INTO this distraught land Genghis Khan led his Mongol tribesmen in 1220 and they laid it waste, massacring hundreds of thousands of people. A new dynasty established by Genghis' grandson Hulago had barely got started when, in the 1370s, Tamerlane arrived to spend 10 years on a murderous, loot-hunting march through the land.

Nevertheless, it was just in this desperate period that Iran produced some of its greatest works. The poet and astronomer Omar Khayyám revised the calendar. A group of Iranian scholars compiled the astronomical tables that still bear the name of Ulugh Beg, a descendant of Tamerlane, who was shahanshah from 1447 until his assassination in 1449. And from the anguish of those days was born Sufism, a mystical movement within Islam that brought forth rivers of lovely poetry. There was Celaleddin Rumi, who sang of the pleasures of sleep; and Hafiz, whose poems praise the beauties of the city of Shiraz; and Sa'di, who mingled his poems with aphorisms such as "Expect not constancy from the nightingale, which will every moment serenade a fresh rose." The present Shahanshah can get wryly angry when he thinks of Sa'di, for the poet also wrote: "A falsehood mingled with expediency is better than a truth that stirs up trouble." The Shah thinks that this graceful excuse for prevarication has been overworked by his countrymen. Indeed, it may be the

philosophical explanation of why Iran's official statistics are so often so far from reality.

The task of pulling the country together fell upon Ismail, first of the Safawid line of shahs who were to rule the land from 1502 to 1736. Ismail started by killing Shaibani Khan, a descendant of Genghis, and having his skull mounted in gold to be used as his drinking cup. Then he led his troops against the first modern army the Iranians had ever seen: Turkey's musketeers backed by artillery and cavalry. The Iranians barely managed to escape. Under the Safawid Dynasty's greatest monarch, Shah Abbas, who ruled from 1587 to 1629, the tables were turned. England's (and Queen Elizabeth's) Earl of Essex, worried over Turkey's aggressions in the Balkans, sent out two Britons, Sir Anthony Sherley and his brother Robert, to set up a powerful country in Turkey's rear. They showed the Iranians how to equip and reorganize their army along modern lines. With his refurbished fighting forces Abbas won back all that Turkey had taken from Iran. And at home he built at Esfahan the most beautiful city in Iran and one of the most beautiful in the world.

As with so many other dynasties, the Safawids degenerated in increasingly weak shahanshahs. Afghans invaded the country and, taking advantage of the resulting turmoil, both Turkey and Russia seized large parts of Iran. In this crisis a strange new chief arose, Nadir Kuli Beg, born in a tent, leader of a band of robbers, and a military genius. He drove the Afghans out of the cities of Iran, defeated the Turks and was just turning north against the Russians when Peter the Great, the Czar who had ordered the invasion of Iran, died. The Russian Government subsequently decided to withdraw from the country. Nadir then turned against the Afghan capital at Kandahar, captured it and invaded India, where he took Delhi and seized among much other loot the solid-gold, jewel-bedecked Peacock Throne, which is now in the museum of Bank Melli in Teheran.

WHEN Nadir died, assassinated by some of his officers, his descendants and generals fought for the throne, which eventually went to Karim of the Zand tribe, and after Karim's death to the Aga Mohammed Khan. The story of this dynasty, which lasted from 1796 to 1925, is one of weak shahs bounced back and forth between the power and commercial rivalries of Britain and Russia, mainly, but with France and Germany also throwing their weight about from time to time. To finance exciting trips to Europe the shahs handed out all manner of enticements: to the British, railroad, trolley car and telegraph concessions, plus exclusive oil and mineral rights; to the Russians, Caspian fishing monopolies, banking rights and special trade concessions. But the shahs' trips opened Iran's eyes to Western progress. Nasir ed-Din Shah, for instance, came home with important news: those railroad engines were not run by a horse hidden inside. He ordered up a five-mile railroad from Teheran to Rey that is still in operation. And he also ordered all the women of his court, even the fat ones, to wear those devastating little white skirts, or tutus, that the ballet dancers wear at the Paris Opera.

BUT things went much further than mere trade concessions. The shahs granted the Russians the right to organize in northern Iran a brigade of Persian Cossacks officered by Russians. To balance that, they permitted the British to form a brigade of Persian Rifles in the south, under British officers. In addition they signed the shameful "capitulations," whereby foreigners charged with crime in Iran would be tried not in Iranian courts but in courts of their own nationalities.

But the winds were changing. One Shah, Nasir, when informed that the people wanted a constitution, a parliament and responsible ministers, growled: "I want ministers who do not know whether Brussels is a city or a cabbage." But Nasir was assassinated in 1896 and his successor, Muzaffir ed-Din, was forced to grant the constitution in 1906 after thousands of Iranians demonstrated by taking refuge in the British Legation and refusing to leave.

Thus, into the current century, history has continued to provide Iranians with excitement. During World War I the Russians and the British occupied the country. Order was maintained in rough-and-ready fashion by the Persian Cossack Brigade, and the South Persia Rifles and British troops fought off a Turkish invasion. In World War II Iran was again occupied by the Western Allies and Russia, and the Reza Shah, suspected of pro-German sympathies, was packed off into exile. With Iranian help, some 4.5 million tons of war matériel was moved through the country (much of it over the Reza Shah's railroad) to Russia.

And World War III came close to starting in Iran in the early 1950s when an eagle-bald and wholly improbable Iranian in pink pajamas, Prime Minister Mohammed Mossadegh, tossed in his bed, weeping, moaning, and at times fainting dead away in a passionate nationalistic and anti-Western fervor while he expelled the Anglo-Iranian Oil Company, watched his treasury drain away in the face of a worldwide boycott of nationalized Iranian oil, chased his Shahanshah into a brief exile in Rome and accepted the support of the Communist Tudeh Party. The Western powers understandably viewed such developments in oil-rich Iran with considerable alarm. There was a distinct possibility that Russia might seize the opportunity to extend its influence southward and that a clash of some sort, possibly leading to war, might be the result.

However, the crisis passed. After a little shooting in Teheran the Shah came home from exile. The wailing Dr. Mossadegh was transferred from his tear-drenched bed to a prison cot for a salutary period of time. He has since emerged from jail to live, mainly perpendicularly and largely dry-eyed, on his country estates. And a new oil concession at rates more favorable to Iran has since been negotiated with an international consortium of oil companies that now includes, besides the British, a number of American firms.

But the Shah who returned from Rome was a different man from the one who had left. He had stood resentfully aside while his father was maneuvered into abdicating. He had treated Dr. Mossadegh gently until he was near abdication himself. Such experiences have their effects, and seldom in Iranian history have more vigorous hands been put to all the country's affairs than those of the present Shah. There would be a revolution in Iran, he decided. And he decided that *he* would make it.

FOR FURTHER READING

Banani, Amin, *The Modernization of Iran, 1921-1941*. Stanford University Press, 1961.
Costa, A., and L. Lockhart, *Persia*. Frederick A. Praeger, 1958.
Marlowe, John, *Iran, A Short Political Guide*. Frederick A. Praeger, 1963.
Pahlavi, Mohammed Reza Shah, *Mission for My Country*. McGraw-Hill, 1961.
Upton, Joseph M., *The History of Modern Iran, an Interpretation*. Harvard University Press, 1960.
Wilbur, Donald, *Contemporary Iran*. Frederick A. Praeger, 1963.

Afghanistan

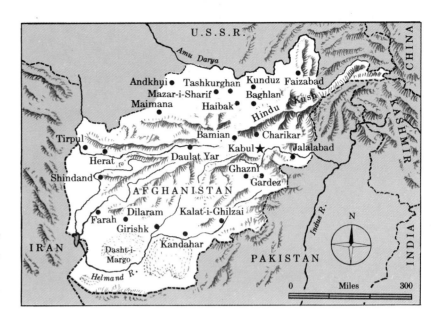

AFGHANISTAN is a starkly beautiful land of bitter extremes. Towering, snow-crowned mountain ranges rise out of precipitous valleys and rocky gorges while orchards and vineyards dissipate in the glittering sweep of barren deserts. The dry countryside can be brutally cold in the winter and suffocatingly hot in the summer. The people who struggle to live in this harsh land cling together in fiercely independent tribes whose heritage is ancient and whose inclination toward change has always been slight. Today, despite new roads and airports capable of handling jets, Afghanistan remains largely a land of caravan trails and nomadic herdsmen.

The estimated 15 million Afghans occupy an area about the size of Texas. It is landlocked and surrounded by nations that are now, or have been, important world powers. Russia abuts to the north along a 700-mile border. To the west is Iran, the modern remains of the Persian Empire. West Pakistan extends along most of the eastern border while Kashmir and Red China touch on the country's northeast projection. Small wonder that this land has grown accustomed to living in long shadows: perhaps proximity to power is a basic cause of Afghanistan's passion for independence.

More than half of Afghanistan is at least a mile above sea level and is marked by many still-unscaled peaks and wild, bare hills. Most of these mountains are in the rugged Hindu Kush range, whose highest summit towers more than 25,000 feet. Hindu Kush means "Hindu killer," an allusion to slaves from India who died while being marched over the treacherous slopes. The mountains and their foothills rest like a giant saddle on the back of Afghanistan, burdening the country with a central terrain extremely difficult to traverse.

North of the Hindu Kush northward-flowing rivers cut across dry steppes providing water to one of the most fertile areas of Afghanistan. Here the country's chief commercial crop, cotton, blossoms in irrigated fields. To the south of the Hindu Kush the plateaus are drier, but there are several fertile valleys, the largest of which surrounds the capital city of Kabul (pronounced Cobble). The city of Kandahar has also grown up in this region of rivers and scattered oases. Irrigation makes possible the cultivation of profitable fruit crops. The orchards produce apricots, apples, melons, pomegranates, dates and figs. Grapes are harvested from vineyards.

Farther south these orchards give way to vicious deserts, including the dreaded Desert of Death, or Dasht-i-Margo, in southwestern Afghanistan. This area, a nightmarish collection of wind-whipped sand dunes, clay soils and coarse gravel, is one of the most desolate and forlorn tracts in the world. But it was not always so. Dotting the plains are ruins of forgotten cities, and the earth is scarred with the remains of vast irrigation systems, relics of an age in antiquity when the region was tamed by man.

Essentially all of Afghanistan is dry. The average rainfall is about 10 inches a year, the wettest sectors receiving about 20 inches annually. (By comparison, Arizona has about 32 inches of rainfall yearly.) The rivers flowing from the Hindu Kush in the north are fed by melting glaciers in the summer and provide a good supply of water. But in other areas the winter snows vanish in a rush of spring floods, leaving the farmers precious little to tap for irrigation. Partly because of this, and partly because of infertile soils, less than 3 per cent of Afghanistan's total area is

An Afghan herdsman lets his pony graze in the Hindu Kush mountains.

cultivated. Water, then, is the key to the lives of the Afghans, 90 per cent of whom are small farmers or herdsmen, usually nomadic. The low rainfall and the inhospitable terrain mean almost constant shortages of food, yet it is said no Afghan has ever died of starvation. The nation of small farmers can apparently always raise enough for its people to subsist.

The major portion of the inhospitable Afghan countryside either is spotted with rough grasses or stands bleakly naked. What plants and trees do manage to survive are immediately threatened by droves of sheep, cattle and, the worst destroyers of all, goats. Man, too, is a major threat to vegetation. Through the ages he has hacked down trees for fuel and building material until the mountains, once resplendent with forests, have become virtually denuded.

Afghanistan is often compared to Switzerland, and indeed the two countries share many circumstances besides rugged, majestic scenery. Both are surrounded by strong nations, and perhaps as a result, both have a long tradition of international neutrality. Both are saddled by major mountain chains; both lack adequate agricultural and mineral resources, and neither has access to the sea.

BUT in contrast to Switzerland, Afghanistan's forbidding terrain has not discouraged invaders. Since earliest antiquity a parade of conquerors has tested armies, equipment and strategies against Afghanistan and its stubborn tribes. Usually Afghanistan has been invaded not for its own modest rewards but because it has been viewed as a corridor to the wealth of India. The most vital part of this corridor is a chink in the mountains of the Hindu Kush which has become rich in legend—the Khyber Pass, gateway to the Indian subcontinent.

It was across one of Afghanistan's many passes that Alexander the Great, while annexing the Persian Empire to his own in about 330 B.C., stormed southward on his way to gather the riches of India. After crossing the Hindu Kush—a feat likened to Hannibal crossing the Alps—the young Macedonian King was set upon in the northern province of Bactria by clever and ferocious mounted bands of guerrilla warriors. He pacified the area at great cost and took a native girl, Roxane, for his bride as a gesture of esteem for the courage the Bactrians had shown in battle. But, so one story goes, the marriage led to his death. Roxane apparently never forgave Alexander

for conquering her people. After a banquet, when Alexander was full of food and wine, she pointed to a cold pool and dared him to swim in it. Alexander plunged in and subsequently contracted the fever that killed him.

The Mongol conqueror Genghis Khan ravaged Bactria at the beginning of the 13th Century, and in the next century Afghanistan was again invaded by a celebrated warrior, Tamerlane, another Mongol leader. The severity of the terrain and weather plus the determination of the native tribes exacted too dear a cost. Tamerlane moved his main force against India, which offered less resistance and, more important to his armies, more booty.

IT was not until the middle of the 18th Century that Afghanistan was able to shake off the effects of invasions and occupations and become its own nation. In 1747 a 23-year-old Afghan who had risen to prominence in the Persian Army was chosen King of Afghanistan by the tribal chieftains. The coronation of this young officer, Ahmed Shah, was humble; the chiefs fashioned a mound of earth for a throne and placed a simple crown of wheat on the new monarch's head. But this coronation did not have the ring of conviction, and Ahmed Shah and his successors were bullied by fractious tribal chiefs for 72 years until finally, in 1819, a civil war engulfed the Crown. A decade and a half of anarchy followed; it was not until 1835 that Dost Mohammed Khan, one of the contending chieftains, secured for himself the title of amir.

Even as the Afghan tribal leaders were fighting among themselves, their land was still being prized by the larger world powers. Czarist Russia and Victorian England imagined their delicate balance of power in jeopardy in Central Asia and the Indian subcontinent. As Afghanistan struggled to settle its own destiny, it was again invaded, this time by Britain seeking to reduce Russia's influence. The British military occupation lasted only from 1839 to 1842, but the country did not become fully independent until the Afghans rose up to expel the last British officials in a brief war in 1919.

In spite of the ceaseless incursions by foreign troops throughout the history of Afghanistan, the influences left by them seem negligible. Another invasion had a far greater impact. From before the birth of Christ until the 10th Century, Afghanistan

Pedestrians and a cyclist cross a rickety bridge toward a busy market street in Kabul, ancient capital of mountainous Afghanistan.

was a forceful center of Buddhism. Then the prose-lytizing fervor of Islam swept across the country, turning it away from Buddha and giving the people, divided in a welter of tribes, a new sense of unity. The mosques and minarets seen in the major cities today demonstrate this religious unity. The glittering tomb of Hazrat Ali, son-in-law of the Prophet Mohammed, in the northern city of Mazar-i-Sharif is radiant evidence of the Afghans' passion for their faith. This common religion has not necessarily drawn the tribes together politically, but it does give them their strongest unifying bond.

Who the original Afghans were and where they came from has been lost in the dust of invasions and migrations. Invaders have included such peoples as the Indo-Aryans, Persians, Greeks, Mongols, Huns and Turks, and many of today's Afghans are descended from them. But the original stock was a people called Pathans, or Pushtoons. The Pathans number more than six million, almost half the country's present population. They speak Pushtu, one of the two major languages spoken in Afghanistan (the other is Persian). Where these people came from is not known. A legend greatly promoted by the Pathans holds that they are the descendants of one of the Ten Lost Tribes of Israel, but there is virtually no anthropological evidence to substantiate this claim.

The Pathans are by tradition exclusively pastoral, either sedentary farmers or nomads living in black felt tents and searching the land for grass for their sheep. They have never shown much interest in trade, industry or other aspects of city living. Now, however, with Afghanistan adjusting to new ways of life, many Pathans have come to the cities to live.

The Pathans are not limited to Afghanistan itself but spill over into neighboring Pakistan. This has prompted the Afghans to dream of carving from their neighbor an independent state of Pushtunistan, with an outlet on the Arabian Sea. This state would enable the Pathans in Pakistan to escape a life under alien rule; it would also provide Afghanistan with a seaport. Since Afghanistan's royal family is of Pathan stock, the argument for Pushtunistan is energetically promoted. From time to time the issue explodes. In 1955 mobs in each country raided the diplomatic missions of the other, causing the border between

Afghan farmers, some mounted on ponies, bring produce to the bazaar in Kunduz, a town in the northern part of the arid country.

Pakistan and Afghanistan to be sealed off for five months. But more acrimony followed. Just six years later, in August 1961, Pakistan closed several Afghanistan consulates, and the Afghan Government retaliated angrily by again sealing the border between the two countries. It took two full years, until 1963, for the border to be opened and trade between the nations to resume.

Of the many other ethnic groups in Afghanistan, the next largest after the Pathans is the Tajiks, some three million strong. They are a Caucasian people, like the Pathans, but speak Persian. There are three million Mongolians, about half of whom are closely related to the people of Soviet and Chinese Turkistan. Some of the lesser tribes live in Afghanistan's most destitute areas: they include the Baluchi nomads, who wander the southern deserts, and the Kafirs and Nuristani, who somehow survive the dour climate and geography of the Hindu Kush.

Farming and herding remain, by custom and necessity, the main occupations of the Afghans, their by-products accounting for 90 per cent of the $70 million yearly export total. Afghan herdsmen keep some 15 million sheep, of which four million are the valuable karakul. Mature karakul sheep are worth little, but the skins of the newly born are highly prized for their fur, which is marketed as Persian lamb. Selling these hides is a large enterprise; it

accounts for about half the country's export revenue. Another famous and profitable product is Afghan wool rugs, which, along with raw wool, account for 20 per cent of the country's exports.

The industrial age has barely dawned in Afghanistan. Several cotton mills, woolen mills and food-processing plants have been built recently, together with a match factory and three cement plants. Most of the implements used every day—farm tools and household equipment—are still made by hand in small workshops or even at home.

Hamstrung as it is by its feudal economy, Afghanistan can today make capital from at least one of its natural resources—its location. The country is still coveted by the major powers of the world: by the West as a buffer between Russia and India and by the East as an entryway to India. The United States has had diplomatic relations with Afghanistan only since World War II, and in the 13 years from 1952 to 1965 sent Afghanistan about $260 million worth of foreign aid. By 1965 the Russians had expended nearly $500 million in the country.

This Cold War competition with money and technical assistance has brought many bounties, some of them unexpected. Both sides have provided money and brains to build new highways and to improve the few that already existed. Each has given Afghanistan a jetport; the Russians built one near Kabul, the Americans near Kandahar. At first these airports were seldom used, but lately domestic flights have been very popular. Thus some Afghans have been able to go directly from camel caravans to jets.

Other projects are equally dramatic. The United States has been the force behind a $50 million irrigation project for the Helmand Valley, while the Russians have blasted a tunnel through the grim Hindu Kush, providing a direct road from north to south.

Afghanistan, borrowing a term from the Communists, has drawn up "five-year plans" for social and economic development, the monies coming not only from the United States and Russia but also from the United Nations and West Germany. A prime object of these programs is education. Until recently almost 90 per cent of the population was illiterate. However, three-year courses have been established in many villages to teach reading, writing and elementary arithmetic. The United States has spent some $15 million on education in Afghanistan, and more than 500 Afghans have been sent to study in United States universities. English is the unofficial third language of the country.

THE journey of the Afghans into the modern world has been beset by a difficult political history. Tribal feuds have hindered national unification, which geography had already made difficult, and the central Government has too often shackled itself with nepotism. King Mohammed Zahir came to the throne in 1933, but for almost three decades actual power was held by his cousin, Prime Minister Sardar Daud. Daud tried hard to bring Afghanistan into the modern era. With one decree he shattered centuries of tradition—his 1959 law permitted women to appear in public without the *chaderi*, the large veil that covers most of the face and flows on as an outer robe. This was a giant step in emancipating the Afghan woman after centuries of virtual imprisonment in the home, and today women are working as nurses or teachers or at other jobs.

But Daud, despite his progressive acts, had an unfortunate tendency to throw into prison all those who did not agree with him. In 1963 King Mohammed Zahir at last replaced Daud and selected as Prime Minister a commoner, Dr. Mohammed Yousuf. To further liberalize the Government, the King in 1964 presented his people with a constitution. This constitution is an honest effort to combine the liberalism of the West with the faith of Islam. It stipulates freedoms previously unimagined in Afghanistan and severs many ties with the feudal past. It guarantees freedom of the press, provides for an independent judiciary and establishes a freely elected Parliament. The right to form political parties is guaranteed, except for those that would violate the spirit of Islam, such as the Communist Party. All members of the royal family (including former Prime Minister Daud) are denied a role in politics. The constitution even clears the way for the King to relinquish many of his personal powers.

Rapidly as Afghanistan is evolving today, many old customs still linger. Strict obedience to Islamic law, for example, forbids the sale of alcohol except to foreigners in private clubs. Sports and games often reach back to the rugged rituals of a more primitive life. One favorite amusement is to pit two butting rams against one another. Men are tested in wrestling and stick fighting, a small wicker shield their only protection. One grisly game, *Buz Kashi*, is a rough-and-ready match between two mounted teams who slug, gouge, kick, butt and even whip one another for possession of a disemboweled goat, which serves as a "ball." When *Buz Kashi* was played by the troops of Genghis Khan in the 13th Century, the goat's role was taken by a live human prisoner.

For the Afghan people the leap from the ways of the past into a modern society is not necessarily easy or even comprehensible. The rituals of games and sports are familiar, but the privileges of democracy are not. One story is characteristic of the difficulty of shifting an attitude. Voting procedures under the new constitution were being explained to a tribe by a Government official. An old man asked that the regulations be repeated because he did not understand. The official gave details again on how to mark the ballot and how to place it in the box, but the old man remained puzzled. At last, he burst out, "But, sir, you haven't told us *who* to vote for yet."

FOR FURTHER READING

Ali, Mohammed, *A New Guide to Afghanistan*. Northern Pakistan Printing and Publishing Co., Kabul, 1958.
Fletcher, Arnold, *Afghanistan, Highway of Conquest*. Cornell University Press, 1965.
Sykes, Sir Percy, *A History of Afghanistan*. Macmillan, 1940.
Wilber, Donald N., and others, *Afghanistan, Its People, Its Society, Its Culture*. Human Relations Area Files, New Haven, 1962.

Pakistan

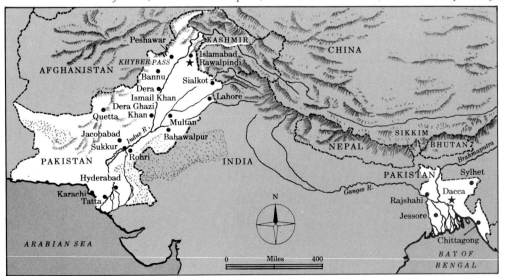

ON the evening of June 3, 1947, the British Viceroy of India, Lord Louis Mountbatten, announced over All-India Radio the impending partition of India and the birth of the new nation of Pakistan. In a swift and brutal effort to cut through years of wrangling, the massive subcontinent was to be divided, not merely in two, but in such a manner that India would become a huge, 1,000-mile-wide wedge splitting the two parts of Pakistan. Instead of just being separated *from* India, Pakistan would be separated *by* India.

"Mutilated, moth-eaten and truncated" was the verdict of Mohammed Ali Jinnah, Pakistan's founding father, on the new nation. But bisected Pakistan was not only a geographic monstrosity; it lacked unity in almost every other essential. Most East Pakistanis spoke Bengali, while West Pakistanis spoke Urdu, Punjabi, Sindi or Pushtu; the East was a green land of monsoon-drenched plains, while the West was arid and semiarid, requiring elaborate irrigation. The smaller part, East Pakistan, with 15 per cent of Pakistan's 365,528 square miles, had a majority of the people—some 55 per cent. The people did not even eat the same foods: the Easterners ate rice,

A street in Sialkot, West Pakistan, teems with laden donkeys, hors...

while the staple of West Pakistan was wheat. They shared only a belief in the Moslem religion and a common fear and hatred of largely Hindu India. But this was only the beginning of Pakistan's difficulties. Its territory contained none of the subcontinent's major cities and only a small fraction of its industry. In the East, Pakistan got half of Bengal province but not its capital and major city, Calcutta; in the West, the Punjab was also halved and its capital city, Lahore, was left in flames by rioters. There was no nucleus around which a new government could be built since there were few

Divided by India, Pakistan has two parts, West and East Pakistan, each with a capital city.

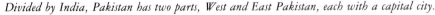

...arts and men bearing produce. Created in 1947 as a homeland for Indian Moslems, Pakistan is struggling to improve its laggard economy.

trained Moslem civil servants. Pakistan was supposed to receive 17.5 per cent of dissolving imperial India's assets, from paper clips to gold; but India's managers and clerks took care of their own first; when the Pakistanis unpacked their share of the "trophies of freedom" they found they had been shortchanged.

Atop it all came an influx of Moslem refugees from India, propelled toward Pakistan by a murderous Hindu-Moslem-Sikh religious war that claimed uncounted thousands of lives. Minorities were butchered on both sides of the new borders, and when they tried to flee, their trains were derailed and the refugees either cut to pieces or abducted. Huge convoys of refugees on foot moved slowly across the countryside, guarded by horsemen armed with spears and with regular troops not far off. During this bloody autumn of 1947, a Punjab magistrate, with a long career in the British service, observed: "The British are a just people. They have left India in exactly the same state of chaos as they found it."

All together, an estimated six million refugees entered Pakistan and were somehow fed and housed at a time when the state itself could barely function. In its triumph over adversity, infant Pakistan seemed indestructible, and sheer ebullience served, at least for a while, to soften its misshapen features.

This low condition of the Moslems is one of history's many dramatic reversals, for once they were the lords of the subcontinent. Islam, with its gospel of the unity of God and the equality of men in His sight, began to penetrate India's caste-bound Hindu society in the Eighth Century. Offering entry into an egalitarian social organism to the Untouchables and to Indians of low caste, who for centuries had huddled on the fringe of the Hindu community, Islam spread through much of northern India, eventually capturing a fourth of the inhabitants.

The new gospel arrived on the point of a sword. Moslem Arab marauders reached the mouth of the Indus River and captured Sind (now part of West

Pakistan) around 712 A.D. The raids became more intense toward the end of the 10th Century. In the 11th Century a Turkish chieftain, Mahmud, whose capital was at Ghazni in Afghanistan, attacked northern India at least 17 times. The Hindus fought back bravely, but they lacked appropriate military tactics and their lumbering war elephants proved no match for the swift and daring horsemen from Central Asia. Mahmud took the Punjab, and another invader, Muhammed Ghuri, expanded farther into India, capturing Delhi in 1192. More than three centuries later, in 1526, still another chieftain, Babur, a descendant of both Genghis Khan and Tamerlane, moved south from what is now Afghanistan and founded in Delhi the stately Mogul Empire.

MOGUL rule reached its golden age under Babur's grandson, Akbar (1556-1605). Internal trade flourished, while good administration increased revenues so that India's people lived as well as those of contemporary Elizabethan England. Surplus wealth at the disposal of the Mogul emperors nourished a cultural flowering. The Taj Mahal, on which 20,000 craftsmen labored for 11 years, and the Jama Masjid of Delhi superbly showed off Mogul architecture, while the Mogul school of miniature painting revealed great sensitivity. Foreigners and scholars of all sorts were welcomed at the enlightened Mogul court, which, like Versailles in Europe, became a cultural focal point for all of India.

Akbar set out not only to promote the arts and create an enlightened court, but also to unify the people and create a rule based on the broad consent of all his subjects, Hindu and Moslem. He abolished the *jizya*, a tax on non-Moslems, made the slaughter of cows illegal, and employed Hindus as generals and ministers.

Akbar's movement toward unity was reversed by his successors, especially by the bigoted, puritanical Emperor Aurangzeb (1659-1707), who spent the first 20 years of his regime restoring Moslem orthodoxy, reimposing the tax on Hindus, killing off Moslem apostates and purging the bureaucracy of nonbelievers. This done, Aurangzeb set out to impose Moslem rule over all India and by 1690 had made himself master of the entire subcontinent. His efforts proved vain, however, and for the last 15 years of his rule Aurangzeb was busy trying to quell the rebellions that his bigotry had roused. After he died, the Mogul

Empire began to fall apart and various governors split off to form their own semi-independent kingdoms. At the same time the power of the Hindu Marathas (a people of northern India) grew, and by the mid-1700s a Maratha Confederation controlled much of central India. India also became the target for parvenu looters. The Persians pushed into Delhi in 1739, massacred the population, and took the crown jewels and the fabled Peacock Throne. Commerce languished, as did agriculture, and the people suffered dreadful deprivations. The once-omnipotent Moguls began waiting, in effect, for a receiver in bankruptcy, and the British East India Company began to move into that role, reducing the emperor to the status of pensioner and slowly claiming one prerogative after another. After the Indian Mutiny of 1857, a direct attack by the Indians on the British, the Government in London stepped in and openly became the ruler of India.

The Moslems thereafter were gripped by an inferiority complex. Distrusted by the British for their leading role in the bloody 1857 mutiny, perceiving for themselves the weaknesses of their old order and the technological superiority of the British structure with its railways, telegraphs and incorruptible civil service, the Moslems fell into a morose decline. British policies furthered this process. In government, for example, the British took the senior posts for themselves, recruited Hindus (who had been quicker to learn English than the Moslems) for the clerical jobs, and used Moslems, if at all, for inferior, manual occupations like running messages and filling inkpots. Denied all avenues of growth, India's Moslems became more and more backward. When Partition came they were a people with a glorious past but a dubious future, lacking in the skills of commerce, industry and banking and in the mastery of the new sciences that the West had brought to India.

THAT this melancholy condition was not worse was due to the efforts of a handful of remarkable men. One of the most remarkable was Sir Sayyid Ahmad Khan (1817-1898), the leader of the "Muslim Renaissance" and a member of the British civil service in India, who urged his people to lay aside their superstitions and embark on a program of regeneration through Western education. Arguing that such a course was not contrary to Islamic belief, Sir Sayyid reminded fellow Moslems that Mohammed

Pakistan's founder Jinnah sits before the flag of the new nation.

had said: "Go even to the walls of China for the sake of learning." Sir Sayyid's efforts resulted in the founding of the Aligarh Anglo-Oriental College in 1875. Modeled after Oxford and Cambridge, its stated purpose was to make it possible for Moslems to "acquire an English education without prejudice to their religion." The first institution at Aligarh was a scientific society, and the college, later a university, became the heart of the Moslem reform movement.

Sir Sayyid believed that the Moslem community could rebuild itself only through a program in which both education and loyalty to the British raj were strongly emphasized. He discouraged participation in the new nationalist movement, symbolized by the Indian National Congress, because it might call into question Moslem India's loyalty to the British and because he feared that the Congress would develop into a movement for Hindu revivalism. As a result, Moslems refrained from organizing themselves politically until, as Sir Sayyid had feared, the Congress began to move in a more Hindu revivalist and decidedly militant direction. Then, in 1906, some Moslem leaders did get together to form the Moslem League to protect their community's interests. Even then, however, a number of leading Moslems, while joining the League, continued to remain members of the National Congress. Mohammed Ali Jinnah, later to become Pakistan's George Washington, was

himself an active member of the Indian National Congress until 1920, Jawaharlal Nehru even calling him "the ambassador of Hindu-Moslem unity."

While independence from Britain remained only a distant dream, Hindu and Moslem nationalists were able to work together. But as the dream came closer to reality, Moslems experienced a growing fear that once British protection was gone they would fare badly at Hindu hands. Violent incidents began multiplying in the 1920s, with 18 serious outbreaks in 1924 alone. Two years later the number of incidents rose to 36, and in one in Calcutta 1,400 persons were killed or injured. Between 1924 and 1927 the death toll in riots was 500. Round Table Conferences in London between 1930 and 1932 failed to calm the antagonism, and in June 1931 the Moslem League president declared that "Moslems would rather die fighting for preservation of their rights than to accept slavery at the hands of the infidels."

With increasing intensity Moslem leaders pressed the British for special safeguards for their community. However, the actual concept of Pakistan, that is, the idea of a separate Moslem state, is surprisingly new. Iqbal (1873-1938), the liberal poet of Moslem nationalism, mentioned it at a 1930 Moslem League meeting, and in 1933 the name "Pakistan" was coined by a group of Indian Moslems who were studying, appropriately enough, at Cambridge University. They made up their name for the Moslem national state with "p" for Punjab, "a" for Afghan (representing the Northwest Frontier Provinces), "k" for Kashmir, "s" for Sind and "tan" from the last syllable of Baluchistan—together the letters spelled a Persian word meaning "land of the pure."

Few people took the idea very seriously until about 1937, when elections to the new representative provincial legislatures recently granted India by the British produced a resounding victory for the Indian National Congress. After that Moslem India moved inexorably toward separation.

THE actual decision to demand a separate Pakistan was made in 1940 in Lahore. There, in an immense wrestling ring on the city's edge, the Moslem League passed the Lahore Resolution, namely that "the areas in which the Moslems are numerically in a majority . . . should be grouped to constitute 'Independent States.'" Jinnah subsequently said that "no power on earth can prevent Pakistan"—although

Pakistan

India's Mohandas Gandhi, hoping to persuade "Brother Jinnah" against separation, sat and talked with him over a period of several weeks in 1944.

The new state of Pakistan actually came into being at midnight on August 14, 1947, 72 days after the British Viceroy had announced that India would be partitioned, with Jinnah as the new state's first Governor General. Jinnah was one of those rare paternalistic authoritarians who act literally like the father of their people. Jinnah bossed and bullied the Pakistanis, and they loved it and called him Quaid-i-Azam (the Great Leader). A remote, severely logical man, Jinnah moved without fear or the need to please, doing what he thought necessary. He named trained British officials as governors in three of Pakistan's four provinces, as commanders of the Army, Navy and Air Force, and as administrators of eight Government departments. He made of his job of Governor General, theoretically a ceremonial post, the most important office in Pakistan during his lifetime and carried the burden of Pakistan's first year on his own thin shoulders, even to reading sentence by sentence the bills that arrived for him to sign. In September 1948 Jinnah died of tuberculosis, aged 72. Dominating obstacles by his sheer refusal to admit them, living by the creed that "failure is a word unknown to me," he had given Pakistan a better start than the turbulent circumstances warranted.

THE land itself was exciting and pretty. The green-and-white Pakistan flag fluttered over the old British forts at the Khyber and Malakand Passes that recalled lines from Kipling; over the breadbasket plain of the Punjab, where fat-tailed sheep grazed; over East Pakistan's Chittagong Hills, where bare-breasted aboriginal girls walked like queens. Outside the provisional capital of Rawalpindi (usually called Pindi) people still lived in earth caves, but Karachi was transforming itself from a small, provincial port into a modern city. Among the shining automobiles, the men in Western clothes and women in smart saris walked fewer and fewer wives in purdah, covered from head to toe in their white *burqas*, peering distrustfully through the eyeholes of their antique shrouds at this new world that Mohammed Ali Jinnah had made for them.

But soon tragedy struck. In October 1951 Liaquat Ali Khan, Jinnah's hand-picked successor and Pakistan's Prime Minister, was assassinated by an Afghan

and in four years Pakistan had lost both its principal leaders. None with equivalent authority and stature came forward to take their place. With the decline of the racial violence that had united all Moslems against Hindus and obscured all other issues, the bitter quarrel between East and West Pakistan came to the fore. The East, with its 55 per cent of the population and its jute and tea plantations that earned 70 per cent of Pakistan's foreign exchange, naturally resented the West, which, possessing the national capital, took by far the larger share of the aid and loans for itself and enjoyed a per capita income that was one third higher. This disparity was a constant theme in East Pakistan politics, and clashes erupted over all sorts of issues. Angry talk and violent demonstrations were provoked by the issue of which of several languages should be adopted as the national tongue. By 1954 the continuing trouble between the two areas led the federal Government to dismiss the elected head of East Pakistan's provincial government, move in 10,000 troops and hold control for nearly a year.

Even Pakistan's sole positive link—the Moslem religion—became a cause for contention. The leaders like Jinnah, who had made Pakistan, were Moslems, but they were also eclectics and Western-minded. While they invoked Islam to justify Pakistan, they avoided defining the role that religion would play in the new state. Personally they saw Islam as the new nation's spiritual nucleus and as the focus of its tradition on which unity and loyalty could be based, but they emphatically did not see Islam as a guide to how to organize the Government. Nor did they discuss this dichotomy lest it create confusion and internal conflict, and in this evasion they were at first tacitly joined by the religious men who also feared dividing the new state. But as one leader put it at the time: "Talking of an Islamic system and thinking in terms of the Western system is an incongruity which is visible all around us. The spirit soars to the lofty heights reached in Omar's time, but eyes are fastened on the spires of Westminster."

THE moves to draft a long-delayed constitution in the early 1950s gave immediacy to the postponed religious issue. Orthodox Moslems wanted a theocratic state, with Pakistan ruled by the letter of Islamic law. They inflamed the people with cries of "Islam in Danger," and in 1953, when they launched a murderous attack on a minority Moslem sect in

128

West Pakistan, the police had to open fire, killing 11.

The economy began to lag. The heroic efforts of the year immediately following independence gave way to a period of growing corruption, inefficiency and black-marketeering. Cabdrivers charged extra, milk sellers added water to their product, food merchants adulterated their goods, and everyone sought quick profits. Persistent fear of India forced Pakistan —despite U.S. military aid—to channel 70 per cent of its budget into defense, leaving little for development. West Punjab, the traditional granary of undivided India, proved incapable of feeding Pakistan's population, swollen by refugees and a high birth rate. The land system was outmoded and favored absentee landlordism, while an equally outmoded tax system that penalized those who worked hard and saved made for a situation in which many thousands of Pakistan's most fertile acres were idle. The Korean War obscured Pakistan's economic plight by raising the world price of its main exports, cotton and jute, giving an illusion of prosperity. But the commodity slide of 1953 shriveled the country's earnings, and by 1958, for lack of foreign exchange to buy spare parts and needed raw materials, the nation's mills were operating at 50 per cent of capacity. By October 1958 the Pakistan treasury was almost empty.

TO these many miseries of life in Pakistan were added the burdens of political instability, maladministration and the absence of a dynamic, unifying leader or force. And lacking a strong leader, the Pakistanis proved unable to properly operate their loose-knit, British-style parliamentary Government. The country had seven administrations in the 11 years between 1947 and 1958, and toward the end of this period prime ministers shuffled in and out of office with bewildering frequency. A second major problem was that the Pakistanis had extended suffrage to all, women included. With a much more advanced citizenry, the newborn U.S. had relied heavily on the Electoral College—a device for indirect elections—to offset the inexperienced electorate. Many politicians, contemptuous of the illiterate populace, worked deliberately for their own ends. Candidates seldom toured the countryside, but handed out a few rupees to this or that headman, buying the ballots of his village. Elective office became a lucrative profession, as politics vied with business as the way to making a fortune. The result was widespread chaos, and parliament became an uninhibited monkey house. In political debates, to accuse an opponent of anything less than treason or to register an objection through anything milder than the threat of holy war, was to be ignored. In the mid-1950s the rampaging members of the East Pakistan provincial assembly clubbed the presiding Speaker to death with inkpots and planks ripped from their desks.

In 1958, after 11 years of independence, the smell of failure hung in Pakistan's air. India's Prime Minister Jawaharlal Nehru complained that he did not know "whom to address" in his chaotic neighbor. Said a Western observer: "What can you do? It's an impossible country. Everybody's fighting India, or the other half of the country, or each other—sometimes all at the same time."

ONE of the men who stood by silently but uneasily and saw all this was the commander of Pakistan's 200,000-man Army. In imperial India the Hindus had provided most of the civil servants but the Moslems had provided some of the best soldiers. General Mohammed Ayub Khan, a Pathan from the northwest frontier, was one of those soldiers. With his clipped British accent and his guardsman mustache, the burly general, a product of Britain's Royal Military Academy at Sandhurst, shared also the British officer's distaste for politics. For 11 years the Army had kept aloof, watching decay set in.

Ayub finally decided to act, and on the evening of October 7, 1958, he and President Iskander Mirza, a fellow graduate of Sandhurst, seized power. They imposed martial law, dissolved the two provincial legislatures and the national legislature, dismissed all ministers, abolished all political parties, abrogated the 1956 Constitution and arrested some 50 persons, including a former Defense Minister (who was later put on trial for automobile black-marketeering). Three weeks later, saying that "somehow or other, people felt that he was as much responsible for the political deterioration as anyone else," Ayub fired Mirza, hustled him off to Europe with a double pension and himself took over as President, ending the era that had almost ended Pakistan. "There was," said Ayub, "no alternative to it except the disintegration and complete ruination of the country . . . our ultimate aim is to restore democracy, but of the type that people can understand. . . . When that will be, events alone will tell. Meanwhile, we have to put this

Pakistan

mess right and put the country on an even keel.''

The Pakistanis celebrated the military coup almost as joyfully as they had hailed independence 11 years before. They began seeing immediate results. The streets were cleared of pimps and the Karachi version of Britain's Teddy boys, who had made a practice of molesting women, and became safer and cleaner. Ayub rigidly enforced such elementary rules as that hospitals must not turn away anyone who is dying, that doctors had to charge "reasonable" fees and that price controls must be firmly enforced. He tackled the political and administrative morass. Some 3,000 corrupt or inefficient Government officials were either demoted or dismissed. When Ayub finished his reforms it was no longer necessary to pay "tea money" to the lowly *chaprasi* to get him to take one's card to the proper official, or to give a bagful of rupees to the official. Tax evaders were allowed to come clean by paying back taxes, more than six million dollars thus being collected. Government spending was reduced to curb inflation. Karachi's teeming refugee slums were razed and some 100,000 refugees from the bloody Partition were rehoused in plain but clean modern colonies.

A foreign newspaperman revisiting Pakistan in 1958 wrote: "For the first time in a number of trips here I have found it pleasant being in the capital.

Their mainsails swollen with wind, wide-beamed transport boats mo

A farmer in Bengal guides a plow pulled by two water buffalo.

Streets are swept clean. Piles of refuse have disappeared, potholes in the roads are filled, shacks have been removed, taxi drivers who would formerly cheat and abuse passengers now docilely accept reasonable fares. People are learning to queue up before buses and shops instead of being a rabble. Police, now able to operate without fear of interference from politicians, are pulling defective vehicles off the road and compelling owners to fix them. Many items are now selling in shops at a third or half the former price.''

Having scoured the stables, Ayub went to work on the main structure. Most importantly, he gave Pakistan—where 75 per cent of the people live from agriculture—long-overdue land reform. More than half the farmland in the Punjab and more than 90 per cent in Sind was held by absentee landlords. Ayub's martial-law regime completely abolished the old, semifeudal landholding systems and restricted landholders to 500 acres of irrigated or 1,000 acres of dry land, confiscating the rest and paying for it with interest-bearing bonds. In all, Ayub redistributed 23 per cent of the land, 3.5 million acres being sold to peasants on easy terms. Grasping the nettlesome population problem, Ayub advocated birth control

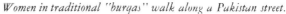
…p the Indus River in West Pakistan on their way to the local markets.

1960, and the food-grain index swelled almost 19 per cent. Ayub gloried in such figures, for he was fundamentally a technician rather than a demagogue and he seemed to shrink from the crowd's adulation. He was certainly a modest and civilized dictator, driving in a white Chevrolet, going about with few guards, laying aside his uniform and marshal's baton in favor of a business suit, a pink shirt and a striped tie. He told a critic of martial law: "Martial law is not a good thing. [But it] was imposed under extraordinary circumstances to save the country. If you think this is bad, go to Iran or other countries where martial law is really in force. Compared to them, Pakistan is a paradise."

From the outset of his benign dictatorship Ayub had been taking a close look at democracy. He liked it but he also distrusted it. It was, he later said, an arrangement for which "above all, you need a really cool and phlegmatic temperament, which only people living in cold climates seem to have. Also it requires a long period of probation. So don't let us kid ourselves and cling to clichés and assume that we are ready to work such a refined system." Nevertheless, boning up on the writings of Thomas Jefferson and surveying the American Constitutional system in a series of talks with the U.S. ambassador, Ayub evolved a creed he called "basic democracy." It was essentially an adaptation of the Western concepts tailored to fit an Eastern society lacking most of the prerequisites for intelligent political participation.

What basic democracy amounted to was a pyramid of power and political participation. Each village would elect a number of its citizens to be "basic democrats." These men would look after the collection of local taxes, see to the maintenance of the village roads and oversee the local police force. In

to his proliferating people, whose 2.1 per cent annual population increase was almost the equal of India's. "Unless we can effectively curb this galloping rate of population growth," he warned, "it will soon outstrip the pace of our economic development, and, believe me, the time may come when man may start eating man."

Despite some economic gains, vast new programs were still needed: less than 20 per cent of the population could read or write; the country had already lost a staggering 10 million acres of arable land to rising salinity and was losing many thousands more each year. In 1961 Ayub ordered experts to draft a 10-year reclamation plan and with characteristic impatience ordered the plan submitted to him in six weeks. Ayub also started construction of a new capital, to be called Islamabad. When completed it is expected to be one of Asia's finest cities. In keeping with his austere, no-nonsense habits, Ayub instructed the planners to make the new presidential palace the kind of place that "one woman can run."

Statistics vindicated Ayub and his bold development program. By 1961 foreign-exchange resources had increased 261 per cent, from $90 million to $235 million. Industrial production rose 16.7 per cent in

Women in traditional "burqas" walk along a Pakistan street.

addition they would send some of their members as representatives to a higher district council, which, in turn, would send representatives to a still higher council, and so on. Each of these councils, according to Ayub's scheme, would have some appointed as well as elected members; as political maturity increased, the number of appointed members would decrease. Thus something like a multileveled electoral college would be created which would insulate the electorate against demagogy and the other weaknesses to which the politically naïve are prone. Ayub also hoped that this hierarchy of basic democrats could be hitched to the national purpose and used to transmit new ideas about farming, sanitation and education from the Government down to the masses.

In December 1959 the first elections took place and 83,000 basic democrats were chosen. They were then asked to vote "in respect of their confidence in the present President of Pakistan." An overwhelmingly positive vote confirmed Ayub in office, and thus given a mandate he immediately set about to prepare a new Constitution that would fit "the genius of the people." Three commission reports were prepared surveying the problem, and on March 1, 1962, a new Constitution, which largely mirrors Ayub's thinking, was promulgated. It gave Pakistan a strong president. He could, for example, veto any act of the National Assembly, dissolve the assembly and discharge the governors of both provinces. In turn the president could be impeached by a three-fourths vote, but woe to the impeachers if they failed to get at least half the assembly votes, for they would automatically lose their own seats.

PAKISTAN'S dormant political life suddenly woke up. Two months after the Constitution was promulgated the basic democrats elected the National Assembly, and in May 1962 they elected the two provincial legislatures. On June 8, 1962, the assembly began meeting, ending three and a half years of martial law. After another two months, political parties were made legal again. By the time the assembly opened its second session, in November 1962, there was even an opposition to Ayub's Government, led by, of all people, Ayub's brother.

Ayub could add to these successes some limited economic gains. Pakistan's second Five Year Plan (1960-1965) did far better than the first plan of 1955-1960, the national income rising 11 per cent in the first two years. However, the continuing worldwide decline in agricultural prices and the rise in manufacturers' prices penalizes countries like Pakistan, some 75 per cent of whose exports are agricultural. In 1961, for example, Pakistan had to export twice as much in agricultural goods to pay for the same amount of manufactured goods as it had imported a decade before.

INEVITABLY, Ayub was also having his troubles with tradition-minded Moslems. Ayub asked the state bank to research Islamic doctrine to find justification for charging interest, an indispensable requisite for raising the capital that Pakistan sorely needs. He ordered more research in the Education Ministry to find Islamic principles to counter the usual conservative arguments. The orthodox, for example, wanted to abolish Ayub's Family Laws Ordinance, which protects the rights of women. Some mullahs (religious scholars) had even gotten their congregations to pass resolutions calling such legislation "un-Islamic." There was a danger that Pakistan, which existed because of religion, could be strangled by it, and Ayub found himself fighting with the mullahs for the allegiance of the masses.

One powerful religious party, the Jamaat-i-Islami, strong in the grassroots, bitterly opposed Ayub on such issues as banking, birth control and removing veils from women's faces. Ayub tried reasoning, telling the superfaithful on one occasion that they had "absolutely no option but to recognize the needs and demands of the present and future. . . . The strength of Islam lies in its progressive nature, its stress on knowledge and discovery. . . ." But the Jamaat persisted in its obstructionist policies, and before dawn one day in January 1964 Ayub's police swooped down on the party leaders and jailed them. Ayub proceeded to ban the party as "subversive."

Many enlightened Pakistanis agreed that the Jamaat-i-Islami Party had been troublesome, but they were concerned over the implications of Ayub's police action. Some observers had been noting Ayub's recent behavior with increasing misgivings. As his term lengthened he seemed to be moving closer to one-man rule. Stringent regulations in 1964 closed down West Pakistan's last opposition paper, and a pro-Government press trust bought up leading papers to make sure that they toed the official line. After a long term in office there were indications that some members of the Ayub team had grown corrupt; the President himself had to explain how his son-in-law had suddenly resigned his Army commission to pop up as one of Pakistan's biggest businessmen.

As the 1965 presidential election rolled around, five opposition parties ranging from ultraleft to ultraright united behind the prestigious figure of Fatima Jinnah, 72, sister of the late Mohammed Ali Jinnah, to oppose Ayub's re-election bid. Taking as her theme Ayub's rationalization for dictatorship —"our greatest need is to maintain stability"—the wiry spinster countered that "you can't have stability through compulsion, force and the big stick." As Miss Jinnah politicked, Ayub seemed to panic. He juggled both the election rules and the date. He need not have, for he won the balloting on January 2, 1965, with 61 per cent of the vote. Hearing the news, Ayub cried, "Thank God! The country has been saved." But more and more Pakistanis were beginning to wonder whether Ayub's long tenure was not proving Lord Acton's dictum about the corrupting effect of power. The Ayub Khan victory motorcade that streamed through Karachi's streets after the election ran down a total of 33 of Miss Jinnah's followers and left a bad taste in many mouths.

SO did a fundamental turn in Pakistan foreign policy. Though a member of SEATO and CENTO, Pakistan had long complained that the U.S. took its allies "for granted." In 1961 Ayub impatiently burst out in public, "At times our American friends seem to question our right even to defend our territory." What Ayub was referring to was his long-nurtured dissatisfaction with what he regarded as Washington's tendency to place India's interests above those of Pakistan. He thought that U.S. military aid for India reinforced Delhi's intransigence over the disputed state of Kashmir. This predominantly Moslem province had been taken by India during Partition, an act of monumental injustice in the eyes of Pakistan. Indeed, Kashmir became a focus not just for the India-Pakistan rivalry, but also for the apparently ineradicable hatred and distrust that exists between Hindus and Moslems. This hatred broke forth violently in 1965 when India's and Pakistan's armies clashed in brief but bloody fighting, each side accusing the other of trying to seize the lovely, jewel-like province.

But even before this short, undeclared war further embittered relations between India and Pakistan, and between Pakistan and the Western world, Ayub had sought friendship with the Communist regime in China. In 1962, when the U.S. abruptly increased its military aid to India following the Chinese attacks on India's northern frontier, Ayub persisted in viewing the move as hostile to Pakistan, as strengthening India's ability to hold Kashmir rather than its ability to resist a bellicose China. In revenge Ayub in 1963 gave China its first air outlet to the non-Communist world, conceding to the Reds reciprocal permission to fly to East and West Pakistan, a route, incidentally, that takes Chinese planes over Indian territory. The eastward turn accelerated in 1964 when China came out openly for Pakistan in the Kashmir dispute. Ayub was grateful, but he also tried to keep a Pakistan foot in both camps, with Karachi continuing to maintain membership in SEATO and CENTO. There was also the matter of U.S. aid to Pakistan, an item of one million dollars a day, which Ayub dearly wanted continued.

Nevertheless, in 1965 Ayub traveled to Peking for a lavish reception and then to Moscow for a lesser greeting. A subsequent trip to Washington was canceled rather unceremoniously, and although President Johnson later did see Ayub it was clear that Pakistan would have a hard time continuing to play with both sides. The new republic was going to have to make up its mind about a couple of vital issues: whether its Government was going to be democratic or one-man rule, and whether its foreign policy would lean toward the West or the Chinese Communists. Obviously, Pakistan's growing pains were far from over.

FOR FURTHER READING

Andrus, J. Russell, and Azizali F. Mohammed, *The Economy of Pakistan.* Stanford University Press, 1958.
Bolitho, Hector, *Jinnah; Creator of Pakistan.* Macmillan, 1955.
Callard, Keith, *Pakistan; A Political Study.* Macmillan, 1957.
Kahin, George McTurnan, ed., *Major Governments of Asia,* 2nd ed. Cornell University Press, 1963.
Spear, Percival, *India, Pakistan, and the West,* 3rd ed. rev. Oxford University Press, 1961.
Stephens, Ian, *Pakistan.* Frederick A. Praeger, 1963.
Symonds, Richard, *The Making of Pakistan.* Faber and Faber, London, 1950.
Weekes, Richard V., *Pakistan; Birth and Growth of a Muslim Nation.* D. Van Nostrand Co., 1964.
Wilcox, Wayne Ayres, *Pakistan; The Consolidation of a Nation.* Columbia University Press, 1963.

Nepal, Bhutan and Sikkim

DREAMING away the centuries on the southern slopes of the great Himalayas north of India, the sealed kingdoms of Nepal, Bhutan and Sikkim were all but unknown to Western man until the 1950s. Before then visitors were not welcomed. In the 19th Century all three countries were forced to accept British (later Indian) advisers, but these officials for the most part were kept residence-bound in the three capitals while the peoples went their own ways untouched by foreign ideas.

Sometimes, for mountain men love mountaineers, a British, Swiss, German or French climbing team was admitted to try its luck on one of the monster mountains, Everest, Kanchenjunga or the others that for 700 miles rim the northern frontiers of these countries. But after burying their dead the climbing parties were expected to move out smartly.

From the few who caught brief but tantalizing glimpses of these aloof countries came charming descriptions of fairy-tale lands incredibly far removed from modern times. There were no wheeled carts or cars in most parts of these Himalayan kingdoms and no roads to roll them on; no radios, no newspapers, no movies, little currency, few towns and no worries worth worrying. It seemed possible to believe that the shy and gentle Lepchas, the original people of Sikkim, had in fact been born of bamboo shoots and that their merry laughter, rising in the cold air, froze into the stars that twinkled down upon the river gorges and mountain ridges.

Here life still retained customs from the distant past. Men strode the mountainsides of Bhutan roaring, "Women, prepare, I am lord of the mountains and I own the sun. Your valley is mine." And from across a ridge would come a mocking female chorus, "But are you a man?" Archery contests were (and still remain) the favorite sport of Bhutan, and elaborately dressed contestants came to the butts each with his chorus of village girls who sang to him, "My beautiful lord, let your arrow fly like a bird, straight to its nest." But his rivals' choruses sang back that there are goats in their villages handsomer than this "beautiful lord."

But change is coming to the mountains and coming fast. The first stirrings came with the independence of India. Emulating the new political activity to the south, political parties and factions appeared, demanding land reform and constitutional government. More important was the appearance of the Chinese Communists in Tibet, just to the north, which brought home the realization that, should China decide to launch a major invasion of India, there are many passes through these mountain kingdoms to the plains below.

LARGEST of these newly imperiled kingdoms is Nepal, whose problems arise mostly from the fact that its rugged geography divides it into many small enclaves. Formed of a number of principalities by Gurkha warriors in the 18th Century, it stretches 500 miles along the Tibetan border and runs some 100 miles down the slopes and valleys of the Himalayas. The three major bands of ridges and valleys run west to east, but great blocks of mountain and river gorges compartmentalize them. In these compartments live some 9.7 million people of 10 or 12 major ethnic groups, and many minor ones, all speaking different languages and dialects.

Transportation between these diverse compartments is very difficult, and most of Nepal's internal commerce still moves on the backs of pack animals or coolies. The people at different altitudes live according to different culture patterns, eating different

An old Hindu shrine stands by a river near Katmandu, Nepal.

foods and keeping different animals. Thus the people think in terms not of the nation but of their *thum,* or county. This local loyalty naturally leads to political apathy on the national level. The situation has been only worsened by King Mahendra, who has dismissed his prime minister and with the help of an advisory council is

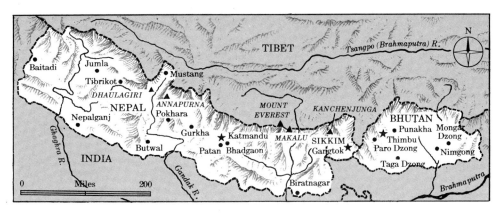

ruling his country alone. This is the reverse of the 100 years ending in the 1950s when Nepalese kings were powerless, the virtual captives of a family of prime ministers, the Ranas.

But the Ranas have lost their hold, and Nepal's isolation has begun to break down. By 1965 diplomatic relations had been opened with 35 foreign countries. Modest but useful loans and grants have been promised on all sides, including $60.6 million from India, $76.4 million from the U.S. and $42.2 million from Communist China. With such sums at hand the King and his advisers have set ambitious goals for the country's progress, including such things as 1,000 miles of new roads, 900 new telephone lines, schools for 60,000 more children, three new hospitals and 10 new health centers.

Second in size of the Himalayan kingdoms is Bhutan, with 18,147 rugged square miles ranging up to 24,000 feet, and 715,000 equally rugged people. Its beginnings are lost in antiquity, although most people date its political existence from about 300 years ago. Until 1907 Bhutan, like Tibet, was ruled jointly by a high lama, revered as a reincarnation of the Buddha, and a temporal leader. In 1907, when the incumbent lama died and a successor could not be found, the Government was taken over by a local governor who had himself elected King. The present King, Jigme Dorji Wangchuk, is this man's grandson. A progressive ruler (who nonetheless prefers the title *Druk Gyalpo*—''Precious Ruler of the Dragon People''), Dorji often leaves Thimbu, the capital, and travels about the country overseeing the medical programs and road-building projects he has sponsored. In domestic affairs he has absolute power, although he listens to an eight-man advisory council and all laws officially originate in a 130-man national assembly. By treaty India controls Bhutan's external

affairs, an arrangement the people of Bhutan accept in the hope that it will deter their aggressive northern neighbor, China. Bhutan's people, although poor in terms of money, live quite satisfactorily. They eat well and are adequately clothed, and most of them not only own land but also have two homes, a winter one in a valley and a summer one higher up.

Third and smallest of the Himalayan kingdoms is little Sikkim, a protectorate of India, which is smaller than Yellowstone Park and has 167,000 people. Essentially, Sikkim, which has an American Queen, the former Hope Cooke, is a trough 40 miles wide between two north-and-south-running ranges of the Himalayas. The western range forms the boundary with Nepal. The eastern range may one day determine Sikkim's history, for through it comes the Natlu-La, a pass that is still one of the easiest invasion routes from Tibet into India.

Sikkim has an Indian prime minister and an Indian finance adviser. Recent finance advisers, and aid from India, have enabled Gangtok, the capital, to rebuild itself in handsome stone houses, modern shops and a refurbished royal palace. The country's chief political issue, the lack of an elected congress, does not seem to be near a solution. One reason is that immigrants from Nepal have become a majority in the country, and the Lepchas and Bhutias, the earlier inhabitants, do not want to be outvoted.

But this issue tends to be lost in a general sense of urgency. At the royal palace, behind grilles designed to ward off demons, typewriters clack and telephones ring. Indian troops drill in Sikkim; Indian engineers have built a road northward from Gangtok to the border areas. Fear of China is galvanizing the country. Perhaps if the Sikkimese and the Indians are successful, they can protect the independence of the never-never lands forever.

Ceylon

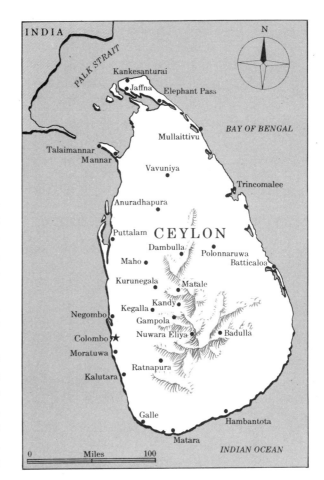

AGAINST a background of Asian turmoil and poverty, the island nation of Ceylon looks at first glance like an oasis. "Isle of Delight" the ancient Moors called it; "Resplendent" is its name in Sanskrit. Marco Polo described it as "the best island of its size in the world." Moslems believe this pearshaped land was the next best thing to paradise and that, after being cast out of Eden, Adam and Eve spent the rest of their lives in Ceylon.

The pleasantly tropical island, cooled by trade winds, is at no point more than 70 miles from the balm of the green Indian Ocean. The Sinhalese, who make up 70 per cent of the 11 million population, are a happy, easygoing people. Rush hour brings traffic jams to Colombo, the capital (pop. 511,000), and parking is difficult around the large downtown department stores, but the way of life seems casual, pleasant and colorful, from the men wearing sarongs and vividly colored shirts to the head-shaven Buddhist monks strolling about in saffron robes, carrying black umbrellas.

Ceylon is densely populated. Since the island has only 25,332 square miles—roughly the area of Ireland—on which live some 11 million people, the density comes to well over 400 people to the square mile. But even this is deceptive since only about a fifth of the island is cultivated. On this basis each square mile of productive land must support about 2,200 people. Most of the people live in the southwestern portion of the island, called the wet zone, and in the central highlands, and both of these are fertile. The northern section and the land along the east coast—the dry zone—are subject to droughts and are for the most part thinly populated.

Despite these drawbacks, the people of Ceylon are better fed, clothed and educated than any others in South Asia. If the people in the little thatch-roofed farming villages—and the overwhelming majority live in such small communities—know few of the conveniences thought essential by people in the

West, they are at least twice as well off as the people of their near neighbors to the north, India and Pakistan. But somehow Ceylon has never quite proved to be the paradise that its advantages would seem to promise, and the island's soft breezes these days often carry the harsh disputation of a divided people, and sometimes the crack of gunfire.

Ceylon's early history is clouded in the mists of legend and mythology. According to the *Mahavamsa,* an ancient Sinhalese chronicle, Ceylon's history began with the landing of a man called Vijaya. A descendant of a union between an Indian princess and a lion (*sinha* means "lion," hence Vijaya's people came to be called Sinhalese), Vijaya was exiled from India because of his evil ways. Wandering to Ceylon with 700 followers, he enlisted the aid of a sorceress to subdue the demon population. Then, turning over a new leaf, he is said to have ruled benevolently for 38 years.

This fantastic legend contains several germs of truth. The arrival of Vijaya probably represents the first important event in Ceylon's history: the coming of the North Indian Aryan immigrants. The demons

Vijaya subdued were most likely aboriginal Veddahs, the first known inhabitants of Ceylon. (There are still some Veddahs in Ceylon's interior jungles, living much as did their Stone Age ancestors.)

The second great event in Ceylonese history was the introduction of Buddhism in the mid-Third Century B.C. The great majority of Sinhalese became, and remain, Buddhists. By this period the Sinhalese kings had established their capital at Anuradhapura, and from there they ruled Ceylon for the better part of the first millennium A.D. From time to time there were palace intrigues and minor revolutions. Occasionally Tamil adventurers from South India invaded Ceylon and usurped the throne for short periods. But until about 700 A.D. the destruction wrought during these periodic upheavals was apparently not so great that things could not be set right during the long intervening eras of peace. Great irrigation works—lifeblood of agriculture in the dry northern area where the Sinhalese were concentrated—continued to be built and extended, and the land continued to produce its wealth.

Stimulated by Buddhism, the early Sinhalese nurtured a great civilization. They built magnificent cities with ornate palaces and parks, large Buddhist monasteries and beautiful shrines called dagobas to house relics of the Buddha. Sinhalese painting of the Fourth to Sixth Centuries attained astonishing excellence. Perhaps the best examples are the frescoes in a fortress built on a precipitous hill at Sigiriya by a king named Kasyapa. The paintings may once have covered an entire face of the rock. Today all that remain are 21 graceful female figures—still glowing in brilliant colors after 1,500 years—located in a cave halfway up the near-vertical cliff. The modern Sinhalese language and script also took shape in these early centuries and a number of poetic works from this era still survive.

AFTER the end of the Sixth Century the armies of South Indian Tamil kingdoms came to Ceylon more and more frequently and with ever greater success. Civil wars also became more frequent. One after another, Sinhalese generals, employing Tamil mercenaries, usurped the throne and moved the capital back and forth between Anuradhapura and Polonnaruwa, 60 miles to the southeast. By the end of the Ninth Century the kings of Ceylon could no longer keep the realm intact, and

in 1017 great armies of the Chola Empire of South India destroyed Anuradhapura, annexed Ceylon and made Polonnaruwa their headquarters.

Periodically thereafter, Sinhalese generals tried to wrest power from the Cholas and briefly, under Vijayabahu I in the mid-11th Century and under Parakramabahu I the Great in the mid-12th Century, they succeeded. Parakramabahu especially renewed the glory of Sinhalese civilization. During his reign gardens and schools, palaces and baths, and Buddhist shrines of great beauty were constructed in Polonnaruwa. But after Parakramabahu's death the civil wars began anew and South Indian armies descended again. In due course the great monuments were laid waste. Irrigation works were destroyed and no longer rebuilt. When drought came the rivers dried into malarial pools. Little by little the defeated population edged its way southward into the forbidding central highlands and jungles of the southwest. By the dawn of the 16th Century the ancient Sinhalese dynasty was reduced to a number of squabbling principalities, with the lowland capital at Kotte near Colombo and the uplanders centered around Kandy. Divided Ceylon was plainly easy picking for the first predator who passed by.

IN the autumn of 1505 some Portuguese galleons dropped anchor off Colombo looking for water. They stayed to do the picking. These first predators came under the guise of helping the Sinhalese kingdom at Kotte fight a number of enemies, especially some Moslem traders who had ensconced themselves in Colombo. What they wanted was to convert the cinnamon industry to their profit and the people of Ceylon to Roman Catholicism. They gained control of the cinnamon-producing wet zone by playing off one rival chieftain against the next. As for their proselytizing activities, the directive to Franciscan missionaries read: "Begin by preaching, but that failing, proceed to the decision of the sword." But the record is not all black. Many missionaries did give devoted service, teaching the people such useful things as how to grow new crops. Their proselytizing, and that of later missionaries, was not unsuccessful, and Ceylon has 718,000 Roman Catholics today. The Portuguese record on the whole, however, is anything but creditable.

In 1658 the Dutch, who had been promised trading concessions by the king of Kandy, ousted the

Portuguese. Then the Dutch stayed on, of course, despite the efforts of the king of Kandy to get rid of these new invaders. The Dutch were naturally not half as concerned about the welfare of the king or of Ceylon as they were with profits. Yet in pursuit of them, the Hollanders set up a creditable colonial framework: they improved communications, established a lasting system of Dutch-Roman jurisprudence, imposed a good amount of law and order, and (predictably) dug canals.

BUT soon the tides of power shifted, and in 1796 the British ousted the Dutch from Ceylon. For the first few years of British rule the island was governed by the East India Company. The Company unwisely replaced the local Sinhalese chieftains, through whom the Portuguese and Dutch had governed, with British and Indian civil servants who were ignorant of Ceylonese customs. Disturbed by this new regime and by its sometimes questionable methods of taxation, the Ceylonese shortly staged a revolt.

This bloody uprising prompted London to take Ceylon away from the East India Company in 1802 and make it a Crown Colony. The country was not yet fully subdued, however. In their mountain fastness the Kandyans remained stubbornly independent, and not until 1815 were British forces able to invade the area successfully. That year the Kandyan king was captured and sent into exile in India, and the 2,300-year-old line of Sinhalese monarchs finally came to an end.

With the country united and largely pacified, the British began to build new roads into the highlands and to encourage European, and particularly British, merchants and entrepreneurs to penetrate into the interior to trade and clear the jungles for coffee plantations. In the mid-1830s adventurous men began to come in droves to cut themselves hearty helpings. In their wake, banking, shipping and other necessary commercial services developed. To establish and run great coffee estates required large capital investments, which few Sinhalese could accumulate. Inevitably they became British economic outposts, often run by retired Army men or civil servants, most of whom made up for their ignorance of coffee by their harshness with their workers. Increasing numbers of Tamils from India were brought in to work the fields, and so exploited were they that for a time their annual death rate was an incredible 250 per 1,000.

It was all very profitable for the landowners, and by 1877 over 250,000 acres of coffee were being cultivated. Then a virulent coffee fungus struck, and within 10 years the burgeoning industry was destroyed. After initial panic the growers tried tea, and it proved successful beyond hope. By 1962 Ceylon was growing 467 million pounds annually, about 20 per cent of the world's supply. The rubber industry, which grew up after 1876, further accelerated the trend toward plantation agriculture and the need for imported Tamil labor. Until 1921 the Indians entered mostly as indentured servants, living in bondage to their plantations until they had repaid their passage money. These late-arriving Tamils made up an unassimilated group that today numbers one million. Ceylon's third most important crop, coconuts, is the only one that is almost exclusively in the hands of Ceylonese rather than foreigners.

The three cash crops—tea, rubber, coconuts—constitute some 95 per cent of the country's exports and have made Ceylon the richest nation per capita in the area. But they have also created a lopsided economy with serious problems. By concentrating on market agriculture, the British failed to develop industry. Further, with two thirds of its cultivable land and population involved in producing and handling the three crops, Ceylon has had to import half of its food. Ceylon's economy is thus dependent to an alarming degree on world market fluctuations.

IF the British were in Ceylon primarily to harvest its resources to their own advantage, and in so doing fostered some great ills, they also must be credited with some great benefits. A *Pax Britannica* spread over the country. The British rebuilt many of the marvelous old dams and built roads and eventually railroads linking all parts of Ceylon. Gradually the administration was overhauled and systematized and an admirable civil service was created. The legal codes and court system were reorganized and the jury system was introduced. Education, too, was stressed, and Ceylon attained a far higher literacy rate than did its great northern neighbor, India.

These reforms, of course, created many of the elements necessary for a modern, independent state. As they did elsewhere, the British created the very forces responsible ultimately for driving them out of the country. Given some voice in their own Government as early as 1833, an increasingly politically minded

In bright skirts and white blouses, girls from a local boarding school take a Sunday stroll along Lake Kandy in central Ceylon.

middle class, Western-educated and full of liberal ideas, came to demand an ever-greater measure of self-government. The more the British reformed, the greater grew Ceylonese pressure for still more reform. Occasionally there were flare-ups, such as the bloody riots of 1848 and 1915, but these were usually spontaneous and not inspired by the politically active Ceylonese, who by and large pursued their goals by strictly constitutional means.

The British recognized as early as 1931 that some sort of self-government for Ceylon was inevitable and granted the country a Constitution with universal suffrage—the first Asian nation to achieve it. The nationalists were not fully satisfied with the new Constitution but accepted it and diligently tried to make it work. The governmental structure, in fact, proved unwieldy, but the 1931 Constitution did provide the Ceylonese with an excellent period of training in the techniques of government that stood them in excellent stead when they finally took complete charge of their country in 1948. As the Union Jack was lowered for the last time and the Sinhalese lion flag was raised, Ceylon slipped easily into independence as a Dominion voluntarily associated with the British Commonwealth.

During Ceylon's first eight years of independence, the country was administered by the United National Party, founded and led (until his death in 1952) by Don Stephen Senanayake, a wealthy plantation and mine owner who had worked hard for Ceylonese independence. Significantly, the party had an English name and its leaders almost without exception were Western-educated and upper middle class. Schooled in English gradualism, these leaders aimed at measured but steady progress. All went fairly well until the outbreak of the Korean War, which caused a sharp rise in the price of rice. Since Ceylon must import large amounts of rice to feed its people, the whole economy was thrown into a turmoil. Rationing had to be instituted and a Government subsidy that had kept down the price of rice had to be discontinued. All this heightened popular dissatisfaction with the Westernized United National Party, a dissatisfaction on which the opposition leaders capitalized.

In 1956 the people of this land of tea terraces and umbrella-shaped shrines went to the ballot box for a democratic revolution. The People's United Front (whose Sinhalese initials are MEP), a strange amalgam of Marxists, Buddhists, supporters of Sinhalese supremacy and plain opportunists, led by Solomon West Ridgway Dias Bandaranaike, swept out the UNP. The MEP victory reflected a growing Sinhalese nationalism directed against the Western-educated and against the Tamil communities. Those Sinhalese educated only in the Sinhalese language, for example, felt at a disadvantage in a country still largely dominated by a Western-educated and English-speaking elite. Peasants were fearful that the continuing growth of the giant plantations meant increasing landlessness for them.

The actions of the Bandaranaike Government, such as the nationalization of the port of Colombo, served only to put the economy into further disarray. Then, after two years, a blowup occurred. The cause was a 1956 law proclaiming Sinhalese the official language in place of English. With that the simmering antagonism between the country's six million Buddhist Sinhalese and its two million Hindu Tamils—an antagonism that had grown during the 450 years of Portuguese-Dutch-British rule but had been submerged by nationalist feeling—forcefully came to the surface. The Tamils, who speak the Tamil language, a Dravidian tongue native to South India, reacted to the new law sullenly. Outbreaks multiplied and then a May 1958 train derailment incident escalated into sharp communal rioting that claimed 300 to 400 lives before the Government restored order by force. A compromise law was passed permitting "reasonable use of Tamil," but the smoldering issue broke out again in 1961 and again had to be met with force.

BY this time, however, Bandaranaike was dead, shot by a crazed Buddhist monk. Bandaranaike's widow, matronly Sirimavo Bandaranaike, who was swept into office on a wave of sympathy, became the world's first woman Prime Minister. She surrounded herself with assorted Marxists and Trotskyites, and the Government blundered leftward. It recognized East Germany, whereupon the West German Government in Bonn cut off its aid. It expropriated without compensation several U.S. and British oil firms, whereupon the U.S. also cut off aid. It spawned 15 socialized enterprises, all but one of which operated at a financial loss. The prices of potatoes, cabbage and dal (tropical pea) rose 50 to 100

per cent, and textiles suddenly became hard to get. As friction increased, Catholics of Burgher background (descendants of the Portuguese and Dutch colonists) began leaving the country for Australia. A Government economist admitted: "We've always lived well and without worry. . . . But now we're in real trouble."

Foreign-exchange reserves in 1964 hit the lowest point since 1941, while prices soared. But if these problems were remediable, not so easy was the phenomenal population increase of 2.7 per cent annually. In 1948, when Ceylon gained independence, there were some seven million persons on the island; 15 years later there were 10.6 million. A tribute to past good government, to the wiping out of malaria and to improved health services, Ceylon's population was outrunning the capacity of the lovely island to feed it. This was especially true in a nation where there was a growing shortage of cultivable land and little progress in shifting to industry. As the rapidly expanding population pressed upon a relatively static resources base, and as it showed a reluctance to enter upon the disciplined time-delimited life that marks highly productive societies, the future of the lovely island was heavily overcast.

A new Government, elected in March 1965, did appear, however, to have some constructive ideas. Headed by Dudley Senanayake, son of the country's first Prime Minister, the new Government proclaimed itself neutralist but decidedly pro-Western, and it took steps to meet some of the nation's problems—and to attract much-needed U.S. aid. In any case, the election was peacefully contested by several political parties and the exchange of power was orderly. Both of these were excellent signs for the future.

FOR FURTHER READING

Bailey, Sydney D., *Ceylon*. Hutchinson's University Library, London, 1952.
Farmer, B. H., *Ceylon; A Divided Nation*. Oxford University Press, 1963.
International Bank for Reconstruction and Development, *The Economic Development of Ceylon*. The Johns Hopkins Press, 1953.
Jeffries, Sir Charles, *Ceylon; The Path to Independence*. Frederick A. Praeger, 1963.
Pakeman, S. A., *Ceylon*. Frederick A. Praeger, 1964.
Tresidder, Argus John, *Ceylon; An Introduction to the "Resplendent Land."* D. Van Nostrand Co., 1960.
Wriggins, W. Howard, *Ceylon: Dilemmas of a New Nation*. Princeton University Press, 1960.

Outer Mongolia

Soviet-trained Mongolian troops, dressed in Russian-style greatco

WHEN Outer Mongolia entered the United Nations in 1961, Westerners began to get their first good look in centuries at the land of Genghis Khan. What they found was a desolate-appearing land that was also a modern state with a surprisingly high standard of living, combining features that would be familiar both to an industrially oriented European and to Marco Polo.

As recently as 1921, when Outer Mongolia became the Soviet-protected Mongolian People's Republic, the most imposing structures in the nation were Buddhist monasteries; today the most impressive buildings are apartment houses and factories. The only medical care and education that existed were the medieval forms practiced in the monasteries, available only to the monks (called lamas); today Ulan Bator, Outer Mongolia's capital, has a university and seven other institutions of higher learning, including a medical school. It is estimated that there is one doctor for every 1,000 people, and almost 100 per cent literacy has been achieved among the younger generation. But despite rapid industrialization and the introduction of modern agriculture, the economy remains, as it has for hundreds of years, predominantly pastoral and nomadic. The difference is that the herdsmen are now organized into cooperatives served by schools and hospitals. The majority of the people live in round, portable tents known as *yurts* or *gers*, just as they did in Genghis' time, but many of the tents are now factory-made and some even have electric lighting.

It was obviously no simple feat to bring Outer Mongolia into the 20th Century. This isolated land, lying between Siberia and China, is one of the most sparsely populated and rugged nations on earth. Covering some 600,000 square miles, it is as large as England, France, Germany, Italy and Portugal combined, but it is inhabited by only about a million people. Most of the country is a vast plateau averaging 3,000 to 5,000 feet in height. In the northwest rises a rough mountainous section; in the southeast the nation takes in 175,000 square miles of the Gobi desert, an area two thirds the size of Texas.

If the countryside, with its *yurts* and herds of livestock, has changed little in appearance since the days of the Khans, neither have the people. In the towns many wear Western dress today, but most still wear the traditional *del*, a long coat of silk, wool or padded cloth. The Mongols are a mixture of many peoples, and the terms "Mongol" and "Mongoloid" are not, strictly speaking, racial terms. Some Mongols, with copper skin, straight noses and high cheekbones, are not unlike American Indians (to whom they may be related). Others have button noses and round faces. What all have in common is a strong feeling for Mongolian tradition. All share a passion for the country's ancient sports—archery, wrestling and long-distance horse racing. Their favorite alcoholic drink is still fermented mare's milk. Virtually all Mongolians are expert horsemen. It was horsemanship, in fact, that first brought this region of Asia to

...ot across a vast square in Ulan Bator, Mongolia's capital. The square is named after a founder of Communist Mongolia, Sukhe Bator.

the attention of the rest of the world. Mongol raiders caused China to build its Great Wall. And in the 13th Century the Mongols rode westward toward Europe and eastward into China to conquer a large part of the known world.

Genghis Khan became king of the Mongols around 1206 and deployed his skilled cavalrymen in all directions. The empire he began eventually took in the territory from Peking to the Danube, from Lake Baikal in Siberia down to the Persian Gulf. The huge empire was relatively short-lived, however. About a century and a half after Genghis' conquests the Chinese pushed the Mongols back and destroyed their capital, and in the late 1500s Inner Mongolia was occupied, never again to emerge from Chinese rule. In the 17th Century the Chinese Manchus occupied

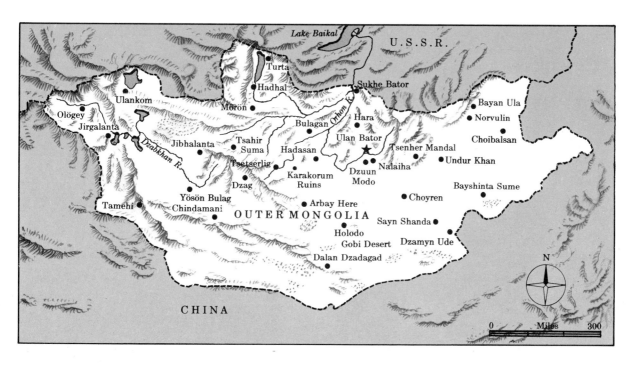

Pedestrians in Ulan Bator wear Western dress and native "dels."

Outer Mongolia and kept control of it until 1911.

Of considerable help to the Chinese in suppressing the Mongols was the rise of Lamaist Buddhism, a religion that perpetuated Outer Mongolia's economic and political stagnation. By the beginning of the 20th Century 750 monasteries were flourishing, and 40 per cent of all Outer Mongolian males were celibate and nonworking lamas. The highest-ranking spiritual, and in effect temporal, authority was the Urga Living Buddha, who, like the Dalai Lama in Tibet, was considered an incarnation of the Buddha. Much of the country's wealth belonged to the monasteries. And the wealth consisted of little beyond livestock, since the lamas told the people that mining and agriculture would annoy the spirits of the earth.

In 1911, at the time of China's nationalist revolution, Outer Mongolia broke away and became an autonomous region under the protection of czarist Russia. But life for most Mongols was little changed. Power was held by petty feudal nobles, by the monasteries, and by Chinese traders and adventurers. The vast majority of Mongolians were illiterate. Since the wealthy preferred not to work, they educated impoverished youths to perform jobs that required special skills—such as staffing the new state's Russian-trained Army or handling clerical work for traders.

It was in such a climate that two young men were able finally to set in motion forces that would transform their land. The first, Sukhe Bator, was conscripted into a cavalry unit and served as an officer until 1919, when the Chinese, reasserting their authority, disbanded the Mongolian Army. Instead of turning in his arms to the Chinese, Sukhe Bator persuaded his men to hide their guns and bullets and thus formed the nucleus of a revolutionary organization. In 1920 he tried to go to Russia to see Lenin, and according to some accounts succeeded. In any case, he received aid from the Red Army. The Government —at that point an alliance between the Urga Living Buddha and a Baltic soldier of fortune—was routed and Mongol independence was declared.

Aiding Sukhe Bator was Choibalsan, an intellectual who in his youth had run away from a monastery, studied at an interpreters' school and gone on to higher schooling in Siberia. In 1917 he had made contact with Russian revolutionaries. Sukhe Bator was the popular leader of the people, beloved almost as much for his feats of horsemanship as for his revolutionary guidance. Choibalsan supplied the ideology and the international Communist connections. Mongolians proudly claim that although they could not have set up their republic without Russian military backing and economic aid, it was their own people who were responsible for the revolution and the way their nation developed afterward.

THEY are not, however, so proud of the way Mongolia's affairs were conducted in the first years. Until the early 1930s, when Choibalsan took personal control of the Government (Sukhe Bator had been poisoned, so it was said, by a lama doctor in 1923), the nation went through what its historians look upon as "deviations" to the right and left. Changes in policy were accompanied by purges, and with each switch many officials were jailed or executed. When Choibalsan took over he announced a "New Turn" following a path between right and left. Until his death in 1952 he ruled Outer Mongolia with the authority and personality cult of a Stalin.

In 1961, to commemorate the 40th anniversary of the Mongolian People's Republic, the Government published a book giving personal accounts of the revolution by 203 of Sukhe Bator's original followers. It is significant that of the 203 only 17 ever joined the Revolutionary Party. Many of the men who made the revolution were only dimly aware of Marxist dogma, a fact that helps explain the slow start in putting the revolutionary goals into practice. Instead of moving against the lamas directly, and risking a split in the ruling coalition, the new Government actually made the Urga Living Buddha the titular head of state. When he died in 1924, the new

Government still avoided a direct attack on the lamas. Instead, it simply announced that Buddhist legends had given no indication that there should be another Urga Living Buddha—and thus the state quietly became a secular republic.

The real attack on the monasteries did not begin until the 1930s, at a time when the Japanese were in control on the Manchurian-Mongolian frontier. The Government had already begun charging the lamas with impeding the advance of modern education and medicine. Many of them were also accused of helping the Japanese cause. Some of the monasteries were disbanded and many lamas were shot. The campaign against the lamas continued after the war, and today in all of Outer Mongolia there are only two or three operating monasteries and a few hundred lamas.

SHORTLY after World War II ended, Outer Mongolia began receiving massive economic and technical aid from the Soviet Union, and the pace of socialization and modernization was sharply accelerated. A visitor to Ulan Bator 20 years ago would hardly recognize today's up-to-date city. Although some of its 220,000 people still live in *yurts*, many live in modern apartments. A full program of concerts, ballet, opera and theater—including many Western works—is performed each year. Films are very popular. Jazz records are produced, including a popular item called "The Waltz of Ulan Bator."

When Mongolia became the People's Republic the country had no industry and virtually no agriculture. Today modern factories, making use of Mongolia's livestock resources, turn out such export items as shoes, textiles and canned meat. Coal is mined on a large scale near the capital. In other regions veins of copper, iron and gold are worked. Oil has been struck in the Gobi desert. A railroad, completed in 1962, connects Ulan Bator directly with both Moscow and Peking.

Outside the towns most of the herdsmen are organized into cooperatives. At the center of the cooperative there is always a school and a hospital. But although their health is improved, and they can read and write, the herdsmen still live a nomadic life, carrying their *yurts* with them as they follow their sheep, cattle, yaks, goats, camels and horses hundreds of miles in search of forage. Most of the livestock is owned by the cooperatives, but many herdsmen also have animals they own themselves. In addition to the cooperatives there are state farms, where strains of livestock have been improved through the latest methods of experimental animal husbandry. In 1959 a large-scale program to grow crops was begun, and by 1961 Mongolia for the first time was able to supply enough wheat for its own people.

Changes in the official party line in Mongolia have never reached the proportions of Russian policy turnabouts, but generally the People's Republic has followed the Russian line. Yumzhagin Tsedenbal, who became Prime Minister after Choibalsan's death in 1952, conducted a campaign against the "personality cult" of Choibalsan at the same time Nikita Khrushchev was attacking the personality cult of Stalin. When Russia and China began to draw apart, the Mongols expelled Chinese laborers who had been helping them with construction projects, and Tsedenbal made it clear that the Mongols would support the Russians against the Chinese. Centuries of Chinese occupation account for the fear in Outer Mongolia of being swallowed up by China—as was the case with Inner Mongolia, which under Chinese colonization programs now contains more Chinese than Mongols. With a population of only about a million, Outer Mongolia would not be able to resist the Chinese without the support of Russia.

The Outer Mongolian state is organized almost exactly the way Russia is organized, with the party playing the dominant role. But Mongolian leaders insist that their revolutionary nation has its roots in nationalism. There are no Red Army detachments in the country; most of the Soviet technicians and teachers have been replaced by Mongols; there are no high-level Russian administrators. The Government has made it clear that on the world scene its first loyalty is to Russia, but in recent years journalists and other visitors from the West have been issued visas and have received a warm welcome from their Mongolian hosts—who still display the curiosity of Genghis Khan about the outside world.

FOR FURTHER READING

Bisch, Jorgen, *Mongolia; Unknown Land*. E. P. Dutton, 1963.
Douglas, William O., "Journey to Outer Mongolia." *The National Geographic Magazine*, Vol. 121, No. 3 (March 1962), pp. 289-345.
Lattimore, Owen, *Nomads and Commissars; Mongolia Revisited*. Oxford University Press, New York, 1962.

Korea

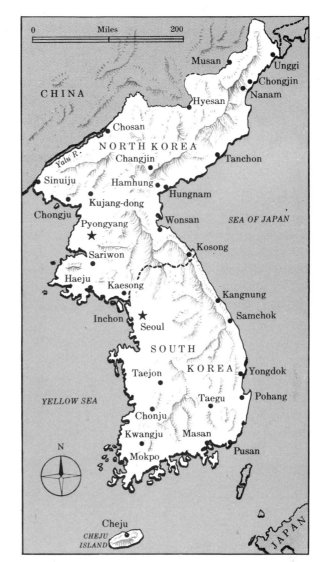

KOREA is a land of heartbreak. Through the centuries it has struggled to maintain its identity as marauding Asian armies have thundered over its mountainous terrain. Japan occupied the country for the first half of this century, its domination and exploitation ending only through its defeat in World War II. During the war Korea was promised freedom, independence and unity by the Allied powers, but before the country could begin to repair the damage, material and psychological, done by long years of Japanese captivity, it was split in two, a Communist regime ruling the country's northern half. Then in 1950 it became a battleground once more, this time for an ugly, frustrating war waged between the forces of the East and the West. The conflict ended three years later with Korea still split politically and geographically and left once more to rebuild from the rubble of ruinous fighting.

Korea's geographic location is largely responsible for its violent history of invasions and occupations. A peninsula jutting off the Asian mainland and aimed toward Japan, Korea was inevitably coveted as a bridge—to Asia by the maritime Japanese, to Japan by the continental armies of Asia. It is a small country, 84,544 square miles, or approximately the size of Minnesota. But its strategic importance becomes evident when its neighbors are considered. Manchuria, China's large northeastern province, fronts on most of Korea's northern boundary. About 120 miles across the Yellow Sea from the Korean peninsula lies China's Shantung peninsula. At about the same distance to the southeast is Honshu, Japan's main island. And for 11 miles in the far northeast Korea shares a border with Russia.

With these powerful neighbors it is not surprising that Korea's history is inextricably bound with the expansionist dreams of Asian powers. The Chinese invaded in the Second Century B.C., then struck again in the Seventh Century A.D. The ferocious Tatars rode in during the early 11th Century, and

the Mongols hit in the 13th Century. The Japanese invaded in the late 16th Century and the Manchus of China in the 17th. The Koreans managed a fitful era of isolation from the 18th Century until they became embroiled in the 1904-1905 Russo-Japanese War. The victorious Japanese war dragon swallowed Korea whole, not to disgorge it until 1945.

This string of foreign incursions has threatened to crush the Korean nation entirely, but somehow the country's spirit has not withered. Korea has been, and still is, peopled by one race with a common language, heritage and culture. It is an old culture. The country's origin, according to Korean tradition, goes back to a spiritual king, Tan'gun, who ruled for 1,000 years, and the Koreans calculate that the year 1965 was the 4,298th year after Tan'gun. Outstanding among the elements that have made up Korean culture has been an indigenous, unique and highly effective form of poetry called *sijo*. *Sijo* poems are brief but often powerful three-line stanzas in which hundreds of poets have expressed themselves since the 13th Century. The golden age of *sijo* was in the 15th and 16th Centuries, but the poems are still written and loved.

Through the spate of invasions the Koreans clung to their ancient culture and ways of life until, at the turn of the century, Japan wrenched Korea out of the past and thrust it into the modern age. Korea had existed as a typical Oriental agricultural society. This meant farms, each with a few acres of scattered fields, usually worked by the entire family. Life was not easy. Korea bulges with mountains, one range succeeding another. Only one fifth of the land is arable, and much of this is in narrow valleys or on thin strips of alluvial plain along both the east and west coasts. The northern part of the country—roughly today's Communist North Korea—is less hospitable than the country's southern provinces. In the north the mountains are more rugged and plated with lava, and the climate is more extreme. Rainfall is uneven. In the interior it may not come to more than 20 inches a year. In the south 60 inches falls along the coast, mostly in the summer. The winters in the north are bitterly cold, while in the south the temperature does not go much below freezing.

ALTHOUGH these geographical differences are significant, Koreans, north and south, evolved as a distinct people—even though they were all influenced by their massive neighbor, China. According to legend a Chinese philosopher with 5,000 followers settled in Korea in 1122 B.C. The kingdom established by this philosopher was called Chosun, or Land of the Morning Calm. The Chinese influence on the native Koreans was pervasive. Rice was introduced and became a main factor in the economy. The religion of Buddha and the moral system of Confucius, with their emphasis on family ties, replaced the native beliefs. In fact, as in China, Confucianism influenced the Korean system of government. Chinese became Korea's governmental and literary language. The local alphabet, *onmun*, which had developed in the 15th Century, did not become popular until after World War II.

Not only was Korea dominated for centuries by Chinese influence, and invaded by one conqueror

after another throughout its early history, but it was also torn by internal strife. Rival warlords battled each other for control of the peninsula. Eventually, in 918 A.D., the Koryo kingdom prevailed and the name Korea was born. In 1392 a Korean general overthrew the Koryo kingdom, changed the name of the country back to its original Chosun and moved the capital to what is now the capital of South Korea, Seoul. The victorious general's name was Yi Taejo and the Yi Dynasty lasted until 1910, when the Japanese occupation began.

KOREA'S old ways were torn asunder by the Japanese, who substituted a money economy for the barter system, thus causing a major upheaval in the Korean economy. The Japanese built roads and highways and cast a web of rail lines throughout much of the peninsula. The ports were opened to large ships bearing imported goods. These manufactured things, such as cheap cloth and home utensils, quickly ruined Korea's home handicrafts, rendering the country's potters, dyers and weavers professionally useless. One unfortunate product of most modern societies, an unskilled labor force, ballooned, and the old self-sufficient life of the rural Korean was disrupted forever.

As the Japanese prepared for war in the 1930s, Korea's mineral resources and other raw materials were heavily exploited. Coal, iron ore, tungsten, copper, graphite, and even silver and gold were dug from the Korean earth for use by the Japanese war machine. At the same time, the Japanese supervised the construction of chemical and textile mills and food-processing plants in Korea. To power these operations the Japanese utilized rivers such as the Yalu in the north for hydroelectric plants.

The Japanese not only took rice and raw materials from Korea, but also for 35 years sent to Korea all the industrial managers and technicians, the Government officials and business leaders needed to run the country. As a result, when the Japanese were expelled, Korea found itself with few skilled workers or educated leaders and even lacked a trained class of civil servants to run the Government bureaus.

After the war Korea also found that, although the country had not been subjected to heavy bombing or invasion, the industrial complexes were in poor repair and Japanese fiscal policies had helped set off an economic inflation. However, Korea had not

A Korean farmer and his wife work near their thatch-roofed house. Korea is largely agricultural despite a paucity of arable land.

been destroyed by World War II, and the Koreans had every right to expect recovery and even prosperity in the modern world to which the Japanese had introduced them. Then politics split the country in half, in effect strangling each half.

The victorious powers of World War II divided Korea along the now-infamous 38th Parallel. The original object, agreed upon between the United States and Russia, was to expedite the Japanese surrender and withdrawal, the Russians clearing the Japanese troops out of the country's northern half. But this line of convenience became an armed political boundary. Elections supervised by the U.N., designed to start Korea on the road to self-rule, were not permitted north of the 38th Parallel. Below the line, the Republic of Korea was formed and, in 1948, elections for a national assembly were held. The assembly, in turn, wrote a constitution and chose Dr. Syngman Rhee as the nation's first President. Korea was now, in fact, two countries, but each half longed for unification on its own terms. Two years later, on June 25, 1950, North Korea mounted an armed invasion against South Korea. The United Nations Security Council ruled

it open aggression, and a United Nations army, with heavy reliance on American troops, landed to aid the Republic of Korea.

During the first summer of the conflict, in 1950, U.N. troops were often outnumbered 20 to 1 by the North Koreans, who, with help from their Communist neighbors, had managed to train and equip an effective army. Before six weeks of war had passed, the U.N. forces, including the Army of the Republic of Korea, had been pushed to a beachhead at Pusan in the southeast corner of the peninsula. On September 15, however, the U.N. armies staged a surprise landing at Inchon on the west coast near the capital city of Seoul. At the same time, U.N. troops broke out of Pusan. The war was dramatically reversed. Republic of Korea and Allied divisions pushed northward, crossing the 38th Parallel, and by mid-November advance scouting parties had reached the Yalu River—the boundary between North Korea and China. Then without warning, a human tidal wave of Chinese Communist "volunteers" surged into battle. Again the U.N. forces were driven back, this time just below the 38th Parallel. After many attacks and counterattacks the battle lines held on

U.N. and North Korean observer teams meet at the demarcation line that has separated Korea's hostile halves since the Korean War.

both sides. The area between the contending armies eventually became the truce zone established on July 27, 1953, the day the fighting ended.

The three years of war caused unimaginable suffering, loss and devastation in Korea. Hundreds of thousands of people died; the major cities were nearly obliterated by bombs and shells. Seoul lost about 85 per cent of its industry, transportation and public utilities. The areas of the heaviest fighting in the countryside were left burned and scarred wastes. Nearly 80 per cent of the textile industry in the south, one of the most important elements in South Korea's economy, was destroyed. In all, the war is believed to have cost the South Koreans three billion dollars in productive goods.

The human suffering was also terrible. Besides the thousands of dead, about five million of South Korea's estimated 21 million people were driven from their homes. These uprooted people enlarged the swell of unsettled humanity made by perhaps two million refugees fleeing North Korea and another one to two million Koreans recently returned

from wartime forced labor in Japan and Manchuria.

Nor was the war easier on North Korea. In 1954 the North Korean radio admitted that the war had inflicted on that country more than one billion dollars' worth of damage. Tens of thousands of people were killed. Production fell to less than 40 per cent of the figure for 1949, the year before the war started. Worst hit were such vital sectors as the chemical industry, electric-power plants, fisheries and forest products.

In the aftermath of this war each half of Korea has been trying to rebuild and to resettle its people. But the country remains divided, the governments of the North and the South irreconcilable, bitter enemies. Since the war South Korea has been kept going mainly by American and United Nations aid programs. The United States expended some $5.2 billion on the little country between 1953 and 1965. This aid, largely in the form of equipment and raw materials, has helped industry grow in South Korea. But there are not enough natural raw materials or native technicians. The lack of investment capital

150

and the low purchasing power of the vast majority of the population also have not encouraged industry. However, the fishing fleet, with new equipment and techniques, is reaping a fine harvest from the sea. The Government has spent a good deal of money, much of it donated by the United States, on modernizing and expanding the railroads, and the production of minerals is on the rise.

These advances, unhappily, are to a large degree nullified by South Korea's fast-growing population. The estimated 27.6 million people now in South Korea have had an inexorable rate of population increase amounting to 2.8 per cent a year, giving the country a population density of 727 per square mile, extremely high even by Asian standards. South Korea has the best farmland on the peninsula, but its agricultural output cannot maintain even the present population. Poverty is therefore nearly universal. As one writer has put it, in Korea only the politicians seem to get rich.

The country is also burdened by a large Army. To guard against another attack from the North, South Korea keeps 600,000 men under arms (their equipment is supplied by the United States). Some pessimists suggest that the Communists need not attack; they can just wait until the country's creaking economy collapses. South Korea can find small solace in international trade. In 1963 its total exports amounted to only $86.8 million while it had to import more than $560 million worth of goods.

IT is not easy to learn about life in North Korea today because the Communist Government there permits few observers to cross the border. According to one recent visitor, however, North Korea does not want to be considered a satellite of either Russia or China, but an independent nation. Pyongyang, the capital, is a brand-new city, completely rebuilt after being virtually wiped out during the war. Wide boulevards, spacious parks, and a minimum of hustle and bustle, mostly due to the scarcity of automobiles, make the city appear neat and orderly. There is no unemployment since everyone is allotted work without choice. Policemen are not noticeable and crime, it is claimed, is nonexistent. But there is no real freedom, and the population must obey orders without question. In short, according to the observer, life is orderly and dull. North Korea's Premier, Kim Il Sung, has boasted

that in 1964 the industrial output of his country was 11 times that of 1949 and 13 times that of 1944. But experts note a great gap between the industrial areas of North Korea and the rural areas, where land is rare and the farmers are unable to grow enough to feed the country's people.

A recent development that makes the North Koreans uneasy is the effort to create more normal relations between Japan and South Korea. Premier Kim denounced it as a fresh intrusion of Japan (this time influenced by the U.S.) onto the Korean peninsula. Also, the Japanese would pay $300 million for reparations to South Korea and advance $200 million in economic credits. This strengthening of the South Korean economy would not advance the Communist cause.

As turbulent as Korea seems today, it has known violence and upheaval before. The people are noted for their diligence and forbearance, which, in spite of occupations by foreign powers, wars and ideological oppression, have always managed to endure and even prevail. A hardy people, quick to laugh, Koreans have made a distinct way of life in a country which, when left to bloom, is rich with beautiful scenery. The sculpted paddies and delicately curving pavilions are representative of the Korean spirit. These symbols of practicality and beauty bear with them the inherent qualities of hope. As the foremost of Korea's present-day *sijo* poets, Yi Un-sang, has put it:

> Stumbling, fragmented,
>   only one shred of entrails left,
> Grasping it, hugging it,
>   there is a people who must go on.
> I want to see the smile of dawn again,
>   bloody though its face may be.

FOR FURTHER READING

Hulbert, Homer B., *History of Korea.* (2 vols.) Hillary House Publishers, 1962.
Lee, Chong-Sik, *The Politics of Korean Nationalism.* University of California Press, 1963.
McCune, George M., *Korea Today.* Harvard University Press, 1950.
McCune, Shannon, *Korea's Heritage; A Regional & Social Geography.* Charles E. Tuttle Co., Tokyo, 1956.
Rees, David, *Korea: The Limited War.* St. Martin's Press, 1964.
Scalapino, Robert A., ed., *North Korea Today.* Frederick A. Praeger, 1963.

Oceania

FOR several centuries the story of the South Sea Islands has been a tale of native peoples—with ancient and in some ways primitive cultures—coming in contact with the outside world. From the time of Magellan and his treasure-bent explorers to World War II and the U.S. Marines, interlopers from far away have been altering the traditional patterns of island life.

The original immigrants to these islands were dark-skinned Stone Age men who began heading east from the Asian mainland thousands of years ago. Eventually other migrants from Asia colonized virtually every inhabitable South Pacific island between Asia and Easter Island, 9,000 miles away. When outsiders from Europe and the Orient finally penetrated the region they found homogeneous societies operating in idyllic settings. It was a situation that for years to come would be a part of romantic folklore—and a situation ripe for exploitation.

The section of the Pacific that has played such a prominent role in the world's imagination covers a seventh of the earth's surface and takes in 10,000 islands, less than half of them inhabited or even named. The total population of those that are inhabited amounts to about 4.7 million people. Most of the islands are the tops of partially submerged mountains rising from the floor of the Pacific. Some, called atolls, are formed of coral limestone and seldom rise more than a few feet above sea level.

Long before the time of the coming of the Europeans, the islanders had mastered their environment by becoming skilled mariners. They had no written records and only the crudest of maps, but they understood the sea below and the sky above. They made use of the Pacific's circular currents to take their big outrigger canoes on voyages sometimes thousands of miles in length. They learned to use sails, and they gained accurate knowledge of the shifting trade winds and the monsoons that blow out from southern Asia. They made sophisticated use of the stars for navigation—and even augmented this skill by learning the routes of migratory birds, so that a flight of birds far off on the horizon could tell them their location on the ocean.

The South Pacific contains three principal ethnic regions: Polynesia, meaning "many islands"; Micronesia, "little islands"; and Melanesia, "black islands." Polynesia, the largest of the groupings, forms a triangle in the central and eastern Pacific, its corners touching Hawaii in the north, New Zealand in the southwest and Easter Island in the southeast. Included are the Austral, Cook, Ellice, Gambier, Marquesas, Samoa, Society, Tonga and Tuamotu Islands, and small, isolated islands such as Pitcairn. The people, who have light-brown skin, are closest in appearance to Caucasians of all the peoples in the Pacific. Scholars disagree on their Asian origins; it is believed that they came in several migrations starting sometime before 1000 A.D. Speaking a common language, they developed an elaborate religious system, complete with an involved ritual and numerous taboos. On the relatively wealthy "high" islands—those formed by mountains—their economy was based on fruits, fish, and such cultivated crops as the sweet potato, arrowroot, taro, yam and turmeric. From breadfruit tree bark they manufactured cloth. On the sparse atolls they made do mainly with fish and coconuts.

THE Micronesians live on small, scattered islands in a region mostly above the equator, west of Polynesia and north of Melanesia. The area of the ocean that they cover is larger than the United States, but their total land area is less than 1,400 square miles. In the northern part of Micronesia are the Mariana Islands; at the western end are the Palaus; and to the east and south the Caroline, Marshall and Gilbert Islands. Some scholars believe that the Micronesians came to the islands later than the Polynesians, who had used these islands as way stations on their eastward migrations. As with the Polynesians, the Micronesians' maritime skills became highly developed, though they did not learn to build the large canoes that the Polynesians used for combat and long voyages. The resources of Micronesia were meager compared to Polynesia, but the people became skilled fishermen. Coconut palms furnished food and drink, and the Micronesians used the leaves to make thatch and matting. Because of the islands' isolation from one another,

Clad in a traditional skirtlike lava-lava, a speaker addresses the Parliament of Western Samoa in its open-sided meeting chamber.

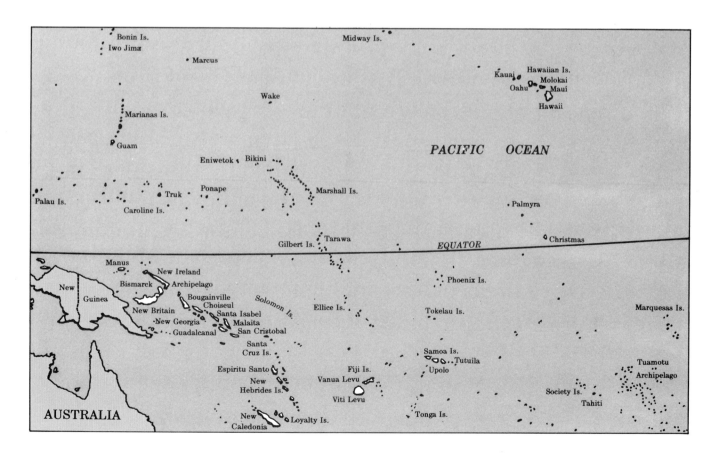

separate, relatively simple cultures grew up and eight different languages developed.

Melanesia, which gets its name from the pigmentation of its primarily Negroid people, is located south of the equator and stretches from New Guinea to the Fijis. It takes in the Solomon, Santa Cruz, New Hebrides, New Caledonia and Loyalty Islands and the Bismarck and Louisiade archipelagoes. A people who have yet to break completely with the Stone Age, the Melanesians formerly practiced headhunting and cannibalism. As in Polynesia and Micronesia, the main agricultural products have always been coconuts, taro and bananas. On the coast most of the people were, and are, fishermen. Pigs are found everywhere and are both a source of food and a proof of wealth. Throughout Melanesia (as in many other Pacific islands) the people have traditionally ornamented their skin.

The outside world first became aware of the civilizations of the South Pacific in 1521 when Magellan, after having sailed across most of the Pacific

A policeman directs traffic in Suva, capital of British-run Fiji.

without coming in sight of a single inhabited island, arrived in the Marianas. Although Magellan was killed in the Philippines, a few of his men got back to Spain and told of what they had found. Over the next 50 years the Spanish established themselves in the Philippines and western Micronesia. The 17th Century saw the emergence of the Dutch as a major trading power in the Pacific, but the 18th Century belonged to the British and the French. Between 1768 and 1779 Captain James Cook sailed over a broad expanse of the Pacific and did such a thorough job of charting the islands that his successors, as a contemporary Frenchman put it, were left "with little to do but admire."

After Captain Cook the islanders began to have consistent contact with the outside world. The explorers were followed by traders and missionaries, beachcombers, whalers and even escaped convicts. The islands were divided up among the major powers of the world. The plantation system was introduced. The majority of the people were converted to various forms of Christianity. In addition to Westerners, numerous Orientals—particularly Indians and Chinese—moved into the area.

THE myth about the South Seas includes the notion that before the coming of the white man the people lived in a kind of paradise. Compared to what happened to them afterward, there is much truth in the myth. Before the white man arrived the South Pacific was largely free of most of the contagious diseases then ravaging Europe. Europeans brought such diseases as syphilis, measles and tuberculosis, which killed off islanders by the hundreds of thousands. In many areas missionaries took over the economic life, and free men suddenly found themselves working for bosses for the first time. Many more were lured away by labor contractors to work in other parts of the world.

On the other side it can be argued that the islanders eventually had to come in contact with people from the continents and that a clash in the ways of life was inevitable. If many missionaries were profiteers, others were dedicated men who fought the casual cruelty of the primitive island societies and took up the cause of the natives when they were oppressed by their colonizers.

And of course the interplay of cultures was not strictly a one-way affair. The writings of Herman

Melville, Robert Louis Stevenson, Pierre Loti and Somerset Maugham were as influenced by the Pacific as were the lives of islanders by the West. The paintings of Paul Gauguin are an enduring reminder of the South Pacific's impact on the consciousness of the world.

THE greatest upheaval in the Pacific, however, did not come until the middle of the 20th Century when remote islands with such now-familiar names as Tarawa and Guadalcanal became bloody World War II battlefields. At the war's start the Japanese controlled all of Micronesia, launched attacks into Polynesia and took over much of Melanesia. The U.S. and its Allies fought bitter campaigns to capture the Japanese-held islands, preparing a strategic position from which an assault on the Japanese mainland could be launched. Both the Japanese and the Allies conscripted the island natives into labor forces to build supply bases and airfields and thus permanently disoriented tens of thousands of people. In the massive air and naval bombardments that preceded the assaults, many natives lost their lives.

Since the war all of the islands have remained in the control of Western powers. Western Samoa, a tiny republic of 119,000 people in western Polynesia, is the only officially sovereign nation in the South Pacific. Independent since 1962, it is closely tied to its former colonial master, New Zealand, which still conducts its foreign affairs.

The natives of Guam in the Marianas have been considered U.S. citizens since 1950. An appointed governor is assisted by an elected unicameral legislature. The residents of American Samoa, six islands in the Samoan archipelago with a capital at Pago Pago, are considered U.S. nationals and have limited self-government. The American Trust Territories in Micronesia, which take in some 2,000 islands (64 of them inhabited), including the Carolines, Marianas and Marshalls, elected their first territorial Congress in the summer of 1965.

Among the British dependencies, Tonga has the greatest degree of self-rule. The 150 islands of the Tonga group were long ruled by the famous Queen Salote Tupou, who was crowned in 1918 and died in 1965. Her son is the present King. External affairs continue to be handled by Great Britain. The Fijis and the British Solomons also enjoy some self-rule. France's holdings in the Pacific are called Overseas Territories, meaning that they have limited self-government and representation in the National Assembly in Paris but are not looked upon as independent states. France's best-known Pacific Territory is French Polynesia. It takes in the Society Islands, which in turn include the Windward and Leeward Islands, the Tuamotu group, the Gambier group, the Australs and the Marquesas. France also controls New Caledonia, a large island in Melanesia.

Tiny Pitcairn Island, still populated by descendants of the *Bounty* mutineers, is controlled by the British; Easter Island, at the extreme eastern end of Polynesia, famed for its gigantic and eerie stone statues, is a colony of Chile. The New Hebrides in Melanesia are administered as a British-French Condominium. The Cook Islands and Niue in Polynesia are New Zealand dependencies.

Until recently the island groups dealt with their problems on a local basis. The first wide-scale official cooperation began in 1928 with the founding of the Central Medical School on Fiji. In 1948 the Western powers involved in the South Pacific formed the South Pacific Commission, an advisory and consultative group which plans programs for the welfare and advancement of the islanders (see page 67).

About 47 per cent of the islanders live in cities, such as France's sophisticated Papeete on Tahiti, or Great Britain's Suva, capital of Fiji. The rest still live in villages. But change is in the air; even remote Easter Island has had the beginnings of a separatist movement. Except for parts of Melanesia, few if any islands have maintained racial purity. On some, native islanders are a numerically smaller group than immigrants, such as Indians. Virtually none have remained untouched by the world beyond the seas.

FOR FURTHER READING

Beaglehole, J. C., *The Exploration of the Pacific*. Adam & Charles Black, London, 1947.

Borden, Charles A., *South Sea Islands*. Macrae Smith Company, Philadelphia, 1961.

Buck, Peter H., *Vikings of the Pacific*. University of Chicago Press, 1959.

Freeman, Otis W., ed., *Geography of the Pacific*. John Wiley & Sons, 1951.

Oliver, Douglas L., *The Pacific Islands*. Harvard University Press, 1958.

Robson, R. W., and Judy Tudor, *Pacific Islands Year Book and Who's Who*. Pacific Publications, Sydney, 1963.

Suggs, Robert C., *The Island Civilizations of Polynesia*. New American Library, 1960.

Credits

The sources for the illustrations in this book appear below. Credits for pictures from left to right are separated by commas, from top to bottom by dashes.

Cover—Farrell Grehan
8—Courtesy the United Nations—Joseph Stonehill
9—Courtesy the United Nations
10—Courtesy the United Nations except right Joseph Stonehill
11—Courtesy the United Nations
12—Courtesy the United Nations except left second from the top and bottom Joseph Stonehill
13—Courtesy the United Nations except bottom left and top right Joseph Stonehill
14—Courtesy the United Nations except top left and center right Joseph Stonehill
15—Courtesy the United Nations except bottom left drawing by John Woods
16—Courtesy the United Nations except top right Joseph Stonehill
17—Courtesy the United Nations except left second from the top drawing by John Woods
18—Courtesy the United Nations except right third from the top Joseph Stonehill
19, 20—Courtesy the United Nations
21—Courtesy the United Nations except top left Joseph Stonehill
22—Courtesy the United Nations except right center Joseph Stonehill
23—Courtesy the United Nations except left and right bottom Joseph Stonehill
24—Courtesy the United Nations except top and bottom right Joseph Stonehill
25—Courtesy the United Nations except right third from top Joseph Stonehill
26—Courtesy the United Nations except left Joseph Stonehill and top right drawing by John Woods
27, 28—Courtesy the United Nations
29—Courtesy the United Nations except right second from the bottom drawing by John Woods
30—Courtesy the United Nations
31—Courtesy the United Nations except bottom left Joseph Stonehill
32—Marvin E. Newman
34—Courtesy the United Nations
35—United Press International
36—Henri Dauman
37—Chart by Nicholas Fasciano
38—Bob Henriques
39—Robert Mottar
40—Courtesy the United Nations
41—Emmett Bright
42—Loomis Dean
43—Chart by Nicholas Fasciano
44—Courtesy NATO
45—Dominique Berretty-NATO Photo
46—U.F.P.
47—Francis Miller
48—N. R. Farbman
50—James Whitmore
51—United Press International
52—Chart by Nicholas Fasciano
53—Farrell Grehan
54—Dominique Berretty
55—Italys News Photo
56—Sabine Weiss for OECD
57—Reportage Bild Stockholm, map by Rafael Palacios
58—Elliot Erwitt from Magnum
60—Eugene Anthony from Black Star
61—John Dominis
63—London *Times*
64—David Moore from Black Star
65—Courtesy the United Nations
66—David Lees
67—Courtesy the South Pacific Commission
68—Dominique Berretty
70—Lawrence Schiller-Don Cravens
71—James Burke—Larry Burrows
72—Farrell Grehan
73—Map by Rafael Palacios
74, 75—Henri Cartier-Bresson from Magnum
77—Farrell Grehan
80—Dmitri Kessel
81—Map by Rafael Palacios
87, 88, 89—Farrell Grehan
92—Marvin E. Newman
93—Map by Rafael Palacios
96—Werner Bischof from Magnum
97—Caj Bremer from Camera Press-Pix
100—Dmitri Kessel, map by Rafael Palacios
101—Hans Wild—map by Rafael Palacios
102—David Lees—map by Rafael Palacios
103—Andy Bernhaut from Photo Researchers—map by Rafael Palacios
104—Charles Rotkin from Photography for Industry
105—Map by Rafael Palacios
106—Leonard Wolfe
107—Map by Rafael Palacios
111—George Holton from Photo Researchers
114, 115—T. S. Satyan
118—David Douglas Duncan
119—Map by Rafael Palacios
121—Esther Bubley
122—James Burke
124, 125—Rene Burri from Magnum—map by Rafael Palacios
127—Margaret Bourke-White
130, 131—Rene Burri from Magnum except bottom left Charles Harbutt from Magnum
134—Leonard Wolfe
135—Map by Rafael Palacios
136—Dmitri Kessel
137—Map by Rafael Palacios
140—Dmitri Kessel
142, 143—Howard Sochurek—map by Rafael Palacios
144—Epoque-Pix
146—John Dominis
147—Map by Rafael Palacios
149—Rene Burri from Magnum
150—John Dominis
153—Christa Armstrong from Rapho-Guillumette—map by Rafael Palacios
154—Christa Armstrong from Rapho-Guillumette

ACKNOWLEDGMENTS

The editors wish to express their appreciation to Marcel Mart, Director of the Information Service of the European Community, New York, for his advice and comment upon the organizations of the European Community.

Index to This Volume

This symbol in front of a page number indicates a photograph or painting of the subject mentioned. NOTE: The Index below does not cover the material contained in the Gazetteer (pages 8-31).

Abadan, Iran, 108
Achaean League, 34
Advertising, in postwar Europe, 53
Afghanistan, 116, *118, 119-123, *121, *122, 126; agriculture, 119-120, 122; bordering nations, 119; Constitution, 123; disputes with Pakistan, 121-122; exports, 122; foreign aid, 122-123; invaders, 120-121; languages, 121; map 119; original stock, 121; people, 120, 121, 122; religion, 120-121; strategic location, 122; terrain, 119; tribes, 122
Afonso I (Afonso Henriques), 74, 76
Africa, 65, 73, 78
Agriculture: Afghanistan, 119-120, 122; Andorra, 101; Ceylon, 139; FAO programs, 41; Iran, 108; Korea, 148, *149; Liechtenstein, 100; Outer Mongolia, 145; Portugal, 74, 75; prices for Pakistan exports, 132; San Marino, 102; tariff disputed in Common Market, 53
Ahmad Khan, Sir Sayyid, 126-127
Ahmed Shah, 120
Akbar, 126
Albania, 47, 58
Alexander I, 94, 95
Alexander II, 95
Alexander III, *quoted,* 95
Alexander the Great, 112, 113, 120
Alfonso VI, 76
Ali Khan, Liaquat, 128
Aligarh Anglo-Oriental College, 127
Alliance for Progress, 60
Allied Command Channel, 44-45
American Trust Territories, 155
Andorra, *101; map 101
Anglo-Iranian Oil Company, 117
Anglo-Persian Oil Company, 108
Anuradhapura, Ceylon, 137, 138
ANZUS Treaty, 49
Arab League, 66
Ardashir I, 113
Arwidsson, Adolf Ivar, *quoted,* 94
Aryans, 112, 137
Asia, 48, 49, 64, 66-67, 134-135. *See also* individual countries
Association of Southeast Asia (ASA), 66-67
Atlantic Charter, 34
Atomic energy: for Europe, 54-55; peaceful uses, 40, 54; power plant, *41; production, 40
Aurangzeb, Emperor, 126
Australia, 39, 49, 62, 63
Austria, *80, 81-86, *87-89, 90-91; *Anschluss,* 90; culture, 86, 90-91; early history, 84-85; economy, 81-82, 83, 86, 90, 91; Habsburgs, 82, 84-85; industry, 81, 83, 91; map 81; people, 81, 82-83, *87-89; politics, 82, 83, 86, 90, 91; *Proporz,* 82, 83; standard of living, 81-82; tourist industry, 81; after World War I, 81, 86, 90; since World War II, 81, 82, 90-91
Austro-Hungarian Empire, 81, 83-86; peoples in, 84-85
Avis, House of, 76
Ayub Khan, Mohammed, 129-133

Babenberg Dynasty, 84
Babur, 126
Bactria, Afghanistan, 120
Baghdad Pact, 47
Baluchi nomads, 122
Bandaranaike, Sirimavo, 141
Bandaranaike, Solomon West Ridgway Dias, 141
Bank for International Settlements (BIS), 56
Banking, international, 40, 41, 56, 90
Belgium, 55, 85
Belgium-Luxembourg Economic Union (BLEU), 50. *See also* Benelux
Belgrade Conference, 69
Benelux, 55
Bengal, 124, *130
Berlin Blockade, 43
Bernini, Giovanni, 105
Bhutan, 134, 135; map 135
Bobrikov, N. I., 95
Borodajkewycz, Taras, 82
Bounty, H.M.S., 155
Brazil, 78
Bretton Woods Conference, 40-41
British East India Company, 126, 139
Brown Shirts, 90
Brussels Treaty, 46
Bucephalus, 112
Buddhism, 120-121, 135, 138, 141, 142, 144, 145, 148
Bulgaria, 43, 47, 59
Bureau of International Expositions (BIE), 70
Buz Kashi, 123

Calcutta, 124
Camões, Luís de, 75
Cão, Diogo, 78
Carlos I, 79
Carmona, António Fragoso, 79
Caroline Islands, 152, 155
Casablanca Charter Organization, 65
Castel Gandolfo, 104

Castle Vaduz, Liechtenstein, *100
Catholic Church. See Roman Catholic Church
Central America, 60, 61; economy, 61-62
Central American Common Market (CACM), 61-62
Central Commission for the Navigation of the Rhine, 69
Central Treaty Organization (CENTO), *47, 48, 133
Ceylon, 62, 64, *136, 137-141, *140; agriculture, 139; art, 138; expropriates foreign oil firms, 141; geography and topography, 137; language controversy, 141; legends, 137-138; map 137; people, 137, 141; political parties, 140, 141; religions, 138, 141; Sinhalese rulers, 138, 139; standard of living, 137; Tamil invasions, 138; Western exploitation, 138-140
Chamber of Commerce. See International Chamber of Commerce
Charlemagne, 84
Charles I of Spain. See Charles V
Charles III, Prince, 103
Charles V, Holy Roman Emperor, 85
Charles VI, Emperor, 100
Château de la Muette, Paris, *56
Chile, 155
China, 143-144, 147, 148; Communist, 35, 37, 47, 58, 119, 134, 135, 145, 149; foreign aid to Nepal, 135; friendship with Pakistan, 133; involvement in Korean War, 149; in Tibet, 134
Choibalsan, 144, 145
Chola Empire, 138
Churchill, Winston, 34, 108, 110; *quoted,* 50
Clemenceau, Georges, 86
Coal, production, 52, 145
Coimbra, Portugal, 74; University of, 76, 79
Cold War, 34, 69. *See also* Communism; Soviet Union
Colombo, Ceylon, 64, 137, 138, 141
Colombo Plan, 64, 66
Colonialism, 65, 73, 126, 138-140, 147, 148, 154
Comecon. See Council for Mutual Economic Assistance
Common Market (European), 50, 51, 52, *53, 54, 55, 58, *61, 62, 65, 91; Asian reaction, 66, 67; Commission, *53; contrasts with European Free Trade Association, 58, 91; crisis over Great Britain, 46, 53-54; meeting, *61; members, 52, 55,

56; rapid expansion, 52; status quo tendency, 53-54; treaty, 52, 53, *55; world's biggest trader, 52. *See also* Central American Common Market
Commonwealth, the, 62-63, 64, 65; common defense, 63; common ties, 63; members, *63
Communications. See European Broadcasting Union; International Radio and Television Organization; International Telecommunication Union
Communism, 47, 48, 49, 60, 64, 96, 97, 102, 134, 144, 151
Communist satellites, 43, 46-47. *See also* individual nations
Confucianism, 148
Congo, the, 35, 38
"Congress of Europe," 50
Cook, Captain James, 154
Cook Islands, 67, 155
Cooperatives, herdsmen, 142, 145
Costa Rica, 59, 60, 61
Council of Europe, 46, 56-57
Council for Mutual Economic Assistance (Comecon), 58
Council on World Tensions, Inc., 38
Crime, international, 70
Cuba, 60
Currency exchange, 41, 61
Cyrus the Great, 107, 110, 112
Czechoslovakia, 43, 47, *58, 59, 84, 85, 86

Da Gama, Vasco, 73, 78
Daniel, 112
Danube Commission, 69
Danube River, 69, 75, 143; canal, *89
Darius, 110, 112
Darius III, 112
De Gaulle, Charles, 45, 53, 54, 55, 58; *quoted,* 45, 54
Delgado, Humberto, 79
Desert of Death (Dasht-i-Margo), 119
Dias, Bartolomeu, 73, 78
Diniz, 75, 76
Diocletian, 102
Dollfuss, Engelbert, 90
Dominican Republic, 60
Dost Mohammed Khan, 120
Dual Monarchy, 82
Dulles, John Foster, 48; *quoted,* 91
Dunant, Jean-Henry, 68
Dürer, Albrecht, 85
Durham, Lord John, 62

Easter Island, 152, 155
Eastern European Mutual Assistance Treaty (Warsaw Pact), 46-47; member, *46
ECLA, 38
Economic Survey for Europe, 38

ECOSOC. See United Nations: Economic and Social Council
Edward VII, 103
Egypt, 35
El Salvador, 61
Elburz Mountains, 107
Electric power, 54, 81
Energy. See Atomic energy; Electric power
England. See Great Britain
Esfahan, Iran, 107, *111, 116
Ethiopia, 36, 65
Eugene, Prince of Savoy, 85
Eurofima, 68-69
Europe: Eastern, 46-47, 70; industry, 53; Marshall Plan, 55; military defense, 43-45, 46; OECD, 55-56; radio and television, 70; World Bank loans, 41
European Atomic Energy Community (EURATOM), 50, 51, 53, 54-55
European Broadcasting Union (EBU), 70
European Coal and Steel Community, 50, *51, 52, 53, 54, 55; description of treaty, 51; High Authority, 51-52; significance, 51
European Community, 50-51, 52, 57; chart 52; map 57; structure, 52
European Conference of Ministers of Transport (ECMT), 68-69
European Defense Community, 46
European Economic Community (EEC). See Common Market
European Free Trade Association (EFTA), 57-58; map 57; "Outer Seven," 56, 91; rebound from Common Market, 57
European Parliament, *50, 51
European Payments Union (EPU), 50
European Recovery Program. See Marshall Plan
Eurovision, 70
Exploration, 73, 138, 152, 154
Exploration, Age of, 76, 78

Ferdinand, Archduke, 86
Figl, Leopold, 91
Fiji (islands), *154, 155
Finland, *92, 93-99, *96, *97; civil war, 95-96; culture, 99; forests, 93, 95; industrialization, 95, 98; language, 93, 94-95; Lapland, *97; Lapua movement, 96, 97; map 93; Russian Grand Duchy, 94; Swedish rule, 93-94; wars with Russia, 94, 97, 98
Fischer von Erlach, Johann, 85-86
Food and Agriculture Organization (FAO), 41
France, 35, 38, 39, 46, 48, 49, 65, 85, 103

Franz Joseph II, 100
Frederich Karl, Prince, 96
Frederick the Quarrelsome, 84
Freud, Sigmund, 90-91

Galvão, Henrique, 79
Gandhi, Mohandas, 128
Gangtok, Sikkim, 135
Gazetteer, 8-31
Gebhard, Hannes, 96
General Agreement on Tariffs and Trade (GATT), 40
General Assembly. See United Nations: General Assembly
General Treaty of Central American Integration, 61
Genghis Khan, 116, 120, 126, 142, 143, 145
Germany, 81, 86, 90; East: 43, 47, 58, 59, 141; West: 43, 46, 51, 81, 123, 141
Ghana, 62, 65
Gheorghiu-Dej, Gheorghe, 47, 59
Gobi desert, 142, 145
Great Britain, 35, 39, 51, 57; advisers in Nepal, Bhutan, Sikkim, 134; Anglo-Persian Oil Company, 108; Commonwealth, 62-63, 65; control over Ceylon, 139-140; given Channel islands, 39; handles Tonga foreign affairs, 155; influence in Iran, 116, 117; intervenes in Lebanon and Jordan, 37; invades Afghanistan, 120; joins Baghdad Pact, 47; leads European Free Trade Association, 56; officials in Pakistani Government, 128; Partition of India, 124, 125, 128; rebuff from Common Market, 53-54; relations with Dominions, 62; as ruler of India, 126; in Western European Union, 46
Greece: ancient, 34, 71, 110, 112; modern, 34, 43, 81
Grimaldi family, 103
Guam, 155
Guatemala, 61
Gustavus IV, 94

Haile Selassie, Emperor, *36
Hallstein, Walter, quoted, 54
Hammarskjöld, Dag, 35, 36; quoted, 36
Harun al-Raschid, 113
Hassan Ali Mansour, 109
Hazrat Ali, 121
Heimwehr, 90
Helmand Valley, Afghanistan, 123
Helsinki, *92, 95, 96, 97, 99; University of, 94
Henry of Burgundy, 76
Henry the Navigator, Prince, 73, 76, 78
Henry the Quarrelsome, 84
Herodotus, 109-110
Herter, Christian, quoted, 45
Hildebrandt, Johann Lukas von, 85-86

Himalayan kingdoms, 134-135
Himalayas, 134, 135
Hindu Kush (mountains), *119, 120, 123
Hinduism, 124, 125, 126, 127, 133, 141; shrine, *134
Hitler, Adolf, 86, 90
Holy Roman Empire, 85, 100
Honduras, 61
Hungary, 35, 43, 82, 83, 84, 85, 86; revolution, 58-59

India, 62, 63, 78, 116, 120, 124, 133, 134, 137; armies invade Ceylon, 138; British rule, 126; Hindu-Moslem incidents, 127; Kashmir dispute, 35, 133; migrants to South Seas, 154, 155; Moslem League, 127; Moslem rulers, 125-126; Mutiny against British, 126; nationalist movement, 127; relations with Himalayan kingdoms, 135; religious war after Partition, 125; trains technicians under Colombo Plan, 64
Indian National Congress, 127
Indus River, West Pakistan, 112, *130-131
Industry: Austria, 81, 83, 91; Central America, 61; Czechoslovakia, *58; Eastern Europe, 58-59; Europe, 52-53; Iran, 108-109; Korea, 148, 150, 151; Liechtenstein, 100; Monaco, 103; Outer Mongolia, 145
Inn River, Austria, *80-81
Inner Mongolia, 143, 145
"Inner Six." See Common Market
Inter-African and Malagasy States Organization. See Monrovia Group
Inter-American Conference, 59
Inter-Governmental Maritime Consultative Organization (IMCO), 42
International Atomic Energy Agency (IAEA), 40
International Bank for Reconstruction and Development (World Bank), 40-41
International Chamber of Commerce (ICC), 69
International Civil Aviation Organization (ICAO), 41
International Commission for Air Navigation, 41
International Committee of the Movements for European Unity, 50
International Criminal Police Organization (Interpol), 70
International Development Association (IDA), 41. See also International Bank for Reconstruction and Development
International Finance Corporation (IFC), 41
International Labor Organization (ILO), 42

International Monetary Fund (IMF), 41
International Olympic Committee, 71
International Radio and Television Organization (OIRT), 70
International Telecommunication Union (ITU), 42
International Union of American Republics, 59
Intervision, 70
Iqbal, 127
Iran (Persia), 34, 47, 48, *106, 107-110, *111, 112-113, *114-115, 116-117, 119, 126, 131; agriculture, 108; Arab rule, 113; culture, 113, 116; economic pacts, 109; foreign concessions, 117; invasions, 112-116; map 107; modernization, 108-109, *114-115; oil, 107, 108, 109, 117; people, 108, 109-112; Persian Wars, 110, 112; religions, 112, 113
Iraq, 47
Islam, 113, 121, 123, 125, 128. See also Moslems
Islamabad, Pakistan, 131
Islands of the South Pacific. See Oceania
Ismail, 116
Israel, 35, 66; Lost Tribes, 121
Italy, 85, 86, 90, 104, 105

Jamaat-i-Islami Party, 132
Japan, 56, 145, 147, 148, 149, 151, 155
Jasomirgott, Duke Henry, 84
Jesuits, 78
Jews, 91, 110. See also Israel
Jinnah, Fatima, 133
Jinnah, Mohammed Ali, 124, *127, 128
João II, 78
João V, 78
João VI, 78, 79
Jonas, Franz, 82
Jordan, 35, 37

Kabul, Afghanistan, 119, *121, 122
Kafirs, 122
Kalevala, Lönnrot, 94
Kanchenjunga, Mount, 134
Kandahar, Afghanistan, 123
Kandy, Ceylon, 138, 139
Karachi, Pakistan, 128
Kashmir, 35, 48, 119, 133
Katmandu, Nepal, 134
Kekkonen, Urho, quoted, 99
Kennedy, John F., 49, *61
Khrushchev, Nikita, 37, 59, 99, 145
Khyber Pass, 120, 128
Kim Il Sung, 151
Korea, 38, *146, 147-151, *149, *150; agriculture, 148; Chinese influence, 147, 148; division of, 147, 149; geography and topography, 147, 148; industry, 148; invasions, 147-148; Japanese

exploitation, occupation, 147, 148; *map* 147; *sijo* poetry, 148
Korea, North, 35, 58; climate and geography, 148; economy, 150, 151; industrial claims, 151; invades South Korea, 149; losses from Korean War, 150; *map* 147
Korea, South, 43; Army, 151; climate, 148; economy, 150, 151; elections, 149; Inchon landings, 149; losses from Korean War, 150; *map* 147; relations with Japan, 151; U.S. aid, 150
Korean War, 34, 43, 49, 60, 129, 140, 147, 149, *150

Labor. *See* International Labor Organization
Lahore, Pakistan, 124, 127
Laos, 35
Lapland, *97, 98
Lapuan movement, 96-97
Lateran Treaty, 104
Latin America, 59-62
Latin American Free Trade Association (LAFTA), 62
Latvia, 43
League of Nations, 34, 42, 62, 86; Mandates, 39; Permanent Court of International Justice, 39
Lebanon, 35, 37
Lie, Trygve, 35, 36
Liechtenstein, *100; *map* 100
Lisbon, *74-75, 76, 78, 79
Lithuania, 43
London Declaration, 34
Lönnrot, Elias, 94
Low Countries, 85
Luxembourg, 55

Macao, 73
Madagascar, 65
Magellan, Ferdinand, 154
Mahavamsa, 137
Mahendra, King, 135
Mahler, Gustav, 86, 91
Mahmud of Ghazni, 126
Malaya, 62, 66
Malaysia, Federation of, 67
Mannerheim, Carl Gustaf, 95, 96, 97, 98
Manoel II, 79
Manoel (the Lucky), 78
Maratha Confederation, 126
Marco Polo, 142
Marconi, Guglielmo, 105
Mariana Islands, 152, 154, 155
Marshall, George C., 55
Marshall Islands, 155
Marshall Plan, 50, 55, 64, 83
Marxism, 144
Masaryk, Thomas, 86
Masjid-i-shah, Mosque of, *111
Maximilian I, 85
Mayence, Convention of, 69
Mazar-i-Sharif, Afghanistan, 121
Medicine. *See* UNICEF; World Health Organization

Melanesia, 67, 152, 154
Memory of Solferino, A, Dunant, 68
Metternich, Prince, 86
Michelangelo Buonarroti, 105
Micronesia, 67, 152, 154
Middle East, 47-48. *See also* Afghanistan; Iran
Military defense organizations, 43-49
Mirza, Iskander, 129
Mogul Empire, 126
Mohammed Yousuf, 123
Mohammed Zahir, 123
Monaco, *103; *map* 103
Mongolia. *See* Outer Mongolia
Mongols, 84, 93, 116, 122, 142-143, 147
Monnet, Jean, 50, 51, 52
Monrovia Group, 65
Monte Carlo, 103
Morocco, King of, *66
Moscow conference (1943), 34
Moslem League, 127
Moslems, 75-76, 78, 109, 124, 125, 126, 127, 128, *131, 132, 137. *See also* Islam
Mossadegh, Mohammed, 117
Mountbatten, Lord Louis, 124
Muhammed Ghuri, 126
Mussolini, Benito, 90
Muzaffir ed-Din, 117
Myrdal, Gunnar, 38

Nadir Kuli Beg, 116
Napoleon I, 78-79, 86, 94
Nasir ed-Din Shah, 117
Nasser, Gamal Abdel, *66
NATO. *See* North Atlantic Treaty Organization
Nauru, 39
Nehru, Jawaharlal, 127, 129
Nepal, 134-135; Hindu shrine, *134; *map* 135
Netherlands, the, 55, 67, 85, 138-139
New Caledonia, *67, 155
New Guinea, 39, 67, 154
New Hebrides, 155
New York World's Fair, 70
New Zealand, 39, 49, 64, 155
Nicaragua, 60, 61
Nicholas I, 95
Nicholas II, 95
Nigeria, 62
Niue, 155
Nordic Council, *57
North Atlantic Treaty, 43
North Atlantic Treaty Organization, *44-45, 46, 47; *chart* 43; disputes over nuclear control, 45; flag, *44; main commands, 44-45; Paris headquarters, *45; structure, 43; success of, 45
Norway, fishing rights, 39
Nuclear energy, 40. *See also* Atomic energy
Nuclear war, likelihood of, 45
Nuclear weapons, 45
Nuristani, 122

Oceania, 152, *153, 154-155; Christian missionaries, 154; disease, 154; economy, 152, 154; ethnic differences among peoples, 152, 154; European colonialism, 154; extent of self-rule since World War II, 155; in literature, 154-155; *map* 153; maritime skills of islanders, 152; migrations, 152; number of islands, 152; Oriental influx, 154; population, 67, 152, 155; South Pacific Commission, 67, 155; Western control since World War II, 155; World War II, 67, 155
Oil, 81, 107, 108, 109, 117, 145
Olympic Games, 70, *71
Omar Khayyám, 116
Organization of African Unity (OAU), 65
Organization of American States (OAS), 59-60; delegates, *60; Meeting of Consultation, 60; supports U.N. in Korea, 60; suspends Cuba, 60
Organization of Central American States (ODECA), 60-61
Organization for Economic Cooperation and Development (OECD), 55-56
Organization for European Economic Cooperation (OEEC), 50, 56
Os Lusíadas, Camões, 75
Ostrogoths, 84
Otto the Great, 84
Ottocar II, 84
Outer Mongolia, *142-143, 142-145, *144; Chinese invasions, 143-144; economy, 142, 145; horsemanship, 142-143; literacy, 142; *map* 143; revolution, 144; Russian sympathies, 145; Ulan Bator, *142-143
"Outer Seven." *See* European Free Trade Association
Outer-space communications, 42
Overseas Territories, French, 155

Paasikivi, J. K., 99
Pacific, islands of. *See* Oceania
Pacific Islands (Trust Territory of), 39, 155
Pago Pago, Samoa (U.S.), 155
Pahlavi, Mohammed Reza Shah, 108-109, 113, 117
Pahlavi, Reza, 108-109, 117
Pakistan, *40, 47, 48, 62, 109, 121-122, *124-125, 124-133, *127, *130-131; Ayub Khan regime, 129-133; basic democracy, 131-132; East Pakistan, 124, 128, 129; economy, 129, 130, 131, 132; elections, 129, 132, 133; established as state, 124, 128; fear of India, 124, 129; foreign policy, 133; geography and topography,
124, 128; government and politics, 124, 127, 128, 129-133; Kashmir issue, 133; language problem, 124, 128; *map* 124; Moslem rule in India, 125-126; nationalism, 127; 1958 coup, 129; origin of name, 127; problems of Partition, 124-125; refugees, 125, 129, 130; role of Islam in state, 128, 132; West Pakistan, 119, 124, 128
Pan American Convention on Commercial Aviation, 41
Pan American Union, 59
Papeete, Tahiti, 155
Parakramabahu I, 138
Paris, 44, 46, *56
Pathans, 121, 129
Peking, 143, 145
Persepolis, *106-107, 112
Persian Empire, 110-112, 120. *See also* Iran
Persian Gulf, 107, 112, 143
Persian Wars, The, Herodotus, 110
Peter the Great, 94, 116
Philippines, 66, 67
Piffl-Percevic, Teodor, 82
Pitcairn Island, 155
Poland, 43, 47, 58-59, 83, 84, 85
Polonnaruwa, Ceylon, 138
Polynesia, 67, 152, 154, 155
Polynesia, French (Overseas Territory), 155
Pombal, Marquis of, 78
Pope Pius IX, 104
Population explosion, 62, 64, 130-131, 141, 151
Porto, Portugal, 74, 78, 79
Portugal, *72, 73-76, *74-75, *77, 78-79; Age of Exploration, 76, 78; architecture, 73-74; area, 74; Burgundian rule, 76; climate, 74; colonial empire, 73, 78, 138; exports, 75; fishing, 74, *76; folk songs, 75; House of Avis, 76; industrialization, 74; language, 75; Lisbon earthquake, 78; *map* 73; Moslem occupation, 75-76; per capita income, 73; population, 74; revolution of 1910, 79; Salazar regime, 79; topography, 73, 74; War of the Brothers, 79; wines, 74-75, 78
Prebisch, Raúl, 38
Punjab, 124, 128, 130
Pusan, South Korea, 149
Pushtunistan, 121
Pyongyang, North Korea, 151

Rainier III, Prince, 103
Raphael, 105
Rawalpindi, Pakistan, 128
Red Cross, International, 68
Refugees, 71. *See also* Pakistan
Reinhardt, Max, 91
Renner, Karl, 90
Rhine Commission. *See* Central

Commission for the Navigation of the Rhine
Roman Catholic Church, 104-105, 138
Roman Empire, 75
Romania, 43, 47, 59, 84, 86, 109
Rome, 41, 104
Roosevelt, Franklin D., *quoted,* 34
Runeberg, Joan Ludvig, 94
Russia. *See* Soviet Union
Russo-Finnish War, 97-98
Russo-Japanese War, 147

Saarinen, Eliel, 99
SACEUR. *See* Supreme Allied Commander Europe
SACLANT. *See* Supreme Allied Commander Atlantic
St. Peter, 104
St. Peter's Basilica, *104, 105
St. Petersburg (Leningrad), 94
Salazar, António de Oliveira, 79
Salote Tupou, 155
Samoa, American, 67, 155
Samoa, Western, 67, 155; Parliament, *153
San Francisco Conference, 34
San José, Costa Rica, 60
San Marino, Most Serene Republic of, 102; *map* 102
San Marino (city), *102
São Paulo, Brazil, 60
Sardar Daud, 123
Savoy, House of, 104
Scandinavia, 57
Schauman, Eugen, 95
Schnitzler, Arthur, 91
Schuman, Robert, 51
Schuschnigg, Kurt von, 90
Schutzbund, 90
SEATO. *See* South-East Asia Treaty Organization
Seattle Exhibition, *70
Security Council. *See* United Nations: Security Council
Senanayake, Don Stephen, 140
Senanayake, Dudley, 141
Seoul, South Korea, *147, 148; heavy war losses, 150
Shah Abbas, 116
Shantung peninsula, 147
SHAPE. *See* Supreme Headquarters Allied Powers Europe
Shipping. *See* Inter-Governmental Maritime Consultative Organization
Shiraz, Iran, 107
Sibelius, Jean, 99
Siberia, 143, 144
Siege of Vienna, 85
Sijo poetry, 148
Sikkim, 134-135; *map* 135
Sind, Pakistan, 125-126, 130
Sinhalese, 137, 138, 139, 141
Sino-Soviet relations, 47, 58
Sistine Chapel, *104, 105
Snellman, Johan Vilhelm, 94
Sobieski, King Jan, 85
Solomon Islands, 154, 155
South Africa, 63

South Pacific Commission (SPC), 67, 155
South Seas. *See* Oceania
South-East Asia Treaty Organization (SEATO), 47, 48-49, 66, 133; members, *48
Soviet Union, 57, 58, 59, 116, 117, 119; agreement with Iran, 109; aids Mongolian revolution, 144; anti-Western objectives, 43; Austrian occupation, 82, 91; foreign aid (to Afghanistan), 122-123; influence in North Korea, 149; postwar expansion, 43; Security Council veto, 34-35, 38, 43; since Stalin, 45; sub bases, 47; in United Nations, 34, 35, 37, 39; wars with Finland, 97, 98; wars with Sweden, 94; Warsaw Pact, 46-47. *See also* Sino-Soviet relations
Spain, 85, 101; relations with Portugal, 73, 76, 78
Statute of Westminster, 62
Steel production, in Europe, 52, 81
Sterling area, 63
Stone Age, 152, 154
Sukhe Bator, 144
Supreme Allied Commander Atlantic (SACLANT), 44, 45
Supreme Allied Commander Europe (SACEUR), 44
Supreme Headquarters Allied Powers Europe (SHAPE), 44
Suva, Fiji, *154, 155
Sweden, 93-94
Swiss Guard, 105
Switzerland, 83, 85, 86, 91, 100, 120

Tagus River, *74-75
Tajiks, 122
Tamerlane, 116, 120, 126
Tamils, 138, 139, 141
Tampere, Finland, 95
Tanganyika. *See* Tanzania
Tanzania, 37
Tariffs, 40, 57-58; within Common Market, 52, 53; Commonwealth preference system, 63; reduced by Central American nations, 61, 62
Technical assistance, 38, 40, 41, 64, 122-123
Teheran, 48, 108, 109, *114-115, 116
Telecommunications, 42
Television, 70, 81
Thailand, 66
Themistocles, 110-112
Thimbu, Bhutan, 135
Tibet, 134, 135
Tonga (islands), 155
Tordesillas, Treaty of, 78
Tourism: Andorra, 101; Austria, 81; Central America, 61; Monaco, 103; Outer Mongolia, 145; San Marino, 102; Southeast Asia, 67

Trade, international, 40, 69; Central America, 61-62; Commonwealth, 63; European Common Market, 52; Latin America, 62
Transportation (European), 68-69
Trujillo, Rafael, 60
Truman, Harry S., *quoted,* 43
Trust Territories, 39
Trusteeship Council. *See* United Nations: Trusteeship Council
Tsedenbal, Yumzhagin, 145
Tunnels: Mont Blanc and Great St. Bernard, 68
Turkey, 43, 47, 81, 116
Tyrol, *80-81, 84

Ulan Bator, Outer Mongolia, *142-143, *144, 145
Ulugh Beg, 116
U.N. *See* United Nations
Underdeveloped countries, aid to, 41, 42, 56, 64, 66. *See also* Technical assistance
UNESCO. *See* United Nations Educational, Scientific and Cultural Organization
UNICEF. *See* United Nations Children's Fund
United Nations, *34-36, 37, *38-42; achievements, 35, 123; background, 34; basic splits, 34, 35; buildings, *32, *65; *chart* 37; Charter, 34, 36; complex structure, 37; delegates, *35; dues issue, 39; Economic Commission for Latin America, 61; Economic and Social Council, 38; Expanded Programme of Technical Assistance, 40; flag, *34; General Assembly, *32, 34, 35, *36, 37, 38; International Court of Justice, *39; Korean War, 149; legal arm, 39; number of members, 36; observers in Korea, *150; Portuguese possessions, 73; San Francisco Conference, 34; Secretariat, *32, 35-36; Secretary-General, 34, 35-36; Security Council, 34, 36-37, *38, 39, 43; technical assistance program, 38; Trusteeship Council, 39; "Uniting for Peace" resolution, 35, 37. *See also* separate agencies
United Nations Children's Fund (UNICEF), 40
United Nations Development Program, 40
United Nations Educational, Scientific and Cultural Organization (UNESCO), 42
United States: Asian commitments, 48; division of Korea, 149; foreign aid, 50, 60, 64, 122-123, 133, 135, 141, 150, 151; foreign relations, 49, 122, 133; intervenes in Middle East, 37; Marshall

Plan, 50, 55, 64, 83; military pacts, 43-45, 47, 48-49, 59; Seventh Fleet, 49; U.N. actions, 35, 37
Universal Postal Union (UPU), 42
Urga Living Buddha, 144-145
U Thant, 35

Valerian, Emperor, 109
Vatican City, *104, 105; art treasures, 105; established as nation, 104; holdings in Rome, 104; *map* 105; St. Peter's, 105; Sistine Chapel, 105; Swiss Guard, 105; works of Michelangelo and Raphael, 105
Versailles, Treaty of, 42, 69, 90
Vicente, Gil, 75
Victor Emmanuel II, 104
Victoria, Queen, 62
Vienna, 84, 85, 86, *87-89, 90; architecture, 85-86; classical composers, 86, 91; Danube Canal, *89; State Opera, *88
Vienna, Congress of, 69
Vietnam: North, 58; South, 48, 49. *See also* Indochina, French
Vijaya, 137-138
Vijayabahu I, 138

Wangchuk, King Jigme Dorji, 135
Warsaw Pact. *See* Eastern European Mutual Assistance Treaty
Weather. *See* World Meteorological Organization
Wellington, Duke of (Sir Arthur Wellesley), 79
Werfel, Franz, 91
Western European Union (WEU), 46
Western Samoa. *See* Samoa
World Bank. *See* International Bank for Reconstruction and Development
World Council of Churches, 70-71; Assembly, *71; membership, 70
World Court. *See* United Nations: International Court of Justice
World Health Organization (WHO), 38, 42
World Meteorological Organization (WMO), 42
World War I, 81, 84, 86
World War II, 50, 67, 81, 82, 83, 90, 97, 98, 147, 155

Xerxes, 110

Yalu River, 148, 149
Yazdegerd III, 113
Yugoslavia, 58, 69, 83, 86

Zagros Mountains, 107
Zarathustra, 112
Zistersdorf, Austria, 81
Zweig, Stefan, 91

Guide to Major Topics in the LIFE WORLD LIBRARY

The following section is a guide to the major subjects, ideas and persons described in the various LIFE World Library volumes. In each case the latest edition of a volume is used. Many items whose inclusion in a specific volume would be obvious (e.g., the Seine River in *France*) have been omitted, as have various general subjects that would be in all volumes, such as agriculture or manufacturing. To use the Guide, note the three-letter code word provided with each entry, find the volume indicated by using the code guide at the bottom of each page of this Guide, and then look up the item in that volume's own index to obtain a specific page reference. Where terminologies differ, some items may be located under a closely related heading.

Abako, **LCO, TAF**
Abbasid dynasty, **TUR**
Abbud, Ibrahim, **ARW**
Abdül Hamid, Sultan, **TUR**
Abdul Ilah, of Iraq, **ARW**
Abdullah, King of Jordan, **ARW, ISR**
Abdullah, Sheik Mohammed, **IND**
Abdül Mecid, Caliph, **TUR**
Abdul Rahman, Caliph, **SPA**
Abélard, Pierre, **FRA**
Aberhart, William, **CAN**
Aborigines, **ANZ**
Abraham (Biblical prophet), **ARW, ISR**
Abyssinia. *See* Ethiopia
Acadia, **CAN**
Achdut Ha'avoda, **ISR**
Achilles, **GRE**
Acropolis, **GRE, SEA**
Adams, Henry, **FRA, USA**
Adams, John, **USA**
Addison, Joseph, **BRI**
Aden, **ARW**
Adenauer, Konrad, **FRA, GER**
Adrianople, **BAL, TUR**
Adriatic Sea, **BAL, ITA, SWI**
Aduwa, Battle, of, **ITA**
Aegean Sea, **BAL, GRE, TUR**
Aeschylus, **GRE, ITA**
Affranchis, **WIN**
Afghani, Jamal al Din al, **ARW**
Afghanistan, **CHI, HBK, IND, RUS**
Afiqim man, **ISR**
Africa, **ARW, BRA, BRI, CHI, FRA, GER, HBK, ITA, RUS, SAF, SCN, SEA, SPA, SWI, TAF, WIN**
Afrikaners, **SAF**
Afyon, **TUR**
Agamemnon, **GRE**
Agassiz, Louis, **SWI**
Agnelli, Giovanni, **ITA**
Agustín I, Emperor, **MEX**
Ahab, King, **ISR**
Ahimsa, **IND**
Ahmadia, **ISR**
Ahmed, Mohammed (the Mahdi), of Sudan, **ARW**
Ahmed Fuad II, of Egypt, **ARW**

Aid, economic, by Great Britain, Russia and the United States, **ANZ, ARW, BAL, BRA, BRI, CHI, FRA, GER, GRE, IND, ISR, ITA, JAP, LCO, MEX, RUS, SEA, SPA, TAF, TUR, USA.** *See also* Marshall Plan
Aircraft industry, **BRI, FRA, IRE, ITA**
Ajax, **GRE**
Akan tribe, **TAF**
Akbar, Emperor, **HBK, IND**
Akhnaton, Pharaoh, **ARW**
Alamán Lucas, **MEX**
Alamo, siege of, **MEX**
Alans, **BAL, SPA**
Alaouite Dynasty, **ARW**
Alaska, **CAN, SCN**
Alba, Dukes of, **LCO, SPA**
Albania, **BAL, GRE, HBK, ITA, TUR**
Albéniz, Isaac, **SPA**
Albert of Hohenzollern, **GER**
Albrecht of Mecklenburg, King of Sweden, **SCN**
Alcántara, Francisco Martín de, **AND**
Alchemy, **CHI**
Alekhine, Alexander, **RUS**
Alem, Leandro N., **PLA**
Alemán, Miguel, **MEX**
Alemann, Roberto, **PLA**
Alemanni, **SWI**
Alencar, José, **BRA**
Alexander I, Czar of Russia, **EEU, HBK**
Alexander II, Czar of Russia, **EEU, HBK, RUS**
Alexander VI, Pope, **ITA, PLA, WIN**
Alexander Obrenović, King of Serbia, **BAL**
Alexander the Great, **BAL, GRE, HBK, IND, ISR, SCN, TUR**
Alexandria, Egypt, **ARW, GRE**
Alexarchus of Macedonia, **GRE**
Alexis, Patriarch, **RUS**
Alföld (plain), Hungary, **EEU**
Alfonso XIII, King of Spain, **CTA, SPA**
Alfred the Great, King, **BRI, IRE, SCN**

Algeria, **ARW, FRA, ISR, SWI, TAF**
Aliyah: First, Second, **ISR**
Allenby, Sir Edmund, **ISR**
Alliance for Progress, **COL, CTA, HBK, PLA, USA**
Almagro, Diego de, **AND**
Almagro the Boy (son of Diego), **AND**
Almogi, Yosef, **ISR**
Almoravid Berbers, **TAF**
Alonso y Trelles, José, **PLA**
Alp Arslan, **TUR**
Alphabets, **ARW, BAL, IRE**
Alps, **BAL, FRA, GER, ITA, SWI**
Alsace, **FRA, GER**
Alsogaray, Alvaro, **PLA**
Altamira caves, **SPA**
Altstadt (Zurich), **SWI**
Althing, **SCN**
Altiplano, **AND, MEX, PLA**
Aluminum, **CAN, IND**
Alvarado, Pedro de, **AND, CTA**
Amahuaca Indians, **AND**
Amazon River, **AND, BRA, COL**
Amber, **IND**
"Amboina massacre," **LCO**
America. *See* United States
American Revolution, **BRA, CAN, COL, FRA, IRE, PLA, USA**
Amerigo's Land, **COL**
Amida Buddha, **JAP.** *See also* Buddha and Buddhism
Amiet, Cuno, **SWI**
Amis, Kingsley, **BRI**
Amritsar massacre, **IND**
Amsterdam, **FRA, LCO**
Amundsen, Roald, **CAN, SCN**
Amur River, **CHI, RUS**
Anatolia (Anadolu), **TUR**
Ancestor worship, **CHI, TAF**
Anders, Wladyslaw, **EEU**
Andersen, Hans Christian, **SCN**
Andes, **AND, BRA, COL, PLA**
Andhra Pradesh, **IND**
Andino, Tiburcio Carías, **CTA**
Andrade, Mário de, **BRA**
Andreassen, Lennarth, **SCN**
Androutsos (Klepht chief), **GRE**
Angelico, Fra, **ITA**
Angiolini, Gasparo, **RUS**

Angkor Wat, **SEA**
Angles, **BRI, GER**
Anglo-Saxons, **BRI, SCN**
Angola, **SAF, TAF**
Angostura, Venezuela, **COL**
Anielewicz, Mordechai, **EEU**
Animism, **SEA, TAF**
Anker, Albert, **SWI**
Ankole, Kingdom of, **TAF**
Ansermet, Ernest, **SWI**
Antarctica, **ANZ, SCN**
Antes, Horst, **GER**
Anticlericalism, **ITA, MEX, SPA**
Antigua, **CTA, WIN**
Antinoüs, **TUR**
Antiochus Epiphanes, **ISR**
Anti-Semitism, **BAL, FRA, GER, ISR.** *See also* Jews and Judaism
Antonescu, Ion, **BAL**
Antonov, Aleksei, **EEU**
Antony, Marc, **GRE**
Anyte of Tegea, **GRE**
Apennines, **ITA**
Aphaia, **GRE**
Aphrodite, **GRE**
Apollo, **GRE**
Appleton, Tom, **FRA**
Apponyi, György, **EEU**
Aqaba, Gulf of, **ISR**
Aquinas, Thomas, **ITA**
Aquino, Maria d', **ITA**
Arabia, **ARW, TUR**
Arabi Pasha, **ARW**
Arabs, **ARW, CHI, HBK, ISR, SAF, SPA, TAF, TUR.** *See also* Mohammed and Mohammedanism
Aragon, Louis, **FRA**
Arakanese, **SEA**
Aramaic, **ISR**
Aramburu, Pedro, **PLA**
Aran Islands, **IRE**
Ararat, Mount, **TUR**
Araucanian Indians, **AND, PLA**
Arawak Indians, **COL, WIN**
Arawa tribe, **ANZ**
Arbenz Guzmán, Jacobo, **CTA, SWI**
Arbroath, Declaration of, **BRI**
Arcadians, **ITA**

AND Andes; **ANZ** Australia and New Zealand; **ARW** Arab World; **BAL** Balkans; **BRA** Brazil; **BRI** Britain; **CAN** Canada; **CHI** China; **COL** Colombia and Venezuela; **CTA** Central America; **EEU** Eastern Europe; **FRA** France; **GER** Germany; **GRE** Greece; **HBK** Handbook; **IND** India; **IRE** Ireland; **ISR** Israel; **ITA** Italy; **JAP** Japan; **LCO** Low Countries; **MEX** Mexico; **PLA** River Plate Republics; **RUS** Russia; **SAF** South Africa; **SCN** Scandinavia; **SEA** Southeast Asia; **SPA** Spain; **SWI** Switzerland; **TAF** Tropical Africa; **TUR** Turkey; **USA** United States; **WIN** West Indies.

Archeology, **BAL, BRI, CHI, CTA, GRE, ISR, MEX, SEA, TUR**
Archimedes, **GRE**
Arctic, **SCN**; Ocean, **RUS**
Arezzo, Guido d', **ITA**
Argentina, **AND, BAL, BRA, ISR, PLA, SPA**
Arguedas, Alcides, **AND**
Arguedas, José María, **AND**
Arias, Arnulfo, **CTA**
Arias de Avila, Pedro, **CTA**
Arias, Gilberto, **CTA**
Ariel, Rodó, **PLA**
Ariosto, Lodovico, **ITA**
Aristarchus of Samos, **GRE**
Aristophanes, **GRE**
Aristotle, **GRE, ITA**
Arizona, **MEX, USA**
Armada, Spanish, **BRI, SPA**
Armagh, **IRE**
Armenia and Armenians, **ARW, ISR, ITA, RUS, SCN, TUR**
Arminius, **GER**
Arnold, Matthew, **IND**
Arnolfini, Giovanni, **LCO**
Arp, Jean, **FRA**
Arrieros, **MEX**
Artemidos, Saint, **GRE**
Artemis, **GRE**
Arthashastra, Kautilya, **IND**
Arthur, King, **BRI, SPA**
Artigas, José Gervasio, **PLA**
Arzú Castillo, José Mariano, **CTA**
Asanuma, Inejiro, **JAP**
Asceticism, **IND**
Asclepius, **GRE**
Ashanti, **TAF, WIN**
Ashdown battle, **SCN**
Ashikaga family, **JAP**
Ashoka, Emperor, **IND**
Ashton-Warner, Sylvia, **ANZ**
Asia and Asians, **ANZ, ARW, BRI, CHI, GRE, HBK, IND, JAP, SAF, SEA, SPA, TAF, USA, WIN**
Asia Minor, **ARW, GRE, TUR**
Aslama, **ARW**
Asperukh (Khan), **BAL**
Asquith, Herbert H., Lord, **IRE**
Assimilados, **TAF**
Assyria and the Assyrians, **ISR, TAF, TUR**
Astrology, **SEA**
Astronomy, ancient, **MEX**
Aswan High Dam, **ARW**
Atahuallpa (Inca ruler), **AND**
Atatürk, Mustafa Kemal, **ARW, BAL, GRE, IND, TUR**
Atheism, **ISR, RUS**
Athelney, Isle of, **SCN**
Athens, **GRE, SPA**
Athos, Mount, **GRE**
Atl, Dr. (Geraldo Murillo), **MEX**
Atlantic Charter, **HBK**
Atlantic Ocean, **AND, ARW, SCN, SPA**
Atomic energy and weapons, **BRA, BRI, FRA, HBK, JAP, LCO, RUS, SCN**. *See also* Nu-

clear power and weapons
Atotonilco, shrine of, **MEX**
Attila the Hun, **FRA, GER, WIN**
Attlee, Clement, **BRI, IND**
Augustinians, **MEX**
Augustus, Emperor. *See* Octavian
Auiti Indians, **BRA**
Aurangzeb, Emperor, **HBK, IND**
Auschwitz, Poland, **EEU, GER**
Australia, **ANZ, BRI, HBK, ISR, JAP, SEA**
Austria, **BAL, EEU, GER, HBK, ISR, ITA, SCN, SPA, SWI, TUR**
Austro-Hungarian Empire, **BAL, EEU, FRA, HBK**
Austro-Prussian War (1866), **GER**
Avars, **BAL, EEU**
Avignon, **FRA, ITA**
Avila Camacho, Manuel, **MEX**
Axum, Kingdom of, **TAF**
Ayacucho, battle of (Peru), **AND**
Ayala, Plan of, **MEX**
Ayin, Operation, **ISR**
Aymara Indians, **AND**
Azanians, **TAF**
Azikiwe, Nnamdi, **TAF**
Azores, **WIN**
Aztecs, **AND, COL, MEX**
Azuchi-Momoyama Period, **JAP**

Baathists, **ARW**
Babur, Emperor, **HBK, IND**
Babylonia and Babylonians, **ARW, ISR, TUR**
Baca tribe, **SAF**
Bach, Johann Sebastian, **GER, ITA**
Bacon, Francis, **BRI**
Badoglio, Pietro, **ITA**
Baer, Richard, **GER**
Baffin Island, **CAN, SCN**
Baffin, William, **CAN**
Baghdad, Iraq, **ARW, BAL, TUR**; Pact, **HBK, TUR**
Bagirmi, Kingdom of, **TAF**
Bahais, **ISR**
Bahama Islands, **SPA, WIN**
Bakongo tribe, **TAF**
Bakr, Abu, **ARW**
Balaguer, Joaquín, **WIN**
Balagnandàs, **BRA**
Balboa, Vasco Núñez de, **AND, COL, CTA**
Balearic Islands, **SPA**
Balewa, Sir Abubakar Tafawa, **TAF**
Balfour, Arthur James, **ARW, ISR**
Bali, **SEA**
Balkans, **BAL, EEU, GRE, TUR**
Ballooning, **SWI**
Baltic Sea, **GER, RUS, SCN**
Balzac, Honoré de, **FRA**
Bananas, **AND, BRA, CTA**
Banda, Hastings, **TAF**
Bandung Conference, **ARW, SEA**
Bank for International Settlements (BIS), **HBK, SWI**
Banks, Sir Joseph, **ANZ**

Banna, Hassan al, **ARW**
Banting, Sir Frederick, **CAN**
Bantu, **SAF, TAF**
Bao Dai, Emperor, **SEA**
Baraka, **TAF**
Barbados, **WIN**
Barbarossa, **GER**; Operation, **BAL**
Bardo, Treaty of, **ARW**
Barents Sea, **RUS, SCN**
Bar-Kokhba, Shimon, **ISR**
Barnato, Barney, **SAF**
Barrientos, René, **AND**
Barrios, Justo Rufino, **CTA**
Barth, Karl, **SWI**
Bartók, Béla, **EEU**
Bartolommeo, Fra, **ITA**
Basaldella, Afro, **ITA**
Basaldella, Mirko, **ITA**
Basil II, Emperor, **GRE**
Basque and the Basques, **COL, SPA**
Basuto, **SAF, TAF**
Bataung tribe, **SAF**
Batavia, **LCO, SEA**
Batista, Fulgencio, **WIN**
Batory, Stephen, King of Hungary, **EEU**
Batthyány, Count Lajos, **EEU**
Battle Hill, Battle of, **SAF**
Baudelaire, Charles, **BRA, FRA**
Baudouin, King of the Belgians, **LCO, TAF**
Bauhaus, **GER**
Baumeister, Willy, **GER**
Bauxite, **COL, WIN**
Baxter, James K., **ANZ**
Bayar, Celâl, **TUR**
Bayezit the Thunderbolt, **BAL, TUR**
Bazile, Castera, **WIN**
Beard, Charles A., **USA**
Beaverbrook, Lord (Max Aitken), **CAN**
Bechuanaland, **SAF, TAF**
Beck, Józef, **EEU**
Becket, Thomas à, **BRI**
Beckett, Samuel, **FRA, IRE**
Bede, **BRI, SCN**
Bedouins, **ARW, ISR, TAF**
Beer, **CTA, GER, IRE, LCO**
Beethoven, Ludwig van, **FRA, GER**
"Beggars Revolt," **LCO**
Behan, Brendan, **CAN, IRE**
Beirut, **ARW, ISR**
Béla IV, King of Hungary, **EEU**
Belaúnde Terry, Fernando, **AND**
Belfast, **BRI, IRE**
Belgium, **BRI, FRA, GER, HBK, JAP, LCO, SCN, SWI, TAF**
Bell, Alexander Graham, **CAN**
Bellini, Giovanni, **ITA**
Bellini, Vincenzo, **ITA**
Bello, Andrés, **AND, COL**
Bellow, Saul, **USA**
Bellows, George, **USA**
Belsen, **GER**
Benalcázar, Sebastián, **AND, COL**
Ben Bella, **ARW**

Benelux, **HBK, LCO, SCN**
Beneš, Eduard, **EEU**
Bengal, **HBK, IND, SEA**
Ben-Gurion, David, **ISR**
Ben-Yehuda, Eliezer, **ISR**
Bequia island, **WIN**
Beran, Josef Cardinal, **EEU**
Berbers, **ARW, TAF**
Berenson, Bernard, **ITA**
Bergman, Ingmar, **SCN**
Bergson, Henri, **FRA**
Beria, Lavrenty, **RUS**
Berkeley, George, **IRE, USA**
Berlin, **BAL, BRI, GER, HBK, RUS, SCN, SWI, USA**
Berlioz, Hector, **FRA**
Bermudez, Cundo, **WIN**
Bernadotte, Count Folke, **ISR, SCN**
Bernini, Giovanni Lorenzo, **HBK, ITA**
Bessarabia, **BAL**
Betancourt, Rómulo, **COL, WIN**
Betjeman, John, **BRI**
Bevan, Aneurin, **BRI**
Beveridge, William, Lord, **BRI**
Bhagavad-Gita, **IND**
Bhakra-Nangal Project, **IND**
Bhave, Vinoba, **IND**
Bhumibol Adulyadej, King of Thailand, **SEA**
Biarritz, **FRA, SPA**
Bible, **BRI, ISR, LCO, SAF, SWI, TUR, USA**. *See also* New Testament
Bicycles, **FRA, IND, ITA, LCO, SEA**
Bidault, Georges, **FRA**
"Big Fourteen, The" (Catorce Grande), **CTA**
Bini tribe, **TAF**
Birth control, **ARW, BRA, CHI, COL, IND, LCO, SPA, WIN**
Bismarck, Otto von, **BAL, EEU, GER, LCO, SCN**
Bizet, Georges, **FRA**
Bjørnson, Bjørnstjerne, **SCN**
Black and Tans, **IRE**
"Black Magic," **TAF**. *See also* *Vodou*
Black Plague (1348-1365), **ITA**
Black Sea, **BAL, GRE, RUS, TUR**
Blake, William, **BRI**
Blenheim, Battle of, **FRA**
Bligh, Captain William, **ANZ**
Bloch, Ernst, **GER, SWI**
Bloch, Felix, **SWI**
Blondel, Maurice, **FRA**
Blood brotherhood, **BAL**
Blood River, Battle of, **SAF**
Blum, Léon, **FRA**
Boccaccio, Giovanni, **GRE, ITA**
Bodh-gaya, India, **SEA**
Bodhisattvas, **SEA**
Boer War, **ARW, IND, LCO, SAF**
Bogomils, **BAL**
Bogotá, Colombia, **AND, COL**
Bohemia, **EEU, GER**

AND Andes; **ANZ** Australia and New Zealand; **ARW** Arab World; **BAL** Balkans; **BRA** Brazil; **BRI** Britain; **CAN** Canada; **CHI** China; **IND** India; **IRE** Ireland; **ISR** Israel; **ITA** Italy; **JAP** Japan; **LCO** Low Countries; **MEX** Mexico; **PLA** River Plate Republics; **RUS** Russia; **SAF** South Africa;

Bohr, Niels, **SCN**
Boleyn, Anne, **BRI**
Bolívar, Simón, **AND, COL, PLA**
Bolivia, **AND, BRA, COL, PLA**
Böll, Heinrich, **GER**
Bonaparte, Joseph, **MEX, SPA**
Bonivard, François, **SWI**
Bonnefous, Edouard, **LCO**
Boon, Louis Paul, **LCO**
Boonzaier, Gregoire, **SAF**
Boorstin, Daniel, **USA**
Bór, General (Tadeusz
  Komorowski), **EEU**
Bora, **BAL**
Borduas, Paul-Emile, **CAN**
Borgia family, **ITA**
Boris III, Czar of Bulgaria, **BAL**
Borneo, **SEA**
Bornu, Kingdom of, **TAF**
Bosch, Hieronymus, **LCO**
Bosch, Juan, **WIN**
Bosman, Herman, **SAF**
Bosnia, **BAL, EEU, TUR**
Bosporus, **BAL, TUR**
Botha, Louis, **SAF**
Botticelli, Sandro, **ITA**
Boucher, François, **FRA**
Boulez, Pierre, **FRA**
Boun Oum Na Champassak,
  Prince, **SEA**
Bourassa, Henri, **CAN**
Bourbons, **FRA, ITA, SPA**
Bourguiba, Habib, **ARW**
"Boxer Uprising," **CHI**
Boyacá, Battle of (Colombia),
  AND
Boyars, **BAL**
Boyne, the, Battle of, **IRE**
Boy Scouts, **SAF, SWI, USA**
Brabant, Duchy of, **LCO**
Bracton, Henry of, **BRI**
Bradman, Sir Donald, **ANZ**
Braemar Games, **BRI**
Braganza, House of, **BRA**
Brahmin, caste, **IND, SEA**
Brahms, Johannes, **GER, SWI**
Bramante, Donato, **ITA**
Brand, Jan Hendrik, **SAF**
Brandeis, Louis D., **ISR**
Brandt, Willy, **GER**
Braque, Georges, **FRA, TAF**
Bratislava, Czechoslovakia, **EEU,
  ISR**
Brazil, **AND, BAL, BRA, COL,
  HBK, PLA, SPA, TAF, WIN**
Brecht, Bertolt, **GER, SWI**
Brehon Laws, **IRE**
Bremen, **GER, LCO**
Brest-Litovsk, **RUS**
Brezhnev, Leonid, **RUS**
Brian Boru, King, **IRE**
Bride price, **TAF**
Bridges, **AND, CHI, LCO**
Briscoe, Robert, **IRE**
Britain. *See* Great Britain
British Commonwealth. *See*
  Commonwealth of Nations
Britten, Benjamin, **BRI**
Brogan, Sir Denis, **USA**
Bronze, **AND, CHI**; Age, **SCN**
Brooke, Rupert, **CAN, GRE**

Brown, James Ambrose, **SAF**
Browning, Robert, **GRE, ITA**
Bruce, Robert, **BRI**
Bruegel, Pieter, **LCO**
Brunner, Emil, **SWI**
Bryant, Sir Arthur, **BRI**
Bryant, William Cullen, **USA**
Bryce, Lord James, **USA**
Buber, Martin, **ISR**
Buccaneers. *See* Piracy
Buchenwald, **GER**
Buck, Sir Peter, **ANZ**
Buckland River riots, **ANZ**
Budapest, Hungary, **EEU, RUS**
Buddha and Buddhism, **BAL,
  CHI, HBK, IND, JAP, SEA,
  WIN**
Buenos Aires, Argentina, **AND,
  PLA**
Buffet, Bernard, **FRA, LCO**
Buganda, tribe, Kingdom of,
  TAF
Building industry, **FRA, GER,
  SPA**
Bukharin, Nikolai, **RUS**
Bulgakov, Mikhail, **RUS**
Bulganin, Nikolai, **BAL, EEU,
  RUS**
Bulgaria and the Bulgars, **BAL,
  EEU, GRE, HBK, ISR, RUS,
  TUR**
Bulge, the, Battle of, **LCO**
Bullfighting, **COL, MEX, SPA**
Bunraku drama, **JAP**
Bunyan, John, **BRI**
Bunyoro, Kingdom of, **TAF**
Burgdorfer, Paul, **SWI**
Burgess, Guy, **BRI**
Burgundy, **FRA, LCO, SPA, SWI**
Burgundy, Duke of (Charles the
  Bold), **SWI**
Burke, Edmund, **IRE**
Burle Marx, Roberto, **BRA**
Burma, **BRI, CHI, RUS, SEA**
Burns, Robert, **BRI, IRE**
Burton, Sir Richard, **TAF**
Burundi, **TAF**
Bushmen, **SAF, TAF**
Bushongo tribe, **TAF**
Bustamante, Alexander, **WIN**
Bustani, Emile, **ARW**
Butler, Guy, **SAF**
Butler, R. A., **BRI**
Butler, Samuel, **ANZ, CAN**
Byron, George Gordon, Lord,
  BRI, GRE, ITA, SPA, SWI
Byzantine Empire and Byzan-
  tium, **ARW, BAL, EEU, GRE,
  ISR, ITA, RUS, SCN, TUR**

Cabot, John, **CAN**
Cabral, Pedro Alvarez, **BRA, TAF**
Cacao, **AND, COL**
Caciques, **MEX, SPA**
Cádiz, **AND, SPA**
Caesar, Julius, **BRI, FRA, ITA,
  LCO, SWI**
Café Filho, João, **BRA**
Cairo, **ARW, BAL, ISR, TUR**
Calcutta, **HBK, IND, SEA**
Calder, Alexander, **USA**

Caldwell, Erskine, **USA**
California, **MEX, USA**; Lower,
  MEX
Caligula, Emperor, **ITA**
Calima Indians, **COL**
Caliph, caliphate, **ARW, IND,
  TUR**
Calligraphy, **ARW, CHI, JAP**
Callejón de Huaylas (valley),
  Peru, **AND**
Calvin, John, and Calvinism, **FRA,
  LCO, SAF, SWI**
Cambodia, **IND, JAP, SEA**
Cambridge, University of, **BRI,
  FRA**
Cameron, James, **BAL, TAF**
Camrose, Viscount (William
  Ewert Berry), **BRI**
Camus, Albert, **FRA, GER, LCO**
Canaan and the Canaanites, **ISR**
Canada, **BRI, CAN, CHI, FRA,
  IND, LCO, SCN, WIN**
Canals, **CHI, CTA, FRA, LCO**
Cañari Indians, **AND**
Canary Islands, **SPA**
Canboulay, **WIN**
Cannibalism, **WIN**
Cano, Juan Sebastián del, **SPA**
Canton, **CHI, SEA**
Cantons, **FRA, SWI**
Canudos, war of, **BRA**
Canute, King, **BRI, SCN**
Cao Dai sect, **SEA**
Capek, Karel, **EEU**
Cape of Good Hope, **ARW, SAF,
  TAF**
Capetian Dynasty, **FRA**
Cape Verde Islands, **BRA, COL,
  TAF**
Capitalism, **BAL, BRA, IND,
  MEX, SEA, SWI**
Capuchins, **COL**
Carabobo, Battle of (Venezuela),
  AND, COL
Caracas, Venezuela, **AND, BRA,
  COL**
Cara Indians, **AND**
Cárdenas, Lázaro, **MEX**
Carías Andino, Tiburcio, **CTA**
Caribbean Sea, **AND, WIN**
Carib Indians, **COL, CTA**
Carlist Wars, **SPA**
Carlos, Don Baltasar, Prince, **SPA**
Carlota, Empress, **MEX**
Carlyle, Thomas, **BRI**
Carolingian Dynasty, **FRA**
Carpathian Mountains, **BAL**
Carr, Emily, **CAN**
Carrancas, **BRA**
Carson, Sir Edward, **IRE**
Cartagena, Colombia, **AND,
  COL, WIN**
Cartels, **GER, SWI**
Carthage and Carthaginians, **ITA,
  SPA, TAF**
Cartier, Jacques, **CAN**
Casablanca, **ARW, TAF**
Casablanca group, **TAF**
Casals, Pablo, **ISR, SPA, WIN**
Casement, Sir Roger, **IRE**

Cashel, Rock of, **IRE**
Casimir III, King of Poland,
  EEU
Caspian Sea, **RUS, SCN**
Cassava, **PLA, WIN**
Castillo Armas, Carlos, **CTA**
Castillo, Ramón, **AND, PLA**
Castles, **LCO, SCN, SPA**
Castro, Fidel, and Castroism,
  **BRA, COL, CTA, MEX, PLA,
  WIN**
"Cathay," **CHI**
Cather, Willa, **USA**
Catherine of Aragon, **BRI**
Catherine the Great, **BAL, COL,
  EEU, FRA, GRE, RUS**
Catholic Church. *See* Roman
  Catholic Church
Cato the Elder, **ITA**
Cattle, **ANZ, BRA, FRA, IND,
  IRE, ITA, MEX, PLA, SAF,
  SWI, TAF, WIN.** *See also*
  Dairy farming
Caucasians, **TAF, WIN**
Caucasus Mountains, **RUS**
Cavafy, Constantine, **ARW**
Cave paintings, **ANZ, TAF**
Cavour, Camillo de, **ITA**
Cayapó Indians, **BRA**
Cayman Islands, **WIN**
Celts, **BRI, FRA, GER, IRE,
  SPA, SWI**
Cemal Pasha, **TUR**
Cement, **CTA, SCN**
CENTO. *See* Central Treaty
  Organization
Central America, **CTA, HBK,
  PLA, SPA, WIN**
Central Treaty Organization
  (CENTO), **HBK**
Ceramics, **CHI, ITA, MEX, SCN**
Cervantes Saavedra, Miguel de,
  COL, SPA
Césaire, Aimé, **TAF, WIN**
Ceylon, **ARW, BRI, CHI, HBK,
  SEA**
Cézanne, Paul, **FRA, TAF**
Chacabuco, Battle of, **AND**
Chaco War, **AND, PLA**
Chad, **TAF**
Chagall, Marc, **FRA, ISR**
Chaka, Mofolo, **SAF**
Chakri Dynasty, **SEA**
Chalcolithic period, **ISR**
Châlons, Battle of, **FRA**
Chamberlain, Neville, **GER, SWI**
Chamorro, Diego Manuel, **CTA**
Champlain, Samuel de, **CAN**
Chamula Indians, **MEX**
Chana Indians, **PLA**
Chandragupta, Emperor, **IND**
Chang Ching-yao, **CHI**
Changpai Mountains, **CHI**
Charlemagne, **FRA, GER, HBK,
  ITA, LCO, SCN, SWI**
Charles I, Emperor of Austria-
  Hungary, **EEU**
Charles II, King of Spain, **PLA,
  SPA**
Charles III, King of Spain, **PLA,
  SPA**

Charles IV, King of Spain, **MEX, SPA**

Charles V, Holy Roman Emperor (Charles I, King of Spain), **AND, COL, CTA, EEU, HBK, ITA, LCO, SPA**

Charles of Austria, Holy Roman Emperor, **SPA**

Charles of Lorraine, **EEU**

Charles the Bold. *See* Burgundy, Duke of

Charro, **MEX**

Charrua Indians, **PLA**

Chartres, Cathedral of, **FRA, GRE, SEA**

Chaucer, Geoffrey, **BRI, GRE, SPA**

Chavan, Yeshwantrao B., **IND**

Chechen tribe, **RUS**

Cheese, **ANZ, LCO, SWI**

Chekhov, Anton, **RUS**

Chemical industry, **BRA, CHI, GER, ITA, SWI**

Ch'eng Huang, **CHI**

Ch'en Tu-hsiu, **CHI**

Chesterton, G. K., **BRA**

Chetniks, **BAL**

Chettyar moneylenders, **SEA**

Chiang Kai-shek, **CHI, RUS, SEA**

Chibcha Indians, **AND, COL**

Chichén Itzá, **MEX**

Chichimec Indians, **MEX**

Chile, **AND, COL, HBK, PLA**

Chimu Indians, **AND**

China and the Chinese, **ANZ, BRA, CAN, CHI, GER, HBK, IND, ISR, JAP, RUS, SEA, TAF, USA, WIN**

Ch'in Dynasty, **CHI**

Chingkangshan, Mao Tse-tung, **CHI**

Chirico, Giorgio de, **ITA**

Chocolate industry, **SWI**

Chopin, Frédéric, **EEU**

Chou Dynasty, **CHI**

Chou En-lai, **CHI, RUS, SEA**

Christianity and Christians, **AND, ARW, BAL, BRA, BRI, CHI, CTA, FRA, GER, GRE, IND, ISR, ITA, JAP, MEX, PLA, SCN, SEA, SPA, TAF, TUR, WIN.** *See also* Protestantism; Roman Catholic Church

Christophe, Henry, **WIN**

Chuang Tzu, **CHI**

Chulalongkorn, King of Thailand, **SEA**

Chupas, Battle of (Peru), **AND**

Churchill, Sir Winston, **ARW, BAL, BRI, GER, GRE, HBK, IND, IRE, JAP, LCO, RUS, TAF**

Churriguera, José, **SPA**

Cid, El, **SPA**

Cimabue, Giovanni, **ITA**

Circassians, **ISR**

Circumcision, **TAF**

City-states, **GRE, ITA**

Civil War, American, **SWI, USA.** *See also* United States

Clair, René, **FRA**

Clark, Peter (Peter Kumalo), **SAF**

Claudel, Paul, **FRA**

Claudius, Emperor, **ITA**

Clay, Henry, **USA**

Clement V, Pope, **FRA, ITA**

Clement VII, Pope, **BRI, ITA**

Clive, Robert, **BRI, IND**

Cloete, Stuart, **SAF**

Clontarf, Battle of, **IRE**

Clore, Charles, **BRI**

Clovis, King of Franks, **FRA**

Clytemnestra, **GRE**

Coal, **BAL, BRA, BRI, CHI, FRA, GER, HBK, IND, ITA, LCO, SAF**

Cocaine, **AND**

Cochrane, Lord, **AND, PLA**

Cockcroft, Sir John, **BRI**

Coconuts, **CTA, WIN**

Cocteau, Jean, **FRA**

Code Noire, **WIN**

Coffee, **AND, BRA, COL, CTA, LCO, WIN**

Co-hong, **CHI**

Coleridge, Samuel Taylor, **FRA, JAP**

Collectives, **BAL, CHI, EEU, ISR, MEX**

Collins, Michael, **IRE**

Collins, Norman, **BRI**

Collins, Patrick, **IRE**

Colombia, **AND, COL, CTA, PLA, WIN**

Colombo Plan, **ANZ, HBK**

Colonialism, **ANZ, ARW, BRI, FRA, GER, HBK, ITA, LCO, MEX, SEA, SPA, TAF, WIN**

Colonna, Vittoria, **ITA**

Columbus, Christopher, **BRA, CHI, COL, CTA, ITA, PLA, SCN, SEA, SPA, TAF, WIN**

Comecon. *See* Council for Mutual Economic Assistance

Comintern, **BAL, RUS, SPA**

Common Market, **BRI, CAN, EEU, FRA, GER, GRE, HBK, IRE, ISR, ITA, LCO, SCN, SPA, SWI, TUR, USA**

Commonwealth of Nations, **ANZ, BRI, CAN, HBK, IND, IRE, SEA, TAF, WIN**

Communalism, **BAL, TAF**

Communes, **CHI, FRA**

Communism, **AND, ANZ, ARW, BAL, BRA, CHI, COL, CTA, EEU, FRA, GER, GRE, HBK, IND, IRE, ISR, ITA, JAP, LCO, MEX, PLA, RUS, SAF, SCN, SEA, SPA, TAF, TUR, WIN.** *See also* Marx, Karl

Communist Manifesto, Marx, **CHI, RUS**

Compiègne, **FRA**

Concentration camps, **GER, SAF**

Confucianism, **CHI, HBK, JAP, SEA, WIN**

Congo and the Congolese, **BAL, HBK, LCO, SAF, SCN, SWI, TAF, WIN**

Congress of Vienna, **COL, EEU,**

LCO, SWI

Congreve, William, **IRE**

Conquistadors (soldiers of fortune), **AND, COL, CTA**

Conrad II, King, **SWI**

Conrad, Joseph, **ARW, EEU, SEA, SWI**

Conscription, **CAN, IRE, SWI**

Conservatism, **BRI, CAN, FRA, JAP, PLA**

Constant Botelho de Magalhães, Benjamin, **BRA**

Constantine the Great (Emperor), **BAL, GRE, ITA, TUR**

Constantinople. *See* Istanbul

Convention of Ocaña, **COL**

Convict settlers, **ANZ, BRA, COL**

Cook, Captain James, **ANZ, CAN, HBK**

Coolidge, Calvin, **CTA, USA**

Coomaraswamy, Ananda K., **IND**

Cooper, James Fenimore, **USA**

Copacabana, **AND, BRA**

Copán, Honduras, **CTA**

Copernicus, Nicholas, **EEU**

Copper, **AND, ANZ, ISR, SAF**

Copra, **CTA**

Copts, **ARW**

Córdoba, Francisco Hernández de (d. 1517), **MEX**

Córdoba, Hernández de (d. 1526), **CTA**

Corfu, **BAL, GRE**

Corn Islands (Caribbean Sea), **CTA, WIN**

Cornwallis, Charles, Lord, **IRE**

Cortés, Hernán, **AND, COL, CTA, MEX, SPA, WIN**

Cosgrave, William, **IRE**

Cossacks, **RUS**

Costa, Joaquín, **SPA**

Costain, Thomas B., **CAN**

Costa Rica, **BRA, CTA, HBK**

Costello, John A., **IRE**

Cotton, **AND, BRA, CHI, COL, CTA, MEX, PLA, SPA, TUR, WIN**

Council for Mutual Economic Assistance (Comecon), **BAL, EEU, LCO, RUS**

Council of Trent, **EEU**

Couperin, François, **FRA**

Couperus, Louis, **LCO**

Coureurs de bois, **CAN**

Cousteau, Jacques, **FRA**

Cracow, Poland, **EEU, ISR**

Crane, Hart, **USA**

Crane, Stephen, **USA**

Cremation, **IND**

Creoles, **AND, COL, MEX, PLA, WIN**

Crete, **BAL, GRE**

Crèvecoeur, J. Hector St. John de, **USA**

Crimean War, **BAL, FRA, TUR**

Cristero movement, **MEX**

Croatia and Croats, **BAL**

Croce, Benedetto, **ITA**

Cro-Magnon Man, **FRA, SPA**

Cromer, Earl of, **ARW**

Cromwell, Oliver, **BRI, IRE,**

WIN

Cronje, Piet, **SAF**

Crusades, **BAL, CHI, GRE, ISR, SEA, TUR**

Cuauhémoc, Aztec Emperor, **MEX**

Cuba, **BAL, BRA, BRI, CAN, COL, HBK, MEX, RUS, SPA, USA, WIN**

Cubism, **FRA**

Cúcuta, Congress of, **COL**

Cuevas, José Luis, **MEX**

Cuitláhuac, Aztec Emperor, **MEX**

Cumaná, Venezuela, **COL, WIN**

Cummings, e. e., **GRE, USA**

Cuna Indians, **CTA**

Curaçao, **AND, WIN**

Curie, Marie, **EEU, FRA**

Curtin, John, **ANZ**

Curzon, Lord, **EEU, IND**

Cyprus, **ISR, TUR**

Cyrenaica, Libya, **ARW, TUR**

Cyrus the Great, King of Persia, **GRE, HBK**

Czartoryski, Adam, **EEU**

Czechoslovakia, **ARW, BAL, EEU, FRA, GER, HBK, ISR, RUS, SAF**

Dada movement, **FRA**

Dahis, **BAL**

Dairy farming, milk production, **BRA, IRE, SCN, SWI.** *See also* Cattle; Cheese

Dakar, **BRA, TAF**

Daladier, Edouard, **FRA**

Dalai Lama, **CHI**

Dali, Salvador, **SPA**

Dalmatia, **BAL**

Damascus, **ARW, ISR, TUR**

Damodar Valley project, **IND**

Dampier, William, **ANZ**

Dams, **CHI, FRA, LCO, SCN**

Danegeld, **SCN**

Danelaw, **BRI**

Danevirke, **SCN**

Danish-Prussian War (1864), **GER**

D'Annunzio, Gabriele, **ITA**

Dante, **ITA, LCO**

Danube River, **BAL, EEU, GER, HBK, SWI**

Danza Negra, Palés Mátos, **WIN**

Danzig, **EEU, GER**

Dardanelles, **BAL, TUR**

Darwin, Charles, **AND**

David, Jacques-Louis, **FRA**

David, King, **ISR**

Da Vinci, Leonardo. *See* Vinci

Davis, Stuart, **USA**

Dawes Plan, **GER**

Dayan, Moshe, **ISR**

Dead Sea, **ISR**

Deák, Ferenc, **EEU**

Debré, Michel, **FRA**

Debussy, Claude, **FRA**

Decius, Emperor, **ITA**

Dedijer, Vladimir, **BAL**

Defoe, Daniel, **BRI**

Degas, Edgar, **FRA**

De Gasperi, Alcide, **FRA, ITA**

De Gaulle, Charles, **BRI, COL, FRA, GER, HBK, JAP, LCO, PLA, SEA, SPA, TAF**
De Grasse, François, Comte, **WIN**
Delacroix, Eugène, **FRA**
De Lesseps, Ferdinand, **ARW**
Delta plan, **LCO**
Demeter, **GRE**
Democracy, **ANZ, BRA, CHI, FRA, GER, GRE, IND, ISR, JAP, LCO, SEA, SPA, SWI, TAF, USA, WIN**
Democritus, **GRE, IND**
De Montfort, Simon, **BRI**
Demosthenes, **GRE**
Denmark, **GER, SCN, SWI, WIN**
Deodoro da Fonseca, Manuel, **BRA**
De Poincy, Phillippe de Lonvilliers, **WIN**
Depression. *See* Great Depression
Derain, André, **TAF**
Dervishes, **TUR**
Desai Morarji, **IND**
Deserts, **ARW, SAF, TAF**
De Soto, Hernando, **AND, TAF**
De Staël, Madame Germaine, **SWI**
Detribalization, **BAL, TAF**
De Valera, Eamon, **IRE**
Devil's Island, **COL**
DEW (Distant Early Warning) Line, **CAN**
Dewey, John, **JAP, USA**
Dharma, **IND, SEA**
Diaghilev, Sergei Pavlovich, **FRA**
Diamonds, **BRA, ISR, LCO, SAF**
Dias, Bartolomeu, **HBK, TAF**
Diaspora, **ISR**
Díaz, Porfirio, **MEX**
Díaz del Castillo, Bernal, **CTA, MEX**
Dibelius, Otto, **GER**
Dickens, Charles, **BRI, FRA, SCN, USA**
Dickinson, Emily, **USA**
Dido, Queen of Carthage, **ARW**
Diem, Ngo Dinh, **SEA**
Dien Bien Phu, Vietnam, **SEA**
Dignidad, **WIN**
Dikes, **CHI, LCO**
Dimitrov, Georgi, **BAL**
Dinaric Alps, **BAL**
Dingaan, Zulu chief, **SAF**
Dinka tribe, **TAF**
Diocletian, Emperor, **BAL, HBK, ITA**
Dipa Nusantara Aidit, **SEA**
Disraeli, Benjamin, **BRI, CAN**
Ditende Yawa Nawezi III, Lunda Chief, **TAF**
Divine Comedy, The, Dante, **ITA, LCO**
Divorce, **ARW, BAL, BRA, IRE, ITA, RUS, SEA, SWI, TUR, USA**
Djakarta, Indonesia, **LCO, SEA**
Djilas, Milovan, **BAL, RUS**
Dmowski, Roman, **EEU**
Dobell, William, **ANZ**

Dobrovský, Josef, **EEU**
Dodecanese islands, **GRE**
Dogon tribe, **TAF**
Dolmens, **IRE**
Dome of the Rock, **ARW, ISR**
Dominican Order, **CTA, FRA, MEX**
Dominican Republic, **HBK, WIN**
Donatello, **ITA**
Don Quixote, Cervantes, **COL, SPA**
Dorians, **GRE**
Dos Passos, John, **USA**
Dostoevsky, Feodor, **RUS**
Doyle, Sir Arthur Conan, **SWI**
Draaiorgels, **LCO**
Drake, Sir Francis, **BRI, SPA, WIN**
Drakensberg range, **SAF**
Dravidians, **IND**
Dreiser, Theodore, **USA**
Drums, **TAF, WIN**
Druses, **ISR**
Dublin, **BRI, IRE**
Dufy, Raoul, **FRA**
Dulles, John Foster, **ARW, HBK, SEA, TUR, USA**
Dumlupınar, Battle of, **TUR**
Dunant, Jean-Henry (Henri), **HBK, SWI**
Duplessis, Maurice, **CAN**
Dürer, Albrecht, **GER, HBK, MEX**
Durham, Lord, **CAN, HBK**
Durrell, Lawrence, **ARW**
Dürrenmatt, Friedrich, **SWI**
Dutch East India Company. *See* East India Company
Dutch East Indies. *See* Indonesia
Dutch Reformed Church, **LCO, SAF**
Duvalier, François, **WIN**
Dvořák, Antonin, **EEU**
Dyaks, **SEA**
Dyewood, **BRA, WIN**

Eakins, Thomas, **USA**
Earthquakes, **AND, JAP, WIN**
Easter, **BAL, GRE**
Easter Week rebellion (1916), **IRE**
East India Company (British), **HBK, IND**; Dutch United East India Co., **IND, LCO, SAF, SEA**
East Indies. *See* Indonesia
Eban, Abba, **ISR**
Ebert, Friedrich, **GER**
Ebony trade, **TAF**
Ecuador, **AND, COL**
Eden, Sir Anthony, **ARW, BRI, CAN**
Edib, Halide, **TUR**
Edict of Nantes (1598), **SWI**
Edmund Ironside, King, **SCN**
Edward VII, King of England, **BRI, HBK, IND, IRE, SCN**
Edward VIII, King of England, **BRI, IRE**
Edward the Confessor, King, **BRI, SCN**

Edwards, Jonathan, **USA**
Egypt, **ARW, BRI, GRE, HBK, ISR, SEA, TAF, TUR**
Ehrenburg, Ilya, **RUS**
Eichmann, Adolf, **GER, ISR, SPA**
Einstein, Albert, **GER, SWI**
Eire. *See* Ireland
Eisenhower, Dwight D., **ARW, BRI, CAN, CHI, COL, IND, ISR, JAP, USA**
Ejido system, **MEX**
Elbe River, **GER, RUS**
El Cid. *See* Cid, El
El Dorado, **COL, PLA**
Electronics industay, **GER, JAP**
Elgin marbles, **GRE**
El Greco. *See* Greco, El
Elijah, **BAL, GRE, ISR**
Eliot, T. S., **BRI, USA**
Elizabeth I, Queen of England, **BRI, IRE, SPA, WIN**
Elizabeth II, Queen of England, **BRI, CAN, FRA, GER, IND, TAF**
El Molo tribe, **TAF**
El Salvador, **CTA, HBK**
Elytis, Odysseus, **GRE**
Emerson, Ralph Waldo, **USA**
Emigration. *See* Immigration
Emmet, Robert, **IRE**
Encomienda system, **COL, CTA, MEX, PLA**
Enesco, Georges, **BAL**
England. *See* Great Britain
Ensor, James, **LCO**
Enver Pasha, **TUR**
Ephesus, **TUR**
Epidaurus, **GRE**
Epstein, Sir Jacob, **BRI**
Erasmus, Desiderius, **LCO, SWI**
Erhard, Ludwig, **GER**
Eric of Pomerania, **SCN**
Eric the Red, **SCN**
Eriksson, Leif, **CAN, SCN**
Erlander, Tage, **SCN**
Ertuğrul, Muhsin, **TUR**
Eshkol, Levi, **ISR**
Eskimos, **CAN**
Estremadura, **AND, SPA**
Eternal Pact (1291), **SWI**
Ethelred, King, **SCN**
Ethelwulf, King of Wessex, **SCN**
Ethiopia (Abyssinia), **ARW, HBK, ISR, ITA, TAF**
Etruscans, **ITA**
Eugene of Savoy, **BAL, HBK**
Eugénie, Empress of France, **ARW, FRA**
Eureka Stockade, episode of, **ANZ**
Euripides, **ARW, GRE**
European Atomic Energy Community, **HBK, LCO**
European Coal and Steel Community, **FRA, GER, HBK, SCN**
European Defense Community, **GER, HBK**
European Economic Community. *See* Common Market

European Free Trade Association, **HBK, LCO, SCN, SWI**
Evans, Sir Arthur, **GRE**
Evatt, Dr. Herbert V., **ANZ**
Everlasting League, the, **SWI**
Ewe tribe, **TAF**
Existentialism, **FRA, GER, USA**
Expansionism, **GER, JAP, RUS, SCN, SEA, SPA, TUR**
Exploration, **COL, HBK, SCN, SPA, TAF**
Explosives, **CHI, SCN**
Expressionism, **FRA, PLA**
Eyck, F. Gunther, **LCO**
Eyck, Van. *See* Van Eyck

Fabergé, **RUS**
Fabian Society, **BRI**
Faeroe Islands, **SCN**
Falange party, **SPA**
Falkland Islands (Islas Malvinas), **PLA**
Falla, Manuel de, **SPA**
Famine, **CHI, IRE, RUS**; relief, **SCN**
Fanfani, Amintore, **ITA**
FAO. *See* Food and Agriculture Organization
Farouk, King of Egypt, **ARW, BRI**
Fasching, **GER**
Fascism, **ARW, BAL, BRA, COL, GRE, ITA, SPA**
Fashion industry, **FRA, ITA**
Fatimid Dynasty, **ARW**
Faulkner, William, **BRA, USA**
Favelas, **BRA**
Fedayeen, **ISR**
Feisal II, of Iraq, **ARW**
Felsöpetény, Hungary: riots in, **EEU**
Ferdinand I, Emperor of Austria, **EEU**
Ferdinand I, Holy Roman Emperor, **SPA**
Ferdinand II, Holy Roman Emperor, **EEU**
Ferdinand II, King of Aragon. *See* Ferdinand V, King of Spain
Ferdinand V, King of Spain (II of Aragon), **CTA, SPA, WIN**
Ferdinand VI, King of Spain, **MEX, SPA**
Ferdinand VII, King of Spain, **CUL, MEX, SPA**
Fermi, Enrico, **ITA**
Fertilizers, **CHI, IND**
Feudalism, **BRI, FRA, ITA, TAF, TUR**
Fianna Fail party, **IRE**
Fielding, Henry, **BRI**
Field of Blackbirds, The, **BAL**
Films, **ARW, GER, IND, LCO, PLA, SAF, SCN**
Fine Gael party, **IRE**
Finland, **GER, HBK, SCN**; Gulf of, **RUS**
Fishing and fisheries, **ANZ, BRA, CAN, IRE, GRE, JAP, LCO, PLA, SCN, SEA, TUR, USA, WIN**

COL Colombia and Venezuela; **CTA** Central America; **EEU** Eastern Europe; **FRA** France; **GER** Germany; **GRE** Greece; **HBK** Handbook; **SCN** Scandinavia; **SEA** Southeast Asia; **SPA** Spain; **SWI** Switzerland; **TAF** Tropical Africa; **TUR** Turkey; **USA** United States; **WIN** West Indies.

165

Fitzgerald, F. Scott, **USA**
"Flag of convenience," **CTA**
Flagstad, Kirsten, **SCN**
Flamenco music, **SPA**
Flanders, Belgium, **LCO, SPA**
Flemings, **LCO**
Flinders, Matthew, **ANZ**
Floods, **CHI, IND, LCO**
Flying Doctor Service, **ANZ**
Folkehøjskole, **SCN**
Fomento, **WIN**
Fonseca e Silva, Valentim da, **BRA**
Fon tribe, **TAF**
Food and Agriculture Organization (FAO), **HBK**
Foraker Act (1900), **WIN**
Ford, Henry, **BRA, USA**
Forests and forestry, **ANZ, BRA, CAN, FRA, ISR, ITA, JAP, MEX, RUS, SAF, SCN, TAF.** *See also* Timber
Formosa. *See* Taiwan
Forster, E. M., **BRI, LCO**
Fouquet, Jean, **FRA**
Fragonard, Jean-Honoré, **FRA**
France, **AND, ARW, BAL, BRI, CAN, CHI, COL, EEU, GER, GRE, HBK, IND, ISR, ITA, JAP, LCO, MEX, PLA, RUS, SAF, SCN, SEA, SPA, SWI, TAF, TUR, USA, WIN**
Francis I, King of France, **COL, ITA, WIN**
Franciscans, **CTA, MEX, PLA**
Franck, César, **LCO**
Franco, Francisco, **ITA, PLA, SPA**
Franco-Prussian War, **FRA, GER, SWI**
Frank, Anne, **LCO**
Frankish Empire, **LCO, SCN**
Franklin, Benjamin, **BRI, JAP, USA**
Franks, **ARW, FRA, GER, GRE**
Franz Ferdinand, Archduke of Austria, **BAL, EEU, GER**
Franz Josef, Emperor of Austria, **EEU**
Frederick II, Holy Roman Emperor, **GER, ITA**
Frederick Redbeard (Frederick Barbarossa), **GER, ITA**
Frederick the Great, **EEU, FRA, GER**
Freemasons, **COL**
Frei, Eduardo, **AND**
French and Indian War, **CAN**
French Revolution, **AND, BAL, FRA, IRE, PLA, SEA, SPA, SWI, TUR, USA**
French Union, **FRA, TAF**
Frescoes, **BAL, GRE**
Frisians, **LCO**
Frondizi, Arturo, **PLA**
Frost, Robert, **BRI, USA**
Fulani tribe and language, **TAF**

*G*achupines, **MEX**
Gaelic language, **BRI, CAN, IRE**
Gagarin, Yuri, **BRA, RUS**

Gainsborough, Thomas, **BRI**
Gaitán, Jorge, **COL**
Gaitskell, Hugh, **BRI**
Galbraith, John Kenneth, **IND**
Galen, **ARW, GRE**
Galicia, Poland, **BAL, EEU**
Galileo, **ITA**
Galíndez, Jesús de, **WIN**
Gallegos, Rómulo, **COL**
Gallia. *See* Gaul
Gallipoli, **TUR**
Gama, Vasco da, **HBK, IND, SEA, TAF**
Gandhi, Mohandas, **ARW, HBK, IND, LCO, SAF**
Gapon, Father Georgi, **RUS**
Garcia, Carlos, **SEA**
García Lorca, Federico, **SPA**
Garcilaso Inca de la Vega, **AND**
Garibaldi, Giuseppe, **ITA**
Garonne River, **FRA, SWI**
Garvey, Marcus, **TAF, WIN**
Gauchos, **BRA, PLA**
Gauguin, Paul, **FRA**
Gaul (Gallia), **FRA, ITA, LCO**
Gautier, Théophile, **SPA**
Gaza, **ARW, ISR**
Gazetteer, **HBK**
Geneva Conference (1954), **SEA**
Genghis Khan, **CHI, HBK, IND**
George I, King of England, **BAL, BRI, GER**
George III, King of England, **BRI, CHI, IRE, USA**
George V, King of England, **BRI, IRE**
George VI, King of England, **BRI, CAN, IND, IRE**
Germany, **ARW, BAL, BRA, BRI, CHI, COL, EEU, FRA, GER, GRE, HBK, IND, ISR, ITA, JAP, LCO, RUS, SAF, SCN, SPA, SWI, TAF, TUR, USA, WIN**
Gerö, Ernö, **EEU**
Gerstner, Karl, **SWI**
Ghana, **BAL, BRI, HBK, SAF, TAF**
Gheorghiu-Dej, Gheorghe, **BAL, HBK**
Ghettos, **EEU, ISR**
Ghibellines, **GER, ITA**
Ghiberti, Lorenzo, **ITA**
Ghirlandaio, Domenico, **ITA**
Giacometti, Alberto, **SWI**
Gibbon, Edward, **BAL, GRE, ITA, SWI, TAF**
Gibraltar, **SCN, SPA**
Gide, André, **FRA, TAF**
Gieseking, Walter, **GER**
Gil Robles, José María, **SPA**
Giotto, **ITA**
Glaciers, **SCN, SWI, TAF**
Gladstone, William, **BRI, GRE**
Glass, **ITA, SCN**
Glubb, John Bagot, **ARW**
Gluck, Christoph Willibald, **FRA, ITA, JAP**
Glueck, Nelson, **ISR**
Goebbels, Joseph, **GER**
Goering, Hermann, **CAN, GER**

Goethe, Johann Wolfgang von, **FRA, GER, GRE, ITA, SWI**
Gogh, Vincent van. *See* Van Gogh
Gogol, Nikolai, **RUS**
Gold, **AND, BRA, CHI, COL, CTA, MEX, SAF, SEA, TAF, WIN**
Gold Coast, **TAF, WIN**
Goldoni, Carlo, **ITA**
Goliad, massacre of, **MEX**
Goliath, **ISR, LCO**
Gömbos, Gyula, **EEU**
Gómez, Juan Vicente, **COL**
Gomulka, Wladyslaw, **BAL, EEU, RUS**
Gordimer, Nadine, **SAF**
Gordon, Charles ("Chinese"), **ARW**
Göreme, Valley of, **TUR**
Görgey, Arthur, **EEU**
Gorki, Maxim, **RUS**
Goths, **BAL, GER, GRE, ITA, SCN**
Gotmateswara, god, **IND**
Gottwald, Klement, **EEU**
Goulart, João, **BRA**
Goya y Lucientes, Francisco de, **SPA**
Graaff, Sir de Villiers, **SAF**
Gran Colombia, **AND, COL**
Grass, Günter, **GER**
Grattan, Henry, **IRE**
Graves, Robert, **BRI**
Great Barrier Reef, **ANZ**
Great Britain (England) (United Kingdom), **AND, ANZ, ARW, BAL, BRA, BRI, CAN, CHI, COL, CTA, EEU, FRA, GER, GRE, HBK, IND, ISR, ITA, JAP, LCO, MEX, PLA, SAF, SCN, SEA, SPA, SWI, TAF, TUR, USA, WIN.** *See also* Commonwealth of Nations
Great Depression, **CAN, FRA, SAF, USA**
Great Trek (1836-38), **SAF**
Great Wall, **CHI**
Greco, El, **GRE, SPA**
Greece and the Greeks, **ARW, BAL, GRE, HBK, IND, ISR, ITA, RUS, SPA, SWI, TUR**
Greek Orthodox Church. *See* Orthodox Church
Greene, Graham, **BRI, GER, IRE, SEA**
Greenland, **SCN**
Gregorian Armenians, **ISR**
Gregory, Lady Augusta, **IRE**
Grieg, Edvard, **SCN**
Griffith, Arthur, **IRE**
Grimm, Jakob and Wilhelm, **GER**
Gris, Juan, **SPA**
Gropius, Walter, **GER**
Grösz, Jozsef, Archbishop, **EEU**
Grotius, Hugo, **LCO**
Grounds, Roy, **ANZ**
Grunewald, Mathias, **GER**
Grunwald, Battle of, **EEU**
Guarani Indians, **PLA**

Guardia, Tomás, **CTA**
Guarnieri, Camargo, **BRA**
Guatemala, **CTA, HBK**
Guelphs, **GER, ITA**
Guianas, **BRA, COL, SPA, WIN**
Guinea, Republic of, **TAF, USA**
Guisan, General Henri, **SWI**
Gujarat, **IND, SEA**
Gulf Stream, **IRE, SCN**
Gupta Empire, **IND**
Gürsel, Cemal, **TUR**
Gustaf VI, King of Sweden, **BAL, SCN**
Gutenberg, Johann, **GER**
Guthrie, Sir Tyrone, **CAN**
Guzmán, Martín Luis, **MEX**
Guzmán Blanco, Antonio, **COL**
Gypsies, **IRE, SPA**

*H*aanstra, Bert, **LCO**
Habe tribe, **TAF**
Habsburgs, **BAL, EEU, GER, ITA, LCO, SPA, SWI**
Hadassah, **ISR**
Hadjidakis, Manos, **GRE**
Hadrian, Emperor, **BAL, ITA, SPA, TUR**
Hafiz, Abdul Halim, **ARW**
Haifa, Israel, **ARW, ISR**
Haiku, poetic form, **JAP**
Haile Selassie, Emperor of Ethiopia, **HBK, TAF, WIN**
Hailsham, Viscount, **BRI**
Haiti, **AND, WIN**
Hakim, Towfik al, **ARW**
Hakluyt, Richard, **WIN**
Hals, Frans, **LCO**
Hamburg, **BRI, GER, LCO, SWI**
Hamilton, Alexander, **USA**
Hamites, **TAF**
Hammarskjöld, Dag, **HBK, SCN**
Hamsun, Knut, **SCN**
Handel, George Frederick, **GER, ITA**
Han Dynasty, **CHI**
Hanna, Mark, **CTA**
Hannibal, **ITA, SPA**
Hanover, House of, **BRI**
Hanseatic League, **SCN**
Hansson, Per Albin, **SCN**
Hanukkah, **ISR**
Hardy, Thomas, **BRI**
Harem system, **ARW, TUR**
Harold, King of England, **BRI, SCN**
Harrison, Brian, **BRI, SEA**
Harsha, Emperor, **IND**
Hashemite clan, **ARW**
Hassidism, **ISR**
Hastings, Battle of, **BRI**
Hatem, Abdul Kader, **ARW**
"Hatikvah," **ISR**
Hauhaus (Maori warriors), **ANZ**
Hausa tribe and language, **TAF**
Havana, Cuba, **SWI, WIN**
Hawaiian Islands, **JAP**
Hawaiki (mythical homeland of Maoris), **ANZ**
Hawkins, Sir John, **TAF, WIN**
Hawthorne, Nathaniel, **USA**
Hay, John, **CHI, CTA**

AND Andes; **ANZ** Australia and New Zealand; **ARW** Arab World; **BAL** Balkans; **BRA** Brazil; **BRI** Britain; **CAN** Canada; **CHI** China; **IND** India; **IRE** Ireland; **ISR** Israel; **ITA** Italy; **JAP** Japan; **LCO** Low Countries; **MEX** Mexico; **PLA** River Plate Republics; **RUS** Russia; **SAF** South Africa;

Haya de la Torre, Víctor Raúl, **AND**
Haydn, Franz Joseph, **ITA**
Headhunters, **AND**
Hearn, Lafcadio, **JAP**
Hearne, Samuel, **CAN**
Heavy water, Norsk Hydroplant, **SCN**
Hebrides, **SCN**
Hegel, Georg Wilhelm Friedrich, **FRA, GER**
Heian Period, **JAP**
Heidegger, Martin, **GER**
Heine, Heinrich, **GER**
Hellespont, **BAL, GRE**
Helpmann, Robert, **ANZ**
Helvetic Republic, **SWI**
Hemingway, Ernest, **USA**
Henlein, Konrad, **EEU**
Henry II, King of England, **BRI, IRE**
Henry IV, Emperor, **GER**
Henry IV, King of France, **FRA**
Henry VI, Holy Roman Emperor, King of Sicily, **ITA**
Henry VIII, King of England, **BRI, IRE**
Henry the Navigator, Prince, **CHI, HBK, SEA**
Hera, **GRE**
Heraclea, **GRE**
Heraclitus, **GRE**
Herakleion, **GRE**
Hercegovina, **EEU**
Hermes, **GRE**
Herod, King, **ISR**
Herodotus, **GRE, HBK, ITA**
Herriot, Edouard, **FRA**
Hertzog, James Barry, **SAF**
Herzl, Theodor, **ISR**
Hesse, Hermann, **GER, SWI**
Heuss, Theodor, **GER**
Heydrich, Reinhard, **EEU**
Heyerdahl, Thor, **SCN**
Heyn, Piet, **WIN**
Hillary, Sir Edmund, **ANZ**
Himalayas, **HBK, IND, SEA**
Himmler, Heinrich, **EEU, SCN**
Hindemith, Paul, **GER, SWI**
Hindenburg, Paul von, **GER**
Hindi, language, **IND**
Hinduism, **CHI, HBK, IND, SAF, SEA, WIN**
Hindustani, language, **IND**
Hippocrates, **GRE**
Hispanic islands, **WIN**
Hispaniola, **COL, CTA, SPA, WIN**
Histadrut, **ISR**
Hitler, Adolf, **BAL, BRI, EEU, FRA, GER, GRE, HBK, ISR, ITA, LCO, RUS, SCN, SPA, SWI**
Hittite Empire, **TUR**
Hobart, Tasmania, **ANZ**
Hobbema, Meindert, **LCO**
Hocas, **TUR**
Ho Chi Minh, **SEA**
Hoetink, Harry, **WIN**
Hofer, Karl, **GER**
Hogarth, William, **BRI**

Hohenstaufen dynasty, **GER, ITA**
Hohenzollern dynasty, **GER**
Holbein the Younger, Hans, **GER, SWI**
Holder, Geoffrey, **WIN**
Holland. *See* Netherlands
Holstein, **GER, SCN**
Holyoake, Keith Jacka, **ANZ**
Holy Roman Empire, **GER, HBK, ITA, SWI.** *See also* Roman Empire
Home, Earl of (Alexander Frederick Douglas-Home), **BRI**
Homer, **GRE, ITA, SEA, TUR**
Homer, Winslow, **USA**
Honduras, **CTA, HBK, MEX, SPA, WIN**
Honegger, Arthur, **SWI**
Hong Kong, **BRI, CHI, SEA**
Hoover, Herbert, **RUS, USA**
Hopman, Harry, **ANZ**
Hopper, Edward, **USA**
Horses and horsemanship, **BRA, IRE, PLA, TUR**
Horthy, Miklós, **EEU**
Hortobágy steppe, Hungary, **EEU**
Hottentots, **SAF**
Houphouët-Boigny, Félix, **TAF**
Houston, Sam, **MEX**
Howe, Clarence Decatur, **CAN**
Howells, William Dean, **USA**
Hsia Dynasty, **CHI**
Hsiung-nu tribe, **BAL, CHI**
Huáscar (Inca Prince), **AND**
Huave Indians, **MEX**
Huayna Capac (Inca ruler), **AND**
Hudson, Henry, **CAN, SCN**
Hughes, Robert, **ANZ**
Hugo, Victor, **BRA, FRA, SEA, SWI**
Huguenots, **FRA, IRE, SPA, SWI**
Huichol, language, **MEX**
Huks, **SEA**
Human sacrifice, **TAF**
Humboldt, Alexander von, **AND, COL, GER, MEX, SPA**
"Hundred Flowers" campaign, **CHI**
Hundred Years' War, **BRI, FRA**
Hungary, **BAL, EEU, FRA, HBK, ISR, RUS, SWI, TUR, USA, WIN**
Huns, **BAL, CHI, FRA, GER, IND, ITA, TUR**
Hunyady, Mátyás (the Just), King of Hungary, **EEU**
Huron Indians, **CAN**
Hu Shih, **CHI**
Hussein, King of Jordan, **ARW**
Hussite movement, **EEU**
Huygens, Constantijn, **LCO**
Hydroelectric power, **BAL, BRA, CAN, COL, FRA, IND, MEX, RUS, SWI, TAF**
Hyppolite, Hector, **WIN**

Ibadan, **TAF**
Iberian Peninsula, **SPA**
Ibn Khaldun, **TAF**

Ibn Saud, Abdul Aziz, of Saudi Arabia, **ARW**
Ibn Tulun, **TUR**; mosque, **ARW**
Ibo tribe, **TAF, WIN**
Ibsen, Henrik, **IRE, ITA, JAP, SCN**
Iceland, **BRI, IRE, SCN**
Icons, **BAL, GRE, WIN**
Iemoto, **JAP**
Iguazú River, **BRA, PLA**
Ikeda, Hayato, **JAP**
Illegitimacy, **BRA, CTA**
Illia, Arturo, **PLA**
Iliteracy, literacy, **ARW, BAL, BRA, CHI, CTA, GRE, IND, ITA, JAP, MEX, RUS, SEA, SPA, TAF, TUR, WIN**
Illyria, Kingdom of, **BAL**
Immigration, emigration, **ANZ, BRA, CAN, FRA, IRE, ISR, ITA, LCO, PLA, SAF, USA, WIN**
Impressionism, **FRA**
Incas, **AND, COL, PLA, SEA**
Independence movements, **BRA, COL, GRE, IND, IRE, LCO, MEX, PLA, SAF, SEA, TAF, WIN**
India, **ARW, BAL, BRA, BRI, CHI, FRA, HBK, IND, JAP, SAF, SEA, WIN**
Indians, American, **AND, BRA, CAN, COL, CTA, MEX, PLA, USA, WIN**
Indochina, **FRA, SEA**
Indo-European language, **ARW**
Indonesia (Dutch East Indies), **ARW, BAL, BRA, LCO, RUS, SEA**
Indra, god, **IND**
Industrial Revolution, **BRI, GER, IND, IRE, SAF, SWI**
Infant mortality, **BRA, SAF, TAF**
Inflation, **BRA, GER, IND, JAP, SAF, SCN, SPA, SWI, TUR**
Inge, W. R., **BRI**
Ingush tribe, **RUS**
"Inner Six." *See* Common Market
Inönü, Ismet, **TUR**
Inquisition, **ITA, LCO, MEX, SPA, WIN**
International Bank for Reconstruction and Development. *See* World Bank
International Criminal Police Organization (Interpol), **HBK**
Inti (Inca sun god), **AND**
Invasions, **BRI, GER, IND, IRE, ITA, JAP, RUS, SPA**
Ionesco, Eugène, **BAL**
Iraq, **ARW, HBK, ISR, TUR**
Iran (Persia), **ARW, BAL, GRE, HBK, IND, ISR, RUS, TUR**
Ireland, **BRI, FRA, IRE, SCN, SPA**
Irigoyen, Hipólito, **PLA**
Iron, **ARW, BRA, BRI, CAN, CHI, COL, FRA, GER, IND, ITA, SAF, SCN**
Iron Gate gorge, **BAL**
Iron Guard, Romanian, **BAL**

Iroquois Indians, **CAN**
Irrigation, **ARW, CHI, IND, ISR, ITA, MEX, SEA, SPA, TUR**
Irving, Washington, **SPA, USA**
Isabella (of Castile), Queen, **CTA, SPA, WIN**
Islam, **ARW, BAL, CHI, HBK, IND, ISR, SEA, SPA, TAF, TUR.** *See also* Mohammed; Moslems
Isolationism, **BRI, JAP, USA.** *See also* Neutralism
Israel, **ARW, BAL, BRI, HBK, ISR, SEA, TUR**
Istanbul (Constantinople), **ARW, BAL, GRE, HBK, ITA, TUR**
Italy, **ARW, BAL, BRA, BRI, CHI, FRA, GER, GRE, HBK, ISR, ITA, LCO, RUS, SAF, SCN, SPA, SWI, TAF, TUR**
Iturbide, Augustín de, **CTA, MEX**
Itzán Indians, **CTA**
Ivan the Great (III), **RUS**
Ivan the Terrible, **EEU, RUS**
Ivory Coast, **TAF**

Jackson, Andrew, **IRE, USA**
Jackson, A. Y., **CAN**
Jacobsen, Arne, **SCN**
Jacobson, Dan, **SAF**
Jade Emperor (Taoist deity), **CHI**
Jagan, Cheddi, **COL**
Jagiełło, King of Poland, **EEU**
Jahangir, Emperor, **IND**
Jainism, **IND**
Jamaica, **AND, BRI, COL, SPA, WIN**
James I, King of England, **BRI, IND, LCO**
James II, King of England, **BRI, IRE**
James, Henry, **BRA, USA**
Jameson, Leander Starr, **SAF**
Jameson Raid, **SAF**
Janissaries, **BAL, GRE, TUR**
Jansenism, **IRE**
Japan, **BRA, BRI, CHI, HBK, IND, JAP, SEA, SWI, USA**
Jason, **GRE**
Java and the Javanese, **COL, IND, SAF, SÉA**
Jazz, **BAL, CAN, GER, RUS, TAF, USA, WIN**
Jefferson, Thomas, **BRA, CHI, FRA, GRE, ITA, TAF, USA**
Jerusalem, **ARW, ISR**
Jesuits, **AND, BRA, CAN, CHI, COL, CTA, FRA, HBK, MEX, PLA, SPA**
Jews and Judaism, **ARW, BAL, BRA, CAN, CHI, EEU, FRA, GER, HBK, ISR, LCO, PLA, RUS, SAF, SPA, TUR, USA, WIN.** *See also* Anti-Semitism
Jibaros, **WIN**
Jinnah, Mohammed Ali, **HBK, IND**
Joan of Arc, **FRA, SEA**

João VI, King of Portugal and Brazil, **BRA, HBK**
Jodrell Bank telescope, **BRI**
John (King of Portugal), **PLA**
John XXIII, Pope, **ITA**
John of Austria, Don, **GRE**
John the Baptist, **ISR**
Johnson, Lyndon B., **TUR, USA**
Johnson, Samuel, **BRI, IRE**
Joliet, Louis, **CAN**
Jordan, **ARW, BRI, HBK, ISR**
Joyce, James, **FRA, GRE, IRE, SWI**
Juan Carlos, Prince of Spain, **GRE, SPA**
Juárez, Benito, **ITA, MEX**
Judah Maccabee, **ISR**
Judaism. *See* Jews and Judaism
Judō, **JAP**
Juju, **TAF**
Julião, Francisco, **BRA**
Julio-Claudian dynasty, **ITA**
Julius II, Pope, **ITA, SWI**
Jung, Carl, **SWI**
Junín, Battle of (Peru), **AND**
Jura Mountains, **SWI**
Justinian, Emperor, **GRE, ITA**
Jutes, **BRI, GER**
Jutland Peninsula, **SCN**

Kaaba, the, **ARW**
Kabardinians, **RUS**
Kabuki, **JAP**
Kádár, János, **EEU**
Kaddous, Ihsan Abdul, **ARW**
Kaffirs, **SAF**
Kafka, Franz, **GER, SWI**
Kahanamoku, Duke, **ANZ**
Kalahari Desert, **TAF**
Kaloyan ("Emperor"), **BAL**
Kamakura Period, **JAP**
Kanem, Kingdom of, **TAF**
K'ang Hsi, Emperor of China, **CHI**
Kanishka, Emperor, **IND**
Kankan Musa, King of Mali, **TAF**
Kannon, deity, **JAP**
Kant, Immanuel, **FRA, GER**
Kappel, Battle of (1531), **SWI**
Karagöz, puppet, **TUR**
Karamojong tribe, **TAF**
Karate, **JAP**
Kariba Dam, **TAF**
Karl III, King of Hungary, **EEU**
Karlsbad (Karlovy-Vary), Czechoslovakia, **EEU, RUS**
Károlyi, Mihály, **EEU**
Karma, **CHI, IND, SEA**
Kasavubu, Joseph, **LCO, TAF**
Kashmir, **HBK, IND**
Kassem, Abdul Karim, **ARW**
Katanga Province, **TAF**
Kathiawar peninsula, **IND**
Kattegat, the, **SCN**
Katyn Wood, **EEU**
Kaufmann, General Konstantin, **RUS**
Kayalıdere, Ahmet, **TUR**
Kayastha, caste, **IND**
Kazakhstan, Russia, **CHI, RUS**

Kazantzakis, Nikos, **GRE**
Keats, John, **BRI, CTA, GRE, ITA**
Keita, Modibo, **TAF**
Keith, Minor Cooper, **CTA**
Kemal Atatürk. *See* Atatürk
Kemari, **JAP**
Kempeitai, **SEA**
Kempis, Thomas à, **LCO**
Kemsley, Lord (James Gomer Berry), **BRI**
Kennedy, John F., **ARW, BRI, COL, CTA, GER, HBK, IRE, LCO, MEX, USA**
Kenya, **SAF, TAF**
Kenyatta, Jomo, **TAF**
Kerenski, Aleksandr, **RUS**
Khachaturyan, Aram, **RUS**
Khaldun, Ibn, **ARW**
Khalifa, of the Sudan, **ARW**
Khamsin, **ISR**
Khan, Mohammad Ayub, **HBK, IND**
Khartoum, **ARW, TAF**
Khmers, **SEA**
Khrushchev, Nikita, **BAL, CHI, EEU, GER, HBK, ITA, RUS, SEA, USA**
Kibbutzim, **ISR**
Kiel, **GER, SCN**
Kierkegaard, Soren, **FRA, SCN**
Kigeri V, King of Ruanda, **TAF**
Kikuyu tribe, **TAF**
Kilimanjaro, Mount, **TAF**
Killam, I. W., **CAN**
King, William Lyon Mackenzie, **CAN**
Kinross, Lord, **TUR**
Kipling, Rudyard, **BRI, IND, SEA**
Kirchner, Ernst Ludwig, **GER**
Kishi, Nobusuke, **JAP**
Kitchener, Lord, **ARW, CAN, IND, SAF**
Klee, Paul, **GER, SWI**
Klephts, **GRE**
Knesset, **ISR**
Kodály, Zoltán, **EEU, SWI**
Kol Israel, **ISR**
Komorowski, Tadeusz (General Bór), **EEU**
Kongo, Kingdom of the, **TAF**
Kono, Ichiro, **JAP**
Koran, the, **ARW, BAL, ISR, TUR**
Koraysh tribe, **ARW**
Korea and the Korean War, **CHI, HBK, JAP, RUS, SEA, SWI, USA**
Korzo, **BAL**
Kościuszko, Tadeusz, **EEU**
Kosovo, Battle of (1389), **BAL**
Kossuth, Lajos, **EEU**
Kosygin, Aleksei, **GER, RUS**
Kovács, Béla, **EEU**
Krages, Hermann, **GER**
Kremlin, the, **BAL, RUS**
Krishna, god, **IND**
Krishnamachari, T. T., **IND**
Krohg, Per, **SCN**
Kronshtadt mutiny, **RUS**

Kruger, Stephanus Johannes Paulus, **SAF**
Krupp, house of, **CAN, GER, GRE**
Kshatriya, caste, **IND**
Kuang Hsu, Emperor of China, **CHI**
Kuan Yin, Goddess of Mercy, **CHI**
Kubitschek, Juscelino, **BRA**
Kublai Khan, **CHI, JAP, SEA**
Kulaks, **BAL**
Kültepe tablets, **TUR**
Kun, Béla, **EEU**
Kuomintang, **CHI, SEA**
Kuo-yu (language), **CHI**
Kupe (legendary warrior), **ANZ**
Kurds and Kurdistan, **ARW, ISR, TUR**
Kush, Kingdom of, **TAF**
Kushan Empire, **IND**
Kuwait, **ARW**
Kuwatly, Shukry, **ARW**
Kwiebus, Kwiebe, mythical philosopher, **LCO**

Labrador, **CAN, SCN**
Lacadónes, tribe, **MEX**
Lace, **BRA, SWI, WIN**
Lacedaemon, **GRE**
Lacerda, Carlos, **BRA**
Ladislas, King of Bohemia and Hungary, **EEU**
Ladysmith, siege of, **SAF**
Lagerkvist, Pär, **SCN**
Lagerlöf, Selma, **SCN**
Lambaréné, **TAF**
Lancaster, House of, **BRI**
Landsgemeinde, **SWI**
Landsmål, **SCN**
Laos, **CHI, SEA**
Lao Tzu, **CHI**
Lapps, **SCN**
Lardarello power plan, **ITA**
Las Casas, Bartolomé de, **COL, CTA, MEX, PLA**
Lascaux, cave paintings of, **FRA**
Las Salinas, Battle of, **AND**
Lateran Treaty, **HBK, ITA**
Latifundios, **CTA, SPA**
Laurel, José, **SEA**
Laurier, Sir Wilfrid, **CAN**
Lausanne, Treaty of, **TUR**
Laval, Pierre, **FRA**
Laver, Rod, **ANZ**
Lavon, Pinhas, **ISR**
Lawrence, T. E., **ARW**
Leacock, Stephen, **CAN**
League of Nations, **ARW, CAN, EEU, GER, ISR, ITA, RUS, SAF, SCN, SWI, TAF**
Leakey, Louis S. B., **TAF**
Leakey, Mary, **TAF**
Lear, Edward, **GRE**
Leavis, F. R., **BRI**
Lebanon, **ARW, ISR**
Le Clerq, François ("Peg-Leg"), **WIN**
Le Corbusier, **BRA, COL, FRA, IND, SWI**

Lee Kuan Yew, **SEA**
Leeward Islands, **WIN**
Léger, Paul-Emile Cardinal, **CAN**
Lemass, Sean, **IRE**
Lenin, Vladimir Ilich (Nikolai), **CHI, EEU, FRA, ITA, RUS, SEA, SPA, SWI, TUR**
Leo III, Pope, **EEU, ITA**
Leo X, Pope, **GRE, ITA**
Leonowens, Anna, **SEA**
Leopardi, Giacomo, **ITA**
Leopold II, King of the Belgians, **LCO, TAF**
Lepanto, Battle of, **GRE**
Leptis Magna, Libya, **ARW**
Lesage, Jean, **CAN**
Lesbos island, **GRE**
Lesser Antilles, **SPA, WIN**
Levantines, **ARW, BRA**
Lévesque, René, **CAN**
Levi, Carlo, **ITA**
Lëvizje Nacionalçlirimtarë, **BAL**
Lewis, Sinclair, **USA**
Lhasa, Tibet, **CHI**
Liberalism, **ANZ, BRA, BRI, CAN, CTA, GER, LCO, SAF, SPA**
Liberia, **TAF**
Liberman, Evsei, **RUS**
Libya, **ARW, BRI, ITA**
Lidice, Czechoslovakia, **EEU**
Lie, Trygve, **SCN**
Likay drama, **SEA**
Lima, Peru, **AND**
Lincoln, Abraham, **ITA, SPA, USA**
Lind, Jenny, **SCN**
Lindisfarne, Holy Island of, **SCN**
Lindsay, Vachel, **USA**
Linear B script, **GRE**
Linen industry, **IRE**
Linga, **SEA**
Lin Piao, **CHI**
Lin Tse-hsu, **CHI**
Li Po, **CHI**
Lippi, Fra Filippo, **ITA**
Lippizaners (horses), **EEU**
Lisbon, **BRA, SEA, TAF**
Li Shao-chun, **CHI**
Li Ssu, **CHI**
Liszt, Franz, **EEU**
Literacy. *See* Illiteracy
Lithuania, **EEU, RUS**
Li (tribe), **CHI**
Liu Shao-ch'i, **CHI**
Livingstone, David, **LCO, TAF**
Livy, **ITA**
Li Yuan, **CHI**
Lleras Camargo, Alberto, **COL**
Lloque Yupanqui (Inca ruler), **AND**
Lloyd George, David, **BRI, IRE**
Loa, **WIN**
Lobengula, Matabele chief, **SAF, TAF**
Locarno, Pacts of, **EEU, GER**
Lofoten Islands, **SCN**
Logia Lautaro (secret Argentine patriotic society), **PLA**
Loi Unique, **LCO**

Lo Lung-chi, **CHI**
London, **BRI, FRA, JAP, LCO, SCN, SPA, TAF**; Treaty of (1915), **ITA**
Longfellow, Henry Wadsworth, **BRA, CAN, ITA**
Long March, **CHI**
López Mateos, Adolfo, **MEX**
Lorca, Federico García. *See* García Lorca
Lorelei, **GER**
Lorraine, **FRA, GER**; Duke of, **SWI**
Lost cities, legends of, **AND**
Lotteries, **ANZ, COL, ITA**
Louis XIV, King of France, **EEU, FRA, LCO, SPA, WIN**
Louis the Pious, **GER, SCN**
Lourenço Marques, **TAF**
Louw, Eric, **SAF**
Lovisa Ulrika, Queen of Sweden, **SCN**
Low Countries, **GER, HBK, LCO, SPA**
Lowell, Robert, **USA**
Lower, A.R.M., **CAN**
Luanda, **TAF**
Luba tribe, **TAF**
Lublin, Poland, **EEU, ISR**
Lucian of Samosata, **GRE**
Lucknow, **IND**
Ludwig, Emil, **GER**
Ludwig, King of Bavaria, **GRE**
Ludwig of Baden, **BAL**
Lumumba, Patrice, **LCO, TAF**
Lund, Battle of, **SCN**
Lunda tribe, **TAF**
Lundi Gras, **WIN**
Luo tribe, **TAF**
Lupescu, Magda, **BAL**
Luther, Martin, and Lutheranism, **BAL, BRI, EEU, FRA, GER, ITA, LCO, SCN, SWI, USA**
Luthuli, Chief Albert, **SAF**
Luxembourg, **FRA, GER, LCO, SCN, SPA**
Lvov, Prince Georgi, **RUS**

Ma'barot villages, **ISR**
Macapagal, Diosdado, **SEA**
MacArthur, General Douglas, **JAP, USA**
Macartney, George, Lord, **CHI**
Macaulay, Thomas B., **FRA, IND**
McAuley, James, **ANZ**
Maccabees, **ISR**
MacCarthy, Cormac, **IRE**
McCarthy, Senator Joseph R., **CAN, USA**
MacCool, Finn, **IRE**
Macdonald, Sir John A., **CAN**
Macedonia, **BAL, GRE, ITA, TUR**
Machado de Assis, Joaquim Maria, **BRA**
Machiavelli, Niccolò, **ITA**
Machinery, **BRA, CHI, GER, IND, ITA, RUS, SWI**
Machismo, **WIN**
Machu Picchu (Inca city), **AND**

Maciejowice, Battle of, **EEU**
MacInnes, Colin, **BRI**
Mackenzie, Sir Alexander, **CAN**
Mackenzie, William Lyon, rebellion of, **CAN**
McKinley, William, **CTA, SEA**
McLaren, Norman, **CAN**
MacLennan, Hugh, **CAN**
Macmillan, Harold, **BRI**
Macumba, **BRA**
Madagascar, **HBK, SAF, TAF**
Madariaga, Salvador de, **COL, SPA**
Madero, Francisco, **MEX**
Madison, James, **CAN, GRE**
Madrid, **FRA, SPA**
Maeterlinck, Maurice, **LCO**
Mafeking, **SAF**
Mafia, **ITA**
Magdalena River, **AND, COL**
Magellan, Ferdinand, **HBK, SPA**
Magersfontein, Battle of, **SAF**
Magic, role of, **TAF**
Magic mountain, philosophy of, **SEA**
Magloire, Paul E., **WIN**
Magna Carta, **BRI**
"Magna Graecia," **GRE**
Magsaysay, Ramon, **SEA**
Magyars, **BAL, EEU, GER**
Mahabharata, **IND, SEA**
Mahatma Gandhi. *See* Gandhi, Mohandas K.
Mahdi, the. *See* Ahmed, Mohammed
Maipú, Battle of (Chile), **AND**
Maize, **CTA, MEX, WIN**
Makarios, Archbishop of Cyprus, **TUR**
Malacca, **SEA**
Malagasy Republic, **TAF**
Malan, Daniel F., **SAF**
Malaria, **CTA, IND, ITA**
Malaya, **BRA, CHI, HBK, RUS, SEA, SPA**
Malenkov, Georgi, **EEU, RUS, SEA**
Maléter, Pál, **EEU**
Mali, **TAF**
Malinchismo, **MEX**
Malnutrition, starvation, **IND, SAF, WIN**
Malraux, André, **FRA, ITA, SEA**
Mama Ocllo (Inca Queen), **AND**
Mamelukes, **ARW, TUR**
Man, Isle of, **IRE**
Manchuria, **CHI, JAP, RUS**
Manchus, **CHI, SEA**
Manco Capac (Inca ruler), **AND**
Mandalay, **SEA**
Mandarin (language), **CHI**
Mandela, Nelson, **SAF**
Manet, Edouard, **FRA**
Manfred, Prince of Taranto, **ITA**
Manganese, **IND, SAF**
Mani, **GRE**
Manichaean heresy, **BAL**
Manila, **JAP, SEA**
Maniots, **GRE**
Manley, Norman Washington, **WIN**

Mann, Erika, **SWI**
Mann, Thomas, **GER, SWI**
Mansfield, Katherine, **ANZ, SWI**
Mantegna, Andrea, **ITA**
Manuel I, King of Portugal, **BRA**
Manzikert, Battle of (1071), **TUR**
Manzù, Giacomo, **ITA**
Maoris, **ANZ**
Mao Tse-tung, **CHI, RUS, SEA, USA**
Maratha Empire, **HBK, IND**
Marathon, Battle of, **GRE**
Marcus Aurelius, **CHI, GRE, ITA, SPA**
Margaret of Austria, **LCO**
Margarita Island, **COL, WIN**
Maria I, Queen of Portugal, **BRA**
María Cristina de Bourbon, **SPA**
Maria (da Glória) II, Queen of Portugal, **BRA**
Maria Theresa, Empress, **EEU, GER**
Marienbad, Czechoslovakia, **EEU**
Marimbola, **WIN**
Marine Corps, U.S., **CTA, WIN**
Markets, **CTA, GRE, PLA, SEA, SPA, WIN**
Maronites, **ARW, ISR**
Marrakesh, Pasha of, **ARW**
Marshall, General George C., **CHI, HBK**
Marshall Plan, **FRA, HBK, ITA, LCO, RUS, SWI, TUR, USA.** *See also* Aid, economic
Martí, José, **WIN**
Martin, Paul, **CAN**
Martinique, **WIN**
Marx, Karl, and Marxism, **AND, CHI, EEU, FRA, GER, HBK, ISR, JAP, LCO, RUS, SEA, SWI.** *See also* Communism
Mary of Burgundy, **SPA**
Mary of Hungary, **LCO**
Maryknoll Fathers (missionaries), **AND**
Masaccio, **ITA**
Masai tribe, **TAF**
Masaryk, Thomas Garrigue, **EEU, HBK**
Masks, **TAF, WIN**
Massey, Vincent, **CAN**
Matabele tribes, **SAF, TAF**
Matisse, Henri, **FRA, SCN, TAF**
Mato Grosso, **BRA**
Matshikiza, Todd, **SAF**
Mattei, Enrico, **ITA**
Maugham, Somerset, **SEA, SWI**
Mau Mau movement, **TAF**
Mauritania, **TAF**
Mauryan Empire, **IND**
Maximilian I, Holy Roman Emperor, **HBK, SPA, SWI**
Maximilian, Emperor of Mexico, **BRA, MEX**
Mayas, **CTA, MEX**
Mayta Capac (Inca ruler), **AND**
Mazzini, Giuseppe, **ITA**
Mboya, Tom, **TAF**
Meat industry, **BRA, PLA**

Mecca, **ARW, ISR, TUR**
Medici family, **GRE, ITA**
Medicine men, **SEA, TAF**
Medina, **ARW, TUR**
Mediterranean, **ARW, CHI, GRE, ISR, SCN, SEA, SPA, SWI, TUR**
Megali Idea, **GRE**
Mehmet I, II, III, V, VI (Sultans of the Ottoman Empire), **TUR**
Meiji, Emperor, **JAP**
Meir, Golda, **ISR**
Melanesia and Melanesians, **ANZ, HBK**
Melbourne, Lord, **BRI**
Mello Franco de Andrade, Rodrigo, **BRA**
Melville, Herman, **AND, GRE, USA**
Memling, Hans, **LCO**
Mencius, **CHI**
Mende, Erich, **GER**
Mendelssohn, Felix, **GER**
Menderes, Adnan, **TUR**
Mendès-France, Pierre, **FRA**
Mendoza, Eugenio, **COL**
Menelaus, **GRE**
Menelik I of Ethiopia, **TAF**
Mennonites, **AND, PLA**
Menon, Khrishna, **IND**
Menorah, **ISR**
Mensheviks, **RUS**
Menzies, Sir Robert Gordon, **ANZ**
Meo hunters, **SEA**
Mercator, Gerhardus, **LCO**
Mercia, Kingdom of, **BRI**
Mérida, Carlos, **CTA, MEX**
Merovingian Dynasty, **FRA**
Meru, **SEA, TAF**
Mesopotamia, **CHI, ITA**
Messaure Dam, **SCN**
Mestizos, **AND, CTA, MEX, PLA**
Metaxas, John, **GRE**
Methuen, Lord, **SAF**
Metternich, Prince of Austria, **EEU, HBK, LCO**
Mexican Revolution, **MEX**
Mexican War, **FRA, MEX, USA**
Mexico, **AND, BRA, COL, MEX, PLA, SPA, WIN**
Miango tribe, **TAF**
Mica production, **IND**
Michael the Brave (Prince), **BAL**
Michelangelo, **HBK, ITA**
Middle Ages, **ARW, FRA, GRE, ISR, ITA, JAP**
Middle East, **ARW, CHI, HBK, ISR, TUR**
Middle Kingdom, **CHI**
Midhat Pasha, **TUR**
Midlands, **BRI, SWI**
Mies van der Rohe, Ludwig, **GER**
Migrations, **CHI, EEU, ITA, MEX, TAF, TUR.** *See also* Immigration
Mihailovič, Draža, **BAL**
Mihiragula, Hun chieftain, **IND**
Mikołajczyk, Stanisław, **EEU**

COL Colombia and Venezuela; **CTA** Central America; **EEU** Eastern Europe; **FRA** France; **GER** Germany; **GRE** Greece; **HBK** Handbook; **SCN** Scandinavia; **SEA** Southeast Asia; **SPA** Spain; **SWI** Switzerland; **TAF** Tropical Africa; **TUR** Turkey; **USA** United States; **WIN** West Indies.

169

Mikoyan, Anastas, **EEU, RUS**
Miletus, **GRE, TUR**
Militarism, **GER, JAP**
Milk production. *See* Dairy farming
Mill, John Stuart, **FRA, GRE**
Miller, Joaquin, **CTA**
Milles, Carl, **SCN**
Milliyet, **TUR**
Milner, Lord Alfred, **SAF**
Milton, John, **BRI, GRE, ITA**
Minamoto family, **JAP**
Minas Conspiracy, **BRA**
Minas Gerais, **BRA**
Mindszenty, Jozsef Cardinal, **EEU**
Minerals, **ANZ, BRA, CAN, EEU, ISR, SAF, TAF, TUR**
Ming Dynasty, **CHI**
Ming Huang, **CHI**
Ming Tombs dam, **CHI**
Minifundios, **CTA**
Min Mahagiri, **SEA**
Minoan culture, **GRE**
Minorca, **SPA**
Min Yuen movement, **SEA**
Miranda, Francisco de, **AND, COL**
Miró, Joan, **COL, SPA**
Miroku, god, **JAP**
Miscegenation, **BRA, TAF**
Missiles, **CHI, COL, RUS, USA, WIN**
Missionaries, **AND, ARW, BRA, CAN, CHI, COL, CTA, MEX, PLA, SAF, SEA, SPA, TAF, USA, WIN**
Missolonghi siege, **GRE**
Mistral, Gabriela, **AND**
Mitchell, Sir Philip, **TAF**
Mixtec, culture, **MEX**
Mixtón War, **MEX**
Moche (Indians), **AND**
Moctezuma, Aztec Emperor, **MEX, WIN**
Modigliani, Amedeo, **FRA, ITA**
Mogul Empire, **HBK, IND**
Mohács, Battle of, **EEU**
Mohammed Ali Pasha, **TUR**
Mohammed and Mohammedanism, **ARW, BRA, ISR, SEA, TUR, WIN**
Mohammed Askia, King of Songhai, **TAF**
Mohammed Ben Youssef, King of Morocco, **ARW**
Mohammed ibn Abdul Wahhab, **ARW**
Moksha, **IND**
Moldavia, **BAL**
Molière, **FRA, SPA**
Mollet, Guy, **FRA, TAF**
Molotov, Vyacheslav M., **BAL, EEU, RUS**
Moluccas, **SEA**
Mombasa, **TAF**
Monaco, **FRA, HBK**
Monarchism, Monarchs, Monarchy, **ARW, BRA, BRI, FRA, SPA**
Mondrian, Piet, **LCO**

Monet, Claude, **FRA**
Mongkut, King of Thailand, **SEA**
Mongolia and Mongols, **ARW, CHI, HBK, JAP, RUS, SEA, TUR**
Monnet, Jean, **FRA, HBK**
Monroe Doctrine, **COL, CTA**
Monrovia group, **HBK, TAF**
Monsoon, **IND, JAP**
Montagne Pelée (volcano), **WIN**
Montagu, Lady Mary Wortley, **BAL**
Mont Blanc, **FRA, SWI**
Montcalm, General, **CAN**
Monte Caseros, Battle of, **PLA**
Montenegro, **BAL**
Montessori, Maria, **ITA**
Monteverdi, Claudio, **ITA**
Montezuma. *See* Moctezuma
Moore, Henry, **BRI**
Moors, **AND, SCN, SEA, SPA**
Moravia, **BAL, EEU**
Moravia, Alberto, **ITA**
Morgan, Henry, **WIN**
Morgarten, Battle of (1315), **SWI**
Moriori (Polynesian people), **ANZ**
Morley, Helena, **BRA**
Mormons, **ANZ, USA**
Moro, Aldo, **ITA**
Morocco, **ARW, FRA, GER, ISR, TAF**
Mosaics, **GRE, ISR**
Moscow, **BAL, CHI, FRA, JAP, RUS, SEA**; Treaty, **USA**
Mosega, Battle of, **SAF**
Moses, **ISR**
Moshavim, **ISR**
Moslems, **ARW, BAL, CHI, GRE, HBK, IND, ISR, RUS, SAF, SEA, SPA, TAF, TUR.** *See also* Mohammed and Mohammedanism
Mosques, **ARW, BAL, GRE, ISR, SEA, SPA, TUR**
Mossadegh, Mohammed, **ARW, HBK**
Mountaineering, **ANZ, SWI**
Mountbatten, Lord Louis, **HBK, IND, SEA**
Mount Olga range, **ANZ**
Mousiké, **GRE**
Mouvement National Congolais, **LCO, TAF**
Movies. *See* Films
Mozambique, **SAF, TAF**
Mozart, Wolfgang Amadeus, **EEU, ITA, SPA**
Mphahlele, Ezekiel, **SAF, TAF**
Muezzins, **ARW, ISR**
Muhammadiyya movement, **SEA**
Mulattoes, **BRA, CTA, TAF, WIN**
Munch, Edvard, **SCN**
Munich, **GER**; Conference, **EEU**
Muñoz Marín, Luis, **WIN**
Murals, **MEX, TAF**
Murasaki, Lady, **JAP**
Murad (Sultan), **BAL, TUR**
Murillo, Bartolomé Estéban, **SPA**
Muromachi Period, **JAP**

Murray, Gilbert, **BRI**
Muscovy, principality of, **RUS**
Mussolini, Benito, **ARW, GRE, HBK, ITA, SPA**
Mustafa IV, **TUR**
Mustafa, son of Süleyman, **TUR**
Mycenae, **GRE**
Mysticism, **ARW, IND, TUR**

Nabataeans, **ISR**
Näfels, Battle of (1388), **SWI**
Nagasaki, **JAP, SEA**
Naga (serpent), **SEA**
Naga tribe, **IND**
Naguib, Mohammed, **ARW**
Nagy, Ferenc, **EEU**
Nagy, Imre, **EEU**
Nahas, Mustafa (Nahas Pasha), **ARW**
Nahuatl, language, **MEX**
Naipaul, V. S., **WIN**
Nanchao, Kingdom of, **SEA**
Nandi tribe, **TAF**
Nansen, Fridtjof, **SCN**
Nanyang trade, **SEA**
Naples, **GRE, ITA, SPA**
Napoleon III, **EEU, FRA, MEX**
Napoleon Bonaparte, **ARW, BAL, BRA, BRI, COL, EEU, FRA, GER, HBK, ITA, LCO, MEX, SCN, SEA, SPA, SWI, TUR, USA, WIN**
Napoleonic Wars, **BAL, FRA, GRE, RUS, SCN, SWI**
Nara Period, **JAP**
Narva battle, **SCN**
Nasser, Gamal Abdel, **ARW, BAL, HBK, ISR, JAP, USA**
Nasution, Abdul Haris, **SEA**
Nationalization, **BRI, FRA, GER, IND**
National Socialism. *See* Nazis and Nazism
NATO. *See* North Atlantic Treaty Organization
Nats (spirits), **SEA**
Natural gas, **AND, CAN, FRA, ISR**
Nauru, U.N. trust territory, **ANZ**
Navarino, Battle of, **GRE**
Nayarit culture, **MEX**
Nazca Indians, **AND**
Nazis and Nazism, **ARW, BAL, EEU, FRA, GER, ISR, SAF, SWI**
Ne Win, General, **SEA**
Neanderthal man, **GER**
Nebuchadnezzar, King of Babylon, **ISR**
Negritos, **SEA**
Négritude, **TAF, WIN**
Negroes, **BRA, COL, CTA, MEX, PLA, TAF, USA, WIN**
Nehru, Jawaharlal, **ARW, BAL, BRI, CAN, CHI, HBK, IND, SEA**
Nelson, Horatio, **BRI, IRE, ITA, SCN, SPA, WIN**
Nemanjíc kings, **BAL**
Nenni, Pietro, **ITA**
Nepal, **HBK, IND**

Nero, Emperor, **ITA**
Neruda, Pablo, **AND**
Nervi, Pier Luigi, **ITA**
Nestorian Christians, **CHI**
Netherlands, the (Holland), **CHI, COL, FRA, GER, HBK, JAP, LCO, PLA, SAF, SCN, SEA, SPA, SWI, TAF, WIN**
Neutralism, **BAL, BRI, IRE, JAP, SCN, SEA, SWI, TUR**
New Castile, **AND, SPA**
Newfoundland, **BRI, CAN**
New Guinea, **ANZ, HBK, LCO, SEA**
New Siberian Islands, **SCN**
New Spain, **MEX**
New Testament, **GRE, ISR.** *See also* Bible
New York, **COL, FRA, JAP, LCO, TAF, USA, WIN**
New Zealand, **ANZ, BRI, SEA**
Nicaragua, **CTA, HBK**
Nicene Creed, **GRE, TUR**
Nicephorus I, Emperor, **BAL**
Nicephorus Phocas, Emperor, **GRE**
Nichiren sect, **JAP**
Nicholas I, Czar of Russia, **BAL, EEU, HBK**
Nicholas II, Czar of Russia, **HBK, RUS**
Nicholson, Ben, **BRI**
Nickel, **CAN**
Niebuhr, Reinhold, **USA**
Niemeyer, Oscar, **BRA**
Niemöller, Martin, **GER**
Nietzsche, Friedrich, **GER, ITA, SWI**
Niger (republic), **TAF**
Nigeria, **BRI, HBK, SAF, TAF**
Nile River, **ARW, TAF**
Nilotic people, **ARW, TAF**
Nirvana, **CHI, IND, SEA**
Nitrates, **AND**
Nkrumah, Kwame, **BAL, BRI, TAF**
Nō drama, **JAP**
Noar Halutzi Lochem, **ISR**
Nobel Peace Prize, **LCO, RUS, SAF, SCN, SWI, USA**
Nolan, Sydney, **ANZ**
Nolde, Emil, **GER**
Nordhoff, Heinz, **GER**
Normandy and the Normans, **BRI, FRA, ITA, SCN**
Norsemen. *See* Vikings
North Africa, **ARW, FRA, ISR, SWI, TAF, TUR.** *See also* Africa
North Atlantic Treaty Organization (NATO), **BRI, FRA, GER, GRE, HBK, ITA, LCO, RUS, SCN, SPA, SWI, TUR, USA**
North Pole, **SCN**
North Sea, **SCN, SPA, SWI**
Northern Ireland, **BRI, IRE**
Northumbria, Kingdom of, **BRI**
Northwest Passage, **CAN, SCN**
Northwest Territories, **CAN**
Norway, **GER, HBK, SCN, SWI**

Nubians, **TAF**
Nuclear power and weapons,
 **BRI, CHI, GER, HBK, ISR,
 ITA, JAP, RUS, USA.** *See also*
 Atomic energy
Nuer tribe, **TAF**
Nuri Said, of Iraq, **TUR**
Nyanda tribe, **SAF**
Nyasaland, **SAF, TAF**
Nyerere, Julius, **TAF**
Nzima tribe, **TAF**

Obeahman (witch), **WIN**
Oberammergau Passion play,
 GER
Oberländer, Theodor, **GER**
Obregón, Alejandro, **COL**
Obregón, Alvaro, **MEX**
Obrenović, Miloš, **BAL**
Ocampo, Victoria, **PLA**
Ocaña, Convention of, **COL**
O'Casey, Sean, **IRE**
Occultism, **TAF.** *See also* Magic;
 Vodou
Oceania, **HBK**
O'Conaire, Padraic, **IRE**
O'Connell, Daniel, **IRE**
O'Connor, Edwin, **IRE**
O'Connor, Frank, **IRE**
O'Conor, Rory, **IRE**
Octavian (Emperor Augustus),
 ITA, TUR
Odessa, **BAL, RUS**
O'Donnell, Red Hugh, **IRE**
Odría, Manuel, **AND**
Odysseus, **GRE**
O'Faolain, Sean, **IRE**
Offa II, King of Mercia, **BRI**
O'Flaherty, Liam, **IRE**
O'Gorman, Juan, **MEX**
O'Higgins, Bernardo, **AND,
 COL, PLA**
Oil (Petroleum), **AND, ARW,
 BAL, BRA, CAN, CHI, COL,
 FRA, HBK, ISR, ITA, LCO,
 MEX, PLA, RUS, SAF, SEA,
 SPA, WIN**
Ojeda, Alonso de, **COL, CTA**
Okinawa, **JAP**
O'Leary, Daniel, **COL**
Olga, Mount (range), **ANZ**
Olivetti, Adriano, **ITA**
Olivetti, Camillo, **ITA**
Olmec culture, **MEX**
Olympia, **GRE**
Olympic Games, **GRE, HBK,
 JAP, RUS**
Omar, **ARW**
Ombudsman, **ANZ, SCN**
Ona Indians, **PLA**
O'Neill, Eugene, **USA**
O'Neill, Hugh, Earl of Tyrone,
 IRE
Opium, **CHI**
Oppenheimer, Sir Ernest, **SAF**
Oppenheimer, Harry F., **SAF**
Oracles, **GRE**; "oracle bones,"
 CHI
Oran, **SPA**
Orange Free State, **SAF**
Orange Order, **IRE**

Orestes, **GRE**
Organization for European
 Economic Cooperation (OEEC),
 HBK, LCO, SPA
Organization of American States,
 COL, CTA, HBK, WIN
Oriente province (Cuba), **WIN**
Oriente (region, Ecuador), **AND**
Orkney Islands, **IRE, SCN**
Orozco, José Clemente, **MEX**
Ortega y Gasset, José, **SPA**
Orthodox Church, **BAL, EEU,
 GRE, ISR, WIN**
Oryia, language, **IND**
Osborne, John, **BRI**
Oseberg ship, **SCN**
O'Shannon, Cathal, **IRE**
Osler, Sir William, **CAN**
Osman, **ARW, TUR**
Ostrogoths, **BAL, HBK**
Otavalo Indians, **AND**
Otomi Indians, **MEX**
Ottawa, **BRI, CAN**
Otto I, Emperor, **GER, HBK**
Ottoman Empire, **ARW, BAL,
 GRE, ISR, TUR.** *See also*
 Turkey and the Turks
Ouro Prêto, **BRA**
"Outer Seven." *See* European
 Free Trade Association
Ovid, **ITA**
Oyana Indians, **COL**

Paccha (Inca Princess), **AND**
Pachacuti Inca Yupanqui (Inca
 ruler), **AND**
Pacific Ocean, **AND, COL, CTA,
 GER, JAP, RUS, SCN**
Packer, Sir Frank, **ANZ**
Paderewski, Ignace Jan, **EEU**
Páez, José Antonio, **COL**
Pai Marire (Maori religious
 movement), **ANZ**
Paine, Thomas, **PLA**
Pakistan, **ARW, BRI, CHI, HBK,
 IND, JAP, TUR**
Palacios, Alfredo, **PLA**
Palacký, František, **EEU**
Palatinate, **GER**
Palermo (Sicily), **BAL, ITA**
Palestine, **ARW, ISR, SWI**
Palestrina, **ITA**
Pali, language, **SEA**
Palmerston, Lord, **CTA**
Pamir steppes, **CHI**
Pampa, **PLA**
Panama, **AND, ARW, COL, CTA,
 MEX, SPA, WIN**
Panchayat, **IND**
Panda (Zulu chief), **SAF**
Panikkar, K. M., **IND**
Panipat, Battle of, **IND**
Pantheon, **FRA**
Panza, Sancho, **SPA**
Papacy, **ITA**
Paper, **BRA, CAN, CHI, MEX**
Papineau, Louis-Joseph, **CAN**
Papua (Australian Territory),
 ANZ
Paraguay, **AND, BRA, PLA**
Paramaribo, Surinam, **COL**

Paraná River, **BRA, PLA**
Pardo, Manuel, **AND**
Pardo Farelo, Enrique, **COL**
Parícutin, **MEX**
Paris, **BAL, FRA, HBK, ITA,
 SCN, SEA, SPA, SWI**
Paris Peace Conference (1919),
 ARW, CHI, EEU, SEA
Parkman, Francis, **USA**
Parma, Duke of, Alessandro
 Farnese, **LCO**
Parnell, Charles Stewart, **IRE**
Parsis, **IND**
Parthenon, **GRE**
Partition (division), **EEU, GER,
 IND, IRE, ISR**
Pascal, Blaise, **FRA**
Pasternak, Boris, **GER, RUS**
Pasteur, Louis, **FRA**
Pasto, Battle of (Colombia), **AND**
Patagonia, **PLA**
Pataliputra (*now* Patna), **IND**
Pathet Lao, **CHI, SEA**
Patil, S. K., **IND**
Patiño, Simón I., **AND**
Patmos island, **GRE**
Patna, **IND**
Paton, Alan, **SAF**
Paul III, Pope, **CTA, ITA**
Paul, Saint, **GRE, TUR**
Pavese, Cesare, **ITA**
Pax Britannica, **BRI**
Paysandú, Uruguay, **PLA**
Paz, Octavio, **MEX**
Paz Estenssoro, Víctor, **AND**
Pazmino, Brother Nicholas, **AND**
Pazoz Kanki, Vicente, **AND**
Pearl Harbor, **BRI, JAP, SEA**
Pearse, Padraic, **IRE**
Pearson, Lester B., **CAN**
Peary, Commodore Robert, **CAN**
"Pedrarias the Cruel," **CTA**
Peel, Robert, **IRE**
Peixoto, Floriano, **BRA**
Peking, **CHI, HBK, IND, JAP,
 SEA**
Pelayo, **SPA**
Pelletier, Gérard, **CAN**
Peloponnesian War, **GRE**
Pembroke, Earl of (Strongbow),
 IRE
Peñalosa, Enrique, **COL**
Penang, Malaya, **SEA**
Penfield, Dr. Wilder, **CAN**
Peninsular War, **SPA**
Penn, William, **WIN**
Pentecostists, **WIN**
Pérez Jiménez, Marcos, **COL**
Pergamum (Bergama), **TUR**
Pericles, **GRE**
Permafrost, **CAN**
Perón, Eva Duarte de, **PLA**
Perón, Juan Domingo, **COL,
 PLA, SPA**
Perpignan, **FRA**
Perry, Matthew, **JAP**
Persia. *See* Iran
Persian Gulf, **ARW, BRI, CHI,
 HBK**
Peru, **AND, COL, PLA, SPA,
 WIN**

Peshawar, **IND**
Pestalozzi, Heinrich, **SWI**
Pétain, Henri Philippe, **FRA**
Peter I Island, **SCN**
Peter of Portugal, Prince, **CHI**
Peter the Great, **BAL, HBK,
 RUS, SCN, TUR**
Pétion, Alexandre, **WIN**
Petkov, Nikola, **BAL**
Petöfi, Sándor, **EEU**
Petra, Jordan, **ARW, ISR**
Petrarch, **ITA**
Petrassi, Goffredo, **ITA**
Petroleum. *See* Oil
Petrov Affair, **ANZ**
Peurifoy, John E., **CTA**
Philip II, King of Macedon, **BAL,
 GRE**
Philip II, King of Spain, **IRE,
 LCO, SPA**
Philippine Islands, **COL, CHI,
 HBK, JAP, RUS, SEA, SPA**
Philistines, **ISR**
Phoenicians, **ARW, ITA, SPA,
 TUR**
Phrygia, **TUR**
Picasso, Pablo, **BRI, FRA, SPA,
 TAF**
Piccard, Auguste, **SWI**
Piccard, Jean, **SWI**
Pichincha, Battle of (Ecuador),
 AND, COL
Piene, Otto, **GER**
Pijper, Willem, **LCO**
Pilate, Pontius, **ISR**
Piłsudski, Józef, **EEU**
Pindar, **GRE**
Pinero, Sir Arthur Wing, **IRE**
Pinta, **SPA**
Pinter, Harold, **BRI**
Piper, John, **BRI**
Piracy, buccaneering, **COL, SPA,
 TUR.** *See also* Privateers
Piraeus, **GRE**
Pirandello, Luigi, **ITA**
Pitcairn Island, **HBK**
Pithecanthropus erectus, **SEA**
Pitt, William, **BRI, IND, IRE**
Pizarro, Francisco, **AND, COL,
 CTA, SPA**
Pizarro, Gonzalo, **AND**
Pizarro, Hernando, **AND**
Pizarro, Juan, **AND**
Planck, Max, **GER**
Plantagenet, House of, **BRI**
Plantations, **BRA, CTA, TAF**
Plassey, Battle of, **BRI, IND**
Platinum, **SAF**
Plato, **BRI, GRE, ITA**
Plautus, **ITA**
Plaza, Leonidas, **AND**
Ploești, Romania, **BAL**
Plunkett, Joseph Mary, **IRE**
Po River, **ITA, SWI**
Pocomania, **WIN**
Podgorny, Nikolai, **RUS**
Poe, Edgar Allan, **GRE, USA**
Poland, **BAL, CAN, EEU, FRA,
 GER, HBK, ISR, RUS, SCN,
 SPA, SWI**
Polaris, **BRI**

COL Colombia and Venezuela; **CTA** Central America; **EEU** Eastern Europe; **FRA** France; **GER** Germany; **GRE** Greece; **HBK** Handbook;
SCN Scandinavia; **SEA** Southeast Asia; **SPA** Spain; **SWI** Switzerland; **TAF** Tropical Africa; **TUR** Turkey; **USA** United States; **WIN** West Indies.

Polish Corridor, **EEU, GER**
Polo, Marco, **CHI, HBK, JAP, SEA, WIN**
Polo, Niccolò and Maffeo, **CHI**
Poltava, Battle of, **SCN**
Polygamy, **ISR, TAF, TUR**
Pomerania, **EEU, GER**
Pompeii, **ITA**
Pompey, **GRE, ITA**
Ponce Massacre, **WIN**
Pondicherry, French trade centers at, **IND**
Poniatowski, Stanislas Augustus, King of Poland, **EEU**
Popayán, Colombia, **COL**
Popenoe, Wilson, **CTA**
Popovich, Pavel, **RUS**
Porfirian Peace, **MEX**
Poros island, **GRE**
Portales, Diego, **AND**
Port Arthur, **ANZ, SEA**
Port-au-Prince, Haiti, **WIN**
Porteños, **PLA**
Portobelo, Panama, **CTA, WIN**
Port of Spain, Trinidad, **WIN**
Port Royal, Jamaica, **WIN**
Port Said, **ARW**
Portugal, **BRA, CHI, COL, HBK, IND, ISR, PLA, SAF, SCN, SEA, SPA, TAF, WIN**
Potash, **ISR**
Potatoes, **IRE, LCO**
Potemkin, Grigori, **RUS**
Potsdam, **EEU, GER**; Conference, **GER, RUS**
Pottery, **BAL, BRA, CAN, CTA**
Pound, Ezra, **USA**
Poznań, Poland, **EEU**
Prague, Czechoslovakia, **EEU, GER, SPA**
Prasad, Rajendra, **IND**
Praxiteles, **GRE**
Prebisch, Raúl, **COL, CTA, HBK**
Přemyslids (ruling family of Czechs), **EEU**
Presbyterians, **BRI, IRE**
Prescott, William Hickling, **AND, USA**
Prester John, **TAF**
Pretoria, **SAF**
Pretorius, Andries, **SAF**
Pridi Phanomyong, **SEA**
Primo de Rivera, José Antonio, **SPA**
Primo de Rivera, Miguel, **SPA**
Prince Edward Island, **CAN**
Princip, Gavrilo, **BAL**
Principalities, **GER, IND**
Principe, island, **TAF**
Pringle, Thomas, **SAF**
Pripet Marshes, **RUS**
Pritchett, V. S., **IRE, SPA**
Privateers, **COL**. *See also* Piracy
Prokofiev, Sergei, **RUS**
Propylaea, the, **GRE**
Prostitution, **BAL, ITA, JAP, SWI**
Protagoras, **GRE**
Protestantism, **BRA, CHI, EEU, FRA, GER, IRE, ISR, LCO, SAF, SPA, WIN**. *See also* Reformation

Proust, Marcel, **FRA, JAP, LCO**
Prussia, **GER, ITA, SCN, SEA, SPA**
Ptolemy, **GRE, SEA**
Ptolemy, temple in Edfu, **ARW**
Pucallpa, Peru, **AND**
Puccini, Giacomo, **ITA**
Puerto Rico and Puerto Ricans, **COL, SPA, USA, WIN**
Pugachev, Emelyan, **RUS**
Puławski, Kazimierz, **EEU**
Punic Wars, **ITA, SPA**
Punjab, **HBK, IND**
Puppet plays, **JAP, SEA, TUR**
Purcell, Henry, **BRI**
Purcell, Joseph, **IRE**
Puritans and Puritanism, **ARW, BRI, COL, IRE, SWI, USA**
Pushkin, Alexander, **RUS**
Pu Yi, Emperor of China, **CHI**
Pygmies, **TAF**
Pylos, **GRE**
Pyramids, **ARW, CTA, MEX**
Pyrenees, **FRA, SPA**
Pyrrhus, **GRE**
Pythagoras, **GRE, ITA**
Pythian games, **GRE**

Quadroon, **WIN**
Quadros, Jânio, **BRA**
Quasimodo, Salvatore, **ITA**
Quechua, **AND, PLA**
Queen Maud Land, **SCN**
Queiroz, Rachel de, **BRA**
Quemoy, island, **CHI**
Querendi Indians, **PLA**
Quesnay, François, **CHI**
Quetzalcoatl, **MEX**
Quimbaya Indians, **COL**
Quintana Roo, **MEX**
Quintilian, **SPA**
Quiroga, Vasca de, **MEX**
Quisling, Vidkun, **SCN**
Quitu Indians, **AND**
Quizquiz (Inca chieftain), **AND**
Quoc Ngu alphabet, **SEA**

Rabelais, François, **FRA, GRE**
Rabia of Basra, Sufi mystic, **ARW**
Rabiblancos (Veinte Familias), **CTA**
Rabie, Jan, **SAF**
Rachmaninov, Sergei, **RUS**
Racine, Jean Baptiste, **FRA, LCO**
Racławice, Battle of, **EEU**
Rada, **WIN**
Radek, Karl, **RUS**
Radhakrishnan, Sarvepalli, **IND**
Radić, Stepan, **BAL**
Raeti, **SWI**
Raffles, Thomas S., **SEA**
Raga music, **IND**
Rahman, Abdul, Tengku, **SEA**
Railroads, **ANZ, BRI, CAN, CHI, CTA, FRA, IND, ITA, LCO, MEX, PLA, SAF, SPA, SWI**
Rain forests, **AND, COL**
Rajk, László, **BAL, EEU**
Rajput rulers, **IND**
Raki, **TUR**

Rákóczi, Ferenc, **EEU**
Rákosi, Mátyás, **BAL, EEU**
Raleigh, Sir Walter, **BRI, WIN**
Rama I, King of Thailand, **SEA**
Ramadan, sacred month, **ARW, TUR**
Ramakian, **SEA**
Ramayana, **SEA**
Rameau, Jean Philippe, **FRA**
Ramos, Graciliano, **BRA**
Ramuz, Charles Ferdinand, **SWI**
Ran, Nazım Hikmet, **TUR**
Randers, Jan, **SCN**
Rangoon, Burma, **SEA**
Ranković, Aleksandar, **BAL**
Rao, Shanta, **IND**
Rapallo, **ITA**; Treaty, **EEU**
Raphael, **HBK, ITA**
Rashid, Haroun al, **ARW**
Rasminsky, Louis, **CAN**
Rasputin, Grigori, **RUS**
Ras Tafari (cult), **WIN**
Ravenna, **BAL, GRE, ITA**
Ray, Satyajit, **IND**
Reactor (nuclear), **LCO, SCN**. *See also* Atomic energy; Nuclear power
Reconquista (Creole defeat of British), **PLA, SPA**
Red Army, **BAL, CHI, RUS**
Red China. *See* China
Red Cross, **HBK, SWI**
Red Sea, **ISR, TAF**
Reform, War of the, **MEX**
Reformation, Protestant, **BRI, COL, EEU, FRA, GER, IRE, ITA, SPA, SWI**. *See also* Protestantism
Refugees, **ARW, CHI, GER, HBK, IND, ISR, LCO, SCN, SPA, SWI**
Regiomontanos, **MEX**
Rehoboam, King, **ISR**
Reichstag, **GER**
Reidy, Affonso Eduardo, **BRA**
Reincarnation, **IND, TAF**
Rej, Mikolaj, **EEU**
Rekrutenschule, **SWI**
Remarque, Erich Maria, **GER**
Rembrandt van Rijn, **LCO**
Renaissance, **BAL, EEU, FRA, GRE, ITA**
Renault, **FRA**
Renoir, Auguste, **FRA**
Renoir, Jean, **FRA**
Reuter, Ernst, **GER**
Rey, Jacobus de la, **SAF**
Reymont, Władysław, **EEU**
Rhadé tribe, **SEA**
Rhineland, **EEU, GER, SWI**
Rhine River, **FRA, GER, SWI**; Commission, **HBK**
Rhoden, Ausser, **SWI**
Rhodes, Alexandre de, **SEA**
Rhodes, Cecil John, **SAF, TAF**
Rhodesias, **SAF, TAF**
Rhône River, **FRA, SWI**
Rhyner, Jakob, **SWI**
Rhyner, Kaspar, **SWI**
Ribera, José de, **SPA**
Ribeyre, Paul, **LCO**

Ricci, Matteo, Father, **CHI**
Rice, **AND, CHI, COL, FRA, IND, JAP, SEA**
Richefeu, Charles, **FRA**
Richelieu, Cardinal, **FRA**
Richler, Mordecai, **CAN**
Richter, Karl, **GER**
Riel, Louis, rebellion of, **CAN**
Riffs, **SPA**
Rift valleys, **TAF**
Riga, Treaty of, **EEU**
Rigi, the, **SWI**
Rig-Veda, **IND, SEA**
Riksdag, **SCN**
Riksmål, **SCN**
Rilke, Rainer Maria, **FRA, SWI**
Rimbaud, Arthur, **FRA**
Rinascimento, il, **ITA**
Rinuccini, Ottavio, **ITA**
Rio de Janeiro, **BRA, COL**
Río Negro, **BRA, PLA**
Riopelle, Jean-Paul, **CAN**
Risorgimento, **ITA**
Rivarol, Antoine de, **FRA**
Rivera, Diego, **MEX**
Rivera, Julio Adalberto, **CTA**
Rivera, Manuel, **CTA**
"Rivonia trial," **SAF**
Robert, Georges, **WIN**
Robert of Clari, **GRE**
Robert the Wise, King of Naples, **ITA**
Roberto Holden, **TAF**
Roberts, Lord, **SAF**
Roberts, Tom, **ANZ**
Roberts, W. Adolphe, **WIN**
Robinson, Edwin Arlington, **USA**
Roces, Alejandro R., **SEA**
Rock dwellings (Göreme), **TUR**
Rocketry. *See* Space research
Rock of Cashel, **IRE**
Rock paintings, **TAF**
Rodin, Auguste, **EEU, FRA**
Rodney, George B., **WIN**
Rodó, José Enrique, **PLA**
Roethke, Theodore, **USA**
Rojas, Fernando de, **SPA**
Rojas, Isaac, **PLA**
Rojas Pinilla, Gustavo, **COL**
Rokossovski, Konstantin, **EEU, RUS**
Roland Holst, A., **LCO**
Roman Catholic Church, **ANZ, BAL, BRA, BRI, CAN, CHI, COL, CTA, EEU, FRA, GER, GRE, HBK, IRE, ISR, ITA, JAP, LCO, MEX, PLA, SAF, SEA, SPA, USA, WIN**
Roman Empire, **ARW, BAL, CHI, EEU, GER, GRE, HBK, ITA, LCO, TUR**. *See also* Holy Roman Empire
Romania, **BAL, EEU, GER, HBK, ISR, ITA, RUS**
Romanovs, **BAL, RUS**
Romans, ancient, **BRI, FRA, GRE, IND, ISR, ITA, JAP, LCO, SPA, SWI**
Romansch (language), **SWI**
Rome, **FRA, HBK, ITA, SWI**; Treaty of, **FRA**

Romero, José Rubén, **MEX**
Romulus, **ITA**
Ronin, modern-day, **JAP**
Röntgen, Wilhelm, **GER, SWI**
Rooke, Daphne, **SAF**
Roosevelt, Franklin D., **CTA, FRA, HBK, RUS, SAF, SCN, USA, WIN**
Roosevelt, Theodore, **BRA, COL, CTA, SEA, USA**
Rootes, Sir William Edward (now Lord), **BRI**
Rosado del Valle, Julio, **WIN**
Rosas, Juan Manuel de, **PLA**
Rose, Murray, **ANZ**
Rosewall, Ken, **ANZ**
Ross, Sir James Clark, **CAN**
Rossellini, Roberto, **ITA**
Rossini, Gioacchino, **ITA**
Rössler, Rudolf, **SWI**
Rote Kapelle, **SWI**
Rothschild family, **CAN, FRA, ISR**
"Rotten boroughs," **BRI**
Rouault, Georges, **FRA**
Roundheads, Cromwell's, **BRI**
Round Table, Knights of, **BRI**
Rousseau, Jean Jacques, **AND, CHI, COL, FRA, PLA, SEA, SWI**
Roy, Alix, **WIN**
Roy, Gabrielle, **CAN**
Royall, Kenneth, **JAP**
Ruanda-Urundi, **TAF**
Rubber, **AND, BRA, LCO, TAF**
Rubens, Peter Paul, **BRI, LCO**
Rudolf II, King of Bohemia, **EEU**
Rudolf of Habsburg, **SWI**
Ruhr, **GER, IND**
Ruisdael, Jacob van, **LCO**
Ruiz, Juan, **SPA**
Ruiz Cortines, Adolfo, **MEX**
Ruiz Novoa, Alberto, **COL**
Ruiz-Tagle, Carlos, **AND**
Rumelian rebellion (1885), **BAL**
Rumi, Celaleddin, **TUR**
Rumiñahui (Indian chief), **AND**
Runa Simi (Inca language), **AND**
Runic writing, **SCN**
Runnymede, **BRI**
Ruskin, John, **IND, ITA**
Russell, George (AE), **IRE**
Russia, **ARW, BAL, BRA, BRI, CAN, CHI, EEU, FRA, GER, GRE, HBK, IND, IRE, ISR, ITA, JAP, MEX, RUS, SCN, SEA, SPA, SWI, TAF, TUR, USA, WIN**
Russian Orthodox Church. *See* Orthodox Church
Russo-Finnish War, **HBK, RUS, SCN**
Russo-Japanese War, **HBK, JAP**
Russo-Turkish Wars, **BAL**
Rustah, Ibn, **SCN**
Ruthenia, **EEU**
Rutherford, Ernest, **ANZ**
Ruusbroec, Jan van, **LCO**
Rwanda, **TAF**
Ryots (peasants), **IND**
Ryukyu Islands, **JAP**

Sá, Estácio de, **BRA**
Saba and Sabeans, **TAF**
Sabah, Abdullah al, **ARW**
Sábato, Ernesto, **PLA**
Sabhuza II, Chief, **SAF**
Sabogal, José, **AND**
Sabras, **ISR**
Sacrifice, religious, **GRE, TAF, WIN**
Sacsahuaman (Inca fortress), **AND**
Sadie, J.L., **SAF**
Sadowa, Battle of, **EEU**
Sáenz, Manuela, **AND**
Saenz, Peña, Roque, **PLA**
Safařík, Pavel, **EEU**
Sahagún, Bernardino de, **MEX**
Sahara, the, **ARW, FRA, SPA, TAF**
Said, Ahmed, **ARW**
Said, Mahmoud, **ARW**
Said, Nuri, **ARW**
Sailendra Dynasty, **SEA**
Sailing, **ANZ, SAF, SWI**
St. Gotthard Tunnel, **SWI**
St. Laurent, Louis, **CAN**
St. Petersburg (Leningrad), **HBK, RUS, SCN**
St. Thomas, **WIN**
St. Ursula, **LCO, WIN**
Saladin, **ARW**
Salamanca, **SPA**
Salamis, Battle of, **GRE**
Salan, Raoul, **FRA**
Salandra, Antonio, **ITA**
Saleem, Jewad, **ARW**
Salinar Indians, **AND**
Salisbury, Marquess of (Robert Arthur James Gascoyne-Cecil), **BRI**
Sallal, Abdullah, of Yemen, **ARW**
Salonika, **BAL, TUR**
Salote, Queen of Tonga, **ANZ, HBK**
Salt, **TAF, WIN**
Saltpeter, discovery of, **AND**
Salvemini, Gaetano, **ITA**
Samadhi, **IND**
Samaritans, **ISR**
Samarkand, **CHI, RUS, TUR**
Samarra, **ARW, TUR**
Samo (medieval Czech ruler), **EEU**
Samoa, Western, **ANZ, HBK**
Sam Po Kong temple, Java, **SEA**
Samudragupta, Emperor, **IND**
Samuel (Czar), **BAL, GRE**
Samuel, Sir Herbert, **ISR**
Samurai, **JAP**
San Andrés, **COL, WIN**
San Blas Islands, **CTA**
Sánchez Cerro, Luis M., **AND**
Sanchez, Ramón Díaz, **COL**
Sandino, Augusto César, **CTA**
Sand River Convention (1852), **SAF**
Sangha monks, **SEA**
Sang Hyang Widhi-Wasa, **SEA**
Sanhedrin tombs, **ISR**
San Jacinto, Battle of, **MEX**

Sanjak, the, **BAL**
San Marino, **HBK**
San Martín, José de, **AND, COL, PLA**
San Remo, **ISR, ITA**
San Salvador, **CTA, SPA, WIN**
Sanskrit, **IND, SEA**
Sansom, Sir George, **JAP**
Santa Anna, Antonio López de, **CTA, MEX**
Santa Cruz, Andrés, **AND**
Santa María, **SCN, SPA**
Santa Marta, Colombia, **AND, COL**
Santiago de Compostela, Cathedral of, **SPA**
Santo Domingo, Dominican Republic, **WIN**
Santomaso, Giuseppe, **ITA**
Santos, Máximo, **PLA**
Sappho, **GRE**
Saracens, **ITA**
Sarajevo, **BAL**
Sarawak, **SEA**
Sardinia, **ITA, SPA**
Sarekat Islam, **SEA**
Sargasso Sea, **LCO**
Sargent, John Singer, **USA**
Sarissa, **BAL**
Sarit Thanarat, Marshal, **SEA**
Sarmiento, Domingo Faustino, **PLA**
Sarto, Andrea del, **ITA**
Sartre, Jean-Paul, **FRA, GER, SEA, USA**
Sassoon, Siegfried, **GER**
Satellites. *See* Space research
Sato, Eisaku, **JAP**
Saudi Arabia, **ARW, ISR, TAF**
Sauerland, **GER**
Saul, King, **ISR**
Savoie, Phillippe de, **GRE**
Savonarola, Girolamo, **ITA**
Savoy, Dukes of, **ITA, SWI**
Saxe-Coburg and Gotha, House of, **BRI**
Saxons, **BRI, GER, SCN**
Scandinavia and Scandinavians, **ANZ, GER, PLA, SCN**
Scarlatti, Alessandro, **ITA**
Scarlatti, Domenico, **ITA**
Schacht, Hjalmar, **GER**
Schéhadé, Georges, **ARW**
Schick, René, **CTA**
Schiller, Friedrich von, **GER, SWI**
Schleswig-Holstein, **GER, SCN**
Schlieker, Willy, **GER**
Schliemann, Heinrich, **GRE, TUR**
Schmid, Carlo, **GER**
Schneiper, Xavier, **SWI**
Schoonmaakdag, **LCO**
Schopenhauer, Arthur, **GER**
Schouwen-Duiveland, island, **LCO**
Schreiner, W. P., **SAF**
Schröder, Gerhard, **GER**
Schröder, Kurt von, **GER**
Schurmann Pacheco, Mauricio, **PLA**

Schutzenfest, **SWI**
Schweitzer, Albert, **FRA, TAF**
Schweitzer, Pierre-Paul, **FRA**
Scotland, **BRI, IRE, SCN, SPA**
Scott, Robert, **SCN**
Scotus, Johannes, **GRE**
Scout movement. *See* Boy Scouts
Scugnizzi, **ITA**
Scutari, Yugoslavia, **BAL**
Seabrook, William, **WIN**
Sedgman, Frank, **ANZ**
Segesta, **ITA**
Segovia, Andrés, **SPA**
Segovia Highlands, **COL**
Sejrø island, **SCN**
Selim I, the Grim, **TUR**
Seljuk Turks, **BAL, TUR**
Selvon, Samuel, **WIN**
Selye, Dr. Hans, **CAN**
Semang people, **SEA**
Semites, **ARW, GRE, TAF**
Sempach, Battle of (1386), **SWI**
Seneca, **ITA, SPA**
Senegal republic, **SEA, TAF**
Senghor, Léopold, **SEA, TAF**
Senj (pirate state), **BAL**
Sentso, Dyke, **SAF**
Senussi sect, **ARW**
Sephardim, **ISR**
Sepoy Mutiny, **IND**
Serbia and Serbs, **BAL, EEU, GRE**
Serfdom, **EEU, MEX, SPA**
Seriat, **TUR**
Seris, tribe, **MEX**
Serraj, Abdul Hamid, **ARW**
Sertão, **BRA**
Sertões, Os, da Cunha, **BRA**
Sesotho language, **SAF**
Seven Years' War, **CAN, GER, PLA**
Sèvres, Treaty of, **TUR**
Seyhülislam, **TUR**
Seyss-Inquart, Arthur, **LCO**
Shadbolt, Maurice, **ANZ**
Shadow plays *(Karagöz),* **TUR**
Shahada, Moslem creed, **ARW**
Shakaika, **JAP**
Shakers, **WIN**
Shakespeare, William, **BRI, SCN, SPA**
Shaku, **JAP**
Shakya tribes, **SEA**
Shamba Bolongogo, Bushongo king, **TAF**
Shangaan tribe, **SAF**
Shang Dynasty, **CHI**
Shango, **WIN**
Shans, **SEA**
SHAPE. *See* Supreme Headquarters Allied Powers Europe
Sharpeville massacre, **SAF**
Shastri, Lal Bahadur, **IND, RUS**
Shaw, George Bernard, **BRI, IRE, SCN, SPA**
Sheba, Queen of, **ISR, TAF**
Sheep, **ANZ, BAL, GRE, IRE, PLA, SAF, SPA, TUR**
Shelley, Percy Bysshe, **FRA, ITA**
Shetland Islands, **SCN**

Shih Ching, CHI
Shih Huang Ti, "First Emperor" of China, CHI
Shiite sect, ARW
Shilluk tribe, TAF
Shimbun Rōren, JAP
Shinto, JAP
Shipbuilding, BRI, CHI, FRA, IRE, ITA, JAP, SCN
Ships and shipping, ANZ, BRA, CHI, CTA, GRE, HBK, ISR, LCO, SCN, SPA, TUR, WIN
Shiva, god, IND, SEA
Shoguns, JAP
Shopi, BAL
Shostakovich, Dmitri, RUS
Showa Period, JAP
Shquipëri (Sons of the Eagle), BAL
Shudra, caste, IND
Siam. *See* Thailand
Siberia, CAN, HBK, RUS
Sicily, GRE, ITA, SPA
Siegfried, André, CAN, SWI
Sierra Leone, TAF
Sierra Madres, MEX
Sierra Maestra (Cuba), WIN
Sigismund I, King of Poland, EEU
Sigismund III, RUS
Sihanouk, Prince, SEA
Sikhism, IND
Sikkim, HBK
Silesia, EEU, GER
Silk, CHI, SEA, SWI
Silver, AND, CAN, CHI, EEU, MEX, WIN
Simenon, Georges, LCO, SWI
Simeon the Great (Czar of Bulgaria), BAL
Sinai, ARW, ISR
Sinchi Roca (Inca ruler), AND
Singapore, BRI, SEA
Singh, Jai, Maharaja, IND
Sinn Fein Party, IRE
Siqueiros, David Alfaro, MEX
Siraj-ud-daula, Prince, IND
Sirikit, Queen of Thailand, SEA
Sisavang Vong, King of Laos, SEA
Sitwell family, BRI
Sixtus V, Pope, EEU, ITA
Siyavuşgil, Sabri Esat, TUR
Sjahrir, Sutan, SEA
Sjöström, Victor, SCN
Skagerrak, the, SCN
Slánský, Rudolf, EEU
Slavery, ARW, BAL, BRA, COL, CTA, MEX, PLA, SAF, TAF, USA, WIN
Slavs, BAL, EEU, GER
Slovakia and the Slovaks, BAL, EEU
Slovenes, BAL
Slums, BAL, BRA, CTA, GRE, SAF, SEA, TAF, WIN
Smerderevo, fortress of, BAL
Smetana, Bedřich, EEU
Smith, Adam, BRI, LCO, USA
Smuggling, LCO, SEA, SPA, WIN

Smuts, Jan Christian, SAF
Smyrna, GRE, TUR
Sneevliet, Hendricus, CHI, SEA
Snow, Sir Charles Percy, BRI
Sobieski, Jan, King of Poland, EEU, HBK
Sobukwe, Robert, SAF
Socialism, BAL, BRI, CAN, CHI, FRA, GER, IND, IRE, JAP, LCO, MEX, PLA, SCN, SEA, SPA, TAF, USA
Society of Jesus. *See* Jesuits
Socrates, GRE
Sodom, ISR
Sofia, BAL, TUR
Sōka Gakkai sect (Value Creation Society), JAP
Sokol movement, EEU
Solís, Juan Díaz de, PLA
Solomon Islands, HBK
Solomon, King, ISR, TAF
Soma, god, IND
Somalia, TAF
Somerset, BRI
Somoza, Anastasio "Tachito," Jr., CTA
Somoza, Luis, CTA
Songhai, Kingdom of, TAF
Sonora, Mexico, Walker's invasion of, CTA
Soong, Ch'ing-ling, CHI
Soong, Mei-ling, CHI
Soong, T. V., CHI
Sophie, Princess of Greece, GRE, SPA
Sophists, GRE
Sophocles, GRE
Sorcery, TAF
Soriano, Juan, MEX
Sosso tribe, TAF
Soto, Jesús, COL
Souphanouvong, Prince, SEA
Souq, ARW
South Africa, ARW, HBK, IND, SAF, TAF, USA
South America, BRA, COL, ISR, PLA, SCN, SPA
South-east Asia Treaty Organization (SEATO), HBK
Southern Cross, BRA
Southern Flevoland, Holland, LCO
South Pole, SCN
South-West Africa, SAF, TAF
Souvanna Phouma, Prince, SEA
Soviet Union. *See* Russia
Spaak, Paul Henri, FRA, LCO
Space research, CHI, RUS, USA. *See also* Atomic energy; Nuclear power
Spahis, BAL
Spain, AND, ARW, BAL, BRA, BRI, COL, CTA, FRA, GER, GRE, HBK, ISR, ITA, JAP, LCO, MEX, PLA, RUS, SAF, SEA, SPA, SWI, TAF, WIN
Spanish-American War, COL, CTA, SEA, SPA, USA, WIN
Sparta, GRE
Spenser, Edmund, BRI
Sphinx, ARW

Spice Islands, SEA
Spices, COL, LCO, SEA, WIN
Spinoza, Benedictus de, LCO
Spitsbergen, SCN
Split, Yugoslavia, BAL
Sputnik. *See* Space research
Srivijaya, Kingdom of, SEA
Stadhouder, LCO
Stalin, Joseph, BAL, CHI, COL, EEU, FRA, GER, GRE, RUS, SEA, USA
Ständerat (Council of States), SWI
Stanislas Augustus, King of Poland, EEU
Stanley, Henry Morton, LCO, TAF
Stanleyville, TAF
Starvation. *See* Malnutrition
Stauffenberg, Graf von, EEU
Steel, ARW, BRA, BRI, CHI, FRA, GER, HBK, IND, ITA, LCO, RUS, SPA, TAF
Steinheim man, GER
Stephen, King of England, BRI
Stephen I, King of Hungary, EEU
Stepinac, Alojzije, BAL
Steppes, BAL, RUS
Stern, Avraham, ISR
Stevens, Wallace, USA
Stilwell, General Joseph, CHI
Stockholm, SCN
Stora Kopparbergs Bergslags Aktiebolag, SCN
Storck, Henri, LCO
Stormberg, Battle of, SAF
Storrs, Sir Ronald, ISR
Storting, SCN
Strauss, Franz Josef, GER
Strauss, Richard, GER
Stravinsky, Igor, RUS, SWI
Strindberg, Johan August, SCN, SWI
Stroessner, Alfredo, PLA
Strongbow (Earl of Pembroke), IRE
Stuart, House of, BRI
Sturmgewehr, SWI
Sturzo, Luigi, ITA
Sublime Porte, TUR
Sucre, Antonio José de, AND, COL
Sudan, the, ARW, TAF
Sudentenland, Czechoslovakia, EEU
Suez Canal, ARW, BRI, CAN, FRA, ISR, ITA, SAF, SEA, USA
Sufis, ARW, TUR
Sugar, BRA, CHI, COL, IRE, LCO, PLA, WIN
Suicide, JAP, SCN, SWI
Sui Dynasty, CHI
Sukarno, President of Indonesia, ARW, LCO, SEA
Suk tribe, TAF
Suleiman II, King of Hungary, EEU
Suleiman the Magnificent, Sultan of Turkey, EEU, TUR
Sullivan, Louis, USA
Sumatra, SEA

Sumō, JAP
Sundiata Keita, King of Mali, TAF
Sung Dynasty, CHI
"Sun-Language" theory, TUR
Sun worship, AND
Sun Yat-sen, CHI, SEA
Supreme Headquarters Allied Powers Europe (SHAPE), HBK
Surinam, COL
Suslov, Mikhail, EEU, RUS
Suttee, IND
Suvarnabhumi, SEA
Suzman, Helen, SAF
Sverdrup, Otto, SCN
Swabia, GER
Swahilis, TAF
Swan Islands, WIN
Swaziland, SAF
Sweden, CAN, EEU, GER, HBK, JAP, RUS, SCN
Swift, Jonathan, BRI, IRE
Switzerland, FRA, GER, HBK, ITA, JAP, SAF, SWI
Sybaris, GRE
Sykes-Picot agreement, ARW
Synge, John Millington, IRE
Syria, ARW, CHI, ISR, ITA, TUR
Szechwan province, CHI
Szigeti, Joseph, EEU

Tabasco, MEX
Table Bay, SAF
Tacitus, Publius Cornelius, BRI, GER, LCO
Tagore, Rabindranath, IND
Tahuantinsuyu (the land of the four regions, Peru), AND
T'ai Chi Ch'uan, CHI
T'ai P'ing, CHI
Taisho Period, JAP
Taiwan (Formosa), CHI, JAP, SEA
Tajín Pyramids, MEX
Taj Mahal, IND
Talat Pasha, TUR
Talleyrand, Prince Charles Maurice de, FRA
Talmud, ISR
Tamayo, Rufino, MEX
Tamerlane the Great, BAL, HBK, IND, RUS
Tamil, language, HBK, IND
Tanganyika, BRI, HBK, SAF, TAF
T'ang Dynasty, CHI
Tanzania, HBK
Taoiseach, IRE
Taoism, CHI
Tara, IRE
Tarahumara, language, MEX
Tariffs, CTA, GRE, HBK, IRE, LCO, SAF, SCN, SPA, USA
Tashkent, CHI, RUS
Tasmania, ANZ
Tassili-n-Ajjer murals, TAF
Tatars, BAL, EEU, ISR, RUS
Taurus Mountains, TUR
Tea, CHI, PLA; ceremony, JAP
Technion, ISR
Tecum-Uman, King, CTA

Teheran conference, **EEU, RUS**
Teilhard de Chardin, Père Pierre, **FRA**
Tel Aviv, **ARW, ISR**
Tell, Wilhelm, **SWI**
Telugu, language, **IND**
Tembu tribe, **SAF**
Temples, **ARW, CHI, CTA, GRE, IND, SEA, WIN**
Teng Hsiao-p'ing, **CHI**
Teotihuacán culture, **MEX**
Te Rangi Hiroa (Sir Peter Buck), **ANZ**
Teutoburg Forest, Battle of, **GER**
Teutonic Knights, **EEU, GER**
Texas, **USA**; Revolution, **MEX**
Texel, island, **LCO**
Textiles, **AND, ARW, BRA, CHI, COL, CTA, GER, GRE, IND, IRE, ITA, MEX, SEA, SWI**
Thackeray, William Makepeace, **BRI, IRE**
Thailand (Siam), **HBK, JAP, SEA**
Thales of Miletus, **GRE**
Thames River, **BRI, SCN**
Thebes, **ARW, GRE**
Thermal pools, **ANZ**
Thermopylae, **GRE**
Thessalonica (iki), **GRE**
Thirty Years' War, **EEU, GER, SCN, SWI**
Thomas, Dylan, **BRI, IRE**
Thoreau, Henry David, **IND, USA**
Thrace, **BRAL, GRE**
Thucydides, **GRE**
Thuringia, **GER**
Thurn, Count Heinrich Matthias von, **EEU**
Tiberius, Emperor, **ITA**
Tibet, **CHI, HBK, SEA**
Tidore island, **SEA**
Tigris River, **ARW, TUR**
Tillich, Paul, **USA**
Ti Malice, **WIN**
Timber, **BAL, BRA, PLA, SCN**
Timbuktu, **TAF**
Tin, **AND**
Tintoretto, **ITA**
Tiradentes (Joaquim José da Silva Xavier), **BRA**
Tiran, Straits of, **ISR**
Titanium, **CAN**
Titian, **ITA**
Tito, Josip Broz, **ARW, BAL, GRE, RUS**
Tlaxcalan Indians, **MEX**
Tobacco, **BRA, COL, CTA, GRE, PLA, TUR, WIN**
Tobago, **WIN**
Tobey, Mark, **USA**
Tocqueville, Alexis de, **LCO, RUS, USA**
Togo, **TAF**
Tokugawa Period, **JAP**
Tolima Indians, **COL**
Tolstoy, Leo, **EEU, GRE, IND, RUS**
Toltec Indians, **CTA, MEX**
Tonantzín, Aztec goddess of earth, **MEX**

Tone, Theobald Wolfe, **IRE**
Tonga, **HBK**
Tongaland, **SAF**
Topa Inca Yupanqui (Inca ruler), **AND**
Torah, **ISR**
Toramana, Hun chieftain, **IND**
Tordesillas, Treaty of, **BRA, HBK, PLA, SPA**
Toro, Kingdom of, **TAF**
Torre Nilsson, Leopoldo, **PLA**
Tortuga island, **WIN**
Toscanini, Arturo, **ISR**
Totems, **CAN, TAF**
Totonac Indians, **MEX**
Toulouse-Lautrec, Henri de, **FRA**
Tour, Georges de la, **FRA**
Touré, Sékou, **TAF**
Tours, Battle of, **ARW**
Towfik, Khedive, **ARW**
Toyotomi, Hideyoshi, **JAP**
Trading posts, European, **IND, TAF**
Trafalgar, Battle of, **BRI, SPA**
Trajan, Emperor, **BAL, ITA**
Transdanubia (province), **EEU**
Transjordan. *See* Jordan
Transkei, **SAF**
Trans-Siberian Railroad, **RUS**
Transvaal, **SAF, TAF**
Transylvania, **BAL, EEU**
Trebizond, **GRE**
Trekboers, **SAF**
Trieste, Free Territory of, **BAL, ITA**
Trinidad, **BRI, COL, WIN**
Triple Alliance, **ITA, PLA**
Tripoli, **ARW, TUR**
Trnka, Jiří, **EEU**
Trojan War, **GRE**
Trollope, Anthony, **USA**
Trollope, Frances, **USA**
Trotsky, Leon, **MEX, RUS, SWI**
Troy, **GRE, TUR**
Trujillo, Rafael, **CTA, HBK, WIN**
Truman, Harry S., **GRE, HBK, ISR, USA, WIN**
Trundholm sun chariot, **SCN**
Tsao Chun (Taoist deity), **CHI**
Tshombe, Moise, **TAF**
Tuareg, **ARW, TAF**
Tugwell, Rexford Guy, **WIN**
Tumtum tribe, **TAF**
Tungabhadra dam, **IND**
Tung Pi wu, **CHI**
Tunisia, **ARW, FRA, ITA, TUR**
Tupi Indians, **BRA**
Turanism, **TUR**
Turgenev, Ivan, **RUS**
Turkey and the Turks, **ARW, BAL, COL, EEU, GRE, HBK, ISR, RUS, TUR, WIN**. *See also* Ottoman Empire
Turner, Frederick Jackson, **USA**
Turner, J.M.W., **BRI**
Tutanekai and Hinemoa (fabled Maori lovers), **ANZ**
Tutenkhamen, tomb of, **ARW**
Twain, Mark, **FRA, USA**
Typhoons, **JAP**
Tyre, **ARW, ISR**

Tzotzil, language, **MEX**
Tz'u Hsi, Empress Dowager of China, **CHI**

Ubico, Jorge, **CTA**
Uganda, **ARW, BRI, TAF**
Ukraine, **BAL, EEU, RUS**
Ulbricht, Walter, **EEU, GER**
Ulster, **BRI, IRE**
Ulysses, Joyce, **FRA, IRE**
Umayyad dynasty, **ARW, TUR**
Unamuno, Miguel de, **SPA**
Unanue, Hipólito, **AND**
Undset, Sigrid, **SCN**
UNESCO. See United Nations Educational, Scientific and Cultural Organization
Ungava iron fields, **CAN**
UNICEF. See United Nations Children's Fund
Union of Kalmar, **SCN**
Union of Soviet Socialist Republics (U.S.S.R.). *See* Russia
Union of Utrecht, **LCO**
United Arab Republic, **ARW, TAF**
United Kingdom. *See* Great Britain
United Nations, **ARW, BAL, BRI, CAN, CHI, FRA, IND, IRE, ISR, ITA, JAP, LCO, SAF, SCN, SEA, SPA, SWI, TAF, TUR, USA**
United Nations Children's Fund (UNICEF), **HBK**
United Nations Educational, Scientific and Cultural Organization (UNESCO). **HBK**
United States, **AND, ARW, BAL, BRA, BRI, CAN, CHI, COL, CTA, FRA, GER, GRE, HBK, IND, ISR, ITA, JAP, LCO, MEX, RUS, SAF, SCN, SEA, SPA, SWI, TAF, TUR, USA, WIN**. *See also* American Revolution
Untouchability, **IND**
Upanishads, **IND**
Upper Volta, **TAF**
Uppland, Sweden, **SCN**
Ur, **ISR**
Ural Mountains, **RUS**
Uranium, **CAN, CHI, GER, SAF**
Urdu, language, **IND**
Uribe Piedrahita, César, **COL**
Uriburu, José, Félix, **PLA**
Urk, island, **LCO**
Uruguay, **AND, BRA, PLA**
Uruguay River, **BRA, PLA**
Urundi, Kingdom of, **TAF**
Uslar Pietri, Arturo, **COL**
U Thant, **HBK, SAF**
Uthman, **ARW**
Utrillo, Maurice, **FRA**
Uzbekistan, Russia, **CHI, RUS**
Uzziah, King, **ISR**

Vaclav, Prince, Ruler of Czechs, **EEU**
Vaishya, caste, **IND**

Vajiradvudh, King of Thailand, **SEA**
Valdemar Atterdag, King of Denmark, **SCN**
Valencia, Guillermo León, **COL**
Valéry, Paul, **BRA, FRA**
Valhalla, **SCN**
Valkyries, **SCN**
Valladolid, **SPA**
Vancouver, Capt. George, **CAN**
Vandals, **GER, ITA, SPA**
Vanderbilt, Cornelius, **CTA**
Van der Post, Laurens, **SAF, TAF**
Van Diemen's Land, **ANZ**
Van Dongen, Kees, **FRA**
Van Dyck, Sir Anthony, **LCO**
Van Eyck, brothers, **LCO**
Van Gogh, Vincent, **FRA, LCO**
Vanilla, **AND**
Van Rensburg, Janse, **SAF**
Van Riebeeck, Jan, **SAF**
Van Wyk Louw, N.P., **SAF**
Vargas, Getúlio, **BRA**
Varuna, god, **IND**
Varus, Publius Quintilius, **GER**
Vatican, **HBK, ITA**
Vaux, Roland de, **ISR**
Vedas, **IND**
Veddoids, **SEA**
Veen, Adriaan van der, **LCO**
Vega Carpio, Lope de, **SPA**
Vegetarianism, **IND**
Velázquez, Diego de Silva y, **SPA**
Veld, **SAF**
Velika Strana Mountains, **BAL**
Venables, Robert, **WIN**
Venda tribe, **SAF**
Venezuela, **AND, COL, SPA, WIN**
Venice and the Venetians, **BAL, GRE, ITA, SEA, TUR**
Ventre Livre, Law of, **BRA**
Ventris, Michael, **GRE**
Verdi, Giuseppe, **ARW, ITA**
Vergil, **ITA**
Verlaine, Paul, **FRA**
Vermeer, Jan, **LCO**
Veronese, Paolo, **ITA**
Verrazano, Giovanni da, **WIN**
Verrocchio, Andrea del, **ITA**
Versailles, **FRA, GER**; Treaty, **HBK**
Verwoerd, Hendrik Frensch, **SAF**
Vespucci, Amerigo, **BRA, COL, ITA**
Vesuvius, Mount, **ITA**
Vickers, Jon, **CAN**
Victoria Falls, **TAF**
Victoria, Island, **CAN**
Victoria, Queen, **AND, BRI, FRA, GER, GRE, HBK, IND, USA**
Victoria (state of Australia), **ANZ**
Vienna, **BAL, EEU, GER, HBK, SWI, TUR**
Vierlingh, Andries, **LCO**
Vietcong, **CHI**
Viet Minh, **SEA**
Vietnam, **CHI, HBK, RUS, SEA, USA**

Vigeland, Gustav, **SCN**
Vijayanagar Empire, **IND**
Vikings, **BRI, SCN**
Villa-Lobos, Heitor, **BRA**
Villanueva, Carlos Raúl, **COL**
Villa, Pancho, **MEX**
Villas Boas, Orlando, **BRA**
Villeda Morales, Ramón, **CTA**
Villehardouin, Geoffrey de, **GRE**
Vinci, Leonardo da, **FRA, ITA, SWI**
Vineyards, **AND, FRA, SAF, TUR**. *See also* Wine
Vinland, **SCN**
Viracocha (Inca god), **AND**
Virgin Islands, **WIN**
Visconti, Luchino, **ITA**
Vishnu, god, **IND, SEA**
Visigoths, **BAL, FRA, ITA, SPA**
Vis, island of, **BAL**
Vistula River, **EEU**
Viticulture. *See* Wine and winemaking
Vivaldi, Antonio, **ITA**
Vix, Celtic tomb at, **FRA**
Vladimir (of Russia), **RUS, SCN**
Vodou, **WIN**
Voegeli, C.A., Bishop of Haiti, **WIN**
Volcanoes, **AND, ANZ, MEX, SAF, TAF, WIN**
Volga River, **RUS, SCN**
Voltaire, **CHI, FRA, PLA, SWI**
Vo Nguyen Giap, General, **SEA**
Voodooism. *See Vodou*

Wadai, Kingdom of, **TAF**
Wadi Araba, **ISR**
Wafd party, **ARW**
Wagenia tribe, **TAF**
Wagner, Richard, **EEU, FRA, GER, ITA, SWI**
Wahhabism, **ARW**
Waiblingen, **GER**
Wakefield, Edward Gibbon, **ANZ**
Walcheren, island, **LCO**
Wales and the Welsh, **BRI, IRE, PLA**
Walker, William, **CTA**
Wallenstein, Albrecht, **EEU**
Walloons, **LCO**
Walpole, Sir Robert, **BRI**
Walter, Bruno, **SWI**
Walvis Bay (Whale Bay), **SAF**
Wari Indians, **AND**

War of 1812, **CAN, USA**
War of the Pacific (1879-1883), **AND**
War of the Polish Succession, **EEU**
War of the Spanish Succession, **PLA, SPA**
War of the Triple Alliance, **AND**
Warsaw, **EEU, ISR**; Pact, **CHI, EEU, HBK**
Washington, George, **BRA, GRE, USA**
Water, **ARW, BRA, CTA, GRE, LCO, SAF**
Water buffalo, **BAL, BRA**
Waterloo, Battle of, **BRI, FRA**
Watutsi tribe, **TAF**
Wayang Kulit shadow plays, **SEA**
Webb, Beatrice and Sidney, **BRI**
Weber, Max, **GER**
Webster, Daniel, **USA**
Wegner, Hans, **SCN**
Weidemann, Guillermo, **COL**
Weik-za, **SEA**
Weimar Republic, **GER**
Weizmann, Chaim, **ISR**
Welensky, Sir Roy, **TAF**
Wellington, Duke of, **BRI, HBK, SPA**
Wentworth, William Charles, **ANZ**
Wessex, **BRI, SCN**
West Indies, **BRI, SPA, TAF, WIN**
Westminster, Dukes of, **BRI**
Westphalia, Treaty of, **GER**
Weyden, Rogier van der, **LCO**
Weyler, Valeriano ("The Butcher"), **WIN**
Whaling, **BRA, SCN**
Wheat, **CAN, CHI, FRA, SPA**
Whistler, James Abbott McNeill, **USA**
White, Patrick, **ANZ**
Whitman, Walt, **GRE, USA**
Whittier, John Greenleaf, **BRA, USA**
WHO. *See* World Health Organization
Wilde, Oscar, **IRE**
Wilder, Thornton, **AND, IRE**
Whymper, Edward, **SWI**
Wiinblad, Bjørn, **SCN**
Wilhelm II, Kaiser, **GER, LCO**
William the Conqueror, **BRI, SCN**
Williams, William Carlos, **USA**

Wilson, Harold, **BRI**
Wilson, Woodrow, **BAL, CTA, GER, SEA, USA**
Windsor, Duke of. *See* Edward VIII
Windsor, House of, **BRI**
Windward Islands, **WIN**
Wine and winemaking (viticulture), **BRA, EEU, FRA, GER, GRE, ITA, LCO, PLA, SAF, SPA, SWI**
Winter, Fritz, **GER**
Witches and witchcraft, **GRE, TAF**
Witwatersrand (Ridge of White Waters), **SAF**
Wolfe, Major General James, **CAN**
Wolfe, Thomas, **USA**
Wool, **AND, BRA, BRI, CHI, PLA, SAF**
Wordsworth, William, **BRI, FRA**
World Bank, **HBK, ITA, SPA**
World Federalist Movement, **ISR**
World Health Organization (WHO), **HBK, IND**
World War I, **ARW, BAL, BRA, BRI, CAN, EEU, FRA, GER, GRE, HBK, IND, ISR, ITA, JAP, LCO, PLA, RUS, SAF, SCN, SEA, SPA, SWI, TUR, USA**
World War II, **ARW, BAL, BRA, BRI, CAN, CHI, COL, EEU, FRA, GER, GRE, HBK, IND, ISR, ITA, JAP, LCO, PLA, RUS, SAF, SCN, SEA, SPA, SWI, TAF, TUR, USA, WIN**
Wright, Frank Lloyd, **USA**
Wu Ti, Emperor of China, **CHI**
Wycliff, John, **EEU**
Wyeth, Andrew, **USA**
Wyszyński, Stefan Cardinal, **EEU**

Xavier, St. Francis, **JAP, SEA**
Xenophon, **GRE**
Xerxes of Persia, **GRE, HBK**
Xhosa tribe, **SAF, TAF**

Yadin, Yigael, **ISR**
Yaguarcocha, Lake (Lake of Blood), battle at, **AND**
Yahuar Huacac (Inca ruler), **AND**
Yalta Conference, **RUS**
Yangtze River, **CHI, SEA**
Yaqui Indians, **MEX**
Yaro Indians, **PLA**

Ydígoras Fuentes, Miguel, **CTA**
Yeats, Jack B., **IRE**
Yeats, William B., **IRE**
Yellow fever, **BRA, CTA, WIN**
Yellowknife, Northwest Territories, **CAN**
Yemen, **ARW, ISR, TAF**
Yevtushenko, Yevgeni, **RUS**
Yoga, **IND**
Yorkshire, **BRI, SCN**
Yorubaland, **TAF**
Yoshida, Shigeru, **JAP**
Youlou, Fulbert, **TAF**
Yuan Dynasty, **CHI**
Yuan Shih-k'ai, **CHI**
Yucatán, Mexico, **CTA, MEX**
Yugoslavia, **ARW, BAL, CHI, EEU, GRE, HBK, ISR, ITA, RUS**
Yukon Territory, **CAN**
Yunnan province, **CHI, SEA**

Zadkine, Ossip, **LCO**
Zadruga, **BAL**
Zambezi River, **TAF**
Zangwill, Israel, **ISR**
Zanzibar, island, **TAF**
Zapata, Emiliano, **MEX**
Zapotec culture, **MEX**
Zarzuelas, **SEA**
Zealand island, **SCN**
Zealotry, **ARW**
Zelaya, José Santos, **CTA**
Zemurray, Sam, **CTA**
Zen Buddhism, **JAP**
Zeus, **GRE**
Zeuxis, **GRE**
Zhdanov, Andrei, **SEA**
Zhivkov, Todor, **BAL**
Zhukov, Georgi, **RUS**
Ziggurats, **ARW**
Zimbabwe, **TAF**
Zinoviev, Gregory, **EEU**
Zionism, **ARW, ISR**
Zog I, King of Albania, **BAL**
Zola, Emile, **FRA, IRE**
Zollverein, **LCO**
Zorin, Valerian, **EEU**
Zoroastrians, **CHI, IND, TUR**
Zorrilla de San Martín, Juan, **PLA**
Zurbarán, Francisco de, **SPA**
Zuiderzee, **LCO**
Zulus, **SAF, TAF**
Zurich, **LCO, SWI, TUR**
Zweig, Arnold, **GER**
Zwingli, Ulrich, **SAF, SWI**

xx

Production staff for Time Incorporated

John L. Hallenbeck (Vice President and Director of Production)

Robert E. Foy, Caroline Ferri and Robert E. Fraser

Text photocomposed under the direction of

Albert J. Dunn and Arthur J. Dunn

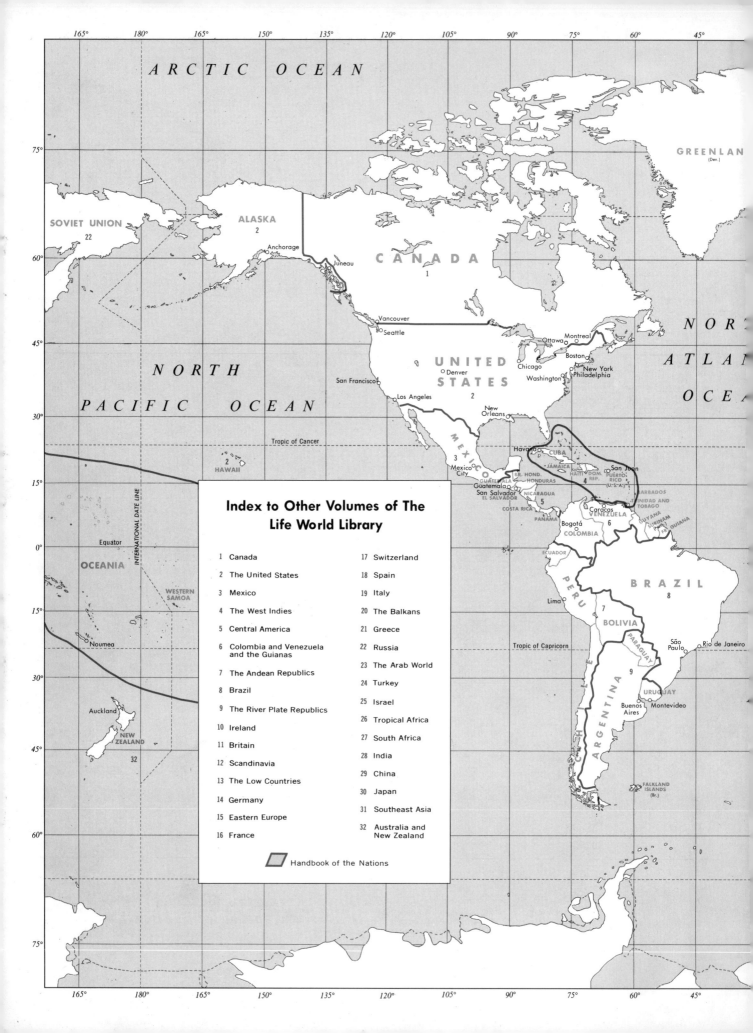

ARCTIC OCEAN

GREENLAND
(Den.)

SOVIET UNION
22

ALASKA
2

CANADA
1

Anchorage

Juneau

NORTH

ATLANTIC

OCEAN

Vancouver

Seattle

Ottawa Montreal

Boston

Chicago

New York
Philadelphia

Washington

UNITED

STATES
2

Denver

San Francisco

NORTH

PACIFIC   OCEAN

Los Angeles

New
Orleans

Tropic of Cancer

Havana   CUBA

MEXICO

HAWAII
2

Mexico
City

GUATEMALA

Guatemala

San Salvador

EL SALVADOR

JAMAICA

HAITI DOM.
REP.

San Juan

PUERTO
RICO
(U.S.A.)

BARBADOS

BR. HOND.

HONDURAS

NICARAGUA
5

TRINIDAD AND
TOBAGO

COSTA RICA

GUYANA

Caracas

SURINAM
(Neth.)

FR. GUIANA

PANAMA

VENEZUELA
6

OCEANIA

Equator

Bogotá

COLOMBIA

ECUADOR

BRAZIL
8

Index to Other Volumes of The
Life World Library

1	Canada	17	Switzerland
2	The United States	18	Spain
3	Mexico	19	Italy
4	The West Indies	20	The Balkans
5	Central America	21	Greece
6	Colombia and Venezuela and the Guianas	22	Russia
7	The Andean Republics	23	The Arab World
8	Brazil	24	Turkey
9	The River Plate Republics	25	Israel
10	Ireland	26	Tropical Africa
11	Britain	27	South Africa
12	Scandinavia	28	India
13	The Low Countries	29	China
14	Germany	30	Japan
15	Eastern Europe	31	Southeast Asia
16	France	32	Australia and New Zealand

Handbook of the Nations

WESTERN
SAMOA

Lima

PERU
7

BOLIVIA

São
Paulo

Rio de Janeiro

Tropic of Capricorn

Noumea

PARAGUAY

9

URUGUAY

Auckland

NEW
ZEALAND
32

ARGENTINA

Buenos
Aires

Montevideo

INTERNATIONAL DATE LINE

FALKLAND
ISLANDS
(Br.)